Follow the Money
Radio Voices for Peace and Justice

Pacifica Radio Network
KPFA's Flashpoints Interviews
2009-2016

by Dennis J. Bernstein

Foreword by Mumia Abu-Jamal
Selected, transcribed and edited by Riva Enteen

Printed in the United States of America

First Printing, 2018

ISBN 978-1-387-36262-2

Left Coast Press
PO Box 16530
South Lake Tahoe, CA 96151

Edited by Riva Enteen

Cover Design by Rael Enteen

Interior Design by Towela Sichinga

First Edition Paperback / February 2018

Dedicated to
late, great Robert Parry,
founder of ConsortiumNews.com,
home of many Flashpoints interviews,
which continues his tradition of true, courageous
investigative journalism.

7/21/18

 To Bill,
for peace & justice,
Rieva Eat—

 To Bill,
I can't imagine
why you'd want my
autograph, but here
it is! Michael B. Kreal

Table of Contents

3

Foreword

Follow the Money evoked in me an odd mixture of feelings: fascination, indignation, awe and rage. I learned a good deal from it, and met people, amazing people, who I had never heard of.

I've got to add another emotion: envy.

Why? Because in Pennsylvania prisons, where some 51,000+ souls reside, Dennis Bernstein's Flashpoints is not heard. We're in Pennsylvania, 3,000 miles away.

Also, there's no internet access in these joints. So, the stirring, soul-touching and moving interviews with Dennis and his guests are lost to us.

That is until *Follow the Money.*

Now that these remarkable interviews are available in print, the vast world of social, ecological, labor, gender, political, national [in]security, legal strategies are open to millions beyond Pacifica's frequencies.

Here, we see that Bernstein has one of the best jobs in the world. He talks to fascinating people from a wide and brilliant array of life, most who are engaged in some of the most challenging struggles of this era, against entrenched state and corporate power. Here, we see activists and participants in the battles against state and corporate snooping on the people, against the growing repression machine (especially versus Black and Brown bodies), against gender/sexual expression, dangerous border wars, global assaults on the world's peoples and environments, the horrors of Palestinian existence under the heels of the Zionist apartheid occupation -- and more, much more.

7

Another feeling: Anger. Why anger you wonder. I've learned of people's struggles that have been largely ignored by the complacent, corporate media. Here, there are hundreds of untold stories that could, and should, be told by the media.

To this date, most of these stories remain untouched and untold. This is an immense disservice to the American public, proving beyond cavil, that the nation's media is primarily the purveyor of infotainment, to dazzle, distract and delude viewers, readers and listeners -- not to inform them.

So, when you read these interviews, and learn of these pivotal events in the life of the nation, how can you not get angry?

How can you not feel that corporate news is little more than a basket of emptiness, of echoing fog? Bernstein's Flashpoints provides a powerful search-light through that fog.

It is common for people, especially young people, to pine for the 'good old days' of the '60s. They often lament the lack of movements in the US today.

No one can read *Follow the Money* and come to such a conclusion ever again, for the nation is bursting with movements.

For people are fighting, with hope, imagination, and deep love against the forces of greed, exploitation, and expropriation by the minions of capitalism, racism, militarism and unjust state power.

Dennis Bernstein has brought some truly remarkable minds, voices and hearts to his listening audiences at KPFAs Flashpoints. Now, these beautiful minds can speak to new audiences of readers (not only in prison, where, by the way, there are voracious readers) across the country, and indeed worldwide.

I found these interviews both enlightening and delightful.
Thank you, Dennis.

Mumia Abu-Jamal

Mumia Abu-Jamal

Acknowledgements

First, heartfelt thanks to Dennis, for his invaluable, essential work, and for giving me this opportunity to "be of use." Sincere appreciation to KJ Noh, who successfully navigated some difficult early waters of the project, tirelessly helped edit the entire manuscript and added color to titles. Enormous thanks to Mumia Abu-Jamal, who agreed to read the manuscript and contributed the power and beauty of his politics and prose to the book. Thanks to Jane Fehlberg, who transcribed many of the interviews. Deep gratitude to all of the interviewees, who contributed their time to read, edit, and grant permission to publish their voices. [Apologies in advance for all errors, all mine.] Interviewees John Pilger, who called the book "eminently publishable," Mattilda Bernstein Sycamore, Seth Holmes and Vernellia Randall gave me strength to keep at it. Many thanks to Sally Goldin, for teaching me how to transcribe; Erica Etelson, Linda Reilly, and Barbara Johnson, for their belief in the book; Scott Fleming, who identified agitprop; Noelle Hanrahan, who said, "Just do it;" Steve Bingham, who showed me I was on solid ground; Karoline Dehnhard, who launched the cover; Roger Stoll, who improved the cover; Deborah Rio Burns, for her keen eye; Kathy Kohberger and Jill Cartoscelli, my Tahoe cheering squad; Ann Garrison for proofreading; and Frances Goldin, for her invaluable professional and comradely advice on publishing. Deep gratitude to Towela Sichinga, my editorial assistant, who allowed this technophobe to produce a book. She is integral to this labor of love. Everlasting appreciation for my two children, Rael and Mara, who gave me their eagle eyes, political acumen, and loving encouragement. Finally, gratitude to the Cuban people, who show us that it can be done. *Si se puede!*

Those who profess to favor freedom and yet depreciate agitation, are people who want crops without ploughing the ground; they want rain without thunder and lightning; they want the ocean without the roar of its many waters. The struggle may be a moral one, or it may be a physical one, or it may be both. But it must be a struggle. Power concedes nothing without a demand. It never did and it never will.

Frederick Douglass, 1857

10

Introduction

This book comes out during the surprise presidency of Donald Trump. All 66 interviews were conducted in the seven years preceding the election and provide the writing on the wall for the toxic stew we now live in. Those who don't know history are destined to repeat it.

The interviews, organized into nine categories, occurred during the period of the first Black US president, one who promised hope and change. Chronologically, they begin with Kevin Cooper, still on San Quentin's death row for a murder he didn't commit, and end with Richard Wolff inviting us to imagine socialism in the US.

I was raised as a Marxist, so *Follow the Money* is a mantra for me. Why are prisons filled primarily with people of color? Why are women second-class citizens? Why is there endless war? Why do we pollute our planet? If we follow the money, we can better answer the question, "Why?"

If war is good for business, we must reshape our paradigm. Since 9-11, endless war against vague groups — many of whom fight with US-made weapons — is the norm. While obscene amounts of money are made for the privileged few. A generation of Americans has grown up in the shadow of endless war — "peace" is a word rarely heard or spoken.

As Malcolm X said, the chickens are coming home to roost. Martin Luther King Jr. said we can't talk about domestic policy without talking about foreign policy, and declared that his government "is the greatest purveyor of violence in the world today." They were both shot for their words.

I am of the generation inspired by Sweet Honey and the Rock's song "We who believe in freedom shall not rest until it comes" and Marge Piercy's poem "To be of use." The voices in this book are songs of courage and hope. They can help guide us as we chart our course through these turbulent seas.

Riva Enteen, editor

The New and Not So New Police State

How the FBI Monitored the Occupy Movement

Mara Verheyden-Hilliard   December 2012

DB: *The FBI and other federal agencies coordinated with banks and local authorities in reacting to the Occupy Movement, which was put in the category of a domestic terrorist threat despite the group's advocacy of nonviolence. Secret FBI documents show not only that the Feds treated the Occupy Movement as a criminal terrorist threat but that the FBI acknowledges that the movement rejected violence as a tactic. Mara Verheyden-Hilliard is the executive director of the Partnership for Civil Justice Fund, which obtained the documents.*

Mara, what motivated the Freedom of Information Act [FOIA] request and what was your initial response to these heavily redacted documents?

MVH: The Partnership for Civil Justice Fund filed a barrage of FOIA requests in the fall of 2011. The movement could see there was a coordinated crackdown against Occupy all over the country. We issued FOIA demands against federal agencies including the FBI, Department of Homeland Security [DHS], the CIA, and others, as well as against municipalities and police departments around the country. When we received these documents, it was very clear the very intense role the FBI played in mass surveillance operations against the peaceful Occupy Movement.

DB: *Many of the documents you received were blacked out. You got a document from as early as Aug. 19, 2011. They were getting ready for this movement.*

MVH: Yes. It says a lot about the FBI's conduct and the role of the American intelligence agencies that the FBI, before a single tent was put up in Zuccotti Park in New York, was meeting with the New York Stock Exchange to discuss the upcoming Occupy protests — as early as August, 2011. Occupy Wall Street started officially on September 17th. While the documents are heavily redacted, it's very clear that it's a limited redaction. They were working with private entities and meeting with businesses to alert them that they were the focus of protests. The documents show the FBI in cities around the country, in different field offices and different joint terrorism task force networks, communicating with the private banks and private security entities — acting as a private security arm of corporations, banks and Wall Street.

DB: *They were working in concert, in conjunction, with some of the major banks. What happened in Indianapolis and the potential criminal activity alert, whatever that is?*

MVH: There was a potential criminal activity alert put out by the Indianapolis Office of the FBI. They were saying they were aware of the Occupy Movement, but they didn't have a date specific for demonstrations or activities in Indiana. Nonetheless, they were putting out these warnings, these alerts. Their documents acknowledge the movement is peaceful.

The FBI has been granted mass license since September 11th under the claims of the need for national security, with billions of dollars poured into the FBI, Homeland Security — and what are they doing? They are turning their sights on a peaceful social justice movement at the same time they are working with the banks and Wall Street — the very focus of people's' demonstrations and organizing because of the economic crisis caused by the corporations, banks and Wall Street. American intelligence agencies are acting as their partners.

DB: *The Occupy Movement had many students and young people involved. What did you learn about spying on campuses?*

MVH: The Campus Liaison Project of the FBI has been very controversial. Many student groups and activists have protested against it, saying it was an abusive program. There is evidence that in Albany, New York the FBI was communicating to many campuses. The documents reference that they were communicating information to 16 campuses — all just from the New York location. A representative from the State University of New York in Oswego reported to the FBI on the campus Occupy Movement, which was made up of students and professors. The documents show an intense collaboration across the country, not just with the banks and Wall Street, but also with state and local law enforcement entities, and the fusion centers. There is an apparatus, which collects huge amounts of information on completely lawful, First Amendment protected — cherished First Amendment protected — conduct in the US and puts it into completely unregulated and very dangerous databases and data warehousing centers.

DB: *Is there any indication that students or teachers were paid to conduct surveillance?*

MVH: I didn't see anything like that. The reference appears to be a representative, so I am assuming it's someone in the administration or campus police. I don't think it was a student or a professor. You can read through these documents and see the activities that are going on at justiceonline.org. There are multiple instances where it appears in the text that there was infiltration, surveillance or undercover operations going on. For example, in Richmond, Virginia, there was a discussion with the FBI conferring with the Federal Reserve, an in-state law enforcement agency and a joint terrorism task force, and reporting from these other entities back to the FBI, giving them updates on planning meetings and general assembly discussions. There's a similar incident in Anchorage where private security, working on behalf of the port in Anchorage, Alaska, is meeting with the FBI over the planned West Coast

Occupy port actions. The private security said they were going to attend the planning meeting of the protestors and report back.

DB: *I became concerned when there were 130 people in an encampment in Oakland and 15 police forces converged. Apparently these police forces were being coordinated by the federal government, which was making deals that if they worked with the federal government they would be able to obtain certain weaponry from the military. This is walking to that border called fascism, when the military and federal government become involved in repression.*

MVH: We've certainly seen that shift of police into paramilitary policing. Our office has litigated a number of cases related to demonstrations and mass demonstrations in the US. In the Occupy context, we're trying to get at this connection and coordination between the federal government and local police agencies. Of course, the federal government always claims they are completely hands off, yet these documents show this relationship over and over again. There is a legal term — *imprimatur* — that means somehow these activities fall under domestic terrorism. That's how the FBI is categorizing it and it's stunning that the FBI is authorized to categorize a social justice movement of peaceful protest, First Amendment free speech activities, as domestic terrorism.

This is happening in this administration. People think if you shift the Democratic or Republican administration, somehow these abuses are not going to occur. But this is full license to have this type of activity going on under the Obama administration. The Tea Party was having rallies across the US where they were openly carrying weapons. They were bringing guns to their rallies, some of them outside where the President of the US was speaking, but what does the FBI do? They are going after the non-violent, peaceful Occupy Movement.

DB: *What is the relationship of the Domestic Security Alliance Council to surveillance?*

MVH: The Domestic Security Alliance Council is the coordinating body between the FBI, Department of Homeland Security, major corporate banking and other interests in the US. One of the documents shows the relationship between these private entities and the federal government anti-terrorism security forces. In this document, which discusses demonstrations and the port actions, there's a routine footnote, which says that nothing within this entity, this communication, should be disclosed to the public or to the media. It's to be kept internally between private corporate entities, the DHS and the FBI.

DB: *When the FBI and these federal agencies work with corporate institutions like banks and the Federal Reserve, what's the problem?*

MVH: Having US government intelligence agencies acting as private security with corporations, banks and Wall Street — the very entities that are the focus of people's social justice activism and their attempts to change the status quo in the United States — is not what our billions of tax dollars are supposed to go to. It is the negation of democracy to have the government act arm-in-arm with corporations, banks, and Wall Street, against the people. For most people in the movement, this doesn't come as a shock, but it's being so plainly revealed here that the FBI and Department of Homeland Security don't even feel they have to explain it, apologize or say it's a mistake or an anomaly. It's enshrined in what they are doing.

DB: *What was the Jackson, Mississippi Joint Terrorism Task Force doing when they issued a counterterrorism preparedness alert?*

MVH: Throughout the documents there are repeated references to domestic terrorism and counterterrorism alerts. The FBI joint terrorism task forces met in Biloxi with private banks to discuss an upcoming demonstration they'd heard about where people were protesting — it was "bad bank sit-in day." They met with

16

these banks privately. One of the documents has the FBI domestic terrorism discussions referencing three groups in its domestic terrorism capacity: the Aryan Nation, Occupy, and Anonymous. The FBI's perspective on social justice organizing is that they put it side-by-side with racist, violent, terrorist organizations like the Aryan Nation.

DB: *The Tea Party is coming, openly, to their meetings with weaponry. It would seem to require some attention. Do you plan to keep pushing forward, given that so much was redacted, or blacked out?*

MVH: Yes, we're filing an appeal. We're challenging both the redactions and the scope of production. When you read the text of the document, it's plain there is a lot more information that was being gathered, collected — memos on meetings that we don't have and intend to get. We have these materials from the FBI, Department of Homeland Security and local police departments, and we've made them all available and searchable on our website. We did this because the people of the US have the right to control the intelligence agencies and these kinds of government activities. They have the right to stop it. But first we have to know about it. As long as the government can act under this cloak of secrecy, in the dark, they are going to continue to get away with these actions. Exposure is the first necessary step to try to halt and bring an end to these abuses. People need to see what's happening and be able to take action.

Please come to our website, justiceonline.org, where you can see these documents. As soon as we get material, we send out email alerts to let people know that new documents are available.

Nobel Peace Prize to Chelsea Manning?
Jeff Cohen   April 2013

[On January 17, 2017, during his final days in office, President Barack Obama commuted Chelsea Manning's sentence and she was released on May 17. *Ed.*]

DB: *As the Iraq War's architects and boosters remain respected figures in Official Washington, whistleblower Chelsea Manning faces possible life in prison. To counter this injustice, media critic Jeff Cohen thinks Manning should get the Nobel Peace Prize. The grassroots activist group, RootsAction.org, drafted a petition addressed to the Norwegian Nobel Committee calling for the Nobel Peace Prize to be awarded to imprisoned US whistleblower, Pvt. Chelsea Manning. According to RootsAction co-founder Jeff Cohen, the response to the petition has been swift and substantial. More than 30,000 people signed on in a matter of days.*

Manning was arrested nearly three years ago on charges that she provided a large number of classified documents to the anti-secrecy group WikiLeaks. Cohen is the founding director of the Park Center for Independent Media at Ithaca College.

Jeff, why the Nobel Prize? Why does it connect up for you?

JC: The prize, as it was originally intended by Alfred Nobel's will, is supposed to go to the person who shall have done the most or best work for fraternity between nations through the abolition or reduction in standing armies. Chelsea Manning has been an unbelievable whistleblower for the cause of peace. Manning was an Army private, and saw many documents that showed war crimes, such as the US official order not to intervene when allies in Iraq were torturing people. The civilian death toll is documented, although the government has always said they are not keeping track of civilians. Chelsea Manning released documents that show they are. We saw the videotape of Apache helicopter personnel almost seeming to enjoy the fact that people were being killed on the ground in Iraq. It turned out to be civilians and at least one or two Reuters journalists. There's much evidence of war crimes, of official misbehavior by both the US Defense Department and the US State Department.

In the cause of peace, as originally intended by Alfred Nobel, there are many worthy candidates this year, but it's hard to see anyone being more worthy than the person who might be spending the rest of her life in prison for educating not only the US public, but also the world, about some of the atrocities that are happening in the so-called US War on Terror.

DB: *The corporate press participated in the release of certain WikiLeaks documents. Everybody went, studied, and published. But all of a sudden, WikiLeaks and anything associated with it became persona non grata. Would you talk about the role the corporate media plays in misinforming the public on something like Chelsea Manning?*

JC: There's no doubt the US mainstream media turned against WikiLeaks; they did not defend WikiLeaks, a publisher of documents received from Chelsea Manning, and from many other whistleblowers inside the government or the corporate world. It reflects how far the US mainstream media has declined since the Pentagon Papers, when, in 1971, newspapers from the *New York Times* to the *Washington Post* to the *Boston Globe* basically engaged in civil disobedience against the Nixon administration.

As soon as one newspaper was stopped from publishing the Pentagon Papers, another newspaper started publishing. These were highly classified documents from Daniel Ellsberg about the Vietnam War, much higher classification than what Chelsea Manning released.

Compared to 1971, today the US mainstream media is uninterested in whistleblowers, unwilling to come to their defense, and will only discuss how the documents that Chelsea Manning or WikiLeaks is releasing are going to affect US policy. It's how the documents are going to undermine the establishment, rather than what a journalist should ask, which is "How did these documents shed light on what the government is doing in the name of the American people, which the American people need to know about?"

These documents showed that the US State Department was aligned with the corporate interests in Haiti trying to stop a minimum wage in the poorest country in our hemisphere. That's news. The documents showed that when there was a military coup in Honduras, the US State Department and embassy there knew immediately this was an open-and-shut case. It was an illegal military coup d'état against a democratic president. But that's not what they were saying outside Washington.

These are huge stories, and are being covered as huge stories across the globe, but our mainstream media has a sort of ho-hum attitude with Chelsea Manning, who is now 25 years old, looking at perhaps life in prison — in fact, quite likely life in prison. People who know the true story of Chelsea Manning have rushed to RootsAction.org — signature numbers are exploding today.

Norman Solomon wrote a column of comments from Americans who believe Chelsea Manning deserves a peace prize. The Nobel Peace Prize was originally intended to give cash, so the people who received the peace prize could continue working for peace. It's a long shot, but if the Nobel committee ever gave a peace prize to Chelsea Manning it would say something to the US war machine about where international opinion is moving on the so-called War on Terror.

DB: *One of my favorite reporters is Amira Hass, who works for Ha'aretz and reports from the West Bank. She says the job of the media is to monitor the centers of power, whether they are in the government or corporations — wherever it happens. Instead, the media is one of the centers of power, and they appear to believe that their job is more as patriots than reporters.*

JC: I used to work in mainstream television, and the higher you go up in mainstream media, the more the people see themselves as part of the establishment. Editors of *Newsweek* have admitted, "We are part of the Establishment — that's how we see things. We don't want the boat rocked." There's no doubt that as the media have become bigger and more corporate, there's less willingness to go out on a limb and question something that the two parties are doing together. That's the essence of the problem.

When the two parties agree on a military adventure like invading Iraq or trying to get a confrontation going today with Iran, when the two parties are in alliance, as they usually are on foreign policy — there's obviously a lot of fighting about domestic policy, but on foreign policy there's often a lot of alliance between the two parties — the mainstream corporate media acts as part of the Establishment and doesn't address the issues. Anyone who does is considered liberally or progressively biased. If you think there's a problem with the thrust of the War on Terror, you must be one of those people, those Pacifica-Manning-WikiLeaks-type people. The Establishment knows that since the two parties aren't in an active fight about US foreign policy, there's no story here.

DB: *I used to be an investigative reporter for some mainstream newspapers, which at that time had some decent editors. Back then, it meant a great deal to a journalist doing these hard stories to get a document, because just an eyewitness' account could be questioned unless you had the document.*

For instance, we were covering the first Gulf War and we got a document that said the public information part of the military was going to lie about the obvious chemical exposure the vets would be exposed to during the first Gulf War. The US knew it, because they sold the material to Iraq. We loved those documents because you couldn't question. Yet, with Manning, the media laugh at the documents. It's as if they've been hoodwinked by giving a document that reveals a crucial story that the people need to know about.

JC: The journalists used to salivate over documentation because the people in power can't deny it's true. You've got the document, which shows someone in power talking to someone else in power. But instead of wanting to grab onto these documents, there's been a sense in the mainstream media that "Oh, okay, this is problematic." What the Manning, WikiLeaks documents show is the US mainstream media has been asleep at the wheel the last decade. That's the point. If you've been in mainstream media, whether National Public Radio or whatever, to grab onto these documents now might make people question "Well, why weren't you on the story before?" These documents show the US leaning on democratic governments in Europe to prevent them from prosecuting CIA agents who engaged in kidnapping and abetted torture. That's serious. These are huge stories in the German, Spanish and British mainstream media — stories about the US war effort, the so-called War on Terror. But they haven't been a big story in the country where the public needs to know what is being done in our name.

DB: *If independent, small, internet journalists are putting out a crucial story based on significant information, the corporate press has a lot to lose, including their credibility — what's left of it. So the corporate press has to walk all over it, pooh-pooh it. They have to pretend that the folks working in smaller organizations are crazy and shouldn't be believed — or they look really bad.*

JC: No doubt about that. WikiLeaks — and I hope there will be many successors to WikiLeaks — has abrogated, diminished the gate-keeping function of the mainstream media. That's another resentment. Many small outfits have gone to town on these documents, and thank God for WikiLeaks as the original releaser. There's a sense in the mainstream media that they are losing their power, losing their ability to control what gets out to the public and what doesn't. If you look at the evolution from Daniel Ellsberg in 1971 to Chelsea Manning today, and the way the *New York Times* and *Washington Post* oriented toward Ellsberg and the way they orient to Chelsea Manning, who was so mistreated in custody — it's night and day.

The good news, though, is that independent media are stronger than ever. As long as the internet remains free and there's community radio, stories are getting out. In the last ten years, the corporate mainstream media has lost some of its clout. They've certainly lost credibility. The mainstream media was largely wrong about the invasion of Iraq, factually. It wasn't an ideological thing — they got the facts wrong. They also missed the story of the financial meltdown on Wall Street. There are many people who don't trust the mainstream media anymore, and that's a good thing. Many of those people are looking for independent outlets, alternatives to the mainstream media. As long as the internet remains free — and that's a big if — and as long as community radio continues to exist, which depends on people's' donations, independent media will continue to grow. That's one of the few bright spots in our society — the growth of independent media and the decline of corporate mainstream media.

DB: *People often think that community media is National Public Radio. You wouldn't agree with that, would you?*

JC: No. I've not been a big fan of National Public Radio's national programs. They sometimes have some great local shows. But think about the run-up to the invasion of Iraq we were just referring to. Who was the NPR reporter who distinguished him or herself during that period? There weren't any.

DB: *No, they were all quoting Judith Miller.*

JC: Right. The *New York Times* and NPR have always enjoyed a special relationship. Who was the NPR reporter who distinguished him or herself on the Wall Street meltdown and the housing crisis? They missed it. I think NPR, at the national news level, is intimidated by Right-wing and corporate forces. It's become bland corporate centrist reporting. There's very little investigative reporting because the Right-wing in Congress is always threatening to cut off their funds.

DB: And a lot of corporate sponsorship.

JC: No doubt. It's sad. In other countries, the mainstream media is more vibrant because they have genuine public insulated funding for genuine public broadcasting, and public broadcasting sets a tone for the more commercial, corporate media. We've never had that. We've always had weak public TV and public radio. The big media corporations have never allowed it to be genuinely public — they've always hemmed it in.

The National Association of Broadcasters has always been the main foe of public broadcasting. It has an audience of millions and millions of people. The news coverage, which I listen to every day, is so bland. If you place yourself between the two parties scrupulously and you believe you are on the 50-yard line, you are not paying attention. If you put yourself between the elites of the Democratic and Republican parties, you may be somewhere between the 10- and 20-yard lines. But if you pretend that's mid-field, which is what gets done on NPR, it's not really solid reporting. Solid reporting has to somehow, sometimes, take itself out of Establishment group think and go outside of what the two or three major political parties are in a society. Our public radio news seems to be embedded inside the elites of the two-party system and rarely wanders outside. That's not helpful to the public.

FBI Targets Judi Bari of Earth First!
Darryl Cherney   May 2013

DB: *Darryl Cherney was with Judi Bari in 1990 when their car was bombed. He was a co-plaintiff in the lawsuit against the FBI and is the producer of the film* Who Bombed Judi Bari? *Darryl, can you remind people who Judi Bari is?*

DC: Judi Bari was a feminist, Earth Firster, labor organizer, fiddler, mother of two children, and carpenter who worked tirelessly to defend the ancient redwood forest, which is probably what she is most known for. She was car bombed in Oakland along with myself in 1990, and was the target of that bombing for her work organizing Redwood Summer. Then we were arrested by the FBI and Oakland police for bombing ourselves. We sued them and won four million dollars, but not before Judi Bari passed from cancer in 1997. Her story is one of victory, inspiration, humor and song. She still has that gift to give us — even after her passing.

DB: *The documentary shows how Judi Bari nailed the FBI and Oakland police, along with you, Darrell, from her deathbed. It was her deathbed deposition that nailed this precedent setting case against the Oakland police and FBI.*

DC: Yes. The FBI and Oakland police tried hard to stop Judi from giving her testimony. After accusing both of us of bombing ourselves, they never once attempted to talk to Judi, even after they had the right to take her deposition after we sued them. In other words, right up to her dying day, the FBI never had a single question to ask of Judi Bari, probably because they knew the answers they would get. That woman could nail you to the wall if you were on her case, and she'd get on your case ten times harder.

DB: *The film is not only a compelling portrait of Judi and what went on with the investigation, but this is a live wire case. The bomber is still free.*

DC: Yes. It wasn't just that they blamed us, but they covered up the tracks of the bomber. The person who covered up the tracks, first and foremost, was special agent Frank Doyle, the chief of the bomb and terror division of the San Francisco division of the FBI. Frank Doyle immediately got to the scene, 20 minutes after the bombing, and told everybody there that the bomb was in plain sight, that we must have known we were carrying it. After various names, the lawsuit was titled *Bari v. Doyle*. Who instructed Frank Doyle to blame us? He didn't know who we were and he was not operating in a vacuum. He must have had some background intelligence in order to not only blame us, but also cover up the tracks of the bomber, which, in my opinion, makes him an accomplice, either witting or unwitting.

DB: *Where is the case now?*

DC: As part of our lawsuit victory, we won the right to test evidence. We have that evidence in a laboratory in the Bay Area. It's a laborious process with over 200 pieces photographed and catalogued. Our lawyers inspected them and we will start testing pieces of duct tape that could contain fingerprints or DNA or both, of the bomber him or herself. I say "herself," because there is the possibility of female involvement in this action. I believe the plot to bomb Judi Bari was a group effort, not the act of a single individual.

DB: *Darryl, can you tell us about Judi Bari day?*

DC: After special agent Frank Doyle left the FBI, he went to work for Mythbusters, a television show on the Discovery Channel. He's still there, and has been on 12 episodes — in the flesh. He builds bombs and blows them up on television. He's been interviewed recently on the Boston bombing, having become a kind of TV consultant.

DB: *He knows a lot about bombs.*

DC: Yes. Frank Doyle showed up at the bomb scene in front of Oakland High School, and, in front of a video camera, looked at the car and said, "This is the final exam." He had just finished teaching a bomb analysis school, which they call a bomb school, in Humboldt County. One of the students was there on-site. At the bomb school, 30 days before the inside of Judi's car was blown up, Frank Doyle was blowing up the inside of cars with pipe bombs, essentially creating the very crime that he was to show up to 30 days later and blame us for. He turns to one of his students, most likely bomb tech Sergeant Myron Hanson of the Oakland Police Department, and says, "This is it. This is the final exam." He created the scene 30 days before, and it happened exactly as he had devised it, which certainly leads to some suspicion, especially with his final exam remark, which he now denies making. There is an audio of him saying it, but not a visual. So we are challenging Mythbusters to bust the myth about their own cast member. Did Frank Doyle show up at the bombed car and say, "This is the final exam?" Mythbusters have voice recognition machines and are always into these kinds of adventures. So let's make the adventure about one of its own cast members, Frank Doyle. He testified under oath that he didn't say it, so not only did he lie about the nature of the bomb and attempting to frame Judi and myself, he might have perjured himself as well, by lying about what he said at the bomb scene.

DB: *Judi Bari Day is May 24. What is the best way for people to track the documentary,* Who Bombed Judi Bari?

DC: The website is whobombedjudibari.com

Surveillance, Secrecy, and the Constitution
Shahid Buttar   June 2013

DB: *Americans got a rare glimpse into the breadth of US government surveillance of their communications with new revelations that phone and internet providers have been turning over vast amounts of data to be mined for "terrorism" investigations. We will discuss this with Shahid Buttar, human rights attorney and executive director of the Bill of Rights Defense Committee.*

Glenn Greenwald, reporting in the UK Guardian this week, revealed a secret US court document ordering Verizon, one of America's biggest telecom providers, to turn over telephone records of millions of US customers. It also seemed clear that other telecom companies had received similarly broad subpoenas. President Barack Obama then insisted that the collected data was limited in nature because it did not include the actual content of the calls, and he maintained that this tradeoff of privacy for security was necessary if the American people want to be protected from acts of terrorism. Further, he argued that Congress and the Judiciary had oversight of the program. However, civil liberties advocates challenged the government's assurances, noting that the secrecy that has enveloped such programs has prevented any serious debate about the tradeoffs.

Shahid, what happened here? Is this a big deal?

SB It's a big deal, particularly because the document disclosed is a secret court order issued by the FISA court giving the FBI the authority to monitor and spy on millions of Americans, at once, in a single order, under section 215 of the Patriot Act. This document provides evidence for the first time of what whistleblowers, and even members of Congress, have long said — the government is essentially waging an all-out war on the rights of we, the American people.

Senator Ron Wyden, a Democrat from Oregon, said that Americans would voice widespread outrage if we knew what the government was doing, in secret, under the Patriot Act. While this particular order did not allow for content to be captured by the government, other surveillance programs do, outside the context of this particular order. This single order is the tip of the iceberg, and even the tip is terrifying. The whole iceberg we haven't come close to grappling with yet.

DB: *Thomas Drake, a whistleblower from the National Security Agency [NSA] was just vindicated. He says he's been hollering into the deep, dark shadows of the surveillance state since October 2001, and then via the press starting in 2006, about this Orwellian threat. Today he said, "Now we have an order for all call records for millions upon millions of Verizon subscribers without probable cause, just because the government wants them. That's about profiling." What does he means by profiling and what doors does this open?*

SB: I would say it's the inverse of profiling. Profiling is when you select people for arbitrary scrutiny, perhaps on the basis of race or religion, which is illegitimate. This is equally illegitimate for the opposite reason. People have not been selected at all — it's a blanket dragnet. Dragnet versus profiling — they're both offensive but for somewhat opposite reasons. He talks of the potential dangers — in the past, simply the possibility that this sort of power could be misused was sufficient reason for we the people in the US to not accept these kinds of programs. Some people suggest, "This program is supposedly helpful for national security." But that's not the point. Even if it were helpful for national security, which remains unconfirmed, no one's given the public any facts to confirm that talking point the government officials have been saying. Even if it were helpful for security, however, there are grave threats to democracy that this kind of power presents.

In the very recent past, the government has gone after the Associated Press, Occupy and the Tea Party. So it doesn't matter where you are coming from on the political spectrum. If you are an activist, you are a target. You don't even have to be an activist. You can just be a member of the press, and you are a target. And if that's the case, the ability of the government to conduct pervasive, dragnet surveillance, enabling agencies like the FBI or NSA to map social networks, creates the very real, I dare say, inevitable likelihood of these powers being bent on nefarious purposes. That's why courts are important, to make sure that people in the Executive Branch aren't pursuing personal piques or political crackdowns — that they are using their authority in the ways they are supposed to. It's precisely because the secret FISA court is a mere rubber stamp that we can't have any confidence of that kind of good-governance practice in these surveillance programs.

DB: *This happens under a so-called liberal administration, a Democrat. It appears that Obama is hell bent on an intensive program to suppress any open flow of information and to seriously punish whistleblowers who try and break this open.*

SB: Absolutely. It's an additional reason to be concerned, and most news outlets, quite frankly, haven't picked up on it. I'm glad you seized upon it. We know about this document because some whistleblower somewhere is risking their career so that we, the public, can know what is happening. At the moment, the Obama administration is already our nation's far-and-away most aggressive anti-press administration. More national security whistleblowers faced prosecution in the last five years than in the entire preceding 225-year history of the Republic. It is likely that whoever leaked this document to Glenn Greenwald at the UK *Guardian* will become an object of prosecution. Recently the President spoke in a very welcome speech, with great rhetoric, about the need for transparency and checks and balances to keep the government honest. That rhetoric flew in very sharp contrast with the reality. While the President very appropriately suggested — though it's ironic given the FBI's assault on the Associated Press — support for a reporter's shield law, what he did not discuss — and what this document makes very clear we need — is a robust protection for whistleblowers as well as members of the press to ensure that Congress, the courts, and the public have the vital information needed to explore and an opportunity to investigate whether or not these kinds of powers are being misused.

DB: *Glenn Greenwald writes: "Under the Bush administration, officials and security agencies had disclosed to reporters the large-scale collection of call records data by the NSA, but this is the first time significant and top secret documents have revealed the continuation of the practice on a massive scale under President Obama." You must see this as a battlefield of free speech. This attempt to shut down any independent information coming from whistleblowers and government officials is showcased in the Chelsea Manning trial — how the administration has suppressed information that is clearly shown to be in the public interest.*

SB: Absolutely. Chelsea Manning is Exhibit A in the government crackdown on whistleblowers. Not only was she detained and is now facing prosecution, but she was tortured, despite having done nothing wrong. She simply, unlike most people in the intelligence apparatus, complied with her responsibility under international law to reveal evidence of war crimes. WikiLeaks first released Chelsea Manning's video of US service members gunning down journalists. That's absolutely something we need to know about — it is not an appropriate secret. Anytime I see claims of government secrecy, the first thing that pops into my head is that someone is trying to cover something up. Secrets are not secrets for any particular reason, and most of the time we see blatant over-classification, where most of the classified documents aren't classified for any legitimate purpose. We see this time and time again.

The Reynolds case before the Supreme Court, which established the States Secrets Privilege, was the first time the courts came up with this notion that they would defer to executive claims of secrecy. That case itself was a cover-up, and many of the cases, at least since then, are similar. We've seen the States Secrets

Privilege used to suppress evidence of corporate complicity in torture. We've seen the States Secrets Privilege used to suppress evidence of mass NSA warrantless wiretapping of the sort not unlike this document revealed to the UK *Guardian*. We've seen the States Secrets Privilege used to hide evidence of FBI infiltration of mosques around the country.

Congress has fallen down on the job and is not conducting the assertive, aggressive oversight necessary to bring these issues into the public view. The Senate Intelligence Committee was founded because in the 1970s there was a several-year investigation led by Senator Frank Church, which uncovered decades of constitutional abuses by the FBI, CIA and the Pentagon — spying on the American people. Now the Senate Intelligence Committee — chaired by Senator Dianne Feinstein from California — like the secret FISA court, is basically a rubber stamp. It is supposed to be a check and balance on the Executive, but there's never been even an attempt at uncovering the facts. Even when drone strikes were in the headlines and Senator Rand Paul was filibustering the nomination of the CIA director, even then the Intelligence Committee was settling for just getting memos. I'm past the point of being interested in memos — let's see some facts.

This is the first time anyone has seen any facts about the government monitoring millions of us, en mass, without any pretext of justification. It's a clarion call for all three branches of the government, the media, and most importantly we the people of the US, to raise our voices and demand that our rights are restored, and these illegitimate surveillance operations either be ended, or at least finally subjected to transparency and oversight.

DB: *Thomas Drake was a senior executive of the US National Security Agency. He was threatened and prosecuted, almost on espionage charges, for what?*

SB: Fraud and waste by the Pentagon, not even misinformation. What he revealed was true and related to fraud and waste — it had no operational benefit to our nation's enemies and yet he was prosecuted...

DB: *...to the full extent of the law. Unbelievable!*

SB: Even beyond the full extent of the law. He was prosecuted so viciously that at his sentencing hearing, the federal judge who sentenced him scolded not Thomas Drake, but the Justice Department, for wasting taxpayer funds and years of everyone's lives chasing someone who had done nothing wrong and merely performed his public duty. A federal judge talked back to the prosecutors, saying this is ridiculous — why are we wasting our time chasing this man around? He's a national hero, not a criminal.

The criminals, unfortunately, are the agencies, administration, Congress and the courts that have all failed to mind their oaths of office to defend the Constitution against all enemies, foreign and domestic. The biggest enemies of the Constitution are, unfortunately, the FBI, NSA, Congress, and apparently, the Obama administration. I should add the secret FISA court in there too.

DB: *Describe the FISA court. We hear that a court is part of these secret proceedings and they will mitigate our concerns about secrecy.*

SB: The secret FISA court is not a court at all. There is this notion, "Oh, this is reviewed by the courts." It's not a court if it's secret, right? Courts are premised on the idea that a decision is transparent, and that it can be reviewed by another court, which could compare the facts before it to the facts before the other court. But, when the decisions are secret, that can't happen. It's not jurisprudential legal decision-making. It's political rubber-stamping. We see that confirmed by the particular order that was released to the UK *Guardian*. There's no conceivable way in which millions of Verizon customers are appropriately up for grabs for the government to look at.

Let's be clear here; it's not just Verizon. Verizon happens to be the one company from which we've gotten the leaked document. All the telecom companies are up to their necks in this. To our knowledge, there is one company that has resisted a national security letter — separate tool, same kind of abuse. No one knows who it is, because if they reveal themselves, they would be prosecuted. There's a lot of speculation that it's Credo Mobile, which used to be Working Assets, but neither the company nor anyone else can confirm that. So it's not just Verizon — almost the entire industry is in bed with the FBI and NSA. In 2008, when the Foreign Intelligence Surveillance Act was amended, one of the central issues was "Would Telecom companies get immunity?" Congress, at the time, gave corporations a massive subsidy in the form of legal amnesty for all their abuses against the American public — just the tiniest bit of which we've seen in this document disclosed to Glenn Greenwald.

At the very least, the Senate and House intelligence and judiciary committees should all conduct investigations. We've seen that the intelligence committees are basically captured by the agencies, and we can't expect meaningful review from them. The judiciary committees are nominally more independent. Even if they don't have oversight over the NSA, they do have oversight over the FBI. They certainly have oversight of any government agency that systematically violates the constitutional rights of the American people. There must be wide-ranging, long overdue, furious, fact based — not just legal analysis — investigations by these committees. In addition, there must be long overdue transparency at the FISA court. The latest issue with secret courts was raised by Senator Feinstein, who — to her vast discredit — suggested more secret courts, particularly to evaluate the uses of drones to kill Americans abroad. We see confirmed by this document that secret courts aren't a check and balance on Executive abuses — they are a political rubber stamp.

Reform of that process, to bring those court opinions into the public, would be nice to see, but I don't have any hope of that happening. I would like to see some people get fired from the NSA and the FBI. The statutes empowering those agencies need to be revisited. Every time Congress looks at the Patriot Act, they re-authorize it — it's been extended at least three times since the Obama administration came into office. The last time Congress looked at the Foreign Intelligence Surveillance Act, it was extended for five years. There must be some meaningful process on these bills, instead of just Congress, like the FISA court, rubber-stamping them. Nobody wants to force the government to justify these surveillance measures because the intelligence officials say, "They're necessary to protect the country against terrorism." We don't need these kinds of measures. They don't help provide security and they do, in fact, lay waste to the constitutional rights that have long made our country great. The reason we have transparency at the root of democratic accountability, the reason democracy and transparency are so tied together, is because secret government is inevitably a pathway to oppression. The more secrecy that emerges in the counterterrorism regime, the greater and greater risk we have of slipping into an authoritarian situation.

None of this should surprise us. President Eisenhower warned of this 60 years ago. This is what a military-industrial complex looks like, and we're seeing it now turn its fangs on the American people. The Defense Department has already, for instance, tortured people around the world — the CIA has as well. What is the result of that? Changes to the law to give the agencies the authority to hide evidence of their criminal trial. When the NSA started violating the Foreign Intelligence Surveillance Act to spy on Americans in the years following 9/11, what happened? Congress bent over backwards to change the law, to give the agency the opportunity to continue those abuses. A fundamental issue we see reoccurring is they change the law to accommodate the agencies, instead of reining in the government programs to comply with the law.

What's at stake here is, quite literally, whether we will live in a free country or not. We can think we live in a free country, but when the Associated Press is essentially invaded in the dead of night by the Justice Department and its sources identified through covert espionage tactics, essentially we're not free. We see millions of Americans monitored by our own government, using our own taxpayer dollars without any individualized suspicion required by the Constitution. We're not free when we see activist groups infiltrated by the FBI and local police around the country. We're not free. We can sing the anthems at all the baseball games that we want, but the idea that America leads the free world is getting harder and harder to sustain. Even the claim that we are part of the free world, I think, is a stretch, and this document that was released to the UK *Guardian*, again, is just the initial case in point. Unfortunately, I think there's a lot more to be found, should we ever have an opportunity to examine the rest of the iceberg.

The Spillover from Data-Mining
Christopher Simpson   June 2013

DB: US Government officials, and many mainstream pundits, assure Americans that there's nothing to fear from the electronic surveillance aimed at "terrorists," but some intelligence experts say the new techniques could ultimately intimidate people from participating in democracy, as author Christopher Simpson asserts. The disclosures by whistleblower Edward Snowden have given Americans a window into the national surveillance state that took shape under George W. Bush in the years after the 9/11 attacks, and that has continued under Barak Obama.

Christopher Simpson, the author of Blowback *and other books on the history of US intelligence agencies, has called these current National Security Agency programs "more dangerous to democracy than intercepting phone conversations" because of their indiscriminate nature.*

Professor Simpson, you said the newly public National Security Agency's PRISM and similar operations are more dangerous to democracy than intercepting phone conversations. California Senator Dianne Feinstein assured us the opposite was the case — that it's not more dangerous because they are not listening to the conversations. Could you please respond to this?

CS: Let's take the simplest possible approach and assume the basic description the NSA and the President have given of what's being recorded is true. What he's saying is the signals data, which is to say the "to" number, the "from" number, the amount of time on-line, the particular channels it's traveled through and so on — that's what's being captured. There are several problems with this claim.

That data is searched through a process of data mining, which selects pieces of technical data that analysts think might be related to terrorism — that's what gets captured. Here's a scenario. Suppose they have suspect A who they think is a bad person — is involved in espionage, terrorism or some other offense against the state. They go and get all of A's records, and that second round of contacts of A, or A's contacts, become a new round of suspects — suspects B. Then they look at B's records, all the different B's, and they get yet another round, the C's, and so on down the line. This is done at the speed of light — mathematically. It's not the same algorithm as Google, but it's essentially the same process by which Google claims to have searched literally millions, sometimes tens of millions of records in a second or two. Those records are then cross referenced, so to speak, to see if there are additional linkages either with the subject A, or among the B's, or among the C's, or to see if there are loop backs between the C's and the A's. Do you follow me here?

DB: *I follow you to implications that might get a whole bunch of people in trouble who never did anything wrong.*

CS: That's exactly right.

DB: *Could you talk about the dangers here?*

CS: The danger is that each of these search probes never disappears. If you turn up as a subject B in connection with the original A suspect, that's noted, even if there is no other information that you have any association with subject A. Subject A might have been calling a pizza parlor, his brother-in-law — he might be calling anybody. Nevertheless, that gets captured as someone who is associated with subject A, the suspected bad guy. It goes throughout the C's and so forth, and so on. Those black marks are not lost — those probes which continue 24/7, 365 days a year, are of the same numbers and contacts shown in relationship to various other suspects, and even non-suspects. The numbers that are showing up become more suspect, so what happens is literally the creation of a network where no actual network exists. It's a creation of a network of people who are supposedly linked to each other through their telephone communications, but who in fact may have no relationship with each other.

The reason this is more dangerous than telephone conversations is at least in the old days if you intercepted a telephone conversation and somebody was talking to Aunt May, wishing her a happy birthday or something of that sort, presumably an analyst would say "No, Aunt May, well she might be involved in this, but this phone call doesn't prove it."

DB: *If it was a mafia hit you'd hear "We're going to hit JoJo" ... or some suggestion of an action that you would actually hear on the phone. Right?*

CS: That's right. So what is happening here is a very important, legal transformation from identifying somebody with some kind of substantial cause who may be complicit in a crime, to assuming that the people who have been contacted for any reason whatever, have some degree of guilt associated with them, whether or not they do. It is the algorithms' work to attribute responsibility to the contacts rather than to identify specific acts that may or may not be legal or compromising.

There's another layer to this too, and that has to do with how suspect A gets identified in the first place. I live in the national capital area. There are at least five different people who have my name who live in this same telephone area, and I get calls quite regularly for other people named Chris Simpson, who somebody is trying to call. That means I'm in touch with people who get nailed for talking to me, or I get nailed for talking to them, when the whole interaction was based on misinformation that I was the person they were trying to call.

Another example — how often do you get junk mail addressed to your house, but addressed to somebody else? It happens because people in the US move all the time, on average once every five years. That means there are addresses out there on computer lists that have the wrong information about your house. When these types of searches are done for suspected terrorists, either prior or subsequent to the telephone records search, they draw on all sorts of public records, any type of media mention — Facebook, Twitter, social media — that's gathered.

That means that at about the same rate you get mail that's not addressed to you, your name is being associated with something you had nothing to do with. That's a serious problem with the reliability of the records that are used to compile dossiers on suspects. The problem for democracy now is there is no way to know whether you have been pinged in this fashion — there's no way to inspect the file or correct it. Equally important, there's no way the government that claims to know everything and to be treating people fairly, can know and correct what they've got wrong.

DB: *So if you get stuck in this nightmare, you wouldn't even know where to begin to clear your name?*

CS: Absolutely. You would not necessarily even know that your name was pinged. What are the results? There is increased attention about your use of your passport, or any type of crossing borders. We have clear examples from the case of the man who was accused of spreading germs in the wake of 9/11. The FBI was after him for years, harassing him day after day. There are other cases of that sort. The way investigative agencies work, and this is well known, is they settle in on a target, and they build a case about that person. Some agencies are more professional, some are less professional, some police are more honest, and some are less honest. That's how the policing process works. The role of the courts, supposedly, is to protect citizens from that. But in the on-line intelligence collection business, these associations are generated automatically by algorithm, at the speed of light, with no accountability for who gets sucked up in these lists, and who doesn't.

DB: *Professor Simpson, you suggest these programs aren't new — we just know a bit more about them. What can we say about those who have been the stewards of these programs? Have they been lying to the American people? How come we don't know more about this, and didn't know a lot more, sooner?*

CS: I think KPFA listeners are probably aware of this type of thing. But in terms of the mainstream media, it's a big revelation. One of the modern revelations was an order from a secret court that established, or continued, these types of operations — that was a breakthrough. There have been whistleblowers going back at least to the Bush administration years that brought the basics of this system to light. Anybody familiar with data-mining can recognize the basic properties of how it is done, and how algorithms are used to identify what in commercial terms are people you might sell to, but in intelligence terms, are people suspected of crimes. It's possible to take the known information about the NSA, for example, and compare it to what is basic to data-mining and get a reasonably clear picture of how this goes on.

Not long ago, one of the members of the Senate Intelligence Committee, a senator from Oregon, asked very directly the Director of National Intelligence James Clapper, "Are there any programs in which the intelligence community captures data about millions of Americans?" Clapper said "No. No. Oh, well, wait, excuse me, we might do it inadvertently sometimes but on purpose, no." Some people would call that dissembling, others would call it lying, but it is clearly false. You get this same type of falsehood, and in many cases, misunderstanding, even from political figures such as [House Minority Leader Nancy] Pelosi, who confuses different aspects of these programs with one another, who makes claims about being briefed, but who, based on their comments, don't seem to understand what they were briefed on, or what we know the facts to be.

We've got a big problem where not only are there powerful, secret programs that are themselves unaccountable, but the people who are held up as being accountable, such as the congressional intelligence committees and so forth, either don't understand or are not telling the truth about what they've been told of these programs. It's a situation in which there is no recourse, although there is no probable cause for the collection of this information about Americans, or for that matter anybody else. There's no way to identify errors in these databases, and provide correct information.

When people have sued these agencies and attempted to get information about themselves, those cases have been tossed out of court on what's called a state's secret claim, in which the government in essence tells the courts, "Go away, don't interfere in this matter. It's a government intelligence matter." The courts don't have jurisdiction either.

DB: *Professor Simpson, can you reflect on the implications of the level of spying and government interference that's taking place now?*

CS: It's not surprising that people who feel vulnerable to these sorts of programs, ordinary people, will shy away from political activity and political involvement. They've got kids maybe, they're worried about their job — they don't want to get involved. That's called a chilling effect, and it's very dangerous for democracy. On the other hand, now is exactly the time to stand up and to be noisy, frankly, about how these programs operate — to push and make clear this is a Fourth Amendment issue, contrary to what Representative Pelosi has to say. It is important that people's right to privacy is respected.

Frequently you hear — even President Obama said this recently — that you can have security or you can have privacy, but you can't have both. I'm paraphrasing. That is a basic misunderstanding, and a misleading way to frame the question. In a democracy, privacy means the right to be left alone by the state — at least that. Some people say it means more, but we'll start with that basic idea — to be left alone by the state if you have not broken a law. What is being institutionalized here is a surveillance system that is so pervasive, there is no such thing as being left alone by the state, even if you are abiding by the laws. That's dangerous. How it's going to play itself out in a modern democracy, I don't think anybody knows, but it's a form of intrusion into people's lives that is different from what we read about in those *1984*, *Brave New World*, or cyberpunk fiction sorts of things. It's different, but it is more pervasive and more pernicious.

DB: *We're talking about getting more noisy, speaking out. It seems that while the government is increasing, expanding, and intensifying this kind of surveillance activity, they're also intensifying the punishment they offer and threaten whistleblowers who want to tell the truth. It seems like a two-pronged policy here.*

CS: Absolutely. It's predictable that's how things would unfold. Yet look at the history of the women's movement, the African American movement, the gay movement, and all sorts of movements. What has worked is standing up, speaking out — *not* standing up and *not* speaking out does not work. It doesn't protect anybody. I think the lessons of history show that now is the time to stand up, speak out, and exercise your rights because if millions of people are exercising their rights, the state does not have the capacity to punish all of them.

Snowden's Case for Asylum

Marjorie Cohn   June 2013

DB: *Despite US government pressure, Russian President Vladimir Putin is balking at demands that he extradite Edward Snowden from Moscow to face espionage charges for leaking secrets about America's global surveillance operations. The US government is putting on a full-court press to prosecute Edward Snowden for blowing the whistle on the National Security Agency's massive collection of data on phone calls by Americans and internet use by foreigners.*

But Marjorie Cohn, professor at Thomas Jefferson School of Law, says international law may give the 30-year-old systems analyst a path to political asylum. Professor Cohn, can you begin with an overview of the case?

MC: Edward Snowden revealed a secret program of massive spying on Americans and people around the world and he turned documents over to the *Guardian* and *Washington Post*. Then he went to Hong Kong, which is where he was until he left for Russia. The US government is likely to charge him under the Espionage Act with crimes that could garner him 30 years, or even life in prison, if they decide to add extra charges.

The Obama administration has gone after whistleblowers in an unprecedented manner, filing charges against eight people under the Espionage Act — more than twice the number of charges filed by all prior presidents combined.

Snowden could be extradited and sent back to the United States for trial. Russia and the US do not have an extradition treaty, but the US has extradited seven Russian prisoners in the last two years. A country can refuse extradition when the offense is political in nature. He would be charged under the Espionage Act and espionage is a classic political act that gives rise to a refusal of extradition, so Russia could refuse extradition on those grounds.

There's also a provision in the Convention against Torture called *non-refoulement,* that forbids extradition of a person to a country where there are substantial grounds to believe he would be in danger of being tortured. Since Chelsea Manning, another prominent whistleblower, was tortured by being held in solitary confinement for nine months, a country could conclude that Snowden might be subjected to the same fate, and deny extradition on that ground.

A country also has an obligation to refuse extradition when it would violate fundamental rights. The right to be free from torture and cruel treatment is a fundamental right. Under the Refugee Convention, any country could grant Snowden political asylum if he can show he has a well-founded fear of being persecuted in the United States due to political opinion. He probably could make that showing.

The Johannesburg Principles of national security, freedom of expression, and access to information, which were issued in 1996 provide, "No person may be punished on national security grounds for disclosure of information if the public interest in knowing the information outweighs the harm from the disclosure." It's important to be talking about that. What did Snowden do? His disclosures were clearly in the public interest. Did he harm national security?

There have been claims that terrorist attacks were thwarted by the massive dragnet surveillance Snowden exposed, but Senators Mark Udall and Ron Wyden of the Senate Select Committee on Intelligence looked at this classified information for years, and say it's not true. The intelligence that is the most useful for foiling these plots is traditional intelligence — not a dragnet surveillance where they listen to people's phone calls and track the places they visit on the internet.

Even if they are not listening in on the content of the phone calls or reading the content of the messages, the fact that they are profiling, coming up with so-called patterns based upon the websites people visit or the people they call could be a tremendous invasion of privacy and lead to a lot of false intelligence.

DB: *The scuttlebutt in the press is about how Snowden's lack of character is reflected by his choice of going to one of the US enemies — Ecuador, Cuba or Russia.*

MC: Quite frankly, if the US didn't have such an antagonistic and ill-advised policy against countries like Venezuela and Cuba, even Ecuador, these countries would probably be extraditing him back to the United States. But when the US pursues the kinds of policies it does in Latin America, it alienates progressive governments. In the 70s and 80s, the US was supporting the tyrannical countries in Latin America that were kidnapping, disappearing, torturing and murdering people. So it's hard to blame these governments for not being willing to do whatever the US says. According to Michael Ratner, a lawyer for Julian Assange, the Obama administration is bullying countries all over the world so they can get Snowden rendered to the US where he can be prosecuted.

Certainly the US government is known for its bullying. It has bullied countries that signed the Rome Statute for the International Criminal Court [ICC] — bullied them into not turning Americans over to the court if Americans are found in those countries. Even the Obama administration has influenced Spain to drop charges against the six Bush torture lawyers. That could be a form of bullying.

The US has been notorious for bullying countries, especially smaller countries, for years — they are blackmailed into believing they will lose foreign assistance from the United States if they don't do what the US wants. When Americans are asked in the polls about what Edward Snowden did, and they think about it personally — do we want the government monitoring our personal communications — they are very much against these massive spying programs and not so critical of Snowden.

It's important that the independent media bring what is happening to the people so they are not just left with sound bites from the corporate media that paint Snowden as a traitor because he violated national security policies that keep us safe from terrorist attacks. We heard that all through the Bush administration, and these policies didn't make us any safer. They probably make us less safe since there's so much hatred against the US since we invaded and killed so many people in Iraq and Afghanistan. The extensive torture, Guantanamo, and the drone strikes, which have been stepped up during the Obama administration, have all created much more hatred against the United States.

DB: *Is there any precedent that this man acted for the greater good of society?*

MC: Daniel Ellsberg leaked the Pentagon Papers, which revealed the truth about what the US government was doing in the Vietnam War; his revelation ultimately helped to end that war. You could say that was for the greater good. Also, Chelsea Manning leaked evidence of war crimes — the collateral murder video, among other things — that showed commission of war crimes, as defined by the Geneva Conventions, by people in the US Army. Yes, there is precedent for this.

DB: *Would the US be breaking international law if they sent a pick-up team to get him, wherever he was?*

MC: Yes, they would. He needs very tight security, wherever he is, because it's not beyond belief to think some thugs could kidnap him and render him to the US.

DB: *Is there any legal justification for the US to do that?*

MC: No, but somebody could do it and say they weren't working for the government. The government could say he's a traitor and we need to bring him to justice in our country and he is being shielded.

DB: *So he can be kidnapped and left somewhere the US could get him? The US could say, "We didn't get him. We found him here."*

MC: That's possible.

Breaking the Surveillance Security State
Birgitta Jonsdottir   June 2013

DB: The US government's "War on Terror" and its companion "surveillance state" have become troubling issues not only for the civil liberties of Americans, but even more so for the rest of the world where popular movements are arising to challenge the electronic penetration of people's information and violation of their privacy. Iceland Member of Parliament Birgitta Jonsdottir of the Pirate Party is also Director of the International Modern Media Institute and co-producer of the WikiLeaks' "Collateral Murder" video, which revealed the slaughter of Iraqis in 2007 by a US aerial weapons team.

Birgitta, you are a member of Iceland's Parliament. I wish we could have an elected official like you in this country.

BJ: You could have a person run for Congress just like me. I think many people in the US are ready for more transparency, accountability and maybe more direct democracy. None of these are alien concepts. People told me, before I entered Parliament four years ago, that because I was quite active, have always been an activist, and considered myself to be an activist in Parliament, I would be marginalized for my actions, which was mostly being a spokesperson for activist groups on environmental issues, against the war in Iraq, and for Tibet. I met so many capable people in this country who I would love to see enter into the belly of the beast, to understand how it works. It is our civic duty to do so. I had many discussions with people while here in the US in the last couple of weeks, about what we can do — we know what is wrong with our systems. The system in Iceland is just as broken as the system in the US. It takes a different formation, but it is broken All our systems are broken, and we all know it. That's why we have uprisings — all the movements, from Occupy Wall Street to Turkey. It is all about broken systems. I am very interested in finding out what we want instead.

DB: *How did you get involved in "Collateral Murder"?*

BJ: I was working with spokespersons for WikiLeaks in 2009. They came to Iceland and spoke at a Freedom Society event where I was also speaking. They talked about an idea that originated in this area of the world, from John Perry Barlow, who, a year earlier, in the wake of our financial collapse, said that Iceland could become a safe haven for freedom of information, expression and speech. Julian Assange and Daniel Ellsberg talked about the same concept, and it was ripe. I was elected to Parliament, the only geek in Parliament at the time. I approached them after the conference and we began to work on this project, which is to look at the best functioning laws in the twenty-first century that protect freedom of information, expression and speech. The reason I chose to work with WikiLeaks was they had hands-on experience in keeping things up on-line no matter what. They had released some documents from the Church of Scientology, and anybody who knows anything about the Church of Scientology knows that it's very difficult to keep things up because they have very good lawyers. They managed to keep their bible up and you can still access their bible through the internet because they have archive versions of the WikiLeaks website before the big leak, which came later.

As I was working with them and some other people, we came up with what politicians and people who want to increase civil liberties can do, and that is to get experts from all over the world to cherry pick the best laws that have proven to function. We wrote it on an "etherpad" in English, and then translated it into Icelandic. For some mysterious reason that I can't comprehend, maybe because there is such a need for it, not only in Iceland, but everywhere, I got unanimous acceptance for it in Parliament. That is equivalent to both the Senate and House of Representatives voting yes on something. The government of Iceland has been working on creating these laws. We have the best source protection in the world, and a very good freedom of information act for the twenty-first century, with transparency about media ownership, etc. The ministry is working to have the best whistleblower laws in the world put into place.

DB: *Tell me about your response to the content of the "Collateral Murder" video shown on WikiLeaks.*

BJ: I was one of the millions of people around the world who tried to stop the war in Iraq before it began and were nearly successful. We coordinated through the internet. I was one of the few who kept protesting after the war, such as against the atrocities in Fallujah. One man posted the horrible things that were happening there. I was following the Iraq body count and knew what was happening — but you can't express it enough to get people to feel the compassion or empathy that is needed to act. When I saw the video that Julian Assange showed me at a cafe opposite the Icelandic Parliament, I wept. I wept many times over this video. It is painful not only to see the war crimes that happen in this video. Particularly troubling for me was when I looked at the wounded man who was trying to get up, and good Samaritans came to help, just ordinary citizens. Imagine there was an accident on the road here, and someone would come and try to take the wounded to the hospital — just like in this video. They had kids in their car and they were killed, slaughtered. It was a murder of innocent people who were trying to do a decent thing, by saving somebody who was dying, and the way the soldiers spoke about it was horrifying.

DB: *There was almost a gleeful hysteria.*

BJ: It was, "Look at the dead bastards. Line them up, nice. It's their fault to bring their kids to war." Who brought the war to Iraq? It certainly wasn't these people — it was from a country far, far away. I knew when I helped release this video that my life would never be the same afterwards. I knew that I was participating in making world history and never thought twice about doing it. If I would be in the same situation tomorrow, I would do it without thinking about it.

DB: *How did it change your life?*

BJ: It changed in both positive and more disturbing ways. I felt I had done something that would make me feel I did something important with my life, because it had a tremendous impact on so many people, all over the world. It helped bring voices to the voiceless. People in Iraq are trying to tell how it is and what is happening there every day, and nobody pays attention. It was so important to me to show the truth to the families of these people who were killed in the video. It is an incredible gift to somebody to be able to do that.

On the other hand, I had an unexpected visit by the FBI. They came into my home, and went through everything, looked at letters I had been sending to my kids and my mother. They looked at who I was with and where and for how long. They went through everything, everything. But they didn't come through my front door — they came through my back door, the internet. They demanded that there would be no knock. Instead, they demanded that Twitter hand over all their metadata, IP numbers and messages, without my knowledge, within three days. Twitter took them to court and managed to unseal a secret document that said what a very scary person I am, a terrible terrorist. I wasn't able to take them to court, but I was advised to contact the EFF [Electronic Frontier Foundation] and the ACLU. I contacted them, and they offered to help and take this to court pro bono. In the first ruling, which was not reported in either the US or Europe, the judge said that I, as an individual, or you, or any individual who listens to this program, do not have the right to look after our own back when it comes to our information that is being stored and kept by social media companies like Gmail and Skype. We have to trust these companies to look after us, and some of them have a very bad track record. I'm talking about social media companies, the new generation — Google, Facebook, Skype and phone companies as well. When the FBI entered my home, this is exactly what happened. There are four more companies that I cannot possibly get unsealed by your courts, although we took this to three different court levels. This goes hand-in-hand with what has now been revealed with the NSA, which is that I cannot un-shield the companies that apparently are in all these documents. There are four others that handed over my information.

The Department of Justice demands that it's kept sealed because of an investigative thing, but I am not the subject of any criminal investigation. I am a Member of Parliament of a sovereign country, yet your government feels they need to find something about me, which compromises everybody who communicates with me, and I communicate with a lot of people. It also compromises their private information to me, so it's not only about me — it's about all of us. I took this to court so now we can see — if they can do this to me, they can do it to anybody.

I am so thankful to the whistleblower in the NSA case, Edward Snowden, because he got the entire world to pay attention to what many of us have been saying of the NSA — suspicions of abuse. I learned much from Thomas Drake, an NSA whistleblower who they tried to put in prison. It's important that people wake up — your government is not only prying into US civilians' private data, but into every person on the planet who uses Facebook or smart phones. You have become like China, Russia, and you must roll it back because you still can. Europe is thinking about building a digital fortress around itself to protect the civilians in Europe against tyranny — not against China, Iran or North Korea, but against the US surveillance state.

DB: *The video transformed the nature of the war effort in Iraq and forced the US hand to get some soldiers out of the country more quickly. Talk about what Julian did, and what happened to him.*

BJ: Julian and I share a similar vision that it is not enough to talk about problems — we need to figure out solutions, work on them, and try to inspire others to do it. I worked with him for five months, so we got quite well acquainted and it was very stimulating to talk with him and brainstorm. I would leave him at midnight and wake up at 6, and he would still be sitting in the same position, not having had anything to drink, just working. He is very dedicated to the cult of transparency.

Julian and the WikiLeaks team are making it possible. They brought into the public debate a very necessary discussion that has been ongoing — the status of freedom of information in our world. When Chelsea Manning managed to get into the discussion, it highlighted the necessity of whistleblowers. This word has almost been forgotten since Daniel Ellsberg, who says, "I was Chelsea Manning." It is uncanny to think about Snowden, the newest whistleblower coming forward from the NSA, who looks almost like Daniel Ellsberg, and had access to the same security clearances as Ellsberg, at the same level. I heard somebody say, "Daniel Ellsberg is back."

It is a tremendous service these people have given to our societies. Julian Assange is among them. He has had lots of controversy about his person, and I don't want to go deeply into that. I want to see the message that he is delivering. I watched him give a speech by Skype at an event for a company called Thoughtworks. He was so right on it. He wrote an excellent book with three other very important people called *Cyber Punk*. Another important book about the history of cryptography is called *This Machine Kills Secrets* by Andy Greenberg, who writes for *Forbes*. That book is both very creepy and very inspirational. If people want to get a crash course in the persons behind the cryptography movement and the leaking culture that has been developing after WikiLeaks, they should read these books.

DB *We know that the US government is engaged in a system of permanent war and is supported by a military-industrial communications network. Chelsea Manning is facing life. Some people want to kill her for telling the truth. What guides you through all this?*

BJ: Most of us are brought up to have the ethics of "if we witness a crime, we are supposed to tell about it." If you see somebody stealing a very expensive perfume, would you look the other way? If you see somebody abusing children, would you look the other way? If you see somebody killing somebody, would you look the other way? If you see somebody committing war crimes, would you look the other way? I am brought up to tell the truth. I am brought up that if I see a crime, I am supposed to report it. Most of the world is a part of the Geneva Convention, except the US. If the people of the US want to earn respect, trust and compassion from the rest of the world, they need to start cleaning up their garden. It is absurd and very depressing that nobody has been questioned or held accountable for the murders that we witnessed in the "Collateral Murder" video, except Chelsea Manning, who showed it to us — who had the guts, heart and ethics to put it out there.

DB: *We have the First Amendment and the example is you can't shout fire in a crowded theater if there's no fire. If there is a fire in that theater and you turn and walk away, then you are responsible for what happens in the aftermath. We live by that on Flashpoints. We believe that information is power and that it's important to get this information out. It's important for people to understand how essential it is to have somebody like Daniel Ellsberg and Chelsea Manning.*

BJ: Yes, and let's not forget about the journalist Barrett Brown. They managed to character-assassinate him by saying he threatened the FBI people who were harassing him. He was taken into the TrapWire that has now been revealed in the NSA leak. I encourage people to look at what TrapWire is. Brown was digging deeper than they wanted him to dig. WikiLeaks has the spy files, much of them now revealed by the NSA. Those of us who know of these things, have been trying to warn the public. Barrett Brown was too close for comfort, so he's in prison for submitting a link to leaked files. Jeremy Hammond, sometimes called the Robin Hood of the internet, is in prison and facing probably ten years for getting the files from Stratfor. Stratfor is a private surveillance company contracted by the government to look after us — or look at us — without our knowledge. There was an attempt to undermine and spy on WikiLeaks and people associated with it. Jeremy Hammond revealed this.

This is all interconnected — WikiLeaks, Chelsea Manning, Jeremy Hammond, Barrett Brown, Thomas Drake. There are many more. I encourage people to look at these people, because it all falls under the category of mass surveillance and a mass secrecy state. They are surveilling everything about us, and in particular in the US and Europe, we don't have a clue about who is doing it. I heard that 70 percent of the surveillance state is contracted with private firms. Imagine how much money is spent on this, when infrastructure is absolutely collapsing — health care, education, even bridges are collapsing because there's no money to be put in there. It's all being paid to private firms that are dancing in the revolving door.

DB: *We build advanced weaponry, and bug each other, while the kids die, the bridges fall, and the wars continue.*

BJ: While you have the revolving door, and accept it as the right way to govern, something is wrong. Do people want this? Do they want Monsanto to genetically modify our food, killing farmers in India and the US? They are taking their own lives because they don't see any future, and they are frankensteining our food. If people will not change, they need to think of the issue we can unite around — what is the single most important thing the American people can do to put a crack in the system? That is the task.

Bush's Foiled UN Blackmail Scheme

Katharine Gun   June 2013

DB: *In early 2003, as the US and British governments were seeking international acquiescence to their aggressive war on Iraq, the plot was foiled when an unexpected cog was thrown into the propaganda machine — the disclosure that the National Security Agency [NSA] was spying on UN Security Council members in search of blackmail material. The revelation received little attention in the mainstream US news media, but the disclosure received wide international attention and stopped the blackmail scheme. US President George W. Bush and British Prime Minister Tony Blair were forced to abandon a UN resolution and invade Iraq with a ragtag "coalition of the willing."*

Several months later, the identity of the leaker was revealed — a brave young British intelligence officer named Katharine Gun who worked as a linguist at the NSA's UK counterpart, British Government Communications Headquarters [GCHQ]. Gun lost her job and was charged under British secrecy laws, but the case was dropped because the court would have required the Blair government to disclose that it also had twisted the arms of legal advisers to extract an opinion endorsing the invasion. Now, a decade later, Edward Snowden, a young American systems analyst working for the NSA, has leaked documents revealing a global surveillance network and prompted another international debate — about government spying vs. personal privacy.

Katharine, what was your position when you decided to leak the document?

KG: My title was linguist analyst. I was a Mandarin Chinese speaker. We translated interceptions and produced reports for the various customers of GCHQ, which are normally the Foreign Office or MI5 and MI6.

DB: *Can you explain the document you released and the significance of the timing?*

KG: It was released at the end of January 2003, just before the invasion of Iraq. I saw an email that had been sent from the NSA to GCHQ. It was a request for GCHQ to help the NSA intercept the communications of six nations that sat on the Security Council at that time. The request was to intercept their domestic and office telecoms in order to obtain all the information we could about the delegates, who the US could then use to achieve goals favorable to US interests. They called for the whole gamut of information, which made me think they would potentially use the information to blackmail or bribe the UN delegates.

DB: *This bugging took place at the United Nations?*

KG: Presumably, yes. Or it could involve the United Nations headquarters or also their domestic residence.

DB: *The idea was to get the necessary information one way or the other to influence key members to support the US quest for war in Iraq?*

KG: Yes. At the time, if you were not working for the intelligence services or the foreign offices of the US or UK you would probably assume that the goals of [President George W.] Bush and [Prime Minister Tony] Blair at that time were to work diplomatically to reach a solution. But we now know, after several leaks over the years about the run-up to the war in Iraq, that war was the agenda all along. When I saw the email it made me think, "This is evidence that war is the agenda." That's why I decided the public needed to know.

DB: *GCHQ is the equivalent of the NSA. You were working there in the lead-up to the Iraq War. What governments were bugged?*

KG: Six nations, smallish countries: Angola, Cameroon, and Pakistan, I think. Mexico was mentioned, and possibly Chile as well. They were countries that are generally not known for their big powerful positions at the UN.

DB: *How did you make this courageous decision to leak this information that also changed your own life? It changed history a bit.*

KG: I was very concerned. I had informed myself about the realities of Iraq and the situation there because I grew up during the first Gulf War and the following years of sanctions. It was in the back of my mind that Iraq was a country that was virtually destroyed, and the people were living in impoverished conditions. It made me think that another attack on them would not be fair and justified because there was nothing about Iraq that was a threat to either the US or the UK. So when I saw the email and realized that what was going on behind closed doors was an attempt to get the UN to authorize what would then have become a preemptive strike on a country, I thought the public should know, because it angered me.

DB: *What happened after you made this information available? Were you intimidated, attacked?*

KG: Initially I tried to remain anonymous, but when I realized the information revealed in the newspaper at the time was identifiable to GCHQ, I decided I didn't want to lead a double life at GCHQ and pretend I had nothing to do with it. I confided to my line manager and said it was my leak. Then I was arrested under suspicion of breaking the Official Secrets Act, questioned, and released on bail for eight months.

In November 2003, much to our surprise, they decided to charge me, despite having waited so long. After discussions with my legal team, which included Liberty, an organization very similar to the ACLU [American Civil Liberties Union], we decided I would plead not guilty, because I felt that although I did the act, I didn't feel guilt because I didn't feel I had done anything wrong. Our defense would have been to establish the defense of necessity, which is not yet tested in a court of law. My legal team then asked for all the legal advice leading up the war, and at that point, the prosecution decided to drop all charges against me.

DB: *What do you think made them decide to prosecute you, and what information made them drop the charges? Were they trying to backpedal?*

KG: It's speculation on my part because obviously they haven't disclosed. I suspect one of the reasons they charged me was to make an example of my actions to try to deter people from doing something similar. On the other hand, when they dropped the charges, I suspect there may have been a variety of reasons. When we asked for the legal advice from the then-Attorney General, his legal advice was not fully disclosed.

During the run-up to the war, Blair asked for legal advice. The first draft was about 13 pages long. The language was very cautious — it didn't say there was a definite reason for war. There were many legal terms of caution, and at some point Blair was told the legal advice was not good enough. He needed a watertight case. The Attorney General then re-drafted his advice, and condensed it to a single page that was then issued to the House of Commons. That is what persuaded all the MPs in the House of Commons to vote for Britain's involvement in the war. Eventually information came out, not from myself, but from other means, and it became apparent that the legal advice had not been at all watertight to start with.

DB: *Daniel Ellsberg said your most important and courageous leak is the only one ever made in time to avert an imminent war. Was your desire to avert war?*

KG: Yes, I was hoping the British ministers would see the truth and question the actions of Blair and the secret negotiations he was having with Bush at the time. I wanted more transparency on the issue. I wanted people to question what was going on and challenge this bandwagon for a preemptive strike against a country that was already very impoverished and no threat to anybody whatsoever.

DB: *Did you ever hear from folks who, based on your revelations, learned they were bugged?*

KG: No.

DB: *So you didn't receive thanks from that part of the world?*

KG: No. At the time of the leak, my name didn't come out. Eight months later my name was made public.

DB: *Did it change your life?*

KG: I lost my job. The secure, full-time, long-term employment was no longer possible. That made an impact, primarily financially, on my life and my family's life.

DB: *We are now seeing extraordinary NSA leaks from Edward Snowden.*

KG: I think Snowden is probably a lot more clued-up than I was at the time. My leak was a single issue. Snowden had a long period of time working within the US intelligence services. He's obviously a very technically savvy professional. I admire him for taking this tremendous step, which he thought out very carefully and methodically. He has made some very good points. These kinds of issues should be in the public domain because it involves innocent members of the public. We, the public, should be able to have a measure of a say in these matters.

DB: *We hear that people like you and Snowden are putting people's lives in jeopardy, endangering the people. We hear that secrecy is necessary to prevent terrorist attacks, and that many attacks have been prevented by the secrecy, investigation, wiretapping, and bugging that's going on now.*

KG: There is absolutely no evidence that my leaks in any way endangered anybody else.

DB: *But you were accused of that.*

KG: Yes, they love to throw accusations around — there's no doubt about that. But in my case, the majority of views supported my actions. In Snowden's case, people who have a fair and just understanding of the issues at-large are supportive of his actions, as they would be of Private Manning, who is currently on trial.

DB: *Did you lose any friends or associates, over this?*

KG: Ironically, not really. Many of my friends and colleagues from GCHQ have also left GCHQ, partly to progress in their professions. They didn't see much chance for their linguistic skills progressing much further within GCHQ, and I continue to be in touch with them.

DB: *If you had it all to do over again, would you?*

KG: That's a difficult question. Now I'm married and have a child. I would hope that I would still do it, but perhaps I would be more savvy about how I did it. Snowden was very clued-up and seems to know exactly what he should be doing — how to stay safe and keep out of the way of being unjustly arrested and tried without due process of law.

The Class War

Splitting Open the World: Voice for Domestic Workers
Ai-Jen Poo   April 2012

DB: For 20 years, Ai-jen Poo has been fighting for the rights of domestic workers in the United States, an organizing task that many labor experts thought impossible, given the sketchy information about who these housekeepers and caregivers are and where they work. But she has scored some stunning successes. This week, Time *magazine named Ai-jen Poo, director of the National Domestic Workers Alliance, to the 2012* Time 100, *the magazine's annual list of the 100 most influential people in the world. Poo is the co-director of National Domestic Workers Alliance. Her organizing of domestic workers has included a decade-long struggle that culminated in the passage of the groundbreaking Domestic Workers Bill of Rights in New York State, which earned her the informal title of "the Nannies' Norma Rae." In 2007 she co-founded the National Domestic Workers Alliance to bring dignity and respect to this growing, yet undervalued, workforce nationally.*

She is also the co-director of Caring Across Generations (CAG), a national movement of families, caregivers, and over 200 organizations working for culture and policy change to value caregiving relationships and to meet our nation's changing care needs. Her first book, The Age of Dignity, *calls attention to the need for a new, sustainable and dignified approach to care as the nation's population ages.*

The Time 100 *list spotlights the activism, innovation and achievement of the world's most influential individuals. As* Time *Managing Editor Richard Stengel has said of the list in the past, "The* Time 100 *is not a list of the most powerful people in the world, it's not a list of the smartest people in the world; it's a list of the most influential people in the world. They're scientists, they're thinkers, they're philosophers, they're leaders, they're icons, they're artists, they're visionaries. People who are using their ideas, their visions, their actions to transform the world and have an effect on a multitude of people."*

Congratulations on the honor. Were you surprised?

AP: I was surprised, but I think it's a testament to all the wonderful organizing that's been happening among domestic workers around the country. Finally this is a workforce whose time has come, and an issue that's time has come.

DB: *Tell us about the National Domestic Workers Alliance. Who do you represent?*

AP: The National Domestic Workers Alliance is an alliance of 35 local organizations representing nannies, housekeepers, and caregivers for the elderly, in 19 cities and 11 states around the country. [Ed. Current numbers are 53 affiliates, plus the first local chapter in Atlanta, in 37 cities and 18 states.] These organizations in San Francisco and Oakland have been organizing immigrant women who work as caregivers and housekeepers — domestic workers of all sorts. It's an alliance of all kinds of organizations, all of whom are working to gain respect and recognition for this very important work that we believe is the work that makes all other work possible.

This workforce is incredibly vulnerable. Domestic workers are still excluded from almost every major labor law that exists in this country. The workforce is very isolated, working in individual scattered homes around the country. No one knows where they are or which households have domestic workers — it's not registered anywhere, so there's a high degree of vulnerability and a legacy of exclusion and discrimination. That means workers like Maria work 12, 13, 14 hours a day for low wages, sometimes below minimum wage, usually without overtime pay, and high degrees of vulnerability to abuse, harassment, unjust firing, and denial of basic rights. That's what the organizing has been about; lifting up those stories, building the power of the workforce, and changing the laws to bring respect and recognition to this work.

DB: *These women who do this work are often in grave danger because nobody knows where they are. They are disconnected because often they have no line out to the rest of the world.*

AP: That's right. There's isolation. Think about what it took for the women's movement to educate the broader public and bring the notion that domestic violence is not just a few isolated incidences, but a systemic problem. To break the silence about violence against women that happens behind closed doors, gives a sense of what might be happening behind closed doors in homes around the country, where women are working.

This is an enormous and growing workforce. We estimated at least two and a half million workers are doing this work that makes all other work possible in households around the country. To have that large of a workforce be so invisible, so isolated, and so vulnerable to abuse, is exactly what we are trying to address.

DB: *Since you co-founded the National Domestic Workers Alliance, one very significant victory is the Domestic Workers Bill of Rights in New York State.*

AP: After a six year organizing campaign where hundreds of domestic workers journeyed to the capital of the State of New York, Albany, to tell their stories and assert their dignity and demand justice, we were successful in passing the very first Domestic Workers Bill of Rights in the country, extending basic labor rights to over 200,000 women who do domestic work in the State of New York. It was an historic breakthrough, and last year in Geneva, Switzerland we had our second historic breakthrough when the International Labor Organization passed the first International Convention on Domestic Work, establishing basic labor standards for over 100 million people who work as domestic workers around the world.

We're on our way to the next historic breakthrough, which is to pass a domestic workers bill of rights in the State of California, where again, over 200,000 domestic workers work every day in households helping the families throughout the State of

California and supporting those families and professionals to be able to do what they need to do every day. That workforce is on the brink of another very important victory with the passage of Assembly Bill 889.

DB: *How did you become engaged in this work, to join these women in this battle?*

AP: I come from a long line of very strong women who took care of our family and their community and professionally also did care work. My grandmother was a nurse, and my mother's a doctor, and a lot of the work they did to care for families in their community was not valued for what it is truly worth. I saw that growing up and also saw a tremendous amount of violence against women in our community. So early on I became involved in women's organizations and domestic violence advocacy, which eventually lead to women's organizing to support women to create a different future, a different economy, a different democracy, for all of us. We always say that when you look at the world through the eyes of the women, you see the world much more clearly both in terms of the problems at hand and the solution — the potential solution and the ways forward. I have always followed the leadership of the women who I work with and whom I'm connected to — who have led me along this path.

DB: *There's that wonderful quote from poet Muriel Rukeyser: "What would happen if one woman told the truth about her life? ... The world will split open."*

AP: That's right.

DB: *It takes unbelievable courage to be undocumented, a woman, a person of color, isolated, with not a lot of money, and having to protect your family, and all their lives.*

AP: I see the most incredible acts of courage every single day in our workforce. It takes courage to assert your dignity, assert your humanity, in the face of vulnerability, and the denial and systemic devaluing of your work on a daily basis — and to still take pride in it and bring love, energy, and hope to the work you do and the work of organizing for change. Not only have people denied the value of domestic work, people have said that domestic workers are unorganizable. It takes incredible courage to be able to stand up in the face of all of that and assert our dignity and assert the possibility of power and respect — courage I've witnessed for the last 15 years. Every day it inspires me to get up and do what I do and I know that it's going to continue to make history.

DB: *They got a domestic workers bill of rights passed in New York, and now the battle is in California. If people want more information about your organization, how do they get that?*

AP: Please sign up for our website list at www.domesticworkers.org so we can stay in touch with you. There's a role for everyone in our movement. We need all of us — all of us are connected, and we can all make history and follow the lead of this incredible workforce, which has courageously been paving the way to a more caring, equitable economy for all of us. We need you, and we need your voices in this movement.

[They have now won Domestic Workers Bills of Rights in five states (NY, CA, HI, MA, and OR), and won domestic worker protections in Connecticut. *Ed.*]

Still Fighting: At 50, Cesar Chavez's UFW Legacy

Arturo Rodriguez   April 2012

DB: *A half-century after Cesar Chavez founded the United Farm Workers [UFW], the people who harvest America's crops remain under pressure from both harsh working conditions and draconian immigration laws. The California State Assembly recently passed a resolution recognizing March 31 as Cesar Chavez Day and urging Californians to observe a day of public service. The resolution was authored by California State Assemblyman Luis Alejo of Watsonville, where the UFW farmworker struggle began 50 years ago. "The injustices in the field are not merely a Latino experience," Alejo said. "The struggles that farmworkers faced and continue to face are shared with the African American community, the Filipino and Asian community, members of the Arab community and countless others."*

March 31, 1927 was Chavez's birthday, and this year marks the half-century anniversary of the founding of the UFW. Arturo Rodriguez, you are president of the UFW. Remind us who Cesar Chavez was and why it's important not only to remember him, but also to carry on the work.

AR: Cesar Chavez founded the United Farm Workers in 1962 along with 200 farmworkers. They had a dream, a vision — they knew it wasn't right for farmworkers to continue to get abused, disrespected, paid low wages, and not given the dignity they deserve for producing and harvesting our fruits and vegetables here in the nation.

DB: *He had a dramatic and transformational impact on the whole labor movement.*

AR: Cesar Chavez brought new life to the labor movement, brought to it new tactics, new strategies, new ways of doing things, and yet at the same time, he didn't have the opportunities like so many others in getting a formal education. He was only able to go to the eighth grade, but he was determined, committed, and very practical about his work. He understood that the only way we could build a union for farmworkers was to not only rely upon the sacrifices and the hard work of farmworkers but at the same time depend heavily on consumers throughout the United States, Canada, and other parts of the world to bring economic pressure on employers through the use of boycotts. Never before had boycotts been utilized throughout the labor movement. Today it is very commonplace for millions to utilize boycotts to meet their goals and objectives in regards to getting contracts and improving wages for their work forces.

DB: *He also put his life on the line with life threatening hunger strikes that brought the attention of people in the US and around the world to the plight of the farmworkers.*

AR: Exactly. Cesar Chavez believed in non-violence such as was practiced by Mahatma Gandhi and Martin Luther King. He felt it was important to engage people, and to make sacrifices of his own to get people to respond, to listen so he could demonstrate that this was such an important issue, he was willing to make penance for all the things that farmworkers had to have done throughout the years, in order to bring about change and bring about the determination necessary to be able to form a union — to be able to form an association.

Throughout his life he fasted numerous times, but there were three major fasts -the first one was in 1968 when he fasted for 24 days. Robert Kennedy came and broke that fast with him. Then he fasted in 1972 in Phoenix, Arizona for 24 days and Robert's son came and broke the fast with him at mass. His third fast, in 1988, was his longest fast, and was shortly before he passed away at 61 years old. It took place in Delano, California, and was finalized with a mass. Ethel Kennedy came to break bread with Cesar and mark the ending of that fast.

DB: *It is still a life-and-death battle to have legislation passed in the California legislature that will help prevent farmworkers from continuing to die horrible deaths in the sun, as they pick the fruits and vegetables that we all depend on. Farmworkers continue to die, right?*

AR: Yes. Since 2005, there are documented cases of at least 16 farmworkers who died as a result of heat stroke — just in California. They're horrible deaths, when folks are out there harvesting the fruits and vegetables with temperatures going above a hundred degrees. They are not given the water they need, or the rest they need. They are forced to work at an incredible pace to ensure that the foremen, labor contractors and growers meet production quotas. But sometimes it's impossible.

One of the deaths was a young Oaxacan woman, Maria Isabel Vasquez Jimenez, who died at the age of 17 when she was pregnant. It was impossible for her to maintain the pace that growers forced her to keep while she was harvesting wine grapes in northern San Joaquin Valley near Stockton.

Situations like that that not only inspired us, but motivated us to go after legislation that puts pressure on the State of California, on Cal-OSHA [Occupational Safety and Health Administration] and on Governor Jerry Brown, to ensure that the laws passed by the legislature and signed by the governor are enforced. This is so that farmworkers don't have to needlessly die as a result of just trying to do their job.

DB: *How would California AB 2346 help?*

AR: This is our way of celebrating the legacy of Cesar Chavez. We want to continue doing the work. It's nice that we have streets, buildings, schools, and libraries recognizing the work that Cesar Chavez did, but the way we truly represent and remember his legacy is through continuing to make improvements for the lives of farmworkers. What AB 2346 will do is give farmworkers the authority to make a citizen's arrest if the grower is not abiding by regulations that exist to give farmworkers more drinking water, to provide them rest when they ask for it, and to ensure shade in the fields while they are working in the extreme heat. Also, the growers will be responsible for the actions of the farm labor contractors, or their foremen or supervisors at their particular company. They won't be allowed to just wash their hands. These violations take place constantly and they say, "Look, we didn't know, we weren't aware...How can we keep track of ..."

Of course they can keep track of what's going on in their fields, just as they do production of the product being harvested. They know exactly how much is being produced. By the same token they know what the conditions are like. They can ensure that the farm labor contractors, foremen, or supervisors they are hiring are abiding by the laws we fight so hard to get in this state.

DB: *Governor Jerry Brown bills himself as a liberal Democrat. On the last round for this bill, Brown opposed it.*

AR: Governor Jerry Brown in the 1970s signed historic legislation for farmworkers. The California Agricultural Labor Relations Act allows farmworkers, for the first time, the opportunity to be able to organize and form a union, just like any other worker in the United States. In his second round as governor of California, we need to go and call attention to the various issues that are important to farmworkers. Often times the interest of growers or the interest of people with money far outpace the needs of farmworkers, poor people in the state, especially when they are undocumented workers. And as a result, we find ourselves doing marches, protests, fasting, letter-writing campaigns, and email campaigns. We must get the attention of the governor to insure that he does not forget what the right thing to do is, and does not forget about the sacrifices farmworkers make every single day to be sure he has food on his table, as well as everybody else in this nation.

DB: *Have you spoken to the governor?*

AR: Yes, last year, before we marched to Sacramento in pursuit of ensuring that farmworkers had better organizing rights and opportunities than what was passed and what existed. To ensure that the Agriculture Labor Relations Act was enforced, we marched 200 miles from Madera, California, in the San Joaquin Valley, to Sacramento.

It was August, and extremely hot for the workers who accompanied me. Prior to that march, we sat down for several hours with Governor Jerry Brown and made it very clear to him why we were marching, and why we felt it was necessary to expand the organizing rights of farmworkers. They are not like any other worker in this country. We told him we're up against tremendous opposition, tremendous power on the part of the growers, so we were looking for his leadership, looking for him to do the right thing on behalf of farmworkers in this country. We said he had a legacy of helping poor people, and he should be thinking about that legacy as much as he is thinking about increasing the revenue of this state. Yes, we have spoken with him and made our thoughts very clear. We're going to continue to push for the type of enforcement necessary, and to push for the types of laws that would give farmworkers the same opportunities as other workers in this country — to have a better life, be able to have a living wage, a medical plan for their families, and to take care of their basic needs.

DB: *I hope the governor is listening. He had a show on KPFA, Pacifica radio, where he talked about how important these issues were. He seemed very supportive.*

AR: It's always important and critical to take a moment and let farmworkers know that we appreciate the sacrifices they make every day to be sure we've got fruit, vegetables, the wine we consume — we appreciate that they take the time to do all of it. If these farmworkers weren't doing that work, there wouldn't be anybody else to harvest the crops, no line of people waiting, despite the unemployment that exists in this state. There are not people waiting to get that job in the fields. It's extremely difficult, and requires a lot of talent and skill for someone to be able to endure the circumstances, and simultaneously be able to pick the kind of product that the grower demands, the consumers want, and ensure they pick it at the pace required by the growers.

That is our way of honoring Cesar Chavez. I just returned from the Department of Labor in Washington, D.C where Secretary Hilda Solis honored the five martyrs of the United Farm Workers. This year we celebrate our 50th anniversary, so the Department of Labor inducted the five martyrs of the UFW into the Labor Hall of Honor, which is unheard of. We're so grateful to Secretary Solis for taking the time. Then they named the auditorium at the Secretary of Labor offices in Washington, D.C. after Cesar Chavez.

It was a very emotional event, when the families of those farmworkers were recognized by the Secretary of Labor, the Secretary of the Interior, Ken Salazar, and the Secretary of Agriculture, Tom Vilsack. We are very blessed with a lot of support and thank everyone who is joining us in various activities as we celebrate this year.

DB: *Please tell us the names of the five martyrs.*

AR: The first one was a young Jewish woman named Nan Freeman, who was killed in 1972 on the picket line in Florida. Then two individuals were killed during the 1973 grape strike in the San Joaquin Valley, in the Lamont, California area. One was Nagi Daifallah and the other was Juan de la Cruz.

The fourth, Rufino Contreras, was killed in 1979 during the Salinas and Imperial Valley strike of lettuce, broccoli, and other vegetables. The last was a 21-year-old farmworker from the Fresno area named Rene Lopez. He was killed during a union election, if you can imagine that! The employer's brother-in-law came, pulled Rene over to his car, pulled a pistol out and shot him dead at the election site.

DB: *The folks in Alabama found out how important the farmworkers were, how hard the work was, and the skills needed, when they passed that draconian series of laws. They had a problem, because they almost lost their crops.*

AR: Yes. It didn't only happen in the State of Alabama — Georgia and Arizona are seeing the same thing. There's nobody to pick the crops except for the farmworkers who are here today. Unfortunately, most of us are undocumented and that's why we continue to fight so hard for immigration reform, so that farmworkers can be respected just like any other worker in this nation.

Stealing the Commonwealth: US Post Offices

Gray Brechin   March 2013

DB: *The US Postal Service, which has bound the nation together since its founding, is under intense pressure to privatize, especially from business rivals and libertarians. But there is a growing grassroots movement to save the US Postal Service from Right-wing Republicans who want to privatize it and turn over its most lucrative pieces to the likes of FedEx and United Parcel Service, which have lobbied Congress to make this happen. The resistance is because post offices represent some of America's finest examples of public space and common purpose, says Gray Brechin, project scholar for the Living New Deal at the University of California, Berkeley. Brechin is engaged in the effort to save the US Post Office as a public trust, as well as the people's art commissioned as a part of Franklin Roosevelt's New Deal.*

Gary, you blogged last year that "Thousands of post offices stand to be converted to condos, restaurants, and real estate offices or demolished to cover the Postal Service's largely manufactured deficit. Those that rely on the Post Office are protesting the disappearance of this still vital public service but few have registered what this fire sale represents to the nation's architectural and artistic legacy..." The Post Office is one of the remaining peoples' institutions. Can you provide some history about how the Post Office evolved and why we need a Post Office when we've got the internet?

GB: I never imagined I'd be doing Post Office studies but I got sucked into it because in the last ten years I've been studying the New Deal. We've been inventorying and mapping it, and it got me thinking about The Public in general. The New Deal was a huge expansion of the idea of The Public, or the commonwealth, which is what we *all* own. And very often — as with the Post Office — it's what we've *paid* for, what our parents and grandparents paid for and built.

It also got me interested in the war against the New Deal, against Franklin Roosevelt, which has been going on for thirty to forty years. It gained strength under President Reagan who was the anti-Roosevelt; equally as charismatic but to opposite ends. These neoliberals, as we now call them, and libertarians began taking over under Reagan. In 1986 the White House came up with something called "Starve the Beast." It's interesting to refer to the government as The Beast — it's a great way to begin distancing people from it, and seeing it as the enemy rather than as *us*. Reagan was very good at that. The idea behind Starve the Beast was that you deliberately bankrupt your government through tax cuts and tax shifts; shifting from progressive to regressive taxes. You do this over a long period of time. It's a long march through the institutions, but in doing so you can get rid of The Public. You can make a very nice profit from doing so as you privatize what was the commons and take it away from the public that paid for and built it. That's essentially what's happening with the Post Office.

What's happening to the Post Office is linked to what's happening to public education and public parks. In the 1990s, I was teaching geography and gave a tour of the San Francisco Presidio, which was just being transferred from the Army to the Park Service. As I was taking the students into a building, one of the new rangers took me aside and said, "Watch this very carefully. No other national park has been required to turn a profit. This is the entering wedge for what they are going to do to the national parks."

Sure enough, the Presidio Trust, which is appointed by the President, is mostly real estate people. The Presidio serves as a model of what could happen to other national parks, particularly if we go off the fiscal cliff and there's no money to operate them anymore. That's essentially what happened to the Post Office. In 2006, the Postal Accountability and Enhancement Act was passed by Congress, a Congress paid by UPS, FedEx, Pitney Bowes and other companies.

DB: *A very unprofitable Congress. I don't think they made much money.*

GB: They've actually been making out like the bandits. FedEx is one of the biggest lobbyists and gives huge amounts of money to Congress members — and they want the profitable business of the Post Office. They are backed up by the Right-wing and libertarian think tanks like the American Enterprise Institute, Cato Institute, Independent Institute and the Peter Peterson Foundation. They've all done papers about this, including ALEC, the American Legislative Exchange Council, whose dirty fingerprints I see all over that 2006 Act. Congress is now poisoning and killing the Postal Service so they not only have to cut services, as everybody's noticed, but we're watching the dismantling of this public service under our very eyes.

They're also selling off *our* real estate and *our* art. I say that quite deliberately. It's not theirs; it's *ours* — we all own it, and you should always use the first person plural when speaking about this. It is not theirs, especially the art, which the Roosevelt administration created and is unique to the US.

DB: *Let's talk about what's at stake with these structures — the art and what they mean to people.*

GB: That's how I got into this. As I was looking at those buildings I became more and more amazed at their quality. You go into some of these old Post Offices and they uplift you because they have amplitude, great spaces, wonderful materials and great craftsmanship. It's not accidental.

These are the physical expressions of the federal government across the nation, in every small town. In cities they become palaces. The idea was that the Post Office would represent for people the integrity and public service of far-off Washington, D.C. — what Ben Franklin, the first Postmaster, set up in 1775 to serve everybody. It was required to provide universal service to bind the nation together and do it at a very reasonable price, which it's been doing quite successfully ever since. These buildings, and the art in them, are unique, beautiful, and precious. We can't afford to lose them.

DB: *What is in these Post Offices? When you talk about precious art, that's not hyperbole. This is extraordinary work.*

GB: This is the people's art gallery. They are most famous for the murals, but there are sculptures too. These were meant to reflect Americans back to themselves in public spaces. This had never happened before. Americans could go into their Post Offices — often the most public place in their town — and see the work they do. They would also see their history, their legends. But most commonly they'd see their work conveyed with the dignity of labor — of ranching, farming, mining, and fishing — whatever happens to be the local specialty. It's all about work. That was important during the Depression, of course, when people didn't have work, so they wanted to see what gives their lives meaning — work. It's often art about postal workers, to celebrate the everyday heroism of the work people do to bind the nation together, to communicate with and to serve one another. We don't think of that. I didn't think about what a miracle the postal system is, and the hundreds of thousands of men and women who do that kind of work.

Now I appreciate it enormously and I always thank my postman, because he's about to get a lot more work if they eliminate the Saturday delivery. On Monday he will carry another day of mail if Postmaster General [Patrick] Donahue gets rid of Saturday delivery. Your postman will be getting to some of the houses at eight o'clock at night with a flashlight and looking very, very tired.

DB: *Some noted artists participated in these paintings. Who's up on the walls?*

GB: Many of the artists you probably wouldn't recognize, although they were known in their time.

DB: *But the public will recognize the people in the murals on the walls.*

GB: Yes, they'll see themselves and their surroundings, their myths. There's one in Troy, New York with wonderful murals of the Legend of Sleepy Hollow, because that's where Washington Irving hung out. Some of the artists were quite famous: Paul Cadmus, Adolph Gottlieb. My favorite is Ben Shahn, one of the great social realists of that time. I wrote an article last May for the *Living New Deal* newsletter and said that when the Postal Service management finds out how much the art is worth, they would sell that too. Just a few weeks ago, it announced that it's going to sell the Central Bronx Post Office, a very large Post Office from the New Deal with thirteen Ben Shahn murals in it that are probably worth more than the building and the real estate it's on. There are thirteen murals that show Americans doing work in factories, with jackhammers, etc. He was asked about that, and he said he wanted to show people in the Bronx what kind of work people all around the US do, not just there, but everywhere else. It's a celebration of labor.

DB: *You mentioned in an earlier interview that friends and historians come to the US and do a Post Office tour because they study history through the Post Office.*

GB: Yes. I have friends in Australia who love to come to the US and take road trips so they can see our Post Offices, because you never know what you are going to run into in these small towns. You'll often run into a beautiful building, very often with art in it. It's always a surprise and actually infectious, because now I do the same thing. Whenever I travel I make sure to visit the small town Post Office and sometimes it blows my mind. I recently went to the one in Grants Pass, Oregon, which is paneled in the most beautiful spider-web marble with bronze trimming.

DB: *I'd love to do a tour of interviews of small town postmaster generals...*

GB: Wouldn't that be wonderful?

DB: *We've talked about what we're going to lose and who's going to lose it. Who gains? Are there specific people that we need to know about?*

GB: Yes, there's a lot to gain. United Parcel Service, FedEx, and Pitney Bowes all want the profitable business from their public rival so they were probably backing this unconscionable Act in 2006, which is now very successfully killing the Post Office. Postmaster General Patrick Donahue probably has a very cushy job waiting for him at FedEx.

DB: *That seems pretty obvious.*

GB: That's the old revolving door. The press has shamefully fallen down on this story — it has not seen the big picture. Occasionally the press mentions the 2006 Act as the proximate cause of why this is all happening, but it hasn't noticed the real estate. These post offices were designed for the centers of every town and city because they had to be accessible and serve all the businesses as well as the people. What happens if suddenly all of this goes on the market? It's been conservatively estimated that the real estate portfolio held by the US Postal Service in trust for us is worth about $105 billion. If anybody can get their hands on that they are going to make a very nice profit. Last July, the Postal Service gave an exclusive contract to a giant real estate company called CBRE. Richard Ellis is a giant company, part of a holding company owned by billionaire private equity financier Richard C. Blum, and a regent of the University of California, who has been busy privatizing my university. He also happens to be married to Senator Dianne Feinstein, probably the most powerful senator in Congress. It's an extraordinary conflict of interest, but not uncommon in Senator Feinstein's history. She's had many conflicts of interests that the mainstream press has not investigated, but this is a particularly stinky one. CBRE is busy selling our property, and our art is going with it. It's often a package deal, and the press hasn't noticed it at all.

DB: *As to the conflict of interest, what's Senator Feinstein's position on saving the Post Office?*

GB: She says she's sort of in favor of it. The only paper that's reported on this was the little *La Jolla Light* newspaper, because their downtown Post Office with a very fine mural is for sale.

DB: *Doesn't she have a house out there?*

GB: That's one of the few places they don't have a house. They have about seven or eight — these people do very nicely. Indeed, their mansion in San Francisco is just below the Getty's, with a fine view of the Bay. Her office said that she was trying to help the people in La Jolla save their Post Office and its mural. I can well imagine she was, because La Jolla is filled with a lot of very wealthy people who are campaign contributors.

DB: *They don't want to lose their beautiful mural.*

GB: So she's been very solicitous to the people of La Jolla, but she hasn't been as solicitous to us in Berkeley, Ukiah, Canby, Oregon, and Central Bronx. She's been completely silent on them and I can understand why.

DB: *What's at stake, what is the heart of the matter?*

GB: The heart of the matter is The Public. Everything in our commonwealth is being stolen from us. I was recently threatened with arrest for trying to go into the Philadelphia main Post Office, which had been sold. I said to the guard, "They are taking everything away from us." He said, "Yes, I know. Now get out of here." I was threatened with arrest and confiscation of my camera. This is what is happening — the enclosure of our commons, of everything. The Public is central to a republic. This is what we *all* own. When it is taken away from us, we are all immensely impoverished, and they are immensely enriched. Only a very, very few people will own everything, and govern us. We see that example in Dianne Feinstein and her husband who are getting in at the hog trough, taking away what belongs to all of us, what our parents paid for, the artists painted, the sculptors sculpted. We can't allow this to happen. This belongs to all of us and is central to what America, at its very best, once was. We can't allow them to steal it from us.

Trade Agreements and the Neoliberal World Order
Manuel Pérez-Rocha   June 2015

DB: *Manuel Pérez-Rocha is an Associate Fellow at the Justice on Global Investment Project with the Institute for Policy Studies in Washington DC. What is President Obama's policy with free trade agreements — the TPP and TTIP?*

MR: These are the largest free trade agreements ever seen, negotiated under a strong veil of secrecy. They encompass both the Atlantic and the Pacific and give negotiating power to the executive branch, which only goes to Congress for up or down approval. Organizations such as farmers, unions, environmentalists, and consumers aren't allowed to participate in the negotiations, or even see the text of the two agreements, the TPP [Transpacific Partnership] and TTIP [Transatlantic Trade and Investment Partnership].

Both agreements are not only seen as substitutes for the multilateral democratic mechanism for trade and investment, but are also a response from the US and Europe to continue cementing a world order based on neo-liberalism, which means deregulation of safety standards, environmental standards, investment and trade. What we've witnessed with NAFTA in the past 21 years is what will be magnified by this agreement with Europe and other countries. These agreements are not just about investments and regulations, but are instruments to dictate standards established by corporations onto not only the US, but Europe and developing countries as well. It is a corporate driven agreement affecting the whole world.

DB: *What do we mean about the Global South and how will that part of the world suffer in the deepest way?*

MR: Both agreements are designed to leverage the power of the US and EU in bilateral and interregional negotiations. The trade imperatives and regulation agenda are very contradictory to the development rhetoric, particularly of the EU. Both the EU and

US say they want to help poor countries by providing aid, but in creating these massive blocks of so-called free trade, they are shutting out other countries from their markets. So other countries who might have general preferences to export their products to the US or EU will be strongly affected by the TTIP because the US and EU will trade more with each other.

The purpose of the TTIP is to impose global standards on trade, investment, deregulation of services, and intellectual property rights such as medicines. So if the EU and the US come together to create these higher standards for corporations, this will possibly be easier to impose on developing countries in other regions of the world. In these agreements, the US has a very strong position on weakening state owned enterprises and other government controlled entities, which are seen as a distortion for trade and investment. However, for many countries, these types of state-owned enterprises are still very important for the development of their own industries. We see a big push for deregulation in many areas of economic activity — services, investment, intellectual property rights, etc. We see the cementing of the free trade model that started with NAFTA 20 years ago, but now on a very massive scale, and with the developing countries in the Global South having no say about this new buttressing of world trading blocks.

DB: *How does this free trade on steroids impact immigration from Mexico and Central America?*

MR: Big agribusiness corporations of the US have benefitted from subsidies in agreements like NAFTA and CAFTA. With the removal of tariffs, they've been able to capture most agricultural productions and markets of Mexico and Central American countries, pushing small farmers out of their livelihoods, making it impossible for them to compete. Smaller farmers cannot compete with large transnationals like Monsanto. When NAFTA passed, there was a massive influx of migrants from Mexico into the US because they were desperately looking for jobs. NAFTA did not create enough jobs in Mexico. It was a recurrent myth that NAFTA would create jobs in Mexico — only a tiny fraction of the population might have benefitted by job creation in the manufacturing sector. But many other sectors were destroyed by NAFTA. With this new agreement, we will see increased migration and displacement. There are dramatic images of people escaping from Africa in precarious boats because of the lack of jobs and livelihoods as a result of these Economic Partnership Agreements with Europe, which are basically free trade agreements. We've seen this global phenomenon. It is a recurrent myth that free trade agreements will lift people out of poverty. The images and reality of forced migration illustrate how the increase of neo-liberal policies in the Global South creates more poverty.

DB: *Some say these policies enforce the power of the drug trade in Mexico and their power in the government.*

MR: The drug trade has benefitted in many ways by free trade. The free trade of arms, the influx of arms into Mexico from the US and Europe has been staggering. There is less control of weapons being imported into Mexico. Also, it has benefitted by the very technical clause in the investment chapter of the free trade agreements that prohibits capital controls, which allows drug traffickers to move their money in and out of the country much more easily. The third country in the world with the most illicit transfer of funds is Mexico, which involves moving money into banks in the US and elsewhere.

DB: *So these policies expand the power of major banks — freeing them up to do more with the drug trade?*

MR: Mexico's finance sector is controlled by four big banks; three from Europe and one from the US. Some of these banks have been under investigation about money laundering. Free trade has also influenced or benefitted the drug trade by creating a massive pool of unemployed people in the countryside who have no choice but to join the ranks of the illicit drug cartels, sometimes by having a gun to their head. There is a massive amount of people being forced into this industry because of the destruction of Mexico's countryside social fabric. There are areas where you don't see young people anymore. There are vast areas of the countryside being controlled by the drug cartels. This is what NAFTA did — it destroyed Mexico's rural sector.

DB: *How have the free trade agreements affected the tens of thousands of kids fleeing Mexico and Central America?*

MR: We have seen a dramatic impact from all these experiments in Central America. The free trade zones will give very little back to Honduras. They are there to exploit the cheapest labor possible. This is labor without any social security — very short-term jobs where they employ people from elsewhere, not local communities. Free trade agreements provide a prohibition of any performance requirements to investors. They can operate freely and move their goods without tariffs, so there is very scant return for countries like Honduras. Tariff proposals have always included the possibility of investments, but investments are now gone from these agreements in certain areas, such as technological industries that provide good jobs. The free trade theory is based on competitive advantage. But the only competitive advantages of many developing countries are cheap labor and natural resources. Free trade agreements are there to make use of cheap labor and all the extractive industries they can get — oil, gas and mining. In Mexico alone, in the last 15 years, there's been more coal and silver mining than during the entire colonial period. Drug cartels are also beginning to operate mines. The violence and operations of mining companies and drug cartels are destroying entire ecosystems in the region. This is all facilitated by free trade agreements, and the TPP and the TTIP are only going to make matters worse.

Imagining Socialism in the US
Richard Wolff   January 2016

DB: *We turn our attention to socialism. What does presidential candidate Bernie Sanders mean by socialism and what does it mean for the possibility of having somebody with those ideas as president? Professor Richard Wolff is a visiting professor at the New School University in New York and Economics Professor Emeritus at the University of Massachusetts in Amherst. Professor, let's start off with the fact that there are about 45 million Americans who live in poverty now, yet the word poverty or poor doesn't exist in the lexicon of most of the presidential debates.*

RW: It's amazing that it doesn't exist. It's amazing that indeed the whole world's poverty story doesn't exist. One of the most revered anti-poverty agencies in the world, OXFAM in Great Britain, issued a report about ten days ago, timed to happen during the World Economic Forum in Davos, Switzerland. The point of their report was about poverty. It had two basic statistics, which if there were any justice in the world, would be the number one topic of the presidential debates and campaigns in the US and elsewhere. The first statistic was that the 62 richest individual people — most are Americans — own together more wealth than the bottom half of the population of this planet, three and a half billion people. That is a level of inequality for which you'd have to go back to ancient Egypt and the pharaohs to find comparable kinds of numbers. The second statistic they released was even worse in way. It said that 2015 was a banner year, a turning point year, because for the first time since records were kept, the top 1% of wealth holders in the world own more than the total wealth of the other 99% in the world. This is a level of inequality that is the product of an economic system that has dominated the world for 300 years, named capitalism. It's the system we live in. Any system with a result like that — with the level of inequality and the poverty that goes with it — is a system that ought to be questioned and challenged.

The significance of the Bernie Sanders campaign is what it brings back into American political life and political discussion — the alternative to capitalism. Sanders calls it democratic socialism. The important thing is not the details of what he's proposing, but rather the opening of American politics to finally deal with the topic it should have been discussing for the last 50 years, which is can we do better than capitalism, and if we can, how do we go about it?

DB: *What's the difference between what Bernie Sanders and Hillary Clinton are saying about the economy?*

RW: Hillary Clinton and her husband Bill Clinton are people who came to their high political office, and indeed came to their ways of thinking, in a period of American history — the last three or four decades — when the governing ideology in this country was that capitalism is the greatest thing since sliced bread, that it's a magical ultimate achievement of human civilization which provides growth and prosperity in an endless vista into the future. And therefore, anyone thinking about alternatives must have been asleep at the wheel, must be a backward looking person, maybe even an evil person, but is someone whose thinking and speech we don't have to take seriously. So like everyone else in these dominant positions in America in the last 30-40 years, they spent no time worrying about how to do better than capitalism, and no time learning or exploring the alternatives.

That's no good anymore because capitalism has shown us its vulnerabilities — the inequality I mentioned, the instability, the crash of 2008, and the failure of most Americans to recover in a significant way from that crash. The uncertainty suggests we may have another recession later this year. This is a system whose inequality, instability, and injustice of everything we read about in the papers — from the scandal of the Flint water system to DuPont poisoning the water to the absurd crisis of apartments in New York City — has given us more than enough reason to think about alternatives. The fundamental difference between

Sanders and Clinton is that Sanders is about alternatives and Clinton acts as if they are not necessary because that's the way she and the people she represents have been thinking for 40 years.

DB: *We hear again and again that Bernie Sanders has great ideas about what he wants to do, but it's impossible to afford the $18 trillion dollars it would cost. Hillary Clinton jumps on the bandwagon with the* Wall Street Journal. *Are Sanders' ideas that everybody deserves healthcare, etc, possible or is it ridiculous?*

RW: They are absolutely possible. There's a certain shame that should be attached to Mrs. Clinton's using these arguments. It has been the standard trope, standard argument of conservatives, that if anything sounds good of the sort that liberals, socialists, or radicals propose — if they admit they sound good — the way to get rid of the population's interest is to suggest they are either undoable or too expensive. This is silly. Here is the example from American history that proves the point. In the Great Depression of the 1930s, when the unemployment was much worse than it is today, when the bankruptcy and economic difficulties of cities and towns was much more severe than it is today, it was thought to be a crazy idea in the midst of the Great Depression to come up with extraordinary, new expensive programs to help the mass of people, which is basically what Sanders is proposing now. But in fact, the president of the United States at that time, Franklin Roosevelt, after whom Sanders patterns himself very obviously, didn't believe we couldn't afford it. So he went ahead and said, "I'm going to do spectacular things. I'm going to create the social security system. I'm going to give everybody a check when they're 65 years of age for the rest of their life. I'm going to create the unemployment compensation system and give the millions of then-unemployed people a check every week. I'm going to raise the minimum wage. The really big one is I'm going to hire 15 million unemployed people and pay them a good salary." Where in the world, conservatives said, are you going to get the money? With a wry smile Mr. Roosevelt said what, in effect,

Bernie Sanders is saying, namely "I'm going to go to where the money is, because the money is there. The government doesn't have it but the corporations and rich people of America have it. They have more than they need and I'm going to relieve them of it."

That's exactly what he did. He raised the taxes on corporations and the rich. He created and funded the social security, unemployment and public employment programs. He proved not only that it could be done, and that the money was there — and it's easier to do those things today than it was then — but he made the very important point, and proved it, that doing that got the US out of the Great Depression, helped millions of people, and set the economy on a much more successful course than could have been achieved any other way. So the notion that we can't do it is contradicted by the fact we've already done it. We've been there and we've done it, and all Sanders is saying is let us learn from our history and do this again.

DB: *Professor Wolff, what do you think about the notion, brought up by the nurses and many others, of the penny tax for the stock exchange and a tax on trades?*

RW: It's one of a dozen proposals that are around, all of which have the same function — to go after taxing the wealth where the wealth is. We're coming off a 30-40 year period when the rich have gotten much, much richer. Every statistic done, whether by Piketty and Saez, the leading researchers in this area, or anybody else, shows that we are now at a point where the rich have become so absurdly wealthy, that a proposal to tax some of that wealth will still leave them, if it passes, in a position of great wealth, just not obscene wealth. Taxing transactions in the stock market, where the rich do the bulk of the playing, is a perfectly good way to do that. As would be a much more progressive income tax, and a payroll tax that keeps on rising and doesn't stop at $120,000 a year as it does now, and a return to a proper inheritance tax we once had, and so on. They should be explored and different taxes put together in an effective way that raises the money to begin to correct for the absurd imbalance that has been created by a system that hasn't been reined in, that has allowed capitalism to work its sad function of dividing a society to the point where it becomes explosive.

The reason Bernie Sanders has a response that is surprising so many people is that we've turned a blind eye to the negative dimensions of capitalism. We were too busy leading cheerleading sessions for the system to honestly evaluate its strengths and weaknesses. Had we done that, we wouldn't be as surprised or as shaken as the establishment clearly is, by all the people — left and right — who are no longer willing to go along with business as usual.

DB: *Speaking of business as usual, let's talk about a Goldman Sachs-run America. I hear many times that of course Hillary Clinton, as a senator from New York, had to understand what was going on in the stock market. She represented them so that gives her the knowledge to deal with them.*

RW: I find that an amazing argument. The stock market happens to be physically located in New York City, but it is a national institution. It doesn't rely on the senator from the state where it happens to have its buildings. It's a childish argument. Goldman Sachs and others who are active in the stock market have all kinds of fingers in all kinds of political apparatuses, because that's how they keep their wealth and grow their business. They all do that. They've always done it and there's nothing particular about the New York senator. Indeed, if the New York senator, Mrs. Clinton or anyone else, wanted to become a national figure, you might expect they would act more in the national interest than in the narrow New York interest, or at least blend the two. But to excuse herself that because she happens to live in New York City, she ought to be off the hook for criticism of working with Goldman Sachs strikes me as kind of bizarre. To illustrate this, if I am properly informed, Mr. Cruz, a Republican presidential candidate, took out huge loans to pay for his campaign both from Goldman Sachs and First City Bank in New York. His wife used to work for Goldman Sachs. This posturing that Clinton is to be excused because she is a senator from New York and he's to be excused because he denounces New York is political theater that masks the underlying reality that in a society as unequal as what we have now in the US, it would be sheer insanity for the tiny number of institutions that have become wildly wealthy, to not spend a lot of time and money controlling the political system, because if they didn't, the political system would undo the very wealth they've accumulated.

We have a political system where everybody gets a vote. It would be childishly easy to go to the mass of people and say, use your vote to undo the inequality the economic system has dumped on us. To prevent precisely that from happening, Goldman Sachs, First City Bank, Bank of America and the biggest corporations spend a lot of time and money lobbying and funding the parties, to make sure politics doesn't undo what the capitalist economy has delivered into their hands. Mr. Sanders is precisely important only because he opens that fact up and says look, if you want the government to work differently, you must address who pays for it, who is working ceaselessly to control it. Otherwise, you're making nice gestures and nice pronouncements, the way so many candidates have been doing for 50 years, and nothing fundamental changes.

DB: *I wrote extensively about the deregulation and remember when Reagan was talking about how the deregulation of the Savings & Loans was the beginning of the future for freedom and free trade. We watched it unfold to the big banks, with taxpayers being sucked under, paying out one way or another. Out of the ruins of that is Dodd-Frank. Hillary Clinton, a strong supporter of Dodd-Frank, says it was the answer to the problems.*

RW: That's a perfect illustration of what Hillary Clinton and most of the others of both parties are all about. They like to pretend that the problems are manageable, easily fixed, and that the various bills they are lucky enough to pass, like Dodd-Frank, are an adequate fix to the problem. But this pretense — all it's ever been — is now no longer sustainable. That's why Bernie Sanders gets the response he does. Let me illustrate with Dodd-Frank. One of the biggest problems of the crash of 2008 was the basic act of blackmail that was imposed on the people of the US and upon the government. It was imposed by the ten biggest banks in this country: Bank of America, Wells Fargo, Citibank, Goldman-Sachs, Morgan-Stanley; the names are well known to everyone. They basically said, "You cannot let us fail. We have made bad investments. We cannot collect on our debts. We face bankruptcy and collapse, but if you let us collapse, the system will collapse with us. We'll take it down with us; we are therefore (as the phrase went) too big to fail." OK. This argument worked. The blackmail succeeded. They were given trillions in loans and supports and investments by the federal government and Federal Reserve. Where do we find ourselves today? The exact same banks that were too big to fail in 2008 are now bigger than they were then. If and when a crash comes, they'll have an argument that will be an even stronger blackmail than last time. Dodd-Frank didn't solve that problem.

In addition, we have huge loans, made by these corporations, to a large number of borrowers who, once again, can't pay back. This time it's not people who can't pay off their mortgage. It's whole countries and industries that can't pay their debts. An example in the US right now is that huge amounts of money were lent to the genius oil companies who decided that by frakking, they could bring up shale oil and make a killing. The oil companies, those genius entrepreneurs, were wrong. They borrowed from the biggest banks in America, who lent them a lot of money, and they were wrong. Oil has been a disaster, and those companies going bankrupt now can't pay back the banks, so we face another looming economic crisis. Dodd-Frank didn't prevent that or interfere in that. Whatever virtues Dodd-Frank had — and it had some — are simply too little, too late to deal with the level of problems we have. When Mrs. Clinton and others refer to it as a great achievement, it's once again a spectacle for the rest of us to see they don't get it. They don't see the system as a whole is our problem, and we need to talk about an alternative system because these little band aids we are putting on are failures to recognize that we have a major illness for which a band aid simply isn't enough.

DB: Speaking of Band-Aids and prosecution of economic criminals, on Christmas Eve somebody gets busted breaking into a food mart stealing some steaks, a couple of bags of food, gets into a fight with somebody who tries to stop him and he goes to jail for five years. Somebody else rips off the US Treasury for billions, takes us into trillions. Doesn't that have to be part of an administration, the willingness to have law enforcement go after these criminals to make an example? Should it happen? Will it ever happen?

RW: Some of us have different views about that. I am so impressed by what Sanders has done in the way of raising the question of the system itself, making the question can we do better than capitalism a live political question. I'm afraid to deflect the tension to the crimes of individuals. It's not that I support or excuse what the banksters — as they're called — did. But my understanding of how banks work in our economy has taught me over and over again that if you arrested the top 20 bankers and put them in jail, the people who come after them, such as the vice president, then rise to become the president. These are the same people, subject to the same pattern of rewards and punishments, who will be driven by the nature of their job and what they are paid to do, and the inducements and incentives they face, to make basically the same decisions. That's why it's the system that has to be changed. If all you do is put away the people at the top, the next group of people who rises to the top will in all likelihood make the same decisions. They can't afford not to. They will convince themselves they will do it more cleverly than their predecessors. The better way is to focus less on the individuals who might be punished, and more on changing the system so that we are not forever putting individuals in the position where they do what we see they do and then we come X years later and rap them across the

94

knuckles and put in place the next group who will show us that they can and will do the same.

DB: *I raise it because one of my pet peeves with the current administration is the current Secretary of Commerce, Penny Ptrizker, who herself was a banking bandit. She crashed a bank in Chicago and 1,400 people lost all or most of their life savings. She then helped invent the securitization of bonds, the compiling of bonds they sold on Wall Street that led to the big meltdown. This woman was in the middle of that and then ascends to the Secretary of Commerce. When Obama was first elected, people wondered how he out-fundraised Hillary Clinton. Penny Pritzker. This family has been doing this corruption for generations. But I understand your point.*

RW: I understand the frustration of the American people. The last thing on earth I want to be understood as is excusing them. But the problem is, for better or worse, deeper and broader than these individuals. We must learn this is a systemic problem. Otherwise, it's the old discovery of the Middle Ages, that when there's a horrible king or emperor, when their children ascended to the throne, they would do basically what their parents had done — not because they were good or bad, but because that's how the system works. You have to make fundamental changes rather than focus on individuals.

DB: *You believe it's possible to have a socialist president of the US. You also believe that if there's no remedy during this election, the next person after Bernie Sanders could be more radical.*

RW: Absolutely. We didn't believe that Obama could win when he first began to run, because the thought of an African American being president was simply beyond the realm of possibility. We were wrong. He hasn't proved to be the engine of hope and change that he claimed he would be, so now we have a Mr. Sanders who takes it a whole stage further. But if Mr. Sanders is stymied the way Obama was, either through his own errors or through the opposition he faced so he couldn't move forward, there's no reason to expect the same will not happen to Mr. Sanders.

Of course a socialist could be president. I find it amazing that Americans are even wondering about that. Europe is the perfect proof, with two-dozen capitalist countries — like the US — run by big private corporations, etc. Many of those countries, such as France, Germany, Italy, and Spain have not only had socialists in high office, but have had socialist presidents, and socialist dominated Houses of Parliament. France today has a socialist president and a socialist majority in both houses of its legislature. That hasn't undermined capitalism or overthrown capitalism. Capitalists have long ago come to terms with socialists in political leadership. The idea that, somehow in the US, it isn't imaginable is the same self deluded political thinking we talked about earlier. We need a conversation about the system and alternatives to it. If Europeans can have a Mr. Francois Hollande, the US could certainly have Mr. Sanders as its president. The world is not going to end. These are lots of Chicken Littles screaming here that don't need to be taken seriously.

Domestic Dissent

Blood on the Tracks
Brian Willson   July 2011

DB: *In the 1980s, Ronald Reagan made many Americans feel good again after Vietnam in the 1960s and the Oil Shocks in the 1970s. However, when part of Reagan's "Morning in America" involved death-squad slaughters in Central America, some Americans, like Vietnam veteran S. Brian Willson, refused to stand aside. On Sept. 1, 1987, Willson was purposely run over and almost killed by a US Navy munitions train while he engaged in a nonviolent blockade in protest of weapons shipments going to El Salvador in support of pro-US death squads.*

Brian Willson, congratulations on your new autobiography, Blood on the Tracks.

BW: Thank you. I call it a psycho-historical memoir because I weave in lots of history and psychology to understand my own personal journey in the midst of the incredible conditioning to be part of the plunder of the planet and not even realize it. Why would we realize it when we are growing up with that conditioning?

The story of my journey from being very typical — I call myself an ignorant, dumbed-down person — to various levels of awakening is still happening. It's a journey, not a destination — a long journey of constantly uncovering new wisdom and meeting new people, stumbling on the path, getting back up and taking another step, and the next thing you know, another experience is happening. It's another "Wow" experience that I wouldn't have had if I'd become a lawyer. I would have been set with my career and income and my life-style commensurate with the income. Fortunately, I couldn't be a practicing lawyer, which I thought I would be, because I couldn't follow the protocol of the court. I was blessed with what I initially thought were obstacles, but all continually became new opportunities.

97

DB: *Can you tell us about the government cover-up and the cover of the book? What was happening before this picture?*

BW: The cover of the book has a very dramatic photo of the scene on the tracks about four or five seconds after I was run over. Concord Naval Weapons Station, which it was called at this time, was the largest weapons depot on the West Coast, from which weapons were shipped to various war zones that the US was involved in, including Central America. We were there to bring attention to the fact that these death trains were going on these tracks, and the trucks carrying munitions were on a road parallel to the tracks, every day. There were many announcements in advance about what we were doing, why we were doing it, where and when, and that we were going to block the trains — knowing we would be arrested.

A big sign by the tracks said exactly what the penalty was — I think it was a $5,000 fine and one year in prison. There was no fear that we would be killed or maimed, so we took our positions. I have no memory of being hit, so I have a four-day period of...

DB: *You were out for four days?*

BW: I was talking after I was hit but I have no memory of it. I have what's called retrograde amnesia. The picture on the cover shows the scene within seconds, and there are four people hovering over my very badly wounded body. Two were working on the bleeding in my legs: Jerry Condon, who had been a Green Beret-trained medic who went to Sweden rather than Vietnam, and my partner at the time, Holley Rauen, whose face you can see in anguish over Jerry's right shoulder. Duncan Murphy is hovering over my upper body and face, just holding my energy, and Dave Hartsough is sitting with his left hand on my bleeding head. There are other people with very anguished expressions. Steve Brooks is coming to the scene to help in stopping my bleeding. He was a door gunner in Vietnam and at that time was commander of the VFW [Veteran of Foreign Wars]

98

Wage Peace Post in Santa Cruz. The man talking to the Marines surrounding the train is Pierre Blasé, who was also a door gunner in Vietnam.

DB: *You have no doubt you were hit on purpose to send a message?*

[Also participating in the interview were Francisco Herrera (FH) and David Hartsough (DH), who were eyewitnesses to the train running over Willson.]

FH: Dennis, there's another very interesting detail on the picture. The end of the train, with boxcars, didn't stop or slow down at all — the whole train went through.

BW: The train was surrounded by Marines because there were 350 armed Marines at that base guarding the weapons, trains, and trucks, day and night.

DB: *Spotters on the trains.*

BW: There were two spotters in front to make sure the tracks were clear. The train speed limit was 5 miles an hour, and the FBI established it was going 16 or 17 miles an hour at the point of impact and still accelerating, which it had never done before. We found out the train crew was ordered not to stop that morning, which was a very unusual order — and grotesquely illegal — in violation of standard protocol for dealing with protesters.

DB: *Ordered not to stop?*

BW: Ordered not to stop. We have that in their own statements, even though they stated later they didn't see us ... but we have their statements.

DB: *They looked away when they ran over you.*

BW: We know they didn't stop because there was a fear of us boarding the train, i.e. hijacking, which I'm sure was just a figment of their imaginations used as a rationale for whatever the order was. Duncan, one of the other veterans with me blocking the train, and I were on the Domestic Terrorist Watch List. We know, because an FBI agent, Jack Ryan, from Peoria, Illinois, spilled the beans when he refused his orders to investigate us as terrorists. He was fired after almost 22 years in the FBI for doing that. Putting all that together, it was an attempted murder.

DH: There's no question they saw us. The two spotters on the front were looking right at us. The train had stopped on the other side of the road, then began going faster and faster. I was standing next to the tracks, looking these guys in the eyes, yelling, "There are people on the tracks, stop the train." I was flagging it down, but they were not stopping!

DB: *Francisco, you show up in one of these pictures right after the train hit.*

FH: I was playing the guitar and singing "Peace is flowing like a river." But it wasn't that morning.

DB: *Blood was flowing.*

FH: You could see the train speed up, the sound, and the energy. Everything about the train said, "We're here to do damage." It was very clear, the level of …

BW: … intent. Another piece of evidence was that the Navy ambulance arrived within a few minutes — David would know better because I have no memory — but they refused to help, because my body wasn't technically lying on Navy property. It was on the roadway, so they left. The Navy fire department came shortly thereafter, rendered some assistance, and stayed until the county ambulance arrived to take me to the hospital

DH: Which was about twenty-five minutes later.

DB: *It is such an important decision the government made, to go ahead and take this kind of action to support what every human rights group in the world knew was already a mass-murdering death squad policy, both in El Salvador, Guatemala, and more to come. How did you find out you were run over by a train — somebody had to tell you?*

BW: I'm still very naïve. I could not imagine them doing to me what they do to people in other countries, all the time, which I had documented. I was excited that on the fourth day after I was hit, 9,000 people showed up at the tracks, including Joan Baez, Jesse Jackson, and others. Although what happened next was somewhat in debate as to its propriety, 300 feet of track were ripped up by people who came, as an expression of rage.

DB: *There's a picture of the ripping up ... people went there to send a message as well.*

BW: Although the tracks were repaired within a week or two after that, shipments couldn't move without massive blocks and arrests. Every train and truck at Concord had munitions on it — that was the sole purpose of moving them from the bunkers to Port Chicago, where they were loaded on ships. Because an encampment had emerged on the tracks twenty-four hours a day for twenty-eight months, every train and every truck was stopped.

DB: *How many trains? Hundreds?*

BW: There were over two thousand arrests. Three people, at least, had their arms broken in the arresting process, including David Hartsough. For another ten or twelve years after that first twenty-eight months, many of the trains and trucks were blocked. The twenty-four hour presence wasn't always there, but there were always people there, at some point during the day and night. The government obviously did not intend to have that kind of reaction — they don't think about things very reflectively.

I had been an installation security commander in Vietnam and had been through lots of training about securing military bases from various threats. In my mind, no commander of a military base would run a munitions train over anything on the tracks: a stalled car, a cow, human beings, or some unknown object.

The two spotters would get off the train and investigate, after the train stopped, to allow them off to investigate and remove whatever is there, before the train would continue. That they didn't even do that, which would be the normal protocol — it was so obviously intended to...I don't know if playing chicken is the right word. They knew we were committed to staying there. We knew the speed limit was 5 miles an hour, and that the protocol was to have us arrested. Blockades at Concord go back to the mid-sixties, so it wasn't unique. It was a pattern over the years, with different commanders every year. So I had to be convinced in the hospital by various friends who were visiting me that I was run over by a train, because I could not believe it — I just couldn't believe it.

DH: When I went to visit him in the hospital a few days after this, not only were there no legs, almost every inch of his body was covered with bandages, from broken arms to elbows, to a hole in his head. I could see his eyes, which was about the only thing that wasn't covered.

FH: The engine had a lower piece — a cowcatcher blade. Brian, I remember this clearly, you rolled once the engine went over you — your body kept rolling with the rest of the train, until the train was going so fast, it passed Brian's body and at some point your body stopped rolling.

BW: Well, it was horrendous for all those who were witnesses. My partner at the time had to...here's a picture of her waiting for the train to go over me...

DB: *Oh, my God.*

BW: My slumped body was under the boxcars. We'd had a ceremony about ten days earlier to celebrate our commitment to one another. My partner Holley Rauen and I were living in San Rafael, in Marin County when I was hit. Shockingly, there were so many death threats coming to the hospital towards me, the hospital hired a private security firm to have a guard outside my room, twenty-four hours a day — there were three shifts. Holley was getting death threats at home for being the partner of this crazy guy who was taking on the empire, so she called the San Rafael police to help her feel safe at our apartment. Then David, unbeknownst to me while I was in the hospital, offered an apartment in his house in San Francisco where we could move to, to feel safer.

When I left the hospital after twenty-eight days, we didn't go to our place in San Rafael, as Holley had already terminated the lease. We went to David's house. There are a lot of steps at David's house so it was a little difficult for me to get in, but it was a safe space where we stayed for almost four years.

DB: *Let's talk about your beginnings, and where you are going.*

BW: I grew up in upstate New York, a relatively pleasant upbringing compared to many people. My family was very religious and conservative Right-wing Republican. As a kid I had to go to Sunday school every Sunday.

DB: *And they had a stack of Bibles...*

BW: When they died, I collected the Bibles — over sixty. Half were Jerry Falwell Bibles — his name was on them. It was a very small town — seventeen kids in my eighth-grade class, six boys and eleven girls. I went on to high school with twenty-eight kids in my class — twelve boys and sixteen girls. I loved high school because I was quite proficient at sports, was an honor student, and on the student council. Then I went to college, and wanted to be an FBI agent for a while, then a Baptist minister, then finally decided to go to law school — that's where I got drafted.

DB: *You got caught in a loophole there. You were college bound...*

BW: I was in graduate school in a dual program of a Master's degree in Criminology Corrections and a law degree specializing in criminal law at American University in Washington. I got my draft notice in my fourth semester of this program and thought it was a mistake because I had a school deferment [2-S] — this was pre-lottery. I flew home and met with my Selective Service board in Fredonia, New York. I said, "This must be a mistake." They said, "No, this is not a mistake. You have a preferential school deferment, but this is a farming county — grape and dairy farming. All the young men who work on their family farms have an absolute deferment, and the Pentagon doesn't take that into consideration when they give us the quota for the demographic pool of the county for young men. So we are short of men because there are fewer available for the draft and we had to go into the preferential deferment 2-S." I knew nothing about any of that. I was for the war and killing the commies, so I didn't have any political or philosophical reason to avoid it once I got caught.

DB: *You wouldn't be going to Canada even though it was just around the corner.*

BW: I wouldn't have thought about it. It was not in my consciousness. I enlisted in the Air Force in a four-year officer program to avoid the Army. I went in at twenty-five.

DB: *You went in as a lieutenant?*

BW: I was commissioned a second lieutenant in November of '66.

DB: *Did that feel good?*

BW: It did. On the day of my commission, I bought a Corvette. It was 1966, and the first time in my life that I had money to spend.

DB: *Vietnam is the core of the driving force for you. Describe what you were doing there, your special assignment and what happened.*

BW: The first village I went into was April 12 or 13, 1969. I was trained as a low-level commander in a supposed Air Force Ranger-type unit at Fort Campbell, Kentucky. When I went to Vietnam I had twelve weeks of this training with forty men under my command, and our job was to protect air bases in hostile areas. They meant first, Vietnam, but they also told us we might go to Guatemala or Korea. We got to Vietnam in March of '69 and were at a small base in the Delta, which was getting attacked quite often. We had heavy machine guns, starlight scopes, outgoing mortars, and counter personnel radar. We were supplementing a regular base security unit.

There's a picture of me, taken my first week there, looking and sitting pensively on a pallet. A damaged Polaroid shows me pensively looking at another pallet of body bags. You can't see the other pallet, but I look like, "Wow, how did I get here? What's happening?" Shortly after arrival, I had a special assignment that I didn't have to do, but the Vietnamese base commander asked me to assess the success of bombings of targets.

DB: *US bombings.*

BW: They were ordered by the US. However, I was told these bombings would be carried out by Vietnamese pilots. The US was doing plenty of the bombing, but after Nixon was elected in '69, the code word was Vietnamization. Turn the war over to the Vietnamese, as if they hadn't already been heavily involved in the war — both as soldiers and victims. The commander feared that the new pilots trained in the United States had been infiltrated by the VC — the Viet Cong — who we called the enemy. We have to remember they were people righteously and correctly defending their country from our illegal invasion, but I hadn't figured that out yet. The base commander picked me, I suspected, because I was a sober officer on the base who was always studying intelligence reports in the command bunker, and he would see me studying. Because I'd been a graduate student, about all I knew I could do was study and read, which helped me feel a little safer and a little less anxious.

So I drove my jeep accompanied by one of the commander's lieutenants who guided me to where these bombings happened. It wasn't dangerous to be on the roads in the daytime. We went to five targets in one week in April — I discovered that all were inhabited fishing and farming villages. Almost everybody was struck by planes flying at 300 feet, meaning they wouldn't have to worry about missing anything with their five hundred pound bombs, their Gatling-gun machine guns and their napalm bombs. Everybody in those villages, for the most part, was wiped out. I witnessed lots of bodies — many blackened from napalm — and at least half the bodies were young children. You could see their burned corpses that were three feet, three and a half feet. It was shocking and sickening.

This was the war, and I started realizing slowly, but then more rapidly, that this was all deliberate, intentional acts of war crimes, justified because we were killing the vermin, rodents, and evil commies. I saw people authentically living in their villages and I knew I was no longer an authentic person. I got it. They are in their village, and I'm nine thousand miles from my village, standing over them as a savior of democracy. I knew it was all B.S. and how deeply my conditioning had dehumanized me.

I couldn't walk any further in one village because there were too many bodies. I stopped because the bodies were too intense. The woman at my feet had been holding three children. She was lying on her back, with her eyes looking up, wide open. I thought, "Wow, is she alive?" I realized they were all dead, but the napalm had burned her eyelids off, along with facial skin. Her eyes were staring at me, and when I looked in those eyes, I knew she was my sister. I call that irreversible knowledge that I could not, ever, forget. It wasn't a thought; it was a feeling in my whole body, the visceral, the body — which is undeniable.

That was in the first village I went into. From that moment, I've been on a different path. It's a very clumsy path — it's certainly not linear and it's not neat. I emerged as a new person from that experience — it was an epiphany.

DB: *Did it manifest right away?*

BW: I started talking, speaking to my superiors every day about the illegality, the unconscionable nature of the war, and the intentional bombing of civilian targets. I learned the rules of engagement as an officer: You do not target civilians or civilian infrastructure. When I continually brought it to the attention of my superiors, they laughed. I know they were irritated at me, and I was the night security commander. We were usually attacked at night, and my adrenaline was working, so I was not lax with the duties, but they felt I was affecting the morale with my anti-war rhetoric, which I was not because I didn't talk about my feelings to my enlisted men. I was talking to other officers on the base, many of whom were drinking. I said, "Look, this is the only way I can keep my sanity. I've got to talk about it." I carried out my duties, but after five months I was sent home early, so I was very relieved.

DB: *Do you have any idea who that woman who was at your feet holding the three children...*

BW: I gave her a name. I think of her all the time. I gave her the name Mai Ly. She's my mythological mother, my mythological sister. She's the one who taught me that everything in the universe is totally connected with each other, and with all of life. Although I haven't always lived with those incredible principles, they have kept a certain resiliency in my journey towards honoring this incredible truth that I knew nothing about. Growing up in the capitalist US, I was quite well adapted to be successful according to the definition I had learned. Make money, get your career, get your house, and live happily ever after. I knew that was all B.S. by then, but I didn't know what it meant. I knew I was no longer one of the guys — which was initially a sad thing, because I had always enjoyed being one of the jocks, but I also knew something else was emerging. It's still emerging 42 years later.

DB: *Buddhist monks began to set themselves ablaze — an extraordinary act. In this country, some people thought it was lunacy, but we understood it as the highest form of protest, giving an individual life for the greater good of the people. The guy who burned himself alive near the Pentagon went to your small, tiny high school.*

BW: Norman Morrison, ... seven years ahead of me in school. He was the first Eagle Scout I met. I didn't know him well, because I was ten and he was seventeen at the time. When I realized who he was when he immolated himself in 1965, I thought he had become a kook, since I was a Right-winger at the time. Then in Vietnam, I had dinner with a Vietnamese family after I had openly turned against the war, and they sang me a song called "An Ode to Norman Morrison," telling me that Norman Morrison was an inspiration to the entire country to continue resistance to the US occupation and its devastation of the Vietnamese life and villages. At that point Norman became my hero too.

There were at least 76 monks who immolated themselves during the war in protest of the incredible, incredible, beyond-belief carnage that we were inflicting on that country. There were nine people in the US who immolated themselves — Norman was one, but there were eight others.

You don't know how to express your angst, outrage and grief over policies of murder, occurring day after day, week after week, month after month, year after year, funded by the United States people and their government. It's so criminally insane, it is difficult to know how to respond.

FH: Which sheds a lot of light on the decision Chelsea Manning made.

BW: Yes, when you find out about incredible war crimes, which happen in every war, there are some people who want to reveal it. It's just human.

DB: *It's not going to look good for Chelsea Manning, and even you. The fact that you could prove the government purposefully tried to kill you — that's what made it impossible for you to win. Give us the thirty-second...*

BW: Under the Federal Tort Claims Act, you can only sue the government for negligence of its employees, but not the criminal intent of its employees.

DB: *Let's be clear. If they purposely try and kill you, you can't sue them, but if they make a mistake you've got an opening.*

BW: Correct. And since none of the criminal administration agencies were going to file criminal charges, we had to go into civil court and sue. Our case was so strong we thought — how are we going to lessen the strength of our case in order to win? It screwed up my mind thinking about it. We finally settled, rather taking a chance of losing in court.

DB: *Let's talk about why you're riding your bike, what it means to you, the notion of changing the paradigm, why we are at that crossroads, and you on the bicycle crossing those roads.*

BW: I'm trying to be honest in my journey. Western civilization is on a collision course with life itself. We've all been conditioned to adapt to the mores and values that enable us to be considered okay, successful, or at least reasonable people. In adaptation, we are dehumanizing ourselves because we are adapting to a capitalist society that promotes individualism versus cooperation, competition versus community, acquisition versus inquisition — acquiring things rather than being curious and questioning things. We have become addicted to a material way of life that requires imperial policies to extract all these resources around the world and funnel them to 4.6 percent of the world's population; demeaning, impoverishing, murdering, and maiming people all over the world who are in the way of our precious metals needed for our cell phones and our computers.

This has been going on since the conquest in 1492. Our country is founded on dispossession of hundreds of nations of human beings who lived on this land, what the Indians call Turtle Island.

We're wired socially to be cooperators. That's the only way we've survived four or five million years as a hominid. We've been living for several thousand years as obedient servants to vertical power structures, which we call democracy. I'm interested in developing an eco-consciousness. We're moving from the age of entitlement, enabled by plunder, to the age of consequences, which provides us this opportunity to learn humility on the planet. We may or may not take that opportunity on.

The Vanished Body of War
Phil Donahue   January 2012

DB: *Amid the war fever over Iraq in 2002, legendary talk show host Phil Donahue returned to television with an MSNBC program that allowed antiwar voices to speak — but his corporate chieftains soon pulled the plug, a shameful moment in US journalism. From the early 1970s to 1985, The Phil Donahue Show was broadcast nationally from Chicago. Donahue also co-hosted a compelling political talk show — with Vladimir Pozner of the former Soviet Union — called This Week with Pozner & Donahue from 1991-1994.*

In July 2002, MSNBC hired him to host a freewheeling TV talk show, which hyped the return of Donahue. However, eight months later, during the run-up to war with Iraq, behind-the-scenes pressure from the Bush White House — and a groundswell of conservative outrage — led MSNBC to give the anti-war TV talk-show host the boot. An internal NBC memo stated that Donahue should be fired because he would be a "difficult public face for NBC in a time of war."

Phil Donahue, you came into town to show a very compelling film you produced in 2007 called "Body of War." It's about a young vet named Thomas Young who was paralyzed in Iraq and went through a transformation. How did the film happen?

PD: I discovered Thomas Young at Walter Reed Army Medical Center, 24-years old, pale as the sheet, and whacked out on morphine. His mother told me how paralyzed he was; a T4, paralyzed from the nipples down. Thomas can't cough, has bowel and bladder procedures every morning, and nausea.

Thomas is a warrior turned anti-warrior. He came home from the war absolutely stunned at its horror, knowing that war wasn't necessary. He went to Fort Hood and immediately said, "Why am I going to Iraq, I thought I was going to Afghanistan?" Too late. He is in Iraq for five days, on top of the truck on Main Street in Sadr City, and he takes a bullet through the collarbone, which exited T4 in his spine. He will never walk again.

I realized how sanitized this war was. President George W. Bush said, "Don't take pictures" of the carnage and the whole mainstream press said, "Okay." There was never any push back. The American public did not see the pain inflicted on thousands and thousands of families. These were especially heinous injuries; women had their faces blown off with IEDs [Improvised Explosive Devices], blind kids. Bush successfully threw a blanket over the painful coverage, and media cooperated. I couldn't believe that the land of the free would allow this to happen. So I nominated myself to show as many people as I could the pain of this one family, and tried to make the point that this is just one. There are thousands of other homes out there; the lives of the entire family are turned upside down.

This young man recently had a pulmonary embolism, so now his speech is affected and he has to be fed. He cannot hold the silverware. A twenty-something male impotent? The people who worked on this film will never be the same. We saw some PTSD [Post Traumatic Stress Disorder], saw him struggling because he's a smoker but he can't get out of bed, walk and get his cigarettes. I picked him up once from an airplane and had to help him off the airplane. This is a spiritual experience. That's when you realize how powerless, helpless he is. From the chest down he is a rag doll, unless somebody comes up with a genome answer to this. And the man he fought for, George Bush, would not approve stem-cell research.

This all came colliding down on us. I said, "I want to show the pain here. I don't want to sanitize this at all."

DB: *It was transformational in nature. It is only one example of millions of young people. Imagine, can we have another ten or fifteen years of war with Iran?*

PD: We live in a nation of law, unless we're scared. George Bush, with great fanfare, talked about democracy. He went around the world saying "Democracy! Democracy!" and turned his back on the Bill of Rights. We have people in cages around the world, and no Red Cross. What is American to us? The bedrock of this nation, habeas, *is* gone. You can't be a proud American and waterboard somebody, or deny attorney access to a prisoner. They say they are doing it to protect us. They say the Bill of Rights is a quaint, good, interesting idea but it's not practical at this time, especially now when you never know when somebody is going to drop a bomb on us. This is how they are arguing. We bombed Grenada, Panama! We drop bombs on crowded cities at night where old people and children are sleeping. And Americans watch this on CNN and remain largely mute. That's how we got here.

DB: New York Times *reporter Judith Miller helped lie us into the war with Iraq, and that was the paper of record. We're in trouble if we don't have that Fourth Estate free and willing to question the centers of power. Remind people what happened to you. We were very excited that you were starting a new show on MSNBC in 2002. A wonderful producer named Jeff Cohen, a founder of Fairness and Accuracy in Reporting, was your producer. It was a wonderful show, but it didn't last long.*

PD: I think we signed in August and I was gone in February of the following year, a month before the invasion. MSNBC and its corporate parent, General Electric, were not pleased with my anti-war position, which I was outspoken about. A memo from a consultant hired by NBC News was released and printed by the *New York Times.* "Donahue appears to take delight in his anti-war stance." See how we're marginalized with a word like "delight." I not only opposed the war, I delighted in…. What kind of crass person am I?

If there is another war, corporate media will be on the side of the establishment. It's not good for business to oppose a war. People who oppose wars are scolds, and nobody likes a scold. They are crabby and don't love America. How can you oppose a war when a president is ramping up for one? You embarrass the president in front of the world and the people that we're trying to overcome, and you're disrespectful to the troops. We've sent how many thousands and thousands of Americans to fight for our freedom, including free speech, and when we need it the most, at a time when a president is starting a war, we have millions of people in this country who believe it's unpatriotic to not support the president. That's how war is made easy.

Then if you scare the people you can move an entire population. George Bush took this nation by the ear, led it into the sword, and we let it happen. It's amazing what you can do if you scare the people. Corporate media will always be on the side of whatever the White House wants to do. They don't want anybody mad.

Imagine the money General Electric makes out of these defense contracts while Donahue is on the air making fun of Defense Secretary Donald Rumsfeld. It's counterintuitive for them to want to have me on their television program. When the board of directors went to their country clubs, their golf buddies said "What the hell are you doing with Donahue on the air?" This is 2002. The Iraq War resolution was October 2002, two weeks before an election and less than a year from the 9/11 towers. The resolution passed overwhelmingly on lies — it wasn't true. Saddam had nothing to do with 9/11, but there are millions of Americans who believe he did.

DB: *The same media machine is cranking up for another war. The great Israeli journalist, Amira Hass, who reports for an Israeli newspaper in the West Bank, when asked, "What's the job of a journalist?" says, "To monitor the centers of power, whether they be in the government, the corporation, or the local politicians. It's our job as the Fourth Estate to monitor the centers of power." But now it seems that the media has become its own center of power.*

PD: There's almost a worship of people in power. You never see a peace worker or leader on *Meet the Press*. Established journalists cover established power. I thought journalists could take all kinds of criticism because they dish so much out, but I was wrong. They bleat and pout and never forget you if you say something. I don't mean to be swinging roundhouse barroom generalities here, but how else can we explain the surrender of the reporters at a Rumsfeld briefing? The so-called expert generals — defense people on CNN and the other channels — were managed by the press. One of the few journalists I admire who doesn't care if the White House calls him back is Sy Hersh. You won't see him on *Meet the Press*.

DB: *Not because he wouldn't accept the invitation — he's not going to get the invitation.*

PD: Exactly. We must fix this. Mainstream media convinces the American public that if we criticize a president ramping up for war, we're unpatriotic and don't believe in God. That's the coup de grace. If you criticize after we go to war, you don't respect the troops. If you criticize it after we lose troops, you're defiling the memory of these troops and spitting in the face of their loved ones and their parents. You can't say, "Why did they crash into the towers?" because then you're blaming the victim. At every turn, they are ready for you, and you better shut up and sing or they're going to make life miserable for you. If you're thirty something, with two and a half kids and a mortgage, and reporting to a Republican boss, how much of an outspoken dissenter are you going to be? Everything conspires to open the door wide for a president to march through it with his cruise missiles and aircraft carriers.

The greatest thing Obama could do now is call a press conference and say, "We are here, now and hereafter not going to use drones for military assault. We may want to reserve the right to keep them for surveillance, but we are promising the world now that we will not..." Where is the valor? A guy sits in a cage or a control room somewhere in Maryland or Nevada and he looks in the nose cone camera of the unmanned aerial vehicle. "There's the insurgents." How they know, I'm not sure, but they fire an incendiary device, and kill children — children! This is on

Obama's watch. I don't see how anybody who engages in this kind of killing can claim to be brave. In Grenada we bombed a mental hospital. We don't have ground troops to go in and take care of Morris Bishop, the communist? What about the endangered lives of those medical students?

We don't have to bomb people — it's just easier. I believe that bombing should be a war crime. If a Marine goes into a Fallujah home and blows away the family with an AK 47, that's a war crime. But if we drop a bomb on that house and incinerate the family, it's called collateral damage. We are in denial and are creating language to help us continue to be in denial.

We are endangering the lives of our young adult children. What kind of a world are my grandchildren going to live in? Are they going to keep looking over their shoulder in downtown New York City or Fargo, North Dakota? Are they going to say, "Did I just get on the wrong bus?" Do we expect that we can drop bombs and not pay a price? We executed an American citizen in a foreign land — assassinated him with a drone.

DB: *Tell us about private Chelsea Manning, who the government and military want to put in jail forever. Some people think she should be executed for revealing some of what you were talking about, including a film that showed a US helicopter crew gunning down civilians — with children.*

PD: When so much is happening under the table, administrations feel they have to protect us, and in order to do that efficiently they must keep it secret. I celebrate the courage of Chelsea Manning. Nobody has proven that anybody was killed because of what Manning made public.

Information is the lifeblood of a democracy. There are more victims caused by secrecy than by sunshine. Let's have the disinfectant there. What Julian Assange has revealed is helpful. It raises the possibility that it won't happen again — that's a good thing. A writer, shortly after 9/11, wrote a column that said, "The chickens have come home to roost." Charles

Krauthammer took her head off because she was blaming the victim. You can't even inquire, "Why did they do this?" Any attempt to say, "Hold it." is shut off. They have succeeded because they've made enough people believe they need this secrecy, otherwise they can't protect us, and that is a very difficult thing for an American citizen to oppose.

Some would argue the most important issue in front of us is the economy, and it may be. But when you think of all this military action going on, all the bombs we've dropped and all the countries we've invaded, it's shocking there's no robust debate. That's how we go to war. It blows me away when I see how easily we are seduced into a war, and all of a sudden we have widows getting the folded flag, people crying around the coffin, young men and women coming home. They'll never see a child graduate, never go to a bar mitzvah or first communion. They are irreplaceable human beings, and are dead forever because George Bush wanted to "Bring it on!" We've got horses, swords, military airplanes, and cannons in parks that kids play on! We celebrate war.

How can the American people stand there and allow this to happen? If we create a culture surrounded by things that go "Boom," we can't be surprised if we build our foreign policy on that kind of activity.

When I was on MSNBC, I had people on from Peaceful Tomorrows, citizens who lost family, loved ones in the towers. Their message was, "Don't go and kill other innocent people to avenge the death of my innocent father, or grandfather..." I could see the pain in their faces, an example of moral courage. These people said this in the middle of the war fever. Of course, they were ignored. These people are not alone — now most people agree with us. We weren't popular enough in 2003 when we invaded, but even then there were millions of Americans who opposed the war but were never heard. Mainstream media went along to get along.

Vice President Dick Cheney looked at Bush at a cabinet meeting and asked "You gonna take him out, or not?" This is cowboy talk. It may involve your son or daughter who will come home in a pine box when two officers come up the front walk. The mother looks out the window and often faints before these men get to the front door. This is the pain American people are not seeing. I made this one little attempt with the movie titled "Body of War" to expose the sacrifice of one family.

Alexander Cockburn and the Art of Radical Journalism

Laura Flanders   July 2012

DB: *Sad news for us who love and believe in real journalism. Radical journalist, author and Nation columnist Alexander Cockburn has died. Cockburn wrote the "Beat the Devil" column in* The Nation *magazine and later edited "CounterPunch" with Jeffrey St. Clair. He was born in Scotland, grew up in Ireland, and graduated from Oxford in 1963. Cockburn wrote for many years for* The Village Voice, *most notably his "Press Clips" column. He was axed out of that column, I believe, and I suspect he believed, by those who did not like that he wasn't afraid to tell the truth about the brutal Israeli occupation of Palestine, and how the mainstream media is afraid of that story.*

Laura Flanders is Alexander Cockburn's niece. She is a contributing writer to The Nation *and a regular guest on MSNBC. She's also the host of* The Laura Flanders Show, *continuing the independent media tradition.* The Laura Flanders Show *airs weekly on KCET/LinkTV, FreeSpeech TV, and in English & Spanish in teleSUR.*

Laura Flanders, Alexander was very proud of you. We miss him, and we're glad you could join us to talk and remember him.

LF: What an incredible man, journalist, and radical he was. He would want us to be living in his spirit, which is that big broad grin, and that ability to poke power in the eye. He had the guts to poke in the eye the people we could then kick sharply in the shins. He kept space alive and open for those who wanted to air possibilities and articulate ideas and questions that were disappearing from the public debate. He was, along with Jeffrey St. Clair of *CounterPunch*, responsible for keeping alive a critique that injected oxygen into what had become an incredibly dried out, dreary, he would say "narcotic," news cycle. It's unbearable that he's gone, simply unbearable. For those who didn't know he was sick, I'm so sorry that you should be getting such a shock.

DB: That was a decision Alex made. The L.A. Times *immediately rushed to compare Alexander Cockburn and Christopher Hitchens, saying they did almost the same thing as they came close to dying. Well, they did the exact opposite things.*

LF: Yes, absolutely. Alexander wanted to keep working until the end, for nothing to change in relationship to his work, to the people he loved, and to his audience. He wanted to keep his eye on the prize, and because of the incredible support he'd built at *CounterPunch* with Jeffrey St. Clair and Becky Grant and so many others in Humboldt County, he was able to keep working almost regardless. That's what he wanted to do. He finished a collection of essays, and compiled a wonderful, short book of words that should be confined to the guillotine, *Guillotined: Being a Summary Broadside Against the Corruption of the English Language.* He was working on preparing for re-publication, his father's — my grandfather's — memoir, *I Claud.* There's a lot of work we're still going to see from Alexander in the weeks, months, and years to come.

CounterPunch can be read at counterpunch.org. They recently started an on-air auction that's auctioning, among other things, photographs by Alexander, and art work that he loved, to raise money for the newsletter and the website.

DB: Can you talk about your family, in particular Claud Cockburn, and the tradition of writing and critique in journalism in your family?

LF: Claud Cockburn was Alexander's father, my grandfather. We have a complicated and twisted family tree. We were all inspired by Claud, a journalist who came to prominence in the UK in the 1930s. Among other things, he had an extraordinary run covering the Spanish Civil War, trying to bring to the public what was happening there.

He also wrote a newsletter, which surely inspired Alexander, called *The Week. The Week* was an intentionally grubby-looking mimeographed broadsheet that no one who was in power admitted to reading, but which everybody who was anybody read. These were the appeasement years in England, in the buildup to World War II. Few people were calling out fascism for what it was. *The Week* carried reports from Berlin and Vienna, where Claud had spent a good amount of time, and sounded the alarm. Claud was also a big believer in the power of humor. He wrote later in life for *Public Eye*, the famous, British satirical magazine. I think Alexander was inspired by Claud's courage and extraordinary freshness of voice. Claud loved to tell the story of interviewing Al Capone for the *London Times*, only to have the story never appear in print — because the gangster's views on American capitalism were so indistinguishable from Wall Street and the paper's editorial page.

Alexander worked hard. He got up at five every morning to, as he put it, "bang away" on the keys to get a story out. Alexander never missed a deadline and he was working until the end. I think he got that work ethic, as well as a healthy disrespect for power, from his father.

DB: You came up after Alex. Were you influenced by his work?

LF: Oh my God, a huge amount. I'm almost embarrassed to see how much the work I was involved in during the 80s was influenced by him, especially the type of media criticism I did at FAIR [Fairness and Accuracy in Reporting]. Alex's *Press Clips* columns at the *Village Voice* in the 70s through the 80s were the first to critique the drivel that came out of the corporate media in a consistent, weekly way. Alexander would hold the drivel up against the light of reality and say, "What gives?" Then he would tell you what gives.

He talked about the interests that influenced coverage, and used language that was so refreshingly releasing. It stripped away that veneer of hocus-pocus, and respect for power that weighs much journalism down. Instead, he poked fun, but also made good sense.

I just re-read a *Village Voice* piece Alexander wrote in 1973, shortly after the CIA backed coup in Chile. Most of the press, the *Washington Post*, and the *New York Times*, wrote that it should be assumed that the US had played no role. Alexander wrote, "In the absence of evidence, it might seem journalistically more responsible to assume there *was* American involvement."

Given the coups in Guatemala and Guyana, "There seems little reason, he wrote, "to wait for Kissinger's memoirs or a Congressional hearing in 1984 to get the full story." How right he was.

DB: He made many people angry. He was pushed out of The Village Voice *after rumors that he was taking money under the table from the pro-Palestinian sources and thus writing pro-Palestinian, anti-Israel columns.*

LF: That was no surprise. He was accused of having taken a grant from a foundation whose critics said was pro-Arab. Heaven forbid! The suggestion was that it influenced his coverage. He said it was for a book. The truth is, there was no place in the money media then for the kind of critical reporting on Israel that he did, and there's no place now. He then started his own media outlet, which is often the one recourse journalists have. It's not an easy route. But create independent media is what he did. It's probably what inspired me to create GRITtv and the Laura Flanders Show and many of the other things I've done. Freedom of the press belongs to those who own one. If you want to be free of the shackles of censorship that he was subjected to through his Israel reporting, among other things, then you have to create your own platform.

There are many fights Alexander picked and got into, and people will doubtless have their favorites. There's no question that in his coverage of the Middle East, he raised the curtain on the bias that exists in what I call the money media — the cruel, casual, conventional wisdom that still today permits a completely double standard for human rights abuses by the Palestinian forces and the human rights abuses by Israel. Alexander drew a line in the sand and said it was unacceptable to treat as equals two so unevenly matched parties, the occupiers and the occupied. He wouldn't give up on it and he was right.

DB: *Whenever there's a new manager here, which is fairly often, there's a visit from the Israeli Consulate. They chat with the station manager and say "Can't you be a little bit more reasonable? Can't you tell Bernstein anything about balance?" Talk about balance.*

LF: If you want to talk about balance go and read Alexander's hysterical parody of the McNeil Lehrer News Hour. He did a parody of the famous PBS evening flagship program in which he said, "This is how they would cover cannibalism." They would have on the one hand the pro-eating-people party and on the other the liberal we-should-regulate-eating-people party. The kind of balance served up in the media obscures, rather than clarifies, the issue at hand. Alexander also did a parody of how PBS would have covered the crucifixion of Christ -- without ever getting to the question of whether it's right to crucify a man. He was pioneering thirty years ago the sort of media criticism that's popular today — his satire that would work perfectly on John Stewart's Daily Show.

DB: *That Press Clips column in the Village Voice was in the first two pages, and everybody rushed to get it and read it. For me, it was transformational because I didn't understand how things worked at that point. He was like a magician that showed you the tricks.*

LF: He both pulled back the curtain and provided a kind of shot in the arm, inoculation against the virus of normality that inserts itself into one's bloodstream. He reminded you that the guff you've been consuming was just that — guff. He would cause you to stop and think, "Am I accepting drivel today that I would have rejected five years ago?" He would say that probably the answer is "Yes," because there's been such an uninterrupted flow of it.

His ability to step back and observe from a healthy distance was partly what he gained by living where he did, in Petrolia, in remote Humboldt County. He was very skeptical of New York after his experience there. He told me a few months ago that he left that city because he felt it had become all about money in the early 90s, the late 80s. He never trusted living in Washington. That's what he thought happened to Christopher Hitchens — too long stewing in the brain-melting pot of DC, surrounded by those with power seeking influence. He chose to live in a place that kept him in touch with a different reality, and that was also partly responsible for what some people saw as the quirkiness, to put it kindly, of some of his views. We can talk about some of those. He saw how policy made in Washington played out at the local level, whether it was about environmental regulation or food. He felt how it felt at the bottom and talked to people who were on the receiving end of government policy. At the end of his life, that was the clearest distinction between him and many other commentators. He was the last person writing about reality from truly outside the beltway, who lived outside the beltway, loved life there, and talked to people who were not other members of the "punditocracy."

DB: *Alex made people angry because he approached subjects they would rather hear nothing about. Please talk more about the man.*

LF: Let's talk about some of the conflicts. People have asked me about how he could be a denier about global warming, refusing to embrace the science on global warming. On the science, I am not an expert, so I didn't fight with him about it, but we did talk about it even recently in the last months before he died because I wanted to understand.

On the science, he had a barrage of facts disputing the patterns of warming that most people point to. On the politics, he would study the words. Where many of us think in huge generalities, he got very particular. When he heard about man-made global warming, he would think, "Which men?" When we are talking about human causes, which humans?

I can't say exactly how Alexander would argue it, but here's what I came to see more clearly after living with him for a little while in Petrolia. Look around and ask who was getting blamed for global warming? It's the miners, the farmer driving his tractor, the guy driving or making an American gas-guzzling car. The same people whose lands and livelihoods have been taken by industrial agribusiness and rapacious mining companies, are now being told they are to blame for what's happening in our environment. The same savage companies that took over small family pits and sent people down into huge deadly mines; the same corporations that put family farmers out of business and hired their children now poor to work in industrially-run fields — those companies with their lawyers and lobbyists are now rigging the game one more time to their own benefit. Once again, regular people living around this country are being told by Washington where, what, and how they can work their land.

Many of his opinions were that way. How is this playing out? We have a moneyed, liberal, environmental elite telling rural folks and others what they can build on their land. He would say something about this stinks, and more often than not, it did. I won't defend him on everything. I tend to cover the work being done by grassroots justice groups to change the environmental movement from the bottom up, and make it a movement that's about power, not shame. The conflicts are often cultural — and they're historical.

In the Daniel Shays rebellion in the US in the 1780s, there was a cultural difference between the rebels in the country who took their lead from the community locally, and made their own independent way in this incredible land of ours, as Alexander did, and those who became driven entirely by money, focused on Washington's markets and laws. He often found himself on the anti-market, anti-money, anti-law side of that equation.

That's my best understanding of what brought him to the political position he ended up in, which I think was a fairly anarchical, libertarian point of view. He put it out there. I remember walking on that incredible beach by the Mattole River in Humboldt County a few months ago and saying "I want to learn from you how to have a tougher skin." I take criticism horribly — he never did. He said he learned early on that if he was going to dish it out, he should be able to take it, and he did. It's a pity that people like [the conservative Zionist] David Horowitz so rarely fought with him in person, but instead picked up the poison pen, and do it one more time when he's dead.

DB: *His passing leaves a huge hole in the world of alternative journalism, real journalism, truth telling, telling it like you see it. What are we missing?*

LF: He was a radical — there's no question. It was a radical approach. He went to the root, and as I put on my site today, he dug it up, dusted it off and laid it out clearly for other people to take a whack at it. That was the charm of him. With all his incredibly erudite education, he never lorded it over people, Instead he tried to make a point clearly enough for anyone to grapple with. If they differed with him, he'd take his hits.

DB: *A journalist's job is to monitor the centers of power and report to the people about the government, corporations, military, whatever.*

LF: Alexander, in addition to being an extraordinary journalist, was actually his own kind of environmentalist. He lived in Humboldt County, on the Lost Coast in little Petrolia. I lived there many weeks this year, and saw a man who recycled almost everything. He put every bit of organic anything back into the ground. He cared for horses and cared for the land. He didn't use a shred of paper he could avoid using. I'm sure expense had nothing to do with it! There wasn't a paper towel in the house. He was also part of a community that held annual rituals, many of them on his land.

He endowed a local arts prize at Humboldt State College. He had a commitment to living a different way that he didn't talk much about. He wasn't a big hippie talker, but he did live and create a beloved community of the sort that many people talk about. Many who criticize him and take time in their obituaries of him to talk about how they differed with him, could learn something from how he treated people close up, people he lived among. Sure, he had his differences intellectually, but he cared and was loyal to the end. And I know from experience, that was worth the world.

DB: *Please tell us about the first time you heard and understood who Alexander Cockburn was and how you'd like him to be remembered.*

LF: I'm going to say something else. Dennis, he really liked you, and the degree that he fought with you was an expression of the degree to which he liked you. He even had a pet name for you, which was Thumper. Thumper is the rabbit that beats the ground with his back feet to alert the forest that there's danger down the track. He thought of you that way.

DB: *I had the same problem with Allen Ginsberg; I never seemed to say the right thing at the right time. I'd ask either one of them a question and they'd say "Well, that's not the question...it's something else." Well, what's the question?*

LF: Go to counterpunch.org. We need *CounterPunch* to be around forever.

Executive Murder: The Laws of the Drone Wars

Marjorie Cohn   February 2013

DB: President Obama's defenders say drone attacks on al-Qaeda suspects have ratcheted down the levels of violence left behind by President Bush. New disclosures regarding President Barack Obama's use of armed drones to hunt down and kill suspected al-Qaeda terrorists thousands of miles from the United States raise troubling questions about the US Constitution and international law. Marjorie Cohn, professor at the Thomas Jefferson School of Law and former President of the National Lawyers Guild, joins us.

Professor Cohn, you say the White Paper runs afoul of international and US law. Please explain.

MC: The White Paper allows the government to kill a US citizen who is not on the battlefield, if some high government official, who is supposedly informed about the situation, thinks the target is a senior Al Qaeda leader who poses an imminent threat of a violent attack against the US. How do they define "imminent"? It doesn't require any clear evidence that a specific attack on US persons and interests will take place in the immediate future, so it completely dilutes the idea of imminent threat. Under well-established principles of international law and the UN Charter, one country can use military force against another only in self-defense. But under the *Caroline* case, which is the gold standard here, the "necessity for self-defense must be instant, overwhelming, leaving no choice of means, and no moment for deliberation." That means if we are going to be attacked right away we can use force.

The very nebulous test the White Paper sets forth even allows the targeted killing of somebody who is considered to be a "continuing" threat, whatever that means. The most disturbing part says that US citizens can be killed even when there is no "clear evidence that a specific attack on US persons and interests will take place in the immediate future." So we have a global battlefield, where if there is someone, anywhere, who might be associated with Al Qaeda, according to a high government official, then, on "Terror Tuesday," Obama can decide who he is going to kill after consulting with John Brennan. And it's not even clear Obama himself has to authorize these targeted killings. John Brennan is Obama's counter-terrorism guru who is up for confirmation to be CIA Director — very incestuous. John Brennan has said targeted killings constitute lawful self-defense.

One of the most disturbing things here is the amassing of executive power with no review by the courts — no checks and balances. The courts will have no opportunity to interpret what "imminent" or "continuing" threat means. The White Paper cites John Yoo's claim that courts have no role to play in what the President does in this so-called War on Terror, where the whole world is a battlefield. I say so-called War on Terror because terrorism is a tactic. It's not an enemy. You don't declare war on a tactic. The White Paper refers to Yoo's view that judicial review constitutes "judicial encroachment" on the judgments by the President and his national security advisers as to when and how to use force. The White Paper cites *Hamdi v. Rumsfeld*, which says the President has the authority to hold US citizens caught on the battlefield in Afghanistan as enemy combatants. But in *Hamdi*, the Supreme Court stated that a US citizen who is being detained as an enemy combatant is entitled to due process, which means an arrest and fair hearing. It doesn't mean taking him out with a drone.

Another interesting passage in the White Paper says "judicial enforcement [a court reviewing these kill orders of the executive] of such orders would require the court to supervise inherently predictive judgments by the President and his national security advisers as to when and how to use force against a member of an enemy force against which Congress has authorized the use of force." Does "inherently predictive" mean the court can't review decisions made with a crystal ball because it's too mushy? I don't know. Courts are certainly competent to make emergency decisions under FISA, the Foreign Intelligence Surveillance Act. The FISA Court meets in secret and authorizes wiretaps requested by the Executive Branch. Courts can do this — they act in emergencies to review and check and balance what the executive is doing. That's what separation of powers is all about.

DB: *The White Paper is a restatement of national security documents. Are the Geneva Conventions thrown in the garbage?*

MC: The policy does violate the Geneva Conventions, because they define willful killing as a grave breach, which is punishable as a war crime. Although the White Paper says they are going to follow the well-established principle of proportionality — which means an attack cannot be excessive in relation to the anticipated military advantage — I don't see how they can put that into practice, because the force is going to be excessive, given they are using drones, taking out convoys, and killing large numbers of civilians. Another principle of international law — distinction — requires the attack be directed only at legitimate military targets. We know from the *New York Times* exposé that the "kill list" Brennan brings to Obama to decide who he is going to take out without a trial — basically execute — can be used even if they don't have a name, or if they are present in an area where there are only suspicious "patterns of behavior." These are known as signature strikes, which means bombs are dropped on unidentified people who are in an area where suspicious activity is taking place — that goes even beyond targeted killings, which are considered to be illegal. The UN Special Rapporteur on Extrajudicial Summary or Arbitrary Executions, Christof Heyns, expressed grave concerns about these targeted killings, saying they may constitute war crimes. He called on the Obama administration to explain how its drone strikes comport with international law, and to specify the bases for the decisions to kill rather than capture particular individuals.

The White Paper says one of the requirements before they can take someone out is that capture must be "infeasible." As you go on and read this memo, infeasible begins to look like inconvenient. We have these very mushy terms, with no clear standards that comply with international law. Yet there is no oversight by any court, and Congress has no role either — so we don't have checks and balances.

Even the Authorization for the Use of Military Force (AUMF) that Congress passed a few days after 9/11 doesn't authorize this. The AUMF allows the President to use force against groups and countries that had supported the 9/11 attacks. When the Bush administration asked Congress for open-ended military authority "to deter and preempt any future acts of terrorism or aggression against the United States," Congress specifically rejected that open-ended military authority. Congress has not authorized this, and it's not clear whether Congress *would* authorize it.

DB: *Comparing Obama policy to Bush, essentially Obama has chosen a little less torture, or skip the torture; we'll just kill them.*

MC: Obama expanded these drone attacks far beyond what the Bush administration was doing. Many thorny issues remain, such as indefinite detention, how detainees are treated, and under what circumstances they can be released. The Obama administration evidently feels it's cleaner and easier just to kill them; then they don't have to worry about bad publicity from housing them at Guantanamo, not giving them a fair trial, holding them indefinitely. This goes beyond the torture policy. I'm not saying that killing with drones is worse than the illegal and outrageous invasions of Iraq and Afghanistan that the Bush administration began, in which hundreds of thousands of people were killed or maimed. So I wouldn't say that Obama is worse than Bush, but he is certainly following in the tradition of the Bush administration and John Yoo's expansive view of executive power — whatever the President does is unreviewable.

JFK Attorney General's Long Trek for Justice

Ramsey Clark   March 2013

DB: *There was a time in America when someone like Ramsey Clark could be Attorney General and assert the power of the federal government on the side of civil rights, but that now seems like ancient history. For more than 50 years — in both the public and private sectors — former US Attorney General Ramsey Clark has challenged the abuse of power and taken up the cause of the oppressed. During his tenure at the Justice Department, including serving as Attorney General during the Johnson administration, Clark worked to end racial segregation and played a historic role in support of the American Civil Rights Movement.*

Clark was in charge of enforcing the court order that protected the famous march from Selma to Montgomery; leading the investigation of abuses by police and the National Guard following the Watts riots; and supervising the drafting and passage of the Voting Rights Act of 1965 and Civil Rights Act of 1968. He also opposed electronic surveillance and refused to authorize an FBI wiretap on Martin Luther King, Jr.

After leaving government, Clark provided legal defense to the disenfranchised. His controversial clients over the years included antiwar activist Father Philip Berrigan and Native American political prisoner Leonard Peltier.

An outspoken critic of US foreign policy, Clark has called for an end to the wars in Afghanistan and Iraq as well as a ban on depleted uranium weapons. He fervently opposes the escalating militarization of the United States and is a staunch advocate for victims of constitutional violations and legal travesties in post-9/11 America.

Mr. Clark, today you are here to talk about limits of power, which you have spent a lifetime challenging. First you were an enforcer as an Attorney General. Maybe you didn't change much, but you became the people's defense. In terms of government power and citizens rights, compared to 20 years ago, where are we? Do we have more rights? Are we safer or not safer in terms of the guarantees we are supposedly given under the constitutional amendments?

RC: I'll ignore your 20-year limitation. I think there's been a significant erosion of government respect for fundamental human rights for our own citizens and the security of people abroad. Since the idealism of the 60s, I don't think we've maintained the respect for individual rights or human dignity that we were inspired with. The Vietnam War took a lot of that out of us, but I think the concentration of capital has done more to hurt individual liberties than anything else.

DB: *Really? Could you say a bit more about the merging of the corporate state and corporate power?*

RC: It's not concerned with individual rights. Look at the prison population. It's heartbreaking and staggering. There's no better barometer of how you feel about freedom than how many people you put in prison. We need to find a better way to treat our folks. As you look at the discrimination by numbers, the percentage of young black males in prison and the lives that are severely damaged, it is unbelievable and staggering. It's a shame for the nation that we would ever permit it. That's after the civil rights movement. You get to vote until you go to prison and then you can't vote anymore because you have been convicted of a felony.

DB: *We have admissions from the highest levels of government that the President of the United States has collaborated in a wide-ranging program of assassinations through the drone program. Under national and international law, how would you characterize that?*

RC: Murder. Simple. It ought to be addressed as such. The drones themselves are murder. The US is going into neutral countries, areas far, far removed from war zones, often missing the people who were intended to be hit and hitting a lot of people there was no intention of hitting — they just got in the way. And it doesn't seem to bother the government. What happens on earth when there's no safety anyplace from something in the sky that you can't see until it kills you?

DB: *When you were there, drones were everywhere. People were terrified. Just about everybody on the Gaza strip was vulnerable. Where are we, in terms of warfare and the power of the rich and the elite to control with more and more intense weaponry?*

RC: The plight of Gaza, not to mention Palestine generally, is desperate. I represented the PLO for about 30 years until Arafat left. He only left Gaza about two years before he died, so I'd visit him there regularly. The place was booming. They were producing three crops a year; there was green everywhere. They were almost finished building an international airport. Education was booming. I don't know of another place so intense on education from grammar school through graduate school. It was so spirited. I was there in January. Now it is just awful. It seems like you are at risk at all times. There is no security anyplace. Even agriculture is barren. Hospitals are in terrible shape, lacking medicines for the many injured and sick people. It's a desperate situation and getting worse.

DB: *Is this an ethnic cleansing? It's a methodical attempt to purge Palestinians from their land. If you live in the West Bank, you can't get to the Gaza Strip to see your uncle on a holiday or for the weekend.*

RC: I went a few times. It's a day's trip, even though just a few miles. You can get there. But if you are trying to meet somebody, it takes a lot of time. I went to Gaza to meet some people and didn't have time to go to the West Bank. So they came to see me, but they got there 15 minutes before I had to leave, after waiting there for 24 hours. That's how hard it is.

DB: *It was just the 40th anniversary of the American Indian Movement. You've represented Leonard Peltier, who is still in jail. What are your thoughts on why the US government will not let him out?*

RC: I argued his first parole release, which is decades ago now. The poor medical examiner ordered release and lost his job because of it. One day in 1965, when I was Deputy Attorney General, I was walking across a prison yard in Texas and I saw an old guy slumped over a building. I walked over and asked what he was doing there, but there was no response. I patted him on the back and he seemed senile. I turned to the warden and said, "Why is he here? The sun could kill him." The warden said, "We have been trying to get rid of him for years. Whenever we said we wanted to release him, we'd get a letter back from J. Edgar Hoover, who said that anyone who is convicted of killing an FBI agent will never leave prison." I think that's Leonard Peltier's problem, although of course he was wrongfully convicted, but two FBI agents were killed.

DB: *Two FBI agents killed, so they will never let him go.*

RC: Not as long as the present power prevails. I'm more of an optimist than that. He shouldn't have been in prison in the first place, and it's so desperately over-due.

DB: *What are some of the issues we need to do something about?*

RC: You are asking for a long list. I'd have to start with our wars. We've got to stop these wars. We just had one outrageous, murderous war after another and we are aiming for Iran now, which might be called the last man standing, but it's not the last, because there will be another war after that. Look at the toll of those wars, and the sheer idiocy of going into Iraq. Since 1991 those people have not had a moment of peace — they are always at risk of death. It's as bad now or worse than it's ever been. After Bush's invasion in 2003, I don't see how the people withstood it. They say mankind is a creature that can be accustomed to anything, and they have become accustomed to hell on earth. It's our responsibility, so we have to stop it. We have to prevent it from happening further, and we can't do that until we demilitarize.

DB: *Is that possible? Where do we go?*

RC: It isn't only possible — we'd be so much better off. Think of all the things we could do with the money if that was the only benefit we got from it. We are risking fighting a nuclear war because, after signing it in 1968, we continue to violate the Nuclear Arms Proliferation Treaty, which compels the five or six nuclear powers at the time to work to eliminate their own nuclear weapons in return for the other nations not acquiring nuclear weapons. Instead, it's grown, and today if you have an enemy with a nuclear weapon, you'd better get one yourself, because there is no other protection. You can't fight, because they'll take out all your cities. It doesn't matter how much bigger you are than they are. That's the plight Iran's faced with. How do you protect your people if Israel's got the bomb?

DB: *We're way past 1984, but every time I hear the notion that Israel, the renegade, is restraining itself by not using some of their 500 thermo-nuclear weapons against Iran, it sounds so Orwellian. That is the story carried by mainstream media, including liberal media like NPR. How do we confront this?*

RC: We must stand up and speak out for what it is. I started going to Iran when the Shah was still there. I watched what they did in the Iran/Iraq war. They lost 800,000 kids because the kids would hold a rifle wearing only tennis shoes and pants and charge toward the artillery and aircraft of the Soviet Union, US and all the other powers of the earth backing Iraq in that war. They lost 800,000 young men, but they kept fighting and they won. They finally prevailed in spite of everything. The problem they have is that however courageous they are, if an enemy uses nuclear weapons against them, their cities are gone.

DB: *Ramsey Clark, we have spoken to you around the world, and wherever you are, the people appreciate your presence. You give us hope and an example of how to live. Thank you, and what an honor.*

Surviving and Standing Proud for Indian Rights

Bill Means   March 2013

DB: *Today is the 40th anniversary of the founding of the American Indian Movement [AIM] in Wounded Knee, South Dakota. As AIM leaders come together today on the Pine Ridge Reservation to remember what happened four decades ago, on February 27 1973, as well as to assess the movement today, one key member of the original uprising will be sorely missed — Russell Means. Bill, your older brother Russell was at the center of the AIM movement. Can you remind us what happened 40 years ago, and the role you both played?*

BM: Greetings to the Pacifica family from the American Indian Movement at Wounded Knee, South Dakota. It is a very historical place, because over 300 of our men, women and children were brutally murdered by the Shetland Cavalry of the United States on Dec 29, 1890, a few days after Christmas. In 1973, the most historic event in the history of modern day Indian people of the 20th century, in the past millennium, Indian people from across America came together to make a statement at Wounded Knee. The gathering was directed by our chiefs, who invited us to Pine Ridge to help redress the corruption and massive abuse of civil rights against the American Indian Movement. Some came as guests, and some of us are from here. Our Means family, our father, originally came from here. So we were very honored — many of us were living here at that time — that other members of AIM from around the country joined us to help in the struggle, which became a worldwide struggle for Indian people — eventually for Indigenous Peoples' rights.

I lost two brothers in 11 months — my brother Russell, who passed in October, and last November we lost my twin brother Ted Means. I thank you for having us on your show because this is a historic day in the struggle for Indigenous Peoples' rights. The most profound effect of Wounded Knee was that it woke up the world's populations, governments, people of the world, that Indigenous Peoples, Indian people of America, have the right to

137

be who we are, have the right to survive and have our own human rights agenda. As Wounded Knee brought back the bravery and identity of Indian people, there was a resurgence of activism. It was the catalyst for the Indian movements around the world to become well organized into an Indigenous Peoples' movement of the world. We lost two very important warriors there, as well as many after. We mention Frank Clearwater and Buddy LaMont, who were killed inside Wounded Knee during the 71-day occupation in 1973. We like to recognize them each year, as well as those we lost in 1890. My role at the time, when I came back as a Vietnam veteran, was primarily that of a warrior — to defend the land and people in Wounded Knee, because we had many women, children and elders with us. It wasn't just a bunch of young militant Indians — it was a very wide coalition of Indian tribes and nations from around the country, and indeed our non-Indian supporters, who came together at Wounded Knee to let the government know that John Wayne didn't kill us all.

In that process we were able to make Indian people feel proud again. One of the strongest memories of Wounded Knee was the renaissance of Indian pride and identity. It was the time of the US policies of assimilation and acculturation. Many of our people forgot their languages, no longer knew their ceremonies. They were under the Christian church's influence as far as spiritual awareness and needs. This is the time to re-establish that we as Lakota have our own language, our own way of relating to the creator. This was a time to make people proud to wear long hair again, to wear beadwork, to be proud to be an Indian. That's our biggest accomplishment, as well as showing the world we still survive as Indian people. We built the pride in the people themselves, ourselves, to stand as Indian people.

DB: *It is the 40th anniversary of the founding of AIM and the face-off at Wounded Knee, South Dakota. Today's* Atlantic Monthly *reports that a number of members of this new movement went to Wounded Knee, took the town hostage and demanded rights. How would you state that?*

BM: We demanded our rights, but there were no hostages. They brought in two senators, George McGovern and James Barrass, senators from South Dakota, to talk to the Guildenstern family, who owned the trading post. They admitted on national television that they weren't hostages. They weren't kidnapped, and they stayed there in support of us for several days. The idea there were hostages taken and that people were held there against their will is a stereotype image that is often associated with social movements. Violence is what sells papers. In this case, we were only defending ourselves. So when the BIA [Bureau of Indian Affairs] police began to fire their weapons against women and children, we had to respond, to defend those women and children. This is the true history. One of the largest criminal trials in history lasted about ten months — the trial of Dennis Banks and Russell Means — then was dismissed by the federal judge, Fred Nichol, due to FBI misconduct. It didn't even go to the jury for a guilty or not-guilty verdict. The judge had over 30 counts of misconduct against the FBI, from coercion of witnesses to illegal wiretaps to manipulation of evidence and selective prosecution. Many of the issues were discussed in over 500 different legal cases that were brought as the result of Wounded Knee. There were maybe one or two convictions from over 500 cases. Our legal record — the right or wrong, the legalities of the 71-day occupation — stands on the evidence. It is very clear we were defending ourselves. We were not the aggressor in the 71-day occupation.

DB: *You came back from Vietnam as a veteran and found yourself in a war at home. When I read the introduction to this interview, I almost said AIM was founded 40 decades ago instead of 4 decades ago. But I wouldn't be mistaken at the core, because this did happen many, many, many years ago. When we say Native peoples, you were here first.*

BM: Yes. History is repeating itself, like the 1890 massacre on the very site where we were occupying the village of Wounded

Knee. As a Vietnam veteran I felt more like the Viet Cong [VC] and NLF [National Liberation Front] when they ran up against me as a soldier in Vietnam. All of a sudden, I was the VC, the North Vietnamese fighting for the liberation of their country. I had a conflict of beliefs even when I was in Vietnam. But when you are in a combat situation, the issue is survival, not politics. I got to relive that conflict within myself, but I also felt like I was exonerated. I had the rare opportunity to allegedly defend the US when I was in Vietnam. Then I came back to defend my own people against the US. It was a very ironic situation when, as a soldier, I was perpetuating the policies of the US in Vietnam, and then a very few months later I was fighting against the US government, on our own lands, here on the reservation in South Dakota.

DB: *Bill, what has changed? Poverty, medical care, schools, all the battles back then — are they still alive and necessary?*

BM: Oh yes. I think the educational systems have improved 100% in terms of having our own Indian educators and administrators. A lot of ceremonies have been restored, both within our school system and communities, to make them available to our youth. We have elders involved in education now. But we still have a lot of poverty and problems with alcohol and drugs. Like many of our minority friends and relatives in America, we have issues of poverty — extreme poverty. Shannon County, home of the reservation, is the second poorest county in the US. We were the first poorest 10 years ago, so if moving from the first to the second poorest is improvement, I guess we improved. But in terms of our identity, our people learning their culture, practicing their traditional ways, I think we have been able to turn that corner. We are Lakota, Indigenous Peoples, we continue to fight for our treaty rights, our land, against mining, against many environmental issues of our time, just like the rest of America. At this time we have our own people in place in various institutions that control us, whether it is the government, schools, churches. I think things have improved due to our self-determination. We have a lot more of our people involved. Many of the same social conditions exist, but we have the tools in place now to make fundamental changes that we didn't have before. We have control of our Indian schools on the reservation. All the schools are now under the control of community boards, district councils, under the control of Indian people, rather than the BIA, Department of Interior or the church. In that sense we made some fundamental changes. We fight everyday to improve the conditions under which our people live.

DB: *How did you move into an international framework with the International Indian Treaty Council?*

BM: Our work establishing the International Indian Treaty Council was a direct result of what happened at Wounded Knee. Our chiefs, elders, leaders, realized we had worldwide recognition because of what happened in Wounded Knee. The press was here from throughout the world, so we realized we needed to do something with the attention. We decided to take our treaties to the United Nations, because treaties are a foundation of our legal rights in the international community. We began in 1974 by hosting a conference that was attended by over 94 Indian nations throughout the hemisphere. Through that, in 1974 we formed the International Indian Treaty Council. In 1977 we had our first international conference at the United Nations in Geneva, Switzerland: Racism Against the Indigenous Populations of the Western Hemisphere. We looked at the UN as an instrument for human rights, and realized that Indigenous Peoples were excluded — not even mentioned. The major powers of the UN said we were either ethnic minorities or only populations that were internal matters of existing members of the UN. Therefore, they said, the UN wasn't authorized to interfere with internal issues of member states. That was the position when we first went there. As we dealt with the issues of treaties — even the US Constitution in article 6 says treaties shall be the supreme law of the land — we were able to show we had standing as nations. We took that standing and began our struggle within the institution of the UN. After 30 years, on September 13, 2007, the General Assembly finally passed the Declaration on the Rights of Indigenous Peoples. That was a very important document — the result of 30 years of work. We established the international part of our movement as a natural and mandated outgrowth of our treaty rights.

DB: *We cannot let you go while we remember the founding of AIM 40 years ago without remembering that Leonard Peltier, who as you mentioned earlier is still suffering in prison, has spent decades in prison, and is in physical trouble. Tell us the significance of Leonard Peltier in this movement, why he is* Présente *there in Wounded Knee and why freeing Peltier is an important battle to fight.*

BM: Peltier represents the treatment of Indian peoples by the US government for the last two centuries, since the treaty making times of the 1800s. The case of Leonard Peltier is a great example of the justice system we face, in that the US government takes someone who is an international figure and continues to deny him his legal rights. After countless appeals in this legal process, he still represents the injustice that Indian people suffer by US policy. After 36 years in prison, he remains a political prisoner as recognized by many prestigious international organizations such as Amnesty International and the World Council of Churches, and leaders such as Bishop Desmond Tutu of South Africa. Many have recognized Leonard as a person who did not receive a fair trial, deserves a new trial and certainly should have been acquitted based on the evidence. So Leonard Peltier remains the number one symbol of the United States' treatment of the legal issues of the Indian people.

US Vets Join Gitmo Hunger Strike

Diane Wilson   June 2013

DB: *Of the 166 detainees still at the Guantanamo Bay prison, 104 are on a hunger strike that has lasted over four months as they protest indefinite detentions without trial or even charges. These detainees are now joined by several US war veterans, including former Army medic Diane Wilson. The US war veterans are seeking to close down the Guantanamo Bay prison and demanding the freedom of detainees who face no charges and are not considered security threats. Diane Wilson is a fourth generation shrimper and an environmental activist on the Texas Gulf Coast who has been on a water-only hunger strike for 50 days.*

First of all, Diane, after 49 days ... how are you doing?

DW: A few days ago it was a different story, but I got some electrolytes. Any time you're on a water-only fast this long, you tend to screw up your electrolytes, and I probably wasn't drinking enough water. One of the vets mailed me some electrolytes. It cleared up my thinking, which was like a fog over my brain. It would have been very difficult to interview me then, but I feel much better now.

DB: *I am glad you are feeling better now. You were a medic in the Vietnam War, and then you became a Vietnam War protester, right?*

DW: Absolutely. What I saw as a medic determined how I've felt about war ever since. I was like those young guys who volunteered — you saw those Life magazine pictures of the medics. That's the one I saw — those black and white photos of those medics wounded and reaching for the helicopter and trying to help a soldier and I felt the urge. I was going to be Florence Nightingale and I wanted to go to Vietnam. That's what I wanted to do, and I found out different. I am totally committed to no war.

DB: *What did you learn?*

DW: When the Army takes these young people, and it's a war like the Vietnam War, they must turn them to thinking as the other. Usually it was a dark-skinned person, because there were many movies where they were the enemy — it was a kill, kill, kill mentality. I remember what they would do to get the guys in that type of mentality. I started seeing the guys being air-lifted back, and saw them in the wards. They were totally lost. If you'd walk down the wards, there would be such a fog of marijuana. I mean it was like a fog, a big fog. The only way they could show their gratitude for me helping them, for taking care of them, was by loading down my nurse uniform with dope — Black Mollies, crack, cocaine. They were totally, totally lost. In a very short period of time there was a transfiguration of people. I finally told my colonel, "I'm not playing your game anymore. I'm quitting." She freaked out and told me to salute and go back and do what I was doing, but I got a ticket to Canada. Other WACS were in Toronto, Canada. I absolutely refused to do it anymore. I wasn't a part of a group, and didn't have solidarity with people. It was something I saw and experienced. I said, "This is not right." Eventually I came back and they said I was very un-American. They gave me an undesirable discharge, which I use with pride.

DB: *Diane Wilson, you are a hero to me at many levels, such as your battle to communicate with the people of Bhopal, coming from that part of Texas where you saw the water you loved [the Gulf of Mexico], that you worked on as a fishing boat captain, destroyed in the BP oil spill, and then you made unity with the people of Bhopal. You traveled around the world in the name of peace. So this hunger strike you are on now is a continuation of extraordinary work for the people, for peace. Why is this important enough? Why is the closing down of Guantanamo important enough for you to put your very life on the line? You are not a youngster.*

DW: I'm sixty-five, not a youngster.

DB: *Tell us why you are risking your life.*

DW: I've done a lot of environmental politics because I've been a fisherman, a shrimper all my life. I was at the Dallas dedication of the Bush library on the protest end — there were a lot of

Vietnam vets and CODEPINK activists protesting the dedication of the Bush library. I was aware there were demonstrations with people in the orange jump suits. I had seen it in all those hearings, and people standing back, but I had never really, really gone in depth. So when Medea Benjamin of CODEPINK told me she wanted to start a rolling hunger fast, an international hunger fast for the prisoners over there ... I read what was going on and it killed me because ... I get real ...

DB: *It's okay...Take a deep breath. It's fine. This is love, what you are doing. This is a commitment you've made. Breathe. In the old days of Greece, they said that crying was a sign of wisdom. They actually had crying rooms.*

DW: Because I'm a fisherman, with sometimes so little voice, and because the corporations are so powerful and destructive, I understand what it is like to not have a voice, so I understand why people go on hunger strikes. It is not a whim, it is not your first option — it comes from a different part of your brain. It's not a rational thing — it's from your heart. I totally understand what it feels like to come from your heart because it's so desperate, and, and...

DB: *Take a deep breath. It's okay.*

DW: Because of my fighting the corporations, I have been arrested so many times for non-violent civil disobedience, for just standing up — so I understand a small fraction of what it must be like for those guys to be in that prison. I know how brutal in every mental, physical, and psychological way those prisons can be. For them to be in that situation, feeling that desperate ... and then, also, for it to be my country! I can't tell you how many people think I am unpatriotic because I stand up and protest. They're like, "Well, why don't you go back from where you come from?" And I'm like, "Well, I'll have you know my grandfather was a Native American Indian." I don't know how back home I can be, being in my own country. The American people have to make this country what we believe it to be. What we were doing to those men over there, and what we have done to their families...

145

CODEPINK was recently in Yemen where a lot of the prisoners are from. Even the families, the children of men who are in those prisons, are being discriminated against. They are being ostracized because it is their father or their brother who is over there. Eighty-eight of them were scheduled for release over three years ago. They have been in that prison for eleven years. The CIA finds no cause to prosecute — the FBI, the State Department, the Justice Department, and the Pentagon — and still they stay. For what reason?

I sincerely believe that to make change, you must push it to the edge and get right in their faces. You become the witness and get as close as you can. That's what I did. The only thing I know that can take it as far as those guys are taking it is to do the very same thing. The American people, the President — they can't see the detainees. Has Obama gone to Guantanamo to see those guys? No! So I'll do it right in front of him. If I had a chance, I'd march right in there, and open his door.

DB: *It's amazing this parallel structure you're setting up by fasting. Would it be correct to say the President totally lied to the American people when he said he was going to close down Guantanamo? What would your dialogue, or your message, to the President be?*

DW: He has to have the moral courage, because he can do it today. He should have done it yesterday, and the day before that, but he can do it today. For him not to is a lack of moral courage, that is all.

DB: *As a senior member of the peace movement, what advice would you give a young woman or a young man, particularly a young woman, who said, "Why are you doing this? Why are you fasting? I have my life ahead of me. Why would it be important for me to get involved in these kinds of issues?"*

DW: These issues are about who we are as people. What we have — our jobs, our accumulations, our job title — is not who we are. Who we are is the good we can do to make this country better. There's no excuse — none. People tell me, "Well, when my kids grow up," or "When I get a better job." The Democrats

146

said, "Well, when we get in a better position." It's always an excuse, and there is none. I believe it is about moral integrity, and that's the only valuable thing that you really have.

DB: *We want you to be careful. It is a very incredible inspiration to many people that you take the stand you do. There are many people who love you for it.*

DW: Thank you very much, Dennis. I don't hear that very often in my neck of the woods.

A Foot Soldier Throws Down His Rifle

Brandon Toy   July 2013

DB: *Brandon Toy, an Iraq War veteran and a mid-level project manager at General Dynamics, concluded that what he had done and was doing went against the best principles of the United States — and so resigned with a declaration that if "every foot soldier threw down his rifle," things might change.*

Brandon, how did you become a part of the post 9/11 military industrial complex? Where did that start?

BT: To be honest, Dennis, I saw images of soldiers and war, glorified veterans held up as heroes, flag waving, etc., etc. It got the idea in my head that it was about the highest thing you could do for your country — serve in the armed forces. It snowballed from there. After 9/11, I became a rabid patriot and was all for the Iraq War. I voted for President Bush twice. I enlisted at the end of 2003 after the Iraq War had started, because I believed in the cause. I thought we were going over there to find WMDs and fight terrorism on its own soil, oust Hussein from power and bring democracy to the Middle East — which now seems like a ludicrous concept to me. But I believed it. I got sucked in very deeply, very quickly. Even though I didn't enlist when I was 18 — I was 24 — I still see myself as very young and naive at the time.

DB: *Could you talk about your experiences in the war zone?*

BT: I was a machine gunner in a Humvee unit, stationed at Camp Rustamiyah, formerly called Camp Cuervo. It's on the southeast side of Baghdad. We patrolled, up and down, what's known as Canal Street through Al Masada and Sadr City. We trained, supported and transported Iraqi police officers and Iraqi army personnel. We checked on detainees, transported detainees from the Green Zone to different locations, or from an Iraqi police station to different locations. I was a foot soldier — a machine gunner.

DB: *Did you see the "collateral murder" video that was made available by WikiLeaks through Chelsea Manning?*

BT: I saw it two to three years ago, for the first time.

DB: *And was that familiar, in terms of your own experience?*

BT: The way they carried themselves and talked about the targets on the ground was familiar to me. It was very disturbing.

DB: *Was seeing that video part of your transformation?*

BT: Absolutely. It stood out to me, in the beginning of coming to understand the truth, as the true nature of what we're doing overseas.

DB: *How did that video became a crucial part of your transformation?*

BT: What stuck out in my mind was the disregard that these were actually people on the ground that they are firing at. Then when the van comes to pick up the wounded ... and they almost take joy in, you know, "Please let us shoot." Then shooting the van, then finding out that there were a couple of Reuters reporters who were on the ground there, and children in the van. A tank — maybe it wasn't a tank, but that's how I remember it — ran over one of the bodies on the ground. They kind of laughed about that. It just seemed very callous, uncaring, dehumanizing, like somebody watching a video game. It was very disturbing.

DB: *After your military experience, you became a contractor and worked with General Dynamics, a major defense establishment of the corporate military. Tell us about your work there as a project manager, and what you did there to support the war effort.*

149

BT: I graduated from college in 2008. One of my professors knew somebody there, and got me in. I began as a glorified administrative assistant, then worked my way up to managing small projects. They were developmental engineering projects around combat vehicle issues, different systems, mechanical systems, electrical systems, etc.

DB: When did the work become offensive to you?

BT: It wasn't the work itself that was offensive. There was nothing overtly criminal or anything of that nature, for the work I was doing. It was more that I came to not see that much of a difference between holding a rifle in theater, and sitting behind a keyboard speaking military jargon, basically being a soldier — an appendage of the military industrial complex — from behind a desk and without a uniform on. We had the same bosses that we reported up through. We were supporting the same war effort. It was just a matter of location, and comfort. I was more comfortable than I was in theater. But I was working for the same exact bosses, in the same effort.

DB: *How would you explain the relationship between General Dynamics and the United States military?*

BT: Oh, very close. Tight knit. Almost one and the same thing.

DB: *So in your mind there's no separation between the private corporations making the weaponry, and the military, buying and using it?*

BT: Absolutely. They're so intertwined, all the way up through the leadership. General Dynamics has almost become an appendage of the United States government, as is any other contractor.

DB: *How are these private contractors now heavily interwoven into the fabric of the military? How does that work?*

BT: Well, you've got the revolving door. You've got generals and other officers that move back and forth from the military and then enter civilian life. They have contacts in the military. You go all the way up to the corporate level and these guys are working on each other's board of directors, etc. They're part of the elite corporate state, at that high level. They have a certain amount of budget they need to spend. There are very close relationships between officials on the government's side and within the defense contractors.

DB: *How did Edward Snowden influence you? You made this extraordinary statement: "I have always believed if every foot soldier threw down his rifle, war would end. I hereby throw mine down."*

BT: Edward Snowden is extremely courageous for what he's done. When I listened to the second video that Glenn Greenwald put out, the second part of the interview from Hong Kong, I heard the words "I joined after Iraq, and I didn't like what I was seeing." I'm paraphrasing badly but it was almost like my words coming out of his mouth. I was so awed that he risked his life — certainly his freedom — for a very long time, to let us know from the inside what's going on. Snowdon turned conspiracy theory into conspiracy fact.

We all had a general idea that we were being spied on constantly. It was just something like — yeah, wink, nod — they're watching us all the time. But I don't think we've had anything this substantial or in-depth before, and the way both Glenn Greenwald and Snowden are handling it is very impressive. They're putting on quite a battle.

DB: *Your work inside General Dynamics and your disillusionment with the war effort — is this reverberating inside the company? Are there other folks you worked with who have these concerns, who are*

151

becoming more jittery that what they may be engaged in is not a democratic effort?

BT: I spoke very little about what I was thinking to other people within General Dynamics. There were a few close friends I had conversations with. "Hey, did you see what happened yesterday? Did you see about the drone program? Have you seen Jeremy Scahill's new movie? Did you see *The Dirty War* exposé in BBC Arabic, etc., etc.?" I didn't get much of a response. It's almost like a willful turning away from the actual events within the company. I've heard from a couple of people within the company since I've left that it was quite shocking. They were trying to figure out why I did it, what happened, and some people expressed that I've made them look at things in a different way, which I was very happy about.

DB: *You say you are no longer a foot soldier in the war. What does it mean to you, to resign? Your words are very powerful.*

BT: When I decided to do this I thought, "Oh, I can slink off into the shadows, find another job, and that will be the end of it." But I felt so strongly about what I was seeing, what I was doing, and what I was a part of that I wanted people to hear my voice, because I believe in Thomas Paine-type democracy. I wanted to get it out there — if people didn't listen, at least I said my piece.

DB: *If you were standing before a class of junior high school students in civics, what would you want them to know that you didn't know when you went blindly, as you say, as a patriot, thinking that you're fighting the good fight?*

BT: Don't blindly trust your government. Things are not as they seem. At a very widespread level there are things we're doing that are just plain wrong. They are against what's supposed to be the fabric of this country, everything they teach us in school — the Constitution, the ideals that we're supposed to uphold, the things that we're supposed to be fighting for. They will cover those up and hide those secrets. There's a higher agenda at work here. I'm not sure what it is, but it is not what is being sold.

It's very easy to fall into that other narrative because the voices that are speaking the truth — WikiLeaks, the Assanges, and the Greenwalds — those are drowned out by the mainstream media. It's getting a little better. People are listening a little more, it's getting into the mainstream. For a long time, if you started talking about this you were labeled a conspiracy theorist. Especially when the Iraq War started and we went into this fevered pitch over 9/11, which was a horrible event, but we lost our mind as a country. We lost our bearing. We swallowed a lot that we didn't need to swallow. We didn't need to give up our civil liberties. We didn't need to blindly follow whatever the government shoved down our throats.

DB: *Are you still haunted by what you experienced in the war?*

BT: What most disturbs me is my attitude during the war. I dehumanized the Iraqi people. Pointing rifles at people to get them to stop in traffic, and thinking it's funny. That's pretty common because it's easy to fall into that mindset when you're over there. We completely dehumanized the Iraqi people. There were very few people saying, "These are people, and they matter." It was more like, "Hey, this is our place, we took it over and we're going to do what we want." I feel bad about that. I feel bad about participating and behaving in that way. There are some incidents that stand out in my mind.

DB: *For instance?*

BT: Responding to bombings and having people jump up and down on burnt up cars saying "Death to Americans." At the time I thought, "Why are they doing this?" Now it all makes sense. There are some incidents I saw that haunted me, but overall it's just the deceit, the dishonesty that is impressed upon my mind.

153

A Hard Look at US History

Oliver Stone   *October 2013*

DB: *Many American historians, like their counterparts in journalism, fail the democratic process they are supposed to serve. Both groups tend to put a positive spin on even the nastiest actions of the US government, a process that Oliver Stone challenges in his "Untold History of the United States." Official American history has shaped a national myth that depicts a good and righteous country, which invariably takes actions at home and abroad that are based on fairness and humanitarian principles, albeit with some mistakes made here and there but with no ill intent. To fit with that myth, the darkest chapters of US history get the lightest touch: the genocide and ethnic cleansing of Indigenous Peoples, the institution of slavery as a key early economic factor in building the nation, widespread abuses in factories including child labor, and the atomic bombing of Hiroshima and Nagasaki, to name just a few.*

But this whitewashing of US history has always gotten under the skin of Oscar-winning filmmaker Oliver Stone, leading him to spend much of the last five years working on a unique documentary series, The Untold History of the United States, *along with a companion book, both co-written with American University historian Peter Kuznick.*

The multi-part documentary seeks to counteract some of the biggest lies perpetuated by modern historians about the past century. Mr. Stone, what planted the seeds for this project? Has this marinated for a while?

OS: In my film work I have gone to historical subject matter quite often. I was interested in the big events. Although I was born conservative, raised that way, and went to school that way, I became more progressive as I experimented and talked to people. In 2008, I reached the place, after making more than a dozen films, where I was exhausted by the idea of George Bush having eight years in office. I felt that rather than make another dramatic film, if there was one thing I could do for my kids, it would be to look back at my life, going back to the 1940s, to look at what went wrong.

Peter is an old friend who has studied these issues for more than 30 years. He is a nuclear arms expert, and we combined our forces — dramatist and historian. We went at it, from 1900 to now, and it was a big deal — much bigger than we had in mind. It was a five-year deal as opposed to a two and a half-year deal. We were over budget and over time. The book came out of this series. Once we were into the series, we realized we were in deep, and we wanted to substantiate some of what we said in the book, so Peter and his graduate students turned it on.

DB: *A lot of footnotes in there.*

OS: It is dramatic. The series was fact-checked three times and the book twice.

DB: *I know a lot of this material, but it was revelatory. The way it was presented on screen was extraordinary. Let's talk about some of the content, then the process of how you work. I think it differs from some of the documentarians working today. What surprised me the most was the story about Henry Wallace and the changing of the ticket under FDR. Was that revelatory for you?*

OS: Yes. Peter knew a lot about it, as it was a special subject for him. It grew out of Peter's interest in the atomic bomb. His main study has been why we did not have to drop the bomb on Japan. He has a very sound argument, and you must see the series to understand it. Part of that chain of birth is the idea that Wallace, who was Vice President from 1941 to 1945, was a true, true American progressive, not a liberal. He had a New Deal vision of America in cooperation with the Soviet Union as well as all countries.

Wallace detested the British Empire — that is true. He didn't have any friends with Churchill. Over the course of the war years it was apparent he was progressive and the Democratic bosses, who were very conservative, could not abide him and wanted to get rid of him — and they did. In the 1944 convention — it was very fixed in those days — they backed a non-entity called Harry Truman who managed to squeak in. Wallace's representative was five feet from the podium when the convention was closed the first night — when Wallace would have swept in. It was a very sad moment.

Roosevelt, if he had lived, possibly wouldn't have dropped the bomb on Japan, because there was no need to. We had been fed the myth over the years, driven into our education system, repeated over and over again, so there are misinformed people. There is such a big story about the atomic bomb and the use of our force over the last 70 years, since WW II, and what we became. That is the essence of the series.

DB: *You were in Japan with Peter Kuznick for the 60th commemoration of the bombing of Hiroshima and Nagasaki. Did this come up? Is there knowledge that the atomic bomb became the opening salvo of the Cold War, as opposed to the end of WWII?*

OS: No. It's not there, but it was a very moving experience. There were many survivors — *Hibakusha*, they are called in Japan. We went to Hiroshima, Nagasaki and Okinawa, because bases are still there, and they are building new ones. I went up to Jeju Island in South Korea where the South Korean government and the Pentagon, of course, are building a gigantic naval base. A lot is going on in the Asian Pacific. That is what our journey was about.

When we talked to the Japanese, they were like us. They never got the basic education about how the US military controlled Japan after the war. Everything about the atomic bomb was censored; even the word itself couldn't be used until 1953 or 1954 when Japan started to open up after the rocky dragon incident. The incident in the South Pacific was a hydrogen bomb test gone wrong. It affected the tuna fish, people died — it was a disaster.

The Japanese turned against the bomb because they were the victims of it. Ironically, at this very time Eisenhower was selling the atoms for peace proposal throughout the world — atoms for the peaceful. His first target was Hiroshima and he wanted to

156

build a nuclear power plant there. He didn't, but they did get Fukushima up, and of course that was a disaster for an earthquake-ravaged country. There was a great movie called Japan's Longest Day, which is about the last few days before surrender.

The American people didn't know how prostrated the Japanese economy was — the ports, facilities, and transportation gone from the terror bombing. More than 100 cities were destroyed. Tokyo was burned to the ground. People were starving. Also unknown to the American people is that the Japanese were trying to surrender. We had broken their codes, so Truman, and those in his circle, knew that Japan wanted to surrender. What is also kept from the American people is the Soviet invasion of Manchuria going toward Japan, and its impact of terror on the Japanese. They knew they were sunk, and their only hope was to make a deal with the US.

Once that was known, we were still three months away from an invasion. We didn't have the troops ready to go, so much could have happened during those three months. But Truman wanted to drop the bomb. We spent a fortune building it. He hyped it — we built it, so we must find out if it really works. They picked Hiroshima because it had never been bombed, so it was a pristine target — they could see how much damage this bomb could do.

Truman didn't want to acknowledge the concessions Roosevelt made with Stalin at Yalta, so we went ahead and basically violated the agreement with the Russians. From that point, the Cold War was on. The Russians knew our game. Two weeks after Roosevelt died, it turned icy, with Truman, in an ugly scene, insulting the Soviet Foreign Minister in Washington. Truman was a small man, like George Bush, with a narrow mind. It's a shame that he's been mythologized in American history as a big hero, the subject of a biography that was a Pulitzer Prize winner. People should read this book [*The Untold*

History of the United States], because it opens an alternative way of looking at our history.

DB: *It reminded me of the great work of Howard Zinn. Is he a precursor, setting the tone? Were you influenced by his work?*

OS: I met him a few times. I'm sorry he didn't live to see the series. We didn't always agree with each other, but Peter and I loved his anti-establishment thinking. There are other Cold War historians who shouldn't be ignored. Peter studied with these historians. We did not just find out about this for the first time — it's been out there, at a high level in the college education system. But it's not available in the mass media so we continue the lies at that level.

DB: *Let's fast forward and deal with 9/11, because there's a lot said about that. I always thought it wasn't about the self-demolition, but that many of the people involved in this action were trained in the US and did actions for the US*

OS: It is very disturbing. Once Brzezinski opened the door in Afghanistan in 1978, he was clear it was a trap, saying in a memo to Carter that it would be the Soviet Vietnam. We knew about the Muslim resistance in the Caucasus of southern Russia. Even Bill Casey of the CIA under Reagan was actively encouraging rebellion of the Islamic fundamentalists in Southern Russia — he wanted that. So we backed them from the beginning in Afghanistan, and gave them a lot of money.

The silly movie, "Charlie Wilson's War," gave the idea that we were heroes for financing these people who are dead serious fundamentalist Taliban types, not interested in the reforms the Soviets brought to the educational system, rights of women, basic scientific education. We lost track of them and then they came back and they are after us because we put 500,000 troops in Saudi Arabia under George Bush's father, which was disgusting, disgusting — a violation of everything we learned in Vietnam. Bringing those troops in there sealed our involvement in the Middle East as well as our Israeli policies, and that's what got Al Qaeda against us. We brought it on.

DB: *Robert Fisk, of the* Independent, *did an interview with Osama Bin Laden in which Bin Laden said — he said it in several interviews — you need to know that when we are done here, we are turning these guns toward the West.*

OS: Fisk is good. He was always out in the front lines.

DB: *This is what Bin Laden said. It is troubling what people do not learn in school when they study the history of that part of the world.*

OS: I never got into all the details, but there were so many Saudi Arabians, which makes us now more and more awake to the idea that the Saudi Arabians have a very fundamentalist regime and we are very entrenched in backing those regimes throughout the Middle East. Saudi Arabia's interests are not necessarily our interests.

DB: *You made this film quite a bit different. There is a lone narrator, not a lot of talking heads. Why did you do it that way?*

OS: We wanted to make it fast — 120 years in 12 hours. We had to travel and wanted to stick to the big points, not get stuck with the smaller points, which are important, and were brought into the book. It is hard to simplify. Each chapter is dedicated, in 58 minutes and 30 seconds, to telling a narrative story. We ended up using my voice, which was used as a temp-track, but people were responding positively to it, so we stayed with it, otherwise I would have used Laurence Olivier — just kidding. The archival footage was terrific, with a lot of original material from around the world. Rob Wilson pulled that in. Music was by Craig Armstrong and Adam Peters, both great composers of the original music, which gives the whole series a movie feel — a lift, which is lovely.

We used film clips, which is important to break the tedium of looking only at archival footage — although it may be fascinating, it can be a lot for the mind. We decided to cut away the movies, and add movies of the time, which adds spice, color and flavor to help understand the mood of the country, especially if the film is a propaganda film. We had no talking heads, which is important, because it would have broken the rhythm. At times I realized I was making the series for the level of my children, who are smart and went to good schools. There is a lot of information, so these hours can be watched again. We made it a kind of evergreen, so it can last into the future. It is well worth watching a second time, because you can learn something that you may have missed, since it does go fast.

DB: *The context and continuum are crucial as well. When you see it in a flow, it begins to come together as a whole about the nature of US policy.*

OS: That's right. Don't get stuck in the details, because the details can drive you down. The everyday news in this country, the 24-hours news cycle, is ridiculous. You rarely get a big picture.

DB: *That's how they teach journalism. They don't want you to think. I did a lot of journalism, and every time I wrote a story that tried to give some historical context, first it was the good images — "we don't want any good imagery," then it was the context — "this is just about what happened there, then and now." It's a killer.*

OS: That's the beauty of history — why I have always loved history. It allows you to think and put together events and make sense of them. Often we only react to the tyranny of now. The maps are extraordinary in the film, done by a very good graphic company, and they made a special effort to make the maps live. We sometimes used old maps, but we also put new maps in, which allow you to understand some of the geopolitical moves of, for example, the British Empire, and its reach in 1940. Churchill was fighting to protect much more than England itself.

DB: *Maps have been a key part of deception and lying about history, haven't they?*

OS: Yes. Churchill plays a huge role in the Cold War too. Greece was the first Cold War battle, and that was Churchill's war, which set us up for Truman's Turkish-Greek aid advisors who use the word terrorist as early as 1947 and declare the National Security Agency.

DB: *Speaking of the NSA, and Edward Snowden, do you conduct your life differently now? Do you have more face-to-face meetings?*

OS: During these five years I wasn't able to develop anything long range — only this. It refreshed me in a deep way, like going back to school and getting a PhD. Now I feel like I have a solid foundation to understand all the recent history in the US. I hope I can bring it back to film. After you do something like this, it is hard to settle on one story.

DB: *Maybe those releases, revelations, will in some way change how history is recorded.*

OS: I hope so. It is so difficult to sell something like this to a public that has been brainwashed for so many years. It feels like we are an exception to the rule.

Liberation Wherever the Drum Beats: John Trudell
Miguel Gavilan Molina   December 2015

DB: *Today we honor the life and times of the noted Native American poet, spoken word artist and political activist John Trudell. He passed yesterday into the spirit world. In 1969 he made historic Radio Free Alcatraz broadcasts of the American Indian Movement's [AIM] occupation of the island through KPFA and the Pacifica network.*

From November 11, 1969 until June 11, 1971 a group called Indians of all Tribes occupied Alcatraz Island off the coast of San Francisco in California. The takeover was done to protest federal laws that contradicted historic land treaties with the Indians and which aimed to destroy American Indian cultures, including the right of tribes to self-determination. This occupation was the first of it's kind. On Dec 22, 1969, Radio Free Alcatraz was broadcast to give voice to the Native American struggle in North America. The broadcast from Alcatraz was produced and hosted by a very young John Trudell, a Santee Sioux from Nebraska. With borrowed and donated radio equipment, the broadcasts originated from the main cellblock on Alcatraz.

Flashpoints' and La Onda Bajita producer Miguel Molina now carries out those historic broadcasts from Alcatraz on Indigenous Peoples' Day and Un-Thanksgiving Day. He met John Trudell many times. Miguel, you have carried on the tradition of broadcasting from Alcatraz. You were just there broadcasting a few weeks ago.

MM: Yes, we've picked up the tradition they started. In 1992 I was involved with the west coast chapters of the International Indian Treaty Council and AIM, which under the direction of Tony Gonzalez, launched the 500 years of resistance campaign. This country was getting ready for the age of discovery, when Columbus came and discovered this land with nobody on it. Not true. It was an invasion of the Americas and the destruction of the Indigenous civilization's culture. I was fortunate to meet John Trudell during the 500 years of resistance campaign, which also linked with international Indigenous communities. Once I asked John when he was going to bring back Radio Free

Alcatraz. He said, "You have the voice, little brother." That rang in my head. A few years later, with the support and invitation of Tony Gonzalez, who was at that time the head of the Treaty Council and member of AIM, we were invited to come out there. We've been there ever since, on Indigenous Peoples' Day, October 12, and for Un-Thanksgiving, a day of both mourning and celebration.

DB: *John Trudell bridged the gap between the Indigenous and white communities.*

MM: The radio became the venue, the bullhorn, for people's voices. The occupation of Alcatraz in that first leap made by Richard Oaks and students from San Francisco State brought Native American reality out of the past and into the present. Up to that point all people saw were the John Wayne movies during the 50s and 60s, killing the Indians, always the bad guys, the "raging savages." The blue coats — Cavalry and soldiers — were the good guys protecting the covered wagons. In reality it was a mass invasion of Indian lands, a push westward by white colonial land grabbers who killed Indians in the process. That leap of the occupation of Alcatraz, when Richard Oaks jumped from the boat because he couldn't land on the dock, and swam in that cold, cold water, brought Native Americans out of the past and into the present. Radio Free Alcatraz, with John anchoring it, resonated like a drum. From then was born the idea of wherever the drum beats, we shall liberate.

Alcatraz to date is still viewed as Indian land. Alcatraz isn't an island. It's a mountain that rises from the bottom of the sea and breaks through the waves of the water to reach the sky. It's literally a gigantic rock. John anchored Radio Free Alcatraz, and we at KPFA and Pacifica have made it a tradition to broadcast from the rock. It became the bullhorn to voice people's stories.

DB: *It represented the voice of the voiceless.*

MM: Yes, Radio Free Alcatraz gave Native Indian peoples a voice. Native American singer Buffy Sainte-Marie wrote a song
163

that John played on every broadcast from the rock, which is called "Now that the Buffalo's Gone." In the Native view, death is part of living. John lived. Across Indian land, we've probably lost our greatest warrior in the last 100 years. But he inspired a generation of spoken word artists and performers, and that rhythm and those words will still echo. The American Indian Movement was given its birth at the beginning of the occupation of Alcatraz. John provided the microphone to echo the voices of Native peoples that were forgotten into the past. Bringing them to the present from the rock, through Pacifica, gave rise to countless movements for Native American land rights in the US. Even today, some of the biggest battles against corporations and their destruction of the environment — to extract minerals and other resources — have been led by the tribes. It was the tribes, with support from other groups, which stopped the Keystone pipeline.

DB: *Trudell talked about Keystone and the resistance.*

MM: Native peoples have been taking the lead against fracking, because it's often on Native land, on reservations. There's a legacy. In Native Circles, we see the earth as the Mother and we are her stewards.

[Wherever John Trudell's life led, he could always close his eyes and return to February 1979. Twelve hours after he burned an American flag in front of the FBI building in Washington, D.C., his pregnant wife Tina, her mother and the couple's three children died in a suspicious fire at the home of his parents-in-law on the Shoshone-Paiute Tribes Duck Valley Indian Reservation in Nevada. For Trudell, there was never any question that the fire at his Nevada home was a payback. *Ed.]*

Black Lives

Witness from Death Row

Kevin Cooper   May 2009

DB: Black prisoner Kevin Cooper is for a second time one step away from execution for a murder that he says he did not commit. He was found guilty at a trial that a number of federal judges believe fell short of fairness. If you believe the claims of death row prisoner Kevin Cooper that he is innocent, and there are many reasons to do so, then the State of California should be brought up on charges of attempted murder and false imprisonment.

Eleven federal judges of the Ninth Circuit of Appeals have enough doubt about Cooper's guilt or various violations of his due process, that they opposed the court's recent denial of a rehearing to examine further evidence key to Cooper's case. Cooper has been denied such hearings in the past. In a hundred page-plus dissent, Judge W. Fletcher of the Ninth Circuit warned that the state might be about to execute an innocent man.

Kevin Cooper last spoke to Flashpoints five years ago in 2004; five days after the state came within a few hours of murdering him. Cooper has been on death row for over twenty-five years. He joins Flashpoints from death row in San Quentin.

Leslie Kean also joins us. She's a friend of Cooper's who has been visiting him for over ten years on death row, and has done extensive research on the case. Kevin, what was happening five years ago, several hours before the state tried to kill you?

KC: The situation was hectic. I was locked inside this dungeon in the bowels of San Quentin prison, where they torture and murder. I managed to get a stay of execution from the state, based on a Brady law violation. The state was holding exculpatory evidence. I was able to survive this madness, and now I seem to be right back in it.

DB: *You were within eight hours of being executed by the state.*

KC: Three hours and 42 minutes. I was in a room right next to the death chamber, the death chamber waiting room. At various points in time, I was in different parts of the prison.

DB: *It must have been a devastating experience, coming three hours within your life, knowing you're an innocent man. Could you describe what was going on and the impact it had on you?*

KC: No, I can't. That's how unbelievable it is — you have to experience it to truly appreciate and understand it. It has an effect on you emotionally, psychologically, mentally, and spiritually. It's a life-altering event. It's so real that it seems unreal. There's no way I can honestly describe what happened to me or anyone else who was tortured and murdered by any state in any death house in this country.

DB: *They put you through a ritual in which they're attempting to get your cooperation in your own killing, in your own murder.*

KC: Exactly. They want you to be complicit, to participate. They want you to make them feel good about killing you. I refuse to do that. I couldn't eat their food or do anything they wanted me to do. They told me to choose the method by which I wanted them to murder me by. I couldn't do that. How can I do that? How sick that sounds. They kept asking if I wanted a last meal and, if so, what did I want? I wanted to eat good food. I don't want to choose the method by which they were to murder me — how they were going to torture me. That's for them to decide. I can't deal with that. That's how unreal the situation is.

DB: *In the studio is Leslie Kean. She is a former producer and host of Flashpoints, a friend of Cooper's who has done extensive research on the case.*
LK: Kevin, hi. We've talked about how you came so close to being executed. After it was over and you were back in your cell,

you maintained your position as an activist. How did you recover and bounce back into the struggle you've been carrying on so powerfully ever since?

KC: I've been blessed to have friends such as you who've taken time out of their lives to visit me at this plantation — visit and spend quality time with me. I read a lot of books. I do my artwork, which is therapeutic. It helps me escape the reality of the hectic day-to-day life in this place. It was about willpower, because I knew that if I didn't recover, these people would win. I'm not about to let them win if I can help it. I had to find my inner spirit, and somehow I managed to do it — but it was hard then and it's hard now.

DB: *What are you reading now?*

KC: I just finished Mumia Abu-Jamal's *Jailhouse Lawyers*. I read many books, do a lot of artwork, and write a lot. I do a variety of things in order to live here on death row.

LK: You are an activist. From that cell you're part of a movement in the Bay Area and around the country to abolish the death penalty. Describe the role that activism plays in your life and how that keeps you going in prison.

KC: This activism has allowed me to vindicate myself because I do feel vindicated by those eleven justices on the Ninth Circuit Court of Appeals. Not only do they believe I am innocent — they agreed they have proven my innocence and proven how the State of California went about framing me. It is all in the first 105 pages. The lawyers who took on this case were pro bono — Orrick, Herrington, & Sutliffe. But none of that would have come about without the movement, without this activism. Every person who has ever done anything in this movement, to help expose corruption in any death penalty case, lays the foundation for us to walk on and build what's happening in my filing.

LK: There was a filing on May 11 in the Ninth Circuit Court of Appeals denying you a rehearing, but eleven judges dissented. What was your reaction when you read the dissent?

KC: Vindication! I felt, no matter what happens to me, whether these people go ahead and torture and murder me, no matter what happens to me, I did what I set out to do. We as a movement did what we set out to do — prove that I am innocent. There is no way that eleven federal circuit judges would come to the conclusions they did if it weren't the truth. These people don't deal with lies; they deal with the truth. There are other judges who know the truth, but they haven't said anything. They've either just ignored it or said it was procedurally broad. They never said we were lying, they just said it's procedurally broad, or too late, or a harmless error or this or that. But they've never said I was lying. These eleven judges are Republicans and Democrats. Even the Chief Judge of the Ninth Circuit — a Right-wing conservative Republican — is on my side.

DB: *Judge Fletcher, who wrote the hundred-plus page dissent, said that the state might be about to execute an innocent man. He suggested that the state could become a murderer once again.*

KC: What Judge Fletcher stated was not just present day fact — it's historical fact. History is my teacher. It has exposed all types of things to me — good and bad — about this country. This country was founded and built upon killing innocent people. And it was maintained, and is being maintained, on killing innocent people. It is something this country has always done, which is why they don't ever seem to blink an eye about it. This is how they can say that it's not unconstitutional to kill an innocent person — because they've always done it. When we find a constitutional violation, they seem to get around it. So I'm not surprised that they'll kill me as an innocent man. What I am surprised about is that ten judges agreed with Judge Fletcher, and there are others who didn't say anything, but also agreed with him.

LK: Kevin, what are some examples of corruption in your case? You were convicted in 1983 for murdering four people. From the beginning you stated that you were innocent of this crime.

KC: Yes, I have.

LK: The judge pointed out in this recent ruling that certain evidence in your original trial in 1983 was withheld from the jury, and if that evidence had been introduced, you would very likely not have been convicted. What are some of the key pieces of evidence that were not included?

KC: There was a pair of bloody coveralls that a lady turned over to the police, and told them that her boyfriend — a convicted murderer — left them at her house. They were covered in blood. She and her sister saw him getting out of a car that matched the description of the victim's stolen car. They threw those coveralls away, which prevented the jury from learning about the coveralls and the guy who left them at her house — that he was a convicted murderer. They denied me due process on that. They also withheld evidence that the warden at CIM [California Institution for Men, a medium security prison] at that time, Ms. Carroll, told them that the tennis shoes they tried to say I had were not prison-issue tennis shoes, as they claimed they were. Those tennis shoes were supposed to have matched an imprint they found in blood on the victim's bed sheet that they did not find at the crime scene, but somehow found at the crime lab. It doesn't sound real, but this is so real. They're getting ready to kill me by making evidence disappear. There was a blue shirt that they found — they threw it away and didn't tell anybody. We didn't know it existed until 2004 when we got some police logs that happened to mention that somebody called the police and told them about a blue shirt. The police went and picked it up. On the police log is the evidence of pick up, and the shirt was in connection with the Ryen-Hughes murder.

LK: These are some examples. We see this in other cases in this country, where people are wrongfully convicted. Judge Fletcher wrote in his summary of his 101-page statement, "Given the weakness of the evidence against Cooper, if the state had given Cooper's attorneys this exculpatory evidence, it is highly unlikely that Cooper would have been convicted." Judge Fletcher focused on the issue of evidence having been tampered with, both at the time of the trial and in the years following.

KC: I had some DNA testing on a drop of blood they claimed was found inside the victim's house. It was supposed to be one drop of blood. When the evidence came around, I asked for it. At first the state said, "No." I asked again and they said, "No." I asked again and they said, "No" and then the fourth time, they happened to say, "Yes." But what they didn't tell us was before they said yes, they let the criminalist who was messing with it at that trial, take it out for 24 hours along with my saliva and my blood that they took from me when I was arrested. And they didn't tell anybody. This guy puts it back after having it out 24 hours. We found out about it after the DNA tests were done and the DNA test came back and said it was mine.

One cigarette butt had a yellow filter in 1983, and in 2001 when there was DNA testing, it had a white filter. It was 4 mm in length in 1983, and was 7.7 mm in 2001. How does the cigarette grow after they've taken it apart and tested it? We have photographic evidence of what I'm saying, and this court system ignored everything. They ignored it, acted like it didn't exist, or they made excuses for it. The bottom line is they're giving me the type of trial they gave Dred Scott back in 1857. They're saying I don't have rights that a white man is bound to respect, because they messed over my life — every last single one of them — in order to kill me for something I did not do.

Joshua Ryen — a child at the time — told them when he saw my face on TV, that I didn't do it — that it was three white men. Judge Fletcher mentions that in his dissent. If Joshua Ryen had seen my picture on TV and said, "Yeah, that was him," they would have used that against me. But he said no, it wasn't me. He told his grandmother it wasn't me, he told other people it wasn't me. He told the police it wasn't me.

LK: There were four people murdered. Joshua Ryen was a young boy in the family that was killed. He was not killed, but severely injured during the assault on his family. He was the only living witness.

DB: *The only eyewitness.*

LK: The only living eyewitness was interviewed very shortly after this crime by two different people in the hospital, and he indicated that three white men committed the crime.

KC: They found a police log in 2004, the same time they found the police log about the missing blue shirt, which indicated they were looking for three young males driving the car they took.

DB: *The entire process — jury tampering, messing with evidence, and ignoring an eyewitness account — how does racism play into that?*

KC: San Bernardino County, where this case happened, is one of the most racist counties in this state. Shortly after my arrest, they had a gorilla hung in effigy with a sign that said, "Hang the troglodyte," calling me a troglodyte. They wanted to get their hands on Kevin Cooper so they could mete out justice, the type of justice they always give Black men.

DB: *What about questionable actions by personnel regarding the chain of custody of evidence?*

KC: The head criminalist — the person in charge of all the evidence they used to convict me — was a heroin addict. He was fired shortly after my conviction for stealing five pounds of heroin out of the evidence locker.

DB: *His name?*

KC: William Baird. He was a lieutenant and was using that heroin for his own personal use and to sell to drug dealers. He didn't stand trial. He didn't do time in prison. They let him go. This is the man who had another pair of tennis shoes like the ones they claimed I had, which I didn't have. He had a pair like that in the crime lab. He had all kinds of things in the crime lab. If you read Fletcher's dissent, everything is in there. If somebody takes the time to look it up and read it, it could piss them off so much they might even want to get involved in this movement — if not already in it — to try to help save my life.

This is American justice, old-school style. This is what they used to do to Black men back in the day. This is what they are doing in the twenty-first century. If you believe Judge Fletcher and the other judges going along with him, you must ask yourself a bigger question: "If they did this to Kevin Cooper, and these judges are saying they did, then how many other men and women are on death row or in prison in this country that had the same thing done to them by the same type of people that's doing this to Kevin?" I am not so special that these people will go out of their way to frame me and not anyone else. I'm not the only person who had their evidence tampered with, their evidence thrown away, or their witnesses tampered with. This is in the system so deeply that it will open a person's eyes, if they want their eyes to be opened.

DB: *There is more information about the case at SaveKevinCooper.org.*

LK: On the website there is a link where people can read the recent filing by the Ninth Circuit. It's an historic filing. It's very rare that eleven judges will dissent in 101 pages.

DB: *Kevin, we call the justice system the criminal injustice system because there is a pattern and practice of racism where if you don't have the money to pay for the lawyers, you often end up on death row and die without a proper defense. You are an expert in understanding how the system works, how it is stacked up against poor people and people of color. Can you talk about your research and activities in this regard?*

KC: I had an attorney that was appointed to me by a federal district judge, Marilyn Huff. His name was Robert Amidon. Marilyn Huff is the same judge that Judge Fletcher talks about very badly in his dissent. But this man, who was a criminal attorney, damn near got me executed because everything he did was against my best interests. Nonetheless, he and the people working with him still got paid.

I decided to take matters into my own hands because I have learned — history is my teacher — that people who are locked in prisons have attorneys who, for the most part, don't give a damn about us because all we are to them is a paycheck. I cared about myself enough to get involved with this movement, to get involved with the campaign to end the death penalty from a socialist viewpoint, with Socialist Action and many other organizations and people, and together, we formulated a plan to educate the public. We did this, over and over and over again, for years and years and years.

Just before these people murdered me, I managed to get in touch with The Innocence Project and Santa Clara University. They found a law firm, Orrick, Herrington, & Sutcliffe, who took it pro bono. This law firm was a white collar, corporate law firm, and it saved my life! They're not a criminal law firm. The criminal lawyer, who worked in the criminal justice system, damn near got me killed. This says a lot about this system. Through their hard work, they completely turned this case around. They got me a stay and found all this new evidence — what Fletcher speaks about in his dissent. Most of it we didn't know.

If you don't have a committee of people — lawyers or not — in your corner, you're in trouble. If you don't have people who care about you, who will fight for you and fight with you, you're dead. And if you don't have a powerful law firm who cares, who has money to fight back, you're damn sure dead. I do know this: if you keep on fighting, working and don't give up, there's a chance. I have a chance. The law firm I have now uncovered evidence and discovered constitutional violations, but I'm still one decision away from being tortured and murdered by the State once they restart this killing machine in San Quentin prison. I will be tortured in this prison as will any other person who has been tortured in these death houses across this country. Make no mistake about that. These people tell you they don't torture, because they say it's humane, but you can't believe them. History tells you not to believe them. I do not look forward to being tortured and murdered by the State of California.

DB: *One of the judges who supports your murder is Judge Bybee, a key player in the Bush administration's torture program.*

KC: In 2004, I received a 9-2 decision for a stay. One of the two judges who refused to give me that stay was Judge Bybee, who was also one of the people who wrote those torture memos for the Bush-Cheney administration, allowing torture to happen to criminals or people they consider criminals, whether it is at Abu Ghraib or Guantanamo Bay or any other place around the world. He's fine with them being tortured there, but he's also fine with them being tortured here, because he supports the death penalty. Torture is part of what he believes in. These people he believes in torturing are all poor people, and mostly people of color. He ain't got no problem with that. Yet he can sit his ass upon the Ninth Circuit like some guard, and dictate who should live and who should die and who should be tortured and who shouldn't.

DB: *He may find himself before too long in some kind of dock in the various international tribunals -- facing crimes against humanity.*

KC: Yeah, right. I'll believe that when I see it.

DB: *More and more poor women are on death row. People don't realize there's a death row at Chowchilla, where many women are facing death. Will there be more women facing this similar situation?*

KC: Historically speaking, women have always been on death row, whether that death row has been in their own homes as victims of domestic violence or whether they're shot and killed in the street or in prison. There's never much said about it, but these women are all poor. They have never been given "equal rights" in their entire life. And for the first time in their life, if they do get executed, they'll be given equal rights. They'll have equality of a male death row inmate because they'll get the same amount of poison pumped into their body as I'll get pumped into mine. These women, victims of all kinds of things, suffer in silence today as they have historically. You never hear the news media talk about women on death row in this state. But one day they'll talk about them so proudly. The State of California is going to execute a woman. Other states have as well. It's disgusting what these people do.

LK: We know you have good lawyers, but we also know it's extremely important that people get involved and fight for your case. You need all the help you can get because you're going to face some serious possibility of being executed. Stanley "Tookie" Williams had pretty good lawyers, got a lot of attention, and he was executed. He was also a friend of yours. You helped him out during the years you knew each other. Could you share with our listeners some of the story of your relationship with him?

KC: He is my friend; he will always be my friend. He's my brother; he will always be my brother. He's a good man and it wasn't so much that I taught him anything. I learned more from him than I could ever teach him, except when it came to his going through this ritual death — they wanted to search his arms for his veins, they wanted to send a psychiatrist to his home to mess with him psychologically. He didn't know about that because he'd never been through it before. Before me, everybody else who had been through it ended up dying, so nobody knew what to expect. But because I got that stay, I was there to show him what I went through. That is how I taught him a thing or two. They tortured and murdered him — it came out in Fogel's court that they did — and they're going to do the same thing to me and everybody else, but go about it differently.

DB: *Torture includes a process where they've deceived the public into believing that lethal injection, this three-stage process, is humane.*

KC: If this system were humane, they wouldn't have to lie about — not just in this state, but across the country — who has been tortured in these death houses. If it were humane, the medical society would participate in it. But it's not humane — it's inhumane. People don't even kill animals the same way they're willing to kill us in this state and across the country. The lethal cocktail they use has been banned by the people who murder animals. They won't use that to kill an animal with. This is inhumane; this is torture. You feel the poison they pump in your body. They've got you paralyzed so you can't screw it up. They tell people who witness body contortions and other things, that they didn't see what their eyes told their brain they saw. This system is sick and the people who run it are sick. I do not look forward to being strapped down on that gurney and have them put their needles in my arm and pump their poison in my body. I am an innocent man. I had eleven federal circuit judges telling the world — warning the world, not just telling them — that this state is about to execute an innocent man. Are they gonna step up to the plate and show everyone how humane they are or are they just going to turn a blind eye to my murder like they do to everyone else's?

Any Black Man Will Do: The Execution of Troy Davis

Benjamin Todd Jealous   September 2011

DB: *Georgia's planned execution of Troy Davis is drawing protests from around the world because of grave doubts that he actually committed the murder of an off-duty policeman 22 years ago. If the State of Georgia has its way, Troy Anthony Davis will be executed for a murder that a growing mountain of evidence suggests he did not commit. Davis was convicted on the basis of witness testimony — in which seven of the nine original witnesses recanted or made major changes in their testimony. Other witnesses have also come forward casting doubt on Davis's guilt. Davis has faced down three previous execution dates. NAACP's Benjamin Todd Jealous explores the case.*

[The State of Georgia executed Troy Davis, after a brief delay, on September 21, 2011. *Ed.*]

NAACP's Benjamin Todd Jealous will discuss the case. Mr. Jealous, you said recently, after reviewing the evidence, that you were convinced Troy Davis is an innocent man. You said, "It is appalling to me that with so much doubt surrounding the case, Mr. Davis is set to be executed." What do you find most appalling?

BTJ: Twenty-two years ago, there was a tragedy in the State of Georgia. An off duty-officer, trying to do his duty and keep the community safe, was killed as he tried to protect a homeless man. There were multiple suspects, but eventually nine people came forward and said that one man, Troy Davis, did it. Those nine voices put him on death row. There was no physical evidence. Troy maintained his innocence, as he has for over two decades.

Today, seven of those folks now say they lied. But the ones amongst those seven who said they saw the killer, said the killer is one of the two suspects who have not recanted. Some of the seven say they lied because they were afraid of him. This man's name is Sylvester Coles.

Now, twenty years later, Troy has had three execution dates — this is his fourth. There are letters from not just Archbishop Tutu; or the Pope himself; or from former President Jimmy Carter, favorite son of Georgia; but also from William Sessions, former head of the FBI; Roy Thompson, number two in the Department of Justice under George W. Bush; Tim Lewis, former US court of appeals judge appointed by President Bush one; and others. This is not about what's left or right; it's about what's correct. What's correct is that when it appears our justice system is about to execute somebody who is innocent, we all stand up and say "No."

DB: *Seven out of nine witnesses recanted. You said Mr. Sylvester Coles was one of the two witnesses who did not recant, and tried to intimidate others into silence.*

BTJ: Yes.

DB: *How does a prosecution tolerate a situation where a witness intimidates other witnesses? This is a witness who may well have been the murderer, intimidating other witnesses in a state murder case?*

BTJ: Let's go to the psychology of the moment. In cases like this, where an officer has been killed, there is often a lot of pressure to find the killer quickly, at any cost. Within a day, a mindset developed amongst the Savannah Police Department that Troy Davis was it. They quickly made the facts fit that conclusion, rather than make the conclusion fit the facts. So you see a very powerful rush to judgment. Witnesses who have come forward and recanted their testimony, and others who were silent at the time — some of them minors still in their parent's house, and the parents wouldn't let them talk — say that people were afraid of Sylvester Coles. It was very clear to people that they needed to lie on his behalf, and they say that they did it because they feared him. In three cases, they said they lied because the cops coerced them.

All in all, that's Savannah of that era. Even today, it is a very problematic law enforcement culture. Savannah is one of 159 counties in Georgia, yet about three out of ten death row exonerations in the state come from that county — all of them Black men. This is a county in which it seems that in some instances, any Black man will do.

This is such an urgent case for justice. It has caused so much doubt, again from the former head of the FBI to the Pope. This is an exceptional case. When our country is stumbling towards executing an innocent person, it is incumbent on everyone to stand up and let their voice be heard.

DB: *If you have a witness able to intimidate other witnesses in a murder trial, it seems to pollute the process. How can this be allowed to go forward? Wouldn't the prosecutors and police know this other guy is a potential suspect?*

BTJ: What is more difficult to understand is that, even after the federal court said the case against Mr. Troy is far from ironclad, the DA is standing silently, signing the death warrant. We believe that, if it came in front of the DA today, he would not bring it as a death penalty case. Then why isn't he reopening the case — saying to the judge, "Vacate the death warrant, let's reopen the case and make sure we have the right person behind bars."

Those of us interested in justice aren't just interested in making sure the wrong person doesn't get executed — we also must be interested in making sure that the right person is behind bars. Too many of our poor communities become "free to murder zones," where it's easy for the killer to get away with the crime. The tragedy in this case is we put the wrong person in for the crime, and now he may be killed by our state and by us, as taxpayers.

DB: *And also, if he is not the murderer, the murderer goes free.*

BTJ: The murderer has been free for 22 years.

DB: *What will it mean if the United States of America and the State of Georgia execute an innocent man? What does that say about the system and what's happening in this country?*

BTJ: If Troy Davis is executed, no one should ever be able to say that our country does not execute innocent people. We know mathematically that there must have been many more, given all of the exonerations; there is a wave of DNA evidence which is releasing people from prison and death row that's been going on for the last decade or more. We must come to terms with the fact that we are the only country in the West that still does this. And we do it, quite frankly, with an unexpectedly high degree of error.

DB: *When you go into the prisons and look at death row, it's as if white people don't do these kinds of things.*

BTJ: What you see is a disproportionate number of Blacks, almost exclusively poor. The white people on death row are all poor. The exonerations are even more disproportionately Black men. The bar this country sets for convicting a Black man seems to be much lower than it is even for a poor white person.

It's absolutely true that who gets executed in this country has less to do with what they did, and more to do with where they live, which side of the tracks they were born on, what color they are, even what gender they are. We are much more reluctant to execute women, even when they commit the same crime. It's grossly unfair. In this case it doesn't matter whether you support the death penalty or not. Everybody in this country, no matter what they feel about the issue, should be completely opposed to executing somebody when there is such a wide shadow of doubt as there is in the Troy Davis case.

Race, Guns, Votes, and the Right to Murder

Kevin Alexander Gray   July 2013

DB: Author and Human Rights activist, Kevin Alexander Gray, is the former President of the American Civil Liberties Union in South Carolina and author of Waiting for Lightning to Strike: The Fundamentals of Black Politics *and* The Decline of Black Politics: From Malcolm X to Barack Obama.

Mr. Gray, George Zimmerman will use the "stand-your-ground" defense for his killing of Trayvon Martin. Can you talk about what that means?

KG: I believe in the Second Amendment. When you look at who own guns in the country, it's white men, yet the people they seek to disarm are usually people of color. I don't own a gun. I am a man of peace. The Second Amendment is not about hunting and fishing — they were talking about defending themselves against a tyrannical government. To me, the Second Amendment, though unspoken, is about the people's right to revolt against a tyrannical government.

Nobody wants to talk about whether to get rid of the Second Amendment in an open, sensible way. I believe in the right of self-defense. Most people who believe in the Second Amendment and the right to self-defense don't believe they need stand-your-ground to defend the Second Amendment or to defend their lives. All stand-your-ground does is take away the rights or abilities of the courts and police to make you explain why you shot somebody, rather than just saying, "I was defending myself," and let it be at that. You had to go into court and show how you were defending your life. That's the problem with stand-your-ground, and we have not tackled that.

Over the past 20 years we've seen a buildup of these concealed weapon laws — now up to 15 states have open carry laws. That's where we are moving. Everybody will get in front of the camera and say this guy shouldn't have shot this guy. But when the rubber meets the road, we must challenge this legislatively, and nobody is doing that.

DB: *I remember a group of Black people who wanted to express their belief in the Second Amendment, and that was the Black Panthers. I don't remember the NRA [National Rifle Association] standing up for their rights.*

KG: That's when these guns laws were tightened up — when the armed Black folks were talking about their rights. We are in a different place. Over the last 20-30 years, there's been a proliferation of pro-gun and concealed-carry groups — not just the NRA. There are the Citizens for the Right to Keep and Bear Arms. Over 40 states have stand-your-ground laws. The pro-gun lobby and pro-gun advocates are not just the NRA. There are over 350 million guns in this country on record, the majority owned by whites. There are probably another 100 million guns not on the books. There are a lot of guns in this country. People want to attack the NRA, which has a large constituency base. But vilifying the NRA as a way to tackle this is not the way to go. It may take what the pro-gun lobby and advocates did — going to the state legislatures, bit by bit, adding more gun laws at the state level. We have not tackled that.

DB: *Are there any major pro-gun African American organizations?*

KG: Not that I am aware of. Black folks own guns. I'm in the South and know many people who own guns. They go to the shooting range and get concealed carry permits. My brothers, uncles, nephews — we were all raised with guns. We are at war every 20 years. I was a range officer while I was in the military. We train people to shoot guns, send them to war to shoot guns, then all of a sudden say guns are bad — people are not going to listen.

DB: *They are going to send 120,000 people to a new surge on the border. Guns aren't going anywhere. They are being expanded and available.*

KG: They will go to the southern border where there's a drug war going on. There were 50,000 people killed in Mexico in the drug war last year. The US plans on sending 20, 30, 40 additional border troops to the southern border with Mexico, and now they talk about building a wall. We're not building a wall at the Canadian border or putting troops there. It is blatantly racist, and nobody is talking about that. This country is heading in a terrible direction. Around the world people view us as Nazis. We think we can kill, spy, and assassinate with impunity, and usually it's aimed at people of color, both domestically and abroad.

DB: *Do you think Mr. Zimmerman will get a fair trial?*

KG: I am against the death penalty. I am glad he isn't facing the death penalty, and I hope he can get a fair trial, but I hope he's found guilty, he serves some time and reflects on how imbecilic and monstrous what he did was, for the family, the community, and for himself. I hope he and his family will reflect on how racist their statements sound to the rest of us — that we are animals. Just because a kid is Black, or might smoke marijuana, it doesn't make him a criminal. Not every Black male walking the earth is some punk up to no good.

DB: *Can you talk about the Voting Rights Act?   What did the Supreme Court do?*

KG: They ruled on section 5, which is the preclearance section of the Voting Rights Act. Section 5 requires that nine southern states must go to the Justice Department if they want to make changes to any kind of voting practice or electoral process. I had a case involving a predominantly Black county, which elected a predominantly Black school board and two legislators. They tried to change that mechanism by writing a state law so state legislators could pick school board members. We challenged that in court under the Voting Rights Act and won.

The court just struck that down, saying that in 2009 Congress failed to examine those states that were covered under preclearance to see if they still needed to be under preclearance. The Court said what Congress did in 2009 was lazy, and only looked at what happened in 1965 — it didn't look at the Voting Rights Act now. The court also didn't add any states to those covered under section 5.

The goal of the Right-wing is to get rid of the Voting Rights Act all together. They know the chances of coming to an agreement about which states should be covered under the Voting Rights Act in this Congress are slim to none. That's why people say the Voting Rights Act is effectively dead. I disagree. We need to, again, organize around the Voting Rights Act. Jesse Jackson Jr. talked in his book *A More Perfect Union* about a constitutional amendment that calls for a protected right to vote. Rep. Keith Ellison of Minnesota is picking that up. We must look at those impediments to voting, and from a progressive perspective talk about how we broaden voting rights in this country, rather than lamenting what this court has done.

DB: *Many people don't understand the enforcement nature of that legislation. In 1965, 1995, even 1996, there was the same problem. Even if you pass legislation, you couldn't get federal officers to enforce it, so it was meaningless unless you brought in folks from the north to go down there to enforce it, right?*

KG: Yes. Things are a bit more sophisticated now. There are voter ID laws enacted to slow down the pace of Black and minority voting in the south.

DB: *So it continues. You live in South Carolina. Is the Klan shop still open?*

KG: Oh yes.

DB: *And they flew the confederate flag until when?*

KG: This is the ideological home of white supremacy. We understand that and fight it all the time. That is why preclearance in the Voting Rights Act is a handy tool. We have to

184

fight to use it all the time. It's a procedural mechanism, and it will be interesting to see moving forward what happens when we don't have it.

DB: *We certainly want to move forward. I did a story in 1996 about the old boys' parties organized by federal agents from the ATF [Alcohol, Tobacco, Firearms] and FBI. They had racist parties with signs about watermelon eating contests — these were federal officers in 1995 in the south. When we investigated the church burnings in 1995 and 1996, the federal officers did the same thing they did in 1965 — they showed up and blamed the Black people for burning down their own churches. Now they're accusing them of voter fraud.*

KG: That's right. I was involved in editing a Black newspaper and organizing with the Rainbow Coalition and other groups to bring attention to the church fires. We had congressional hearings on the fires. Many churches were rebuilt and some people were prosecuted. We can't ever depend on anybody else. The victims need to lead their own way out of oppression.

DB: *The investigation in Mississippi was conducted by Jim Ingram, who was number three in COINTELPRO. He was sued for doing illegal activities — trying to disrupt organizing by Black groups. He was in charge in 1966 to find out who was burning the Black churches, while lots of Black people were being hung in prisons. This was not long ago.*

KG: Every 28 hours, a Black person is killed by a police officer in America. Now they want to put a surge of border agents to the southern border of the US. Trayvon Martin, the Voting Rights Act, the wealth gap between whites and Blacks getting ever wider — it's sad. We have a Black president and over 10,000 Black elected officials across the country, all of whom are the direct recipients of the Voting Rights Act. Yet it seems things keep getting worse and worse and worse.

There's obviously something else that needs to happen in the body politic in this country. Minority communities in particular must raise the level of political consciousness and activism to defend themselves. I'm not talking about defending ourselves by grabbing a carbine and getting behind a barricade. How do we move a movement back into the streets, educate people at a local level? I asked some young folks if they knew what happened today with the Voting Rights Act. They didn't know what happened or even what the Voting Rights Act is. They didn't know the Court's decision on the Voting Rights Act was probably as significant as the Dred Scott decision because they didn't know what the Dred Scott decision was.

Many young folk don't seem to think it matters. Somebody must have told them institutional racism doesn't exist. They have no idea what white supremacy or white privilege is. Maybe they will know about it when they are in a crowd of white folks and somebody picks them out, but something needs to happen in our community, to re-politicize our kids to what it is they are losing, and what it will mean for their future if they have one. That's what's missing in Black politics in this country.

DB: *Has it helped to have a Black president?*

KG: I hear a lot of people say, "White folk did it, why can't he do it?" I say, "What are we for, equal injustice for all?" It comes down to whether or not you want to run or change the system. It used to be the Black movement was about changing the system. Now we have over 10,000 elected officials across the country, so we became part of the system. We are running the system — we are the technocrats of the system. So the goal becomes to do the job as well or better than the white person who had the job.

Surveillance — I've had to argue people down on Snowden. I think what Snowden did is heroic and I'm rooting for him. People say to me he ought to go down, go to jail, he's a traitor. A traitor? I say, "The government is spying on you, me and the whole wide world. We have an assassination program going on around the world. You think an assassination program, a secret government, secret police, drones, constant surveillance, trial without jury, and no due process is a good thing?" People respond with, "Well we have to protect ourselves from the enemy." Dude, who is in jail? It's not a bunch of Islamic fundamentalist extremists in jail. It's people of color — Black and Brown folk in jail. Who do you think they are using the surveillance on? Non-violent drug offenders have their phones monitored. That's what is going on. You are the target here, somebody else is the target across the ocean or down below the border.

We must challenge this, but there is no leadership to do so. I watched Chris Hayes on MSNBC — I've even been on his show — and he criticized Snowden possibly going to Cuba "with Castro and the Cubans." So now are we anti-socialist, anti-communist? We need a new movement, new leadership, to challenge the empire. We need to set up Freedom Schools and a different kind of mechanism to re-educate the people who are under the whip, so they realize it's not themselves beating each other up — it's coming from up top.

DB: *The interchange between Glenn Greenwald and David Gregory demonstrates the level of ignorance we see. Self-censorship is so deep that Gregory thinks his job, as a journalist, instead of monitoring the centers of power and reporting to the people, is to defend the State Department.*

KG: These people have been cheerleaders for empire and warmongering. It's seeping into the heart of it all. They are rooting for warmongering and do not realize how the rest of the world is viewing us — as warmongers, an empire that wants to exploit and bully people. We are bullies in this country, with a bully mentality. We must figure out a movement that connects up with the other movements rolling all around the world — Turkey, Brazil, France, Spain, Egypt, Tunisia. That's what the government fears — that it will hit here. It needs to hit here and be led by the people who are the most affected by it — the people who are at the bottom. We must find some mechanism to tweak people's political consciousness so they know who the real enemy is.

DB: *We are closely watching a group called the Dreamers, which includes undocumented young folks and farmworkers who do the hardest work in the fields. They are part of a new civil rights movement.*

KG: When Black and Brown people, Latinos of Central and South America, Blacks of African descent and Indigenous Peoples finally realize they are better together than apart, we'll have a movement. Instead, many Black folk believe Latinos are taking jobs from them. I tell people they don't call New Mexico, New Mexico for no reason. They must realize that workers must come together. When that happens, we'll have a movement. We have Black folk who say the gay rights movement has nothing to do with the civil rights movement. Of course it does. But as the gay community cheers the defeat of DOMA [Defense of Marriage Act], they need to realize in their celebration that yesterday's gutting of the Voting Rights Act was a bad day for those who believe in the rights of minorities and people of color. If they don't understand the significance of what happened, and temper their celebration with the need to go back and rejoin with this other group, they will miss a teachable moment for themselves.

DB: *The Gay Pride March is coming up in San Francisco, and gay whistleblower Chelsea Manning was nominated as the honorary grand marshal. They yanked her name out and said it was a big mistake because they didn't want to give people the wrong impression. This is in progressive San Francisco.*

KG: It says they want to be a part of the system — mainstream, be on TV every night, say the right things about government, get invited to the right parties, hang out with the powerful muckety mucks — don't piss them off. We're with them — we're with the empire. We're not fighting against oppression, or the wrongful deaths of 100s of thousands of Iraqis. Chelsea Manning exposed the monstrous and murderous war in Iraq that we waged based on a lie. Instead of prosecuting Chelsea Manning and chasing down Edward Snowden, we ought to be talking about why it was that George Bush, Dick Cheney, Colin Powell, Donald Rumsfeld, Condoleezza Rice and the rest weren't prosecuted. Why were they not prosecuted as war criminals? Instead, Obama expands executive power and pre-emptive war through assassinations. People are dissing Chelsea Manning and embracing a foreign policy of empire, murder, and lies.

DB: *How do you think Barack Obama will be thought of in the history books?*

KG: Obviously, as the first African American president, he will be in the history books, because that's a big deal. Many of us who write history will call him the assassination president, a failure — somebody who expanded the empire with a Black face and the face of a beautiful Black family. He did nothing more than serve as a cover for the disastrous policies of this country and take one more step toward ruin for this country. Those in the mainstream will write what they write, because they are with the empire. But many of us, at *Counterpunch, The Progressive,* some at *The Nation* — those historians — will call him the assassination president who aided in the erosion of the international rule of law.

Oklahoma's Botched Execution
Michael Kroll   May 2014

DB: *Oklahoma's recent botched execution — when a disputed cocktail of drugs left Clayton Lockett writhing in pain for 43 minutes before finally succumbing to an apparent heart attack — has again put the spotlight on the death penalty and raised the question of whether Lockett was essentially tortured to death.*

Michael Kroll is the first executive director of the Death Penalty Information Center in Washington, D.C. and a specialist on the American criminal justice system with a special emphasis on the death penalty. He wrote The Final Days of Robert Alton Harris *about California's gas-chamber execution of Harris at San Quentin.*

Mr. Kroll, what is your initial response to what happened in Oklahoma?

MK: I think the appropriate adjective for that cocktail is "experimental," which reminds me of Dr. Josef Mengele, who experimented on human beings for the Nazis. This is an experiment because Oklahoma and a growing number of other states are not able to get approved procedures and drugs for killing people — mainly because Europe refuses to supply them as they once did. They are going to secret pharmacies where we can't learn what they are prescribing, how they're orchestrating the procedure, or what mixture it is. It's being done in secret, as an experiment — experimenting on human beings. We definitely tortured this man.

In the execution I witnessed, which went completely according to the book...

DB: *That was Robert Alton Harris.*

MK: That was Robert Harris, by lethal gas. That execution took 16 minutes — absolutely an eternity. This execution took almost three times that long before they killed him. And who knows by what means they actually killed him, since they closed the curtain on the public — very literally. They closed the visual line into what was going on, so they could have hit him in the head with a hammer for all we know.

DB: *Is that illegal? I thought witnesses must observe the entire process.*

MK: I honestly can't tell you what the law in Oklahoma is. The death penalty, except for a very few cases, is a state-by-state process, and each state has its own procedures. A federal judge just said we must know that process, and unless we know that process and that it meets constitutional standards — mainly Eighth Amendment no cruel and unusual punishment — we will not sign off on it.

That did not happen in Oklahoma, where the State Supreme Court first found there were issues about this method, then Governor Mary Fallin said, "I'm going ahead with it whether you tell me to or not." The next day the Supreme Court caved and said, "Well, we withdraw, there are no issues." So they killed Clayton Lockett, and then stopped the next execution, and probably some executions that might follow.

DB: *The governor was so proud. If the justices wanted to delay that first execution, she was gonna give us a double header, wasn't she? It seemed like this was a vindictive response, and it came back to bite her, of course, in the middle of torturing a human being.*

MK: Who knows what goes on in the heads of politicians? They're always looking for the next issue that's going to put them back in the state house or the senate or wherever they want to be. The issue becomes less important than their evaluation of how much it is going to help their political careers. Basically they are willing to torture people to death in order to seek public office and keep it. It's very, very disturbing and disgusting.

DB: *There is a consistency — torture at home, torture abroad.*

MK: Absolutely.

DB: *We accept it in foreign countries.*

MK: We don't call it torture. Dennis, we don't torture in this country. Yes, we kill people slowly. It takes 43 minutes to strangle them to death. Waterboarding. We hit them over the head, but that's not torture, because we say it's not torture. This is really *1984* where words control history — not what is done, but what is said about what is done.

In California, right now, three former failed governors — Wilson, Davis and Schwarzenegger — have a proposal for a ballot initiative in November that would greatly speed the process of executions in California. Yet a report that came out today shows probably more than 4% of those we condemn to death are not guilty of capital murder, so should not be there — a mistake was made. The system makes mistakes. It is human. We make mistakes. To say that we don't is to say that we are gods, and that is how we are acting.

DB: *The cocktails they were using were outlawed. The cocktails they used in Oklahoma this week were devastating, yet you've got these governors hell-bent on going forward to speed up the process. How will they kill these people? The 43-minute torture? Is gas coming back?*

MK: We have no way of knowing, since it's a closed system. They have said this particular process — which gives government THE most awesome power it can exert over individual citizens — does not require that the public, which gave them this power, has any right to know how it's implemented. That's a formula for absolute corruption.

DB: *How do the Democrats compare to the Republicans on this?*

MK: Some years ago the Democrats in the state legislature circulated a letter saying very clearly — one, two, three, four, five — we Democrats should rip the criminal justice issue out of the hands of the Republicans by being for longer sentences, for the death penalty — a litany of things Republicans have become famous for advocating. The Democrats basically said we should advocate for the same thing, so we can get elected.

Things have changed somewhat since then. The public support for the death penalty has dropped fairly substantially, even though it still shows — depending on how you ask the question — a slight majority. If you ask people whether they would prefer the alternative of life in prison without parole, a majority says "Yes." That's what they would prefer.

DB: *There's still enough of an edge that comes out of it, that these hit-hard, no-holds-barred, criminal-justice-type politicians think it's worth playing the death card.*

MK: Absolutely. While they play the death card on their right hand, on the left hand they are opposing any efforts to put very, very modest limits on the ability to gain access to firearms, which kill 20,000-plus people in America each year. We've seen mass shootings by severely mentally ill people who can't get mental health treatment. That seems to be okay on that side, but we've got to kill them on this side. The hypocrisy is so mind boggling I feel schizophrenic sometimes when I read the news, listen to what I hear, and see what I see.

DB: *You watched your friend grovel and suffocate, and die a horrible death. You've spent much of your life fighting this brutality. What does what happened in Oklahoma say about who we are in 2014?*

MK: As a political system, it says we still have not lifted our last foot out of the slime of antiquity. We are still holding on to what have become human sacrifices. The number of people who commit murder in this country — 20,000-plus. The number of people who get sentenced to death. The number of people who actually get executed. This is the very tiny group of sacrifices. We don't mind sacrificing human beings. We condemn the act of taking a life by taking a life. It doesn't require more than a six-year-old to understand the absurdity of that.

DB: *Do we know how many people on death row were rescued — found not guilty, or innocent, or taken off death row?*

MK: According to a study published in a leading scientific journal, *Proceedings of the National Academy of Sciences*, as many as 300 people sentenced to death in the US over a three-decade period were likely innocent. One of the more disturbing aspects — not just that these people on death row were innocent — is that the longer a person stays on death row, the more likely the error will be found. So those quick processes, like what is suggested for California, will almost certainly result in more wrongful executions.

DB: *The White House said the Oklahoma execution "fell short of fairness." Does this open the door to hold these folks accountable, and prevent it by making this kind of torture illegal?*

MK: The President said his authority exists only over federal law, so he has no authority over the laws of Oklahoma, California, or Georgia. He said he has no power to influence what goes on in Oklahoma, other than the power of the bully pulpit. I call it the bloody pulpit, which is more accurate.

However, I'm hopeful that this barbarity, this torture that no one can deny occurred, will at least make judges in states where this information is secret, recognize that there is an issue here. It's an issue about public knowledge and accessibility to government process. If you close that process and say the public has no right to know what the public has authorized, you have moved into a very different kind of government. We call it tyranny.

•

The Urgent Lessons of Ferguson

Walter Riley   December 2014

DB: *All eyes are still on Ferguson and beyond. We're watching the president get involved. Our guest of honor, Walter Riley, is a lifelong civil rights and human rights activist. He is an attorney who practices in the areas of criminal defense, civil rights and police misconduct in Oakland, California. Walter, you grew up in the segregated South, so this ain't nothing new to you. What are your reactions to how the prosecutor used the grand jury to make sure the cop didn't get indicted? What is the bigger picture, and where does it take us?*

WR: I grew up in Durham, North Carolina. The DA's defense of the police officer is an outrage for me, and for so many people I know living in the communities where we face this. It is an outrage for anybody who takes a moment to look at the kind of society we are in — what we think we can be and what we are. We must be outraged by the conduct of the Ferguson police department, the District Attorney, the state, the governor and everybody who participated in this. The DA totally defended the conduct of the police officer in the shooting of Michael Brown, and played the role of the defense attorney in many ways. We must look at him as an individual who did this, look at his background and what we would expect from him. We should look at the system in Ferguson, which is not an isolated incident. I worry that we think about these individual acts, a police officer and how he explained himself, and add them up as a lot, and a lot, and a lot of police officers act this way.

DB: *It's not isolated, but segregated.*

WR: Yes, a segregated system in Missouri. But how different is that from other places that are not so segregated? I live in Oakland and must bring everything back to where I am. As you know, I am politically involved in Oakland, as are many people. Yet in Oakland we have police shootings and police misconduct of an outrageous sort. We have the police shooting death of Oscar Grant that was heard around the world. [Oscar Grant was an unarmed young African American man who was subdued and pinned down flat by two white officers on an Oakland train station platform, then shot to death at point blank range, in front of hundreds of bystanders on New Year's Day. *Ed*.] We don't think we got justice. Oscar Grant is known as a symbol of the injustice for Black people, and people of color, when we're dealing with law enforcement.

We're dealing with these issues when a large portion of our country is reacting to having a Black president. Whatever our criticisms of President Obama are, we know that many people are reacting and ready to take up arms against the system and mobilize. Police departments are putting up racist posters, banners and nooses in locker rooms across the country. Ferguson police officers were making outrageous statements — attacking the nature of our society and attacking the president, because he's Black. The racism that exists in this country must be confronted in many ways — in discussions, new legislation and resolutions, from local, state and national government. It must be confronted by the people on the street taking action against the economic system that is allowed to make profits at a time when so much injustice exists.

I support the demonstrators. I don't find this is a time to be critical of any of it. It's necessary for all of us who are decision-makers with input into our lives, our society, and our government, to understand that there can't be peace without justice. So we need to take to the streets, and use many means to achieve a world that makes us feel safe. Feeling safe for us doesn't necessarily mean other people will feel safe. We don't feel safe now as young people, working people, particularly Black and Brown people, when police officers shoot us down and shoot our kids down, with no retribution. That must change.

There was a period in our society where we took up the fight against racist lynchings that occurred in the South. The NAACP did research, and many political and social justice groups did organizing work in the 30s and 40s to document the 100 years of lynchings. Then we went through a period of race riots, organized by white racists with local and national law enforcement support, into the 40s. We went through the racist segregation in the 50s and the fight to maintain that system of segregation and oppression with the support of law enforcement and political entities, both state and national governments. We went to the fight in the 60s when masses of people began to rise up in different ways from our communities. We found allies from the Black communities and other communities, including in other parts of the world. The student movement sent people to the south, where people with various ethnic backgrounds found unity, and the desire to put their bodies, their lives on the line to make a change in society.

We need to step it up now. We must make some changes. Sometimes there are costs to be paid, but at this point we need to express our anger. We need to figure out how to organize and make it effective, not because we hear a racist comment from a TV reporter or FOX news, but because we decide we have our own people to communicate with, to develop support, to make allies. We must make some real changes, and put pressure on the government. We need to change the police departments, the way we view, organize and work with the police departments. In the 60s when we said we wanted to fight against the war in Vietnam, fight the repressive society that was destroying people in many parts of the world, we said we didn't want to be part of that. We wanted to change that. If it doesn't work for us, it shouldn't exist.

DB: *You are the father of a high profile activist, Boots Riley. Can the father in you talk about your fears, and how you make your children aware that they could die in the process of expressing themselves?*

WR: It happens. I have had guns pulled on me by police officers. My toddler daughter was in the back of my car when I was riding in San Francisco in the 60s, and a cop pulled me over, spread-eagled me on the car, and put a gun on me. I was an activist, organizer and field secretary for the Congress of Racial

Equality [CORE]. Later, my boys, in the 70s and 80s, coming into their adolescence, needed to face a system where they could be attacked anytime. One of Boot's songs says, "I'm 21, I've reached my life expectancy. At any minute I could be killed by some brother or some crazy cop." That's the nature of society that he understood. A lot of kids at that time, their life expectancies were in their early 20s.

It's not so different now. It's because of a repressive police state and a state that doesn't let young people, particularly young Black men, develop. Mass incarceration, the pushing of drugs on our society — we know that comes from government intervention, allowing destruction in our communities. There's lots of documentation of those government actions. My kids grew up in that. I had to teach them the nature of the world they lived in, which means protect themselves with other people, be part of a community, and know how to identify themselves as strong people, Black boys in a society that doesn't appreciate Black boys.

DB: *Did you teach them what to do when approached by a white cop?*

WR: My approach with my boys and other kids I can talk to honestly is that their dignity is as important as any other part of your being, and your family. Don't kowtow. Don't get off the sidewalk because a cop says you have to. In that process you learn how to handle yourself in a particular situation. It's more important to talk about the need for respect, not the need for giving in. Many people today say kids need to give in to the cops, agree with them, and give them what they need. But that's not why they're killing our kids and are so quick to pull the trigger — because the kids disrespect them. It's not from some internal process in the police department's policies that says if the kid doesn't respect you, you can kill him. They are shooting our kids because they believe in a racist system — that it's OK to get away with killing young Black kids. It has little to do with the personal interaction with a particular kid — it's just an opportunity. Every kid must learn this. It's important for my boys, and all kids, to understand how they interact with people, and what their limits are in any interaction, so they can have some control, but not lose their dignity.

DB: *The Ferguson prosecutor had a long history with the Innocence Project, right?*

WR: This guy should not be a prosecutor based on the history we know, and what the shooting and murder of Michael Brown demonstrated. This DA has a long history of support of the police department, and he had wanted to be a cop himself, which leads to questions of bias. Is it OK to have a DA who is pro-cop? OK. But what about a DA who is unfair, dumped material, did not provide information to the grand jury that would have given them an opportunity to evaluate the material given to them? They were even given wrong instructions regarding what the standard was. But he allowed the cop to testify.

DB: *Before the grand jury.*

WR: Yes, I do criminal defense in addition to police misconduct, so have clients indicted, and they don't have the opportunity to tell their story, although some clients want to tell their story. This cop should have the opportunity to defend himself before a jury, with the public hearing their concerns, at a public trial. This DA didn't care what the public wanted. You saw a smirk on his face when he gave his press conference. This DA shouldn't be there, but it's a position that exists other places. Oakland's DA, Nancy O'Malley, is no better. I think we must name the departments across the country that are like that. In Oakland they don't prosecute police officers, and they let them get away with all sorts of things.

I was an attorney observer at the Urban Shield demonstration at the Marriott organized by Buddhists. They were sitting in their meditative positions in front of a door, but other doors were unblocked. A manager decided to go through the line instead of the unblocked door, and as he did, he kicked the sitting

Buddhists. They were prepared to accept that. The police department is supposed to protect demonstrators so they can exercise their free speech. The police department can remove people from sitting in front of a door, but the law is they are not supposed to let them get attacked, assaulted and battered by counter protestors — in this case the manager of the Marriott hotel. When I said that to the sergeant, he said, "I don't have a duty to protect the protestors." He's trained to say that, even though it's unlawful to take that position, and he should be disciplined for it. I told his supervisor, who decided it was unlikely he said that, so there was no consequence. That's how our police department operates.

The Ferguson police department just took it a bit further, making outrageous statements — the DA supporting the police department and the police officer. I think he actually obstructed the prosecution of this police officer through the grand jury. The public never had an opportunity for what might have been some open discussions. The Alameda County DA hasn't had the opportunity to act like they did in Ferguson, but the Alameda County DA hasn't said what happened in Ferguson is ridiculous. Alameda County has many people of color in the DA's department, and they haven't spoken out against this. The Charles Houston Bar Association hasn't made an open statement against it, outlining what it is. We're seeing some Black elected Missouri state officials who said that something needs to happen, but we need a more unified approach in our community. Get rid of this DA and DAs in other counties who act this way. Ask our institutions to step up. Ask our elected officials to step up. Even if we are cynical, we must demand that the system operates. Challenging those systems means we must make demands on them, specific changes that must occur. Fight for that, demand that, in ways that will be varied, but challenging is absolutely in order.

DB: *At the core it's about economic justice. There will not be any kind of equal rights without the right to survive, make a living, and have the protections a little money and food in the refrigerator give you.*

WR: Yes, it's deep and complicated. Yet there's some simplicity to it. Social and economic justice, jobs, respect in the community, and building the kind of world we want. It's about finding allies, all of us together with specific roles and issues we deal with. In Oakland it's housing, gentrification, jobs, health care, as well as police. Look for opportunities for unity, and not the corporate media's images of the actions we engage in. We need more humanity and outrage in the streets. Make specific demands for change.

Church Murders Reflect Structural Racism

Vernellia Randall   June 2015

DB: *We are going to talk about the recent slaughter by a racist white supremacist in South Carolina. During a Prayer Service at Emmanuel African Methodist Episcopal Church, Dylan Storm Roof killed nine African Americans, including Senior Pastor and State Senator Clementa Pinckney. Documents confirm that it clearly was a plan emerging in the mind of somebody who picked up on the collective spirit of the racism that is still pervasive in this country. Professor Vernellia Randall has written extensively about this.*

Professor Randall, the systematic, institutional history is not talked about. This plan emerged from the pervasive racism of the country.

VR: Correct. The discussion from the President to others is that the act was done by an individual — the overt racist. The problem is that he is representative of systematic and cultural racism that allows this sort of overt racism to breed and that significantly affects people of all colors on a daily basis. I wrote a book, *Dying While Black*, which states that 100,000 Black people die every year who wouldn't die if we had the same death rate as whites. That's the result of systemic and institutional racism.

DB: *The most powerful and effective violence is poverty. What is your response to politicians in South Carolina who want the death penalty? The mourners at the church are already talking mercy.*

VR: I am conflicted because I don't believe in the death penalty, and wouldn't want it even for this gentleman. As an issue of human rights, we should not be putting human beings to death. Anyone who understands the issue of the death penalty must understand that you can't call for it when, most of the time, it's done in a racialized, racist manner. So it can't be called for at all. One of the big issues is that when we start to deal with racial crime, there's a tendency to want to label the person as having some kind of aberration such as mental illness. Rather, this person is a product of a system of hate built around him.

People have focused on the Confederate flag. As a person who grew up in Texas with the Confederate flag in the '40s and '50s, I appreciate the symbolism and actual institutional and systemic racism that is occurring by having that flag — the symbol of the Civil War and what it was about. People who engage in this hate are not mentally evil. They are a product of the society — maybe the most extreme overt product in terms of violence — but when you talk about economic violence, the schools to prison pipeline, mass incarceration violence — in every area of Black lives there is racist violence going on. It's not about poverty. When you compare middle class Blacks to middle class whites, middle class Blacks are doing much worse than middle class whites.

DB: *Some of the same forces that drove slavery continue to drive racism.*

VR: Yes. Part of the issue is that we now have an institution of mass incarceration, which by definition is slavery — under the 13th Amendment of the Constitution. It's no accident that a disproportionate number of people in prison are Black and Brown. We have a system of profit-making companies. I wrote a piece for the United Nations about the school to prison pipeline, and the companies that use labor in prison as a way to get cheap labor. We also have a system of oppression outside the prison that continues to follow Black, Brown and Native American people, but largely Black people. One of my great frustrations is the attempt by both Democrats and Republicans — to the extent that they address racism at all — to define it as individual and overt. That will never deal with the basic problem we have in our society, which is systemic and cultural.

DB: *A tremendous amount of organizing in the civil rights movement happened in churches. Yes, there was Christian ideology preached, but there was also an enormous amount of organizing — voter registration and other campaigns — which revolved around the church. White people know this, and they have always destroyed the Black churches.*

PR: Always. One of the few places Africans enslaved in the US could legally gather was in the churches. In those churches they developed ways of communication, planning for freedom. Whites know it. Particularly the AME church in Charleston — it's no accident that this young man went into one of the oldest Black churches, with a strong history of rebellion and Black organizing. Of all the churches he could have picked in that town, he picked the church that was celebrating its 193-year anniversary. That's a church standing since slavery, with membership since slavery. One of the co-founders of the church was hung, murdered by the system, for supposedly organizing a slave revolt.

People need to look at the choices this young man made, and if he made them all by himself. The investigation should be more than just about a hate crime. How did this young man get all these weapons? How did he get this history, to go into this church at this particular time? And none of his friends who knew about his language and hate reported him. Are they co-conspirators in this? Is anybody talking about charging them as accessories because of their knowledge of what was going to happen and their failure to do anything?

Everybody knows the history of Black churches. They have been bombed and burned down since the beginning. The worst bombing and burning was in the 1990s. People think this is old history. Hundreds of churches were burned down during the period between 1990 and 1996. It hasn't only been Black churches — whole towns were burned down. Black Wall Street in Oklahoma was one of the only cities that was aerial bombed. The destruction of the Black community, both economically and through fear of physical violence, has been an ongoing part of our history. That's what this is about, re-instilling fear back in Black people, making us become more obedient. One police chief said he was going to go after Black Lives Matter. When Roof says he wants to take back his country, he's spouting a political ideology that is not limited to him or the South.

DB: *When I traveled the South in 1995 with Ron Nixon, formerly with an excellent publication,* Southern Exposure, *right before I got to Selma, there was an attack in the city in which a crazy man named Larry Schumake had stored up weapons in a downtown, closed-down, fast-food restaurant. He opened fire and killed and wounded 14 people because Mississippi was finally going to ratify the Anti-slavery Amendment. This is 1995, around the time of those church burnings. When they went to his house, there were journals about how there needs to be a white rebellion to purge the Black race. We discovered that the person who investigated the church burnings in Jackson, Mississippi was a man named James Ingram, who was the number three man in the FBI COINTELPRO program. They sent him to Mississippi to find out who was burning down the churches. He previously said that the incident of the kidnapped civil rights workers was just part of a publicity plot of the NAACP. These were the guys investigating those church burnings in the mid-90s.*

VR: Now that I'm in my 70s and have grandkids who are five years old, I fear for the kind of society we have — I think it's getting worse. People say we are becoming a minority society in which there will be nothing but minorities. But nobody talks about whether the historically racial minorities — Black and Brown, Native American, Asian — will have control of the institutions, the economics. Will that be divided among all the various groups equitably? Or will we have a South African apartheid? Everything we see in our society — police brutality, the militarization of police, aggressive behavior of police — all point to preparation for policing in an apartheid type of society. That's the extension of what we see today, taking it a step further.

Solidarity Against Solitary in California
Mohamed Shehk & Marie Levin   September 2015

DB: *Today California prisoners locked in isolation achieved a groundbreaking legal victory in their ongoing struggle against the use of solitary confinement. There was a settlement reached in the federal class action lawsuit originally filed in 2012, Ashker v. Brown. The settlement effectively ends indefinite, long-term solitary confinement and greatly limits the prison administration's use of solitary and their ability to use the practice widely, as torture. Mohamed Shehk, what is the significance of this victory?*

MS: The significance of this settlement is enormous. California has been an outlier in its use of solitary in this country, a country that uses solitary more than anyplace in the world. Under the settlement, prisoners will no longer be sent to solitary for reasons of gang affiliation, security threat groups or anything status-based. They can be placed there only for specific and very limited serious rule violations. It affects the majority of people that have been in solitary for decades, indefinitely, without any terms. So the settlement does away with indefinite long-term solitary confinement.

DB: *Marie Levin, tell us what your brother was subjected to through this policy.*

ML: My brother while at Pelican Bay didn't have the opportunity to see sunlight, to see the wind blow on the grass, and enjoy the outdoors. There were no windows. The only human touch they had was guards putting them in chains, locking their hands. It was sensory deprivation. In Pelican Bay, even the yard doesn't have sunlight. It's a concrete tomb. I visited him there every other month.

DB: *Mohamed, can you give us more details?*

MS: Solitary confinement was instituted as a widely used practice in the 60s and 70s in response to the increasing prison organizing that was going on. There was George Jackson and also the uprising in Attica. Solitary was a severe punishment where people were placed in a parking space-size cell for 23 or more hours a day in order to isolate them from any contact with other prisoners, so they could not organize or have relationships with one another. This has severe damage and implications for the mental health of prisoners. There have been numerous studies, which show that even a month in solitary can have damaging effects for someone's lifetime. Marie's brother spent decades in solitary. In 2011 and 2013, the prisoners in Pelican Bay organized a hunger strike, coordinating with each other. It was one of the most significant prisoner actions against solitary confinement in history. In 2013 over 30,000 prisoners across California refused meals in solidarity with the hunger strikers. It shows the deep solidarity felt, and shared struggles, in the face of treacherous conditions.

DB: *How do you organize when you are in the most repressed solitary confinement cell in the country?*

MS: It took months to organize, to have communication between the prisoners. They communicated through pipelines, through the walls, to be sure their demands were in line with others. It turned into an incredibly successful nonviolent action.

DB: *Marie, how did you feel when your brother told you they were going to organize? Were people afraid of retaliation?*

ML: Yes, they were worried about retaliation but didn't care. Over a period of 10 years they organized, first in the large group of the "worst of the worst," then when broken up, throughout the prison. My brother told me he went on this hunger strike for those coming behind him, even if he had to die. He didn't want the young ones to suffer like he did for 31 years. In 2011, he and the others decided they would go on these hunger strikes, regardless. I don't like the word fear, because they were prepared to die. The guards knew they were settling this case, so when my brother came back to his cell after a yard visit, it was all trashed. They threw all his papers and other property all over his cell. That's retaliation. The guards do this kind of thing to the guys all the time — tearing up property or throwing it away.

DB: *Mohamed, you've heard these stories before?*

MS: Definitely. The prison administration tried to break up the solidarity and movement that was building, so they separated people within the prison, and also scattered people throughout California, making it harder to coordinate these actions. They were also writing people up and making it harder to have a pathway out of solitary — extending the solitary terms. That made it harder for people to communicate, to maintain that unity despite all the efforts to break it up. The prisoner Agreement to End Hostilities was made in 2012, the same year the lawsuit was filed. It calls on all prisoners to end violence across racial lines, and unite to confront CDCR [California Department of Corrections and rehabilitation] as the main source and threat of violence against them. The agreement is still holding and is being used as a tool for solidarity across racial lines.

Voting While Black Doesn't Count

Greg Palast   February 2016

DB: *Greg Palast is one of the most significant investigative reporters of our time. He has several best selling books; among them* The Best Democracy Money Can Buy. *Greg, you sure nailed that one. Talk about the extraordinary role that money may or may not play in the presidential election.*

GP: The Koch brothers will spend 3/4 of a billion dollars on this election. The firepower to knock out voters is being provided by the Kochs and other interests. Why are they? I know some of the Kochs, and they are not racists, but they see that if you knock out voters of color, poor voters, then they can take the White House, keep Congress, and turn those into profit centers. They are not partisan or racist. They use partisan politics and cynically use racism to make a buck. That's what is going on here.

DB: *Greg, you are marked in history as the journalist who nailed down that the 2000 election was clearly stolen. You opened up that door of electronic voter fraud, calling it Jim Crow goes electronic. Are you concerned this year again about the electronic voting machines?*

GP: Yes, it's worse than ever, but my main concern is aimed at their knocking off voter registrations or actually disqualifying ballots. About one in three ballots in America will be mailed in. It's 10:00 PM. Do you know where your ballot is? People are worried about electronic machines, but when you mail in your ballot, it is mailed to guys who don't want you to vote. Your name is on the envelope, so it's not a secret ballot anymore. I'm very concerned.

In 2000 I discovered how [then Secretary of State] Katherine Harris and [Governor] Jeb Bush in Florida knocked off Black voters by tagging them as convicted felons, who have no right to vote in Florida (although they do have the right in most states). It turned out the only crime these 56,000 Black men were guilty of was voting while Black. There was not a single one found to have voted illegally but, they were overwhelmingly Black. The US presidency was decided by 537 votes, excluding those thousands of Black male votes.

This year there is something new called interstate crosscheck. The Greg Palast team found lists of seven million Americans who are tagged as illegal voters because they voted twice. Voting twice is a crime with a sentence of five years. Who votes twice? This means voting in one state, then in another state. It's a crime. With much investigation, they failed to find anyone who does this, but they are threatening to remove the votes of seven million people. Virginia started by removing 41,000 names, almost all voters of color. How did they pull this off? They say you voted twice if someone with your first and last name voted in another state. This is a horrific frontal attack on voting and no one is raising an alarm.

Here's an example. A very common name among Americans is Mohammed Mohammed. First name Mohammed and last name Mohammed. Since there is more than one Mohammed Mohammed in the US, they are saying that every Mohammed Mohammed in the US is the same person voting hundreds of times. I kid you not. They are removing that person's right to vote. If they mail in their ballot and think they are voting, their ballot will be disqualified in those Republican states, which includes the two big swing states in this election, Ohio and North Carolina. There are 675,000 people in Ohio, mostly voters of color, who were tagged for removal by the Secretary of State. It is serious.

I was just in Ohio investigating. I have lists that the Ohio Republican Secretary of State refused to give me because he said these people are criminal, since voting twice is a criminal act, so there is a criminal investigation. We got most of his lists and it's filled with names like John Brown, Jose Rodriguez and Mohammed Mohammed. And there is a new direct threat on another group — Asian voters with names like David Ho, Lee

Kim. Asian voters have turned from mostly Republican 20 years ago to 75% Democratic.

The Democratic Party is completely uninterested in the matter of voters of color losing their vote. Outside of Georgia, which is controlled by Black folk, you can't get a Democratic Party official who gives a darn about the voters of color. That's a very big problem here. Instead of the natural balance of one party watching another, they are happy to go hand-in-hand to go along with the lynching by laptop, which is what's occurring here.

DB: *We'd be better off conducting the entire election like the Iowa caucus.*

GP: Yes, in the Iowa caucus you can walk in and register to vote. In Ohio are people any more criminally inclined to vote twice than in Iowa? Of course Iowa is not filled with voters of color, so there is not the normal resentment. It's 100 years since the film *The Birth of a Nation* was released. It was the biggest film of its time, the first big feature film in 1915. *The Birth of a Nation* was basically about the Ku Klux Klan and it had a long segment about how Black people vote twice, vote illegally, and are criminal voters. This accusation of criminals, aliens, and double voters leveled against voters of color is as old as the Ku Klux Klan. When the film came out, it was very successful in helping the Democratic Party defeat anti-lynching laws. It was the Democratic Party that defeated the anti-lynching laws. It is an old accusation that people of color love to vote illegally, several times.

Stacy Abrams, head of the Democratic Party in Georgia, is one of the few Democrats concerned about this kind of trickery. They say people voted twice? It's very difficult to get people to vote once! Iowa is a white voting system. We have an apartheid voting structure in the US that's different for voters of color than white voters. It's how it is.

DB: *In Alabama in the mid-1990, we were investigating over 100 church burnings. I traveled with Ron Nixon, now of the* New York Times, *then the editor of* Southern Exposure. *The FBI and ATF [Alcohol, Tobacco and Firearms] were investigating the church burnings. They'd show up in the communities where the churches were burned and open up a double investigation. Did you burn your church down and are you the same people involved in voter fraud? Who will talk about their church being burned down when they are also accused of voter fraud? We saw this repeatedly.*

GP: Voter suppression is a crime. It's a crime to stop somebody from voting because of their color or using racially biased methods. But the criminals are the cops. So when Jeb Bush stole the presidential election for his brother, his brother was supposed to investigate Jeb Bush for stealing the White House for him. You might as well put the Mafia in charge of the FBI and racists in charge of the local police.

I was just in Selma Alabama, the birthplace of the Voting Rights Act movement. Americans congratulated themselves last year on the 50 years since Martin Luther King led marches across the Edmund Pettus Bridge. I just walked across that bridge a few weeks ago with several former marchers, including African American Alabama State Senator Hank Sanders. As a Black man 50 years ago, when he marched into Montgomery he couldn't vote. Today he's the state senator but today he can't vote because his name was removed from the voter roles due to crosscheck. He called me up and said I can't vote. We're walking backward over the bridge.

DB: *Are you serious? Hank Sanders was refused his vote?*

GP: Yes, Senator Sanders was also well known because he tore down the Confederate flag off the State Capital. As a senator he was a symbol of the great advance, but he contacted me to say he can't vote. After the US Supreme Court gutting of the key components of the Voting Rights Act in 2013, within hours — not days or months — within hours, Alabama moved to require active photo-driver's licenses to vote, or a state photo ID. However, they closed almost every DMV [Department of Motor Vehicles] office in the 10 Black majority counties. Almost every DMV office was shut down. You need a driver's license to vote but you can't get a driver's license. Obama sued, so Alabama agreed to open the DMV offices once a month — only in the 10 Black majority counties.

Those who complain become targets of investigation. I was just talking to Martin Luther King III who questioned, looking at the demographics of Georgia, why it's not a blue, solid Democratic state. Because Black people are still fighting for the right to vote 50 years after the now ex-Voting Rights Act. An activist group tried to register young Black, Hispanic and Asian voters — almost all registered Democrats — but when they submitted those names, the state held onto them for six months before the tightly-fought 2014 election and the names were never put on the voter roles. The state said they didn't have the budget or time to put them on the voter roles. Instead, the state had the money to open an investigation on the groups collecting the signatures, to see if they followed every single little rule — which they did. They had the money to investigate the people who were registering voters, but not to put names on the voter rolls.

Just because you filled out a yellow registration form, it doesn't mean you are registered. You need to go on-line with the secretary of state and check that they have your name and address correct and that you are properly registered. You may be tagged, eliminated, purged. If you are a voter of color, look out, especially in these 29 Republican-controlled crosscheck states. It is the stealth steal of 2016 and is deeply, deeply racist.

Church, State, Women, and the Criminalization of Sexuality

Roe v. Wade: Past, Present, Future Struggles

Terry O'Neill   January 2013

DB: *The 40th anniversary of* Roe v. Wade, *the landmark Supreme Court decision that recognized women's fundamental right to an abortion, will be observed by opponents and proponents alike. Among its backers will be National Organization of Women [NOW] president Terry O'Neill. Terry, what was life like before* Roe v. Wade, *and where did this battle start?*

TO: In the late 1960s, there was a young woman who was a student at the University of Chicago. She became very concerned about what she saw all around her — friends terrified of becoming pregnant, needing to terminate a pregnancy, and not being able to. That's a microcosmic description of what life was like. Her name was Heather Booth, and in 1969 she formed an organization called The Jane Network, an organization of women that procured illegal but safe abortions for women from 1969 until 1973. They performed about 12,000 abortions that were safe and medically appropriate, albeit completely illegal. In 1973 the Supreme Court decided *Roe v. Wade.*

For decades, prior to the time *Roe* was decided, women who wanted to terminate a pregnancy would eventually wind up either continuing the pregnancy against their will and being forced into childbirth against their will, or if they found someone to perform an abortion, very often it was a predator. You couldn't be sure whether you were going to someone with medical qualifications who could terminate your pregnancy, or someone who was simply a sadistic sociopathic individual preying on women looking to terminate their pregnancies. It was horrific.

DB: *And, it was brutal and bloody.*

TO: It's terrifying. I remember as a child having the impression that pregnancy was the punishment women experienced for having sex. There was not only judgment — but also bloody, terrible, and terrifying punishments if you had sex and then wanted to terminate the pregnancy resulting from sex. It was a ridiculous means of controlling women through terror. That fundamentally is what *Roe v. Wade* was intended to change, and it fundamentally did change.

DB: *The suffering was immense, women were sent off to live with relatives, they were hidden — it was a very easy way to demonize women. This was a key aspect of the battle for women's liberation.*

TO: Absolutely. In upper-middle-class circles, when a girl was sent away, it was universally understood that she was being sent away from home so she could go to an unwed mother's home, be forced to bear a child, then give that child up for adoption. She was not able to terminate her pregnancy, so she had the baby, and often gave it up. That is what happened to the woman who was Jane Roe, in the *Roe v. Wade* case. She decided to give the baby up for adoption, but she simply wanted to hold the baby, have some kind of goodbye. But it was, "Oh, no..." They whisked it away from her. Women were treated either like children, or as if they were less than human, because it was assumed they were not able to take control of their health care needs.

DB: Roe v. Wade *was passed. Tell us about that battle.*

TO: It was interesting, because from the late 1960s until 1973 when the decision came down, there was enormous legislative work and advocacy to decriminalize abortion. State after state had begun decriminalizing abortion. Before *Roe v. Wade* was decided, New York State passed a law decriminalizing abortion, and a number of other states followed suit, even before *Roe*. In fact, one of the criticisms of the case, in later years, was "Hey, the political process was already taking care of decriminalizing abortion. The Supreme Court really overstepped its bounds or shouldn't have decided the case as a matter of fundamental constitutional rights." Obviously, I disagree with that. I think the court did the right thing in *Roe v. Wade*. There was an enormous groundswell from the public, and not just women — men who cared about their wives' and girlfriends' health care were very supportive of decriminalizing abortion. They saw what happened. I've heard so many stories and read memoirs of women whose husbands or boyfriends were with them every step of the way, trying to find someone who would perform the pregnancy termination, terrified they had gotten someone who was not going to perform a safe and medically appropriate procedure. Men were with the women in very large numbers back then, and it's still true today.

With all this political movement, the challenge to the extremely harsh law in Texas came up through the courts, which eventually ended at the Supreme Court. That was the *Roe v. Wade* case and Justice Harry Blackmun wrote a brilliant decision, saying that women's health care includes abortion, period. He also said that healthcare is a private matter, sex is a private matter, sexuality is a private matter. How the woman got pregnant, and what she does once she does get pregnant, the kinds of decisions that she needs to make once she's pregnant — those are only for her to decide under our constitutional law. That was clearly the right ruling.

Almost immediately, Right-wing lawmakers began trying to undo the *Roe v. Wade* decision. Henry Hyde, a Catholic lawmaker from Illinois, was able to push through what we now call the Hyde Amendment, which must be passed every single year as an add-on to an appropriations measure. The Hyde Amendment basically prohibits Medicaid from funding abortions for low-income women who are otherwise eligible for health care through Medicaid.

It has been expanded to exclude the military from paying for service women or women dependents of service members to have abortions. Even the Peace Corps is not allowed to make abortions available to Peace Corps volunteers, even when they are in countries where safe, legal procedures are not available. Henry Hyde was quoted as saying, "Look, I would like to make abortion unavailable to rich women, middle-class women and poor women alike, but unfortunately, the only women I can go after are the poor women." I think what he said was "Unfortunately, all I have available to me is Medicaid" to go after them. So he pressed to prevent federal funding for abortion care. That has had two extremely harmful effects. First of all, you can't pull out one piece of health care and think women will have all the other aspects of health care they need. We've seen in practice that doesn't work.

Today, in the name of the Hyde Amendment, Right-wing lawmakers are trying to shut down family planning clinics because those clinics refer women to abortion clinics or they perform abortions themselves. They are shutting down family planning clinics that give birth control, STD screenings, breast exams, and cervical cancer screenings. It's not possible to isolate abortion as the one piece of health care you are going to deprive women of. When you go down that road, women start being blocked from reproductive health care generally.

DB: *As Henry Hyde was playing that role in the Congress, he was also collaborating with borderline terrorists — Joseph Scheidler was accused of inspiring the killings of abortion doctors. When you mess with Scheidler, as I did when I wrote a book about Henry Hyde, you could end up in the cross hairs of his website as a baby killer, a mass murderer. This extralegal operation cost abortion doctors their lives.*

TO: Absolutely. It hasn't completely stopped but it has been enormously tamped down, and frankly, that's partly because of my own organization and other women's organizations. As you said, these over-zealous advocates against abortion rights use inflammatory language, announcing that anyone who supports abortion rights is a baby killer and deserves to be killed themselves. That kind of inflammatory language falls on the ears of the hinged and the unhinged alike. And it sets the stage for murdering abortion providers, which absolutely happened in the 1980s and the 1990s. It was a terrible time.

The National Organization for Women brought a RICO suit, a Racketeer Influenced and Corrupt Organizations lawsuit against Joe Scheidler, Randall Terry and others in the violent anti-abortion movement. We set out to prove they had a whole network, a corrupt organization that was designed to shut down legitimate healthcare clinics, which was against the law. Because they were conspiring together to shut down legitimate health care providers, it was a conspiracy under the RICO statutes. That lawsuit was fascinating and amazing. The National Organization for Women went to the Supreme Court twice, and won, but the third time we didn't win. That took 14 or 15 years, and in that time period, we were able to get a nationwide injunction against those men, and the level of violence against abortion clinics dropped like a stone. It was dramatic. The violence has not completely gone away, but it is at a much, much lower level than it was at the height of the extremist activities of Joe Scheidler and Randall Terry.

DB: *This still boils under the surface. Where is* Roe v. Wade *today? This is still the law, but it's incredibly difficult, particularly for poor and working-class women, to exercise this right.*

TO: It is much more difficult for poor women, younger women, military women, employees of the federal government, and women who live in rural areas outside of a city to obtain safe, legal, medically appropriate abortion. It's also much harder today for low-income women who are working two jobs, sometimes three jobs, and barely making it supporting their families. It's very difficult to say with a straight face that, even if there were an abortion clinic in their neighborhood that was not being attacked by radicals, there's a real choice going on. What kind of a choice is it if you have to decide about terminating a pregnancy because you can't afford it, because you and your partner are struggling to get by, because wages have been pressed down so far in the past 30 years. So your decision is to

218

terminate the pregnancy, which you might want if you could only afford it. The other choice is to go forward and have the child, whom you can't afford, and it will drag the entire family down.

The concept that *Roe v. Wade* opened up choices is wonderful, excellent, and good. But we need to be mindful of the economic situation today, with the wealthiest people in this country sucking off the increase in the gross domestic product that we've produced in the past 30 years. So for more and more families, to say they have choice is a bit of an exaggeration. I'm trying to bend my own brain around how to make that point to the legislators, especially our friends on the Hill. They need to see the economic implications of what's going on for ordinary families, and increasingly for middle-class families, who don't feel it's giving them that kind of choice — from an economic point of view. Beyond that, on one hand, you have families struggling, and the economics are making their choices unpalatable. On the other hand, you've got Catholic bishops and truly, truly radical, irrational legislators claiming that women routinely lie about being raped just so they can go out and have an abortion. They are absolutely rabid to control women's sexuality and stop women from accessing not only abortions, but also birth control, STD screenings, breast exams, and cervical cancer screenings.

In 2011 alone, 94 anti-abortion measures were passed into law at the state level. The previous record was only 34 in 2005. It's an astonishing spike in anti-abortion legislation. In 2012, the women's and pro-choice movements pushed those numbers down at the state level to only 43 — still the second highest in the history of this country. This is vicious, anti-abortion legislation and it's not letting up. In 2013, we've got legislation coming out of Michigan, Ohio and even New Jersey, where Governor Chris Christie has zeroed the funding of family planning clinics. This war on women's access to reproductive health care is continuing and is just jaw dropping with its ferocity.

DB: *Obama is getting ready for term two. Give us the good news and the bad news about the first administration and then, if they really want to jump in, what the administration should be doing next.*

TO: The bad news about the first four years of President Obama's administration with respect to abortion rights is that, in the health care debate, in order to get the Affordable Care Act passed, the administration gave up on abortion rights for women. Under the Affordable Care Act, insurance companies will not be required to cover abortion care as part of the health care that women ordinarily get. It also opens the door to legislatively prohibit insurance companies from making it easy for women to access insurance coverage for abortion care. It was a betrayal of women's rights.

The bishops insisted on no insurance coverage whatsoever for birth control. The Obama administration stood up to them and said "No." We are now beginning to see studies that show that if cost is not an issue for women, and they have access to the birth control that's best for them, the general health of women improves over time. Not to mention that the cost for insurance companies goes down, because women's health is better and obviously pregnancy and childbirth is quite expensive for insurance companies.

So covering birth control was a big win — the White House took a leadership role and they did a very good job with that. My hope for Obama's second term is that they'll correct the mistakes he made with abortion rights in the Affordable Care Act. I'm not holding my breath, but I think that's what he should do.

The Culture of Rape: Military Sexual Assault

Helen Benedict   January 2013

DB: *Helen Benedict is a professor of Journalism at Columbia and a novelist specializing in issues of social injustice and war. Her most recent books, the novel* Sand Queen, *and the nonfiction book,* The Lonely Soldier, *have focused on women soldiers, military sexual assault, and Iraqi refugees, and she is credited with breaking the story about the epidemic of sexual assault of military women serving in the Iraq and Afghanistan Wars.*

Helen Benedict, let's talk about violence against women in the military.

HB: I've conducted lengthy interviews with more than 40 women who served in the Iraq and Afghanistan wars, and have spoken with many more informally. Repeatedly, they say, "I have to be twice as bad as the boys. I have to work twice as hard to win the same respect. There's an assumption I can't do the job." That's the best of it, because it can also go all the way to being seen as sexual prey. There needs to be a conscious effort on the part of the military to take the epidemic of sexual assault extremely seriously, much more seriously than it does even now.

DB: *A new military study shows that 30%, nearly one in three women in the military have been sexually assaulted while serving. What does that mean?*

HB: According to the FBI, one in six women is sexually assaulted in civilian life over her lifetime. The military rate is double that, and that's only during the years a woman is serving. Imagine a crowd of military women in a room. If two thirds sit down, the remaining third have been sexually assaulted in the military while serving — mostly by people who are supposed to be their comrades-in-arms. It's deeply shocking and is of epidemic proportion.

Sexual assault is different in the military than in a civilian job because you can't escape your assailant by going home. You must live with the people who are harassing you, who sexually assaulted you, who tried to rape you, or have raped you. This can go on day in and day out, month after month, year after year. Usually the assailant is of a higher rank than his victim. He has all the weight that the chain of command in the military gives people. There is no other organization in America that gives individuals as much power over each other as the military does. Finally, everybody in the military is trained to see each other as family — brothers, sisters, fathers, and mothers. They are supposed to replace your original family and you are supposed to trust one another as you would trust beloved members of your family, only it's under circumstances of life and death. So sexual assault can feel like incest and is tremendously damaging psychologically — it's a very destructive problem in the military. It destroys lives, leads to homelessness, suicide, and other tragic consequences, not to mention undermining the morale of the victim and those who know him or her.

DB: *With a few exceptions, there has been a massive cover-up. When women try to come forward in the military, they are persecuted in extreme ways, given the structure of the military you just described.*

HB: Women do not deserve to be dismissed, smothered, shut up, laughed at, blamed, derided or punished when they report a wrongdoing. The blame for sexual assault lies with the men who commit the crime, not the women they prey upon. We can't punish women and exclude them from things because men behave badly. We need to identify sexual predators and get them out of the military. Anybody who has been convicted — while a civilian or in the military — of sexual assault or abuse of any kind should be kicked out immediately and put through the proper system of law, which the military does not currently do adequately. Rape is a repetitive, obsessive crime. A study revealed that one man in the military had about 300 victims. These people need to be tagged and dealt with properly in the military courts and gotten rid of.

DB: *Are women of higher rank less likely to be harassed?*

HB: Once they are of higher rank, yes, but many have histories of having been assaulted and harassed when they were more junior. If you are at the bottom rung, you are picked on more. Most victims are in the lowest ranks or are 21 or younger, according to the Department of Defense's Annual Report, while most assailants are older and of higher rank. But there is also a huge problem of sexual assault and harassment in the military academies that train officers.

DB: *If higher-ranking older officers are more likely to attack, in the buddy-buddy system, it's the higher ups that are supposed to investigate, so they will be covering each other's butts.*

HB: That's exactly what happens. Statistics show that in about 25% of cases, the assailant is a friend of the commander, the person who decides whether to investigate the crime. In another 25% of the cases, the commander IS the assailant. In 33% of the cases, the commander knows the assailant. This is an obviously ridiculous conflict of interest that reveals how the military perpetuates a culture of rape.

DB: *The statistics are horrifying. What happens to the whistleblowers, women who try to tell the truth about what's happening in the military?*

HB: If a woman decides to report a rape, she has two choices. She can do it anonymously, which is called restricted reporting, which means she can get help, but no investigation will be done. Or she can report it using her name, which is called unrestricted, and then the report goes up the chain of command. The guy at the top will decide whether to investigate or not. That's often where the case stops for the reasons I explained above, and where the woman often ends up being punished instead. Statistics show that a woman is more likely to be punished or expelled from the military for reporting a rape than a man is for having committed one.

Liberation Theology Haunts the New Pope
Blase Bonpane   March 2013

DB: Liberation theology holds that Jesus was committed to making society address the needs of the poor, not just giving them charity. But traditional Church leaders condemn it as Marxism in Christian trappings and have sat back as rightist regimes tortured and killed priests and nuns, a history that now haunts Pope Francis. Blase Bonpane, who served as a Maryknoll father in Guatemala until he was expelled by the Right-wing military in 1967, was among the priests and nuns who believed in the teachings of liberation theology, which held that the Catholic Church must address the plight and marginalization of the poor. Bonpane, now director of the Office of the Americas and host of "World Focus" on Pacifica Radio, expressed grave concerns about the silence of the new Pope Francis, who did not speak out publicly against the Argentine junta as it conducted a "dirty war" killing some 30,000 people, including 150 Catholic priests.

Talk to us about the new pope Francis, who has been portrayed widely as a pope of the people, who rides the bus, love sports, and has a lot of sympathy for the poor. How would you describe his background and his relationship, if any, to the Argentine "dirty wars?"

BB: I would say he is a populist conservative. We have a structural problem within the church, which is that the church has generally been subsidiary to the state and gone along with the state in its history since the Council of Nicea in 325 AD. There seems to be no exception in Argentina, where most of the reports we received during the "dirty wars" were of the clerics not speaking out, as they should have. Many of them opposed individual priests who were liberation theologians. In certain cases this led to the arrest of priests, such as Orlando Yorio and Francisco Jalic, who were kidnapped and practically killed by the junta. Afterward, Orlando Yorio spoke about the situation of surviving months of imprisonment. He felt his imprisonment was because the church said he was a liberation theologian and they didn't want to approve of him and his work in the slums of

Buenos Aires. There are many accusations, most of them in the book *The Silence*, which refers to just that, the fact that silence is complicity, and in some cases there is direct participation of clerics together with the junta.

[Junta leader Jorge Rafael] Videla could go to Holy Communion anytime and would be well received by the higher church in Argentina. This is tragic. But look at the situation in the US. Are our bishops speaking out against Guantanamo and that people are being held there? Are they speaking out on behalf of Chelsea Manning? No. There's a silence here as well. There is a history of silence. The Church supported Franco in Spain. We have the terrible situation with Pope Pius XII and his relationship to the Germans in the period of the Third Reich. It's not unusual — it's been a subservient church in many ways. The new pope has not been comfortable with liberation theology. It is possible to speak on behalf of the poor without supporting the real fundamental changes that are present with liberation theology.

DB: *You are somebody who is connected to this in many different ways, and have followed US and global policies and how they impact Central and South America — the Spanish-speaking world. Did this pope ever speak up, was he outspoken on behalf of the people? He was there during the worst parts of the slaughter. What do we know about what he did and did not do?*

BB: There are many allegations, and most of them appear in the book, *The Silence*. It looks like a case of coexistence with a horrible "dirty war." That is tragic. I don't think we should be defensive about it. We aren't in a court of law where we can say we've gone through all the evidence, but there are certainly substantial reports of not speaking out against the junta, and in some cases being aligned. One Argentine priest was so much aligned with the junta that he was arrested when they began arresting the members of the "dirty war." He had to serve time because he was working directly with the junta. In the case of the higher clergy, silence is not acceptable.

DB: *As a high official in the Catholic hierarchy in Argentina at the time that the slaughter was going on, he would certainly not be unaware of what various priests were doing, and the roles they were playing within this "dirty war." So here, complicity is also being a part of a mass murder situation. Silence is complicity, yes?*

BB: One of the priests, Father Yorio, accused Father Bergoglio of effectively handing him and his colleague over to the death squads by declining to tell the regime that he endorsed their work. In other words, he was on the margin. The other priest refused to discuss it and he moved into seclusion in a German monastery.

Bergoglio discussed this incident of two priests being handed over to the death squad in his biography by Sergio Ruben. The claim in the biography is that Bergoglio took extraordinary behind-the-scenes action to try to save these two guys after they were picked up by Jorge Videla's death squad. Whether that claim is true I don't know. This is coming from him and his biographer. He acknowledges these priests were picked up and practically killed. He doesn't accept the fact that it was because of him. At least one of the priests said it was because of him, so these things are going to haunt him for sure. The problem is the church is subservient to the state in many ways. That is true in the US. I think it's true in Argentina. It's true throughout much of the world.

The liberation church says we don't agree with the imperial church, which came about after the fourth century Council of Nicea. We agree with the anti-imperial church that defied Rome and Roman power when it was illegal to be a Christian and defied the death penalty. We are part of that primitive Christianity, and the essence is a focus on a preferential option for the poor. Step one is to focus on the needs of the poor. This applies to both the church and state. States can understand it, such as under [the late Venezuelan President] Hugo Chavez who had a preferential option for the poor. [Cuba's Fidel] Castro had a preferential option for the poor. [Bolivian President] Evo Morales sees it. [President] Jose Mujica in Uruguay. These people served time in prison, they were rebels, and their focus was a preferential option for the poor. If that applied in the United States, the first problem the President would talk about would be one million people sleeping on the streets of the United States every year. So these liberation theologians come along, who I totally support, and they say we want an authentic interpretation of this man we claim to follow, this carpenter from Nazareth. This is the conflict.

DB: *I don't want to belabor this, but this was Argentina when activists, liberation theologists, social workers, teachers, kids, families, anybody, were being disappeared, tortured, executed. It would be rather difficult to believe that he [Pope Francis] wasn't fully knowledgeable about much of what was going on. These were his parishioners, right?*

BB: That is quite correct. There are some 30,000 deceased involved here. To be unaware would be impossible — awareness simply had to be there. We saw similarities with Augusto Pinochet in Chile. He had friends in the clergy as well. Again, you can see Jorge Mario Bergoglio giving Holy Communion to Videla.

DB: *Giving Holy Communion to the mass murderer?*

BB: Yes.

DB: *So a high-level official was purging a head of state and a known mass murderer. Every human rights organization on the face of this earth nailed this down in terms of what was happening in Argentina. This is troubling.*

BB: Very much so. But this is the rule, rather than the exception — this is part of Church history. We saw it with Cardinal Spellman supporting the war in Vietnam, supporting [South

Vietnamese President] Diem, being the military vicar of the United States of America as a cardinal. This is not unusual. The unusual people are Archbishop Romero, Bishop Samuel Ruiz in Mexico. They are the exception and are worthy of being identified as the exception. Romero, in El Salvador, started off in the stereotypical fashion and then he got to the point where he said *"me converte* — the poor converted me to understanding that I was too much aligned with the wealthy and the military." They used to call that the trinity in Latin America; the military, oligarchy and the church. So we are not talking about an exceptional situation.

DB: *We know Romero was essentially shot through the face for speaking out for the poor. This is a huge bit of information that must have been shared with the church leaders in the community. Can we ever expect the new pope to say, "I was wrong, the Church was wrong, we were silent?" Here now, on his new perch he could come clean and say I am going to change history and make a difference, have a real clearing of the air. Can we expect anything like that?*

BB: I have hope, but I would be very surprised if it happened because as we have seen, there has been a tradition of cover-up to protect the image. It's like a corporation saying we must protect the image of Coca-Cola. I don't care about the image of Coca-Cola. I care about the junk that's in it. Protecting an image is not a very transparent way to conduct a Church. I think it's very important to identify the sins of the church. There have been wonderful books written about it by people such as Gary Wills, an active Catholic writer who wrote about the sins of the church in his recent book called *Why Priests?* It's important that the laity, the people who are members of the church, take it upon themselves to identify these crimes. We have a history emanating from the Council of Nicea, which evolved into the Crusades, Inquisitions, and Conquistadores. The Inquisition was present in Mexico in the 19th Century. You can go to the Museum of the Inquisition in Mexico City where Father Hidalgo, the father of the Mexican revolution, was condemned by the

Inquisition and called a Lutheran, a Jew and an atheist. We have quite a problem with history and it doesn't do any good to try to put it under the rug. It certainly didn't do any good to put the pedophilia scandal under the rug. But people like Roy Bourgeois are being told they are a scandal from the holy office. He is my colleague, a Maryknoll and father of the School of Americas Watch.

DB: *The School of the Americas is where they help train the mass murderers who did this kind of thing in Argentina, El Salvador, Guatemala, you name it.*

BB: Absolutely. They trained the people who killed Archbishop Romero. Father Bourgeois was condemned because he was told to recant his opinion that women should be priests. He said I can't recant — it's about conscience. It's the same reason Pope Benedict gave for stepping down. He said in my conscience I have to do this. People should know that conscience is the ultimate norm of morality in the Church. You can't act against your conscience. Roy couldn't act against his conscience. He wanted to see women priests and wouldn't recant, so he's called a scandal. What about the scandal of pedophilia? Are we going to talk about that?

DB: *Before I let you go, that's exactly what I want to talk to you about. Pope Francis I, from Argentina — can we expect him to be bold? Have the priests been better in Argentina than in the United States?*

BB: I think the problem is bad throughout the world. Many areas are very good at covering it up. Latin America was not a place where people were going to talk about it, so I would expect it to be equally a problem in Latin America. I hope they don't attempt to keep this quiet. This goes back to the Lateran Council of the 11th century that gave us a law of celibacy, which has a terrible history. I think that celibacy is wonderful for those who choose it. But a law of celibacy leads to many, many problems and some of them are related to this situation we've had in the US church and elsewhere.

DB: *We know that the former pope, the first one to resign in 600 or 700 years, before he became the pope, was a kind of mister cover-up. He was directing the office that was making sure everybody shut their mouths as these revelations began to unfold.*

BB: Our evidence shows that he insisted every case of pedophilia be sent to his office, the Holy Office. Then, as far as we can record and get the information, he made it clear to the bishops of the world that he wanted to avoid having these cases go to the civil authorities, or even to psychiatrists, who might feel they were bound in some cases to report these cases to the civil authorities. It is a terrible history and may be one of the reasons that he resigned. There may have been others, but that may be one of them. Now that he is pope emeritus he probably could find it easier not to engage in discussing the matter. But the problems go on and they must get dealt with.

What's wonderful is that through decision-making in the base communities, they are going ahead and following their consciences. Women are celebrating the Eucharist because of their convictions that women have been held back throughout the entire world, not only in Christianity, but in Islam, Judaism, and most religions. In most civic life they have been held back, and this is part of their liberation.

["No profit can be legitimate if it puts lives at risk." The Vatican, recently announcing that its duty-free shop and supermarket will no longer sell cigarettes. *Ed.*]

The Grim Sleeper: Serial Murders of Black Women
Margaret Prescod   March 2015

DB: *Margaret Prescod, host and producer of the radio show "Sojourner Truth," is here to talk about a new film,* Tales of the Grim Sleeper. *Margaret, you are one of my heroes. Tell us about the organization you work with, and what it does for murdered Black homeless women.*

MP: In the mid 1980s — that long ago — I founded the Coalition Fighting Black Serial Murders after the Los Angeles Police Department [LAPD] reported that 11 women were victims of a serial killer in a small area of south Los Angeles. They didn't announce it until 11 women were already dead. We then founded the Black Coalition and we've been going ever since. Why is it that across the US, and across the world, serial murders of scores of Black women in South LA since the mid-1980s are unknown? There are about 200 women missing, with perhaps as many as 100 killed. Even in LA, people didn't know about the murders. So it's good that the British filmmaker Nick Broomfield produced *Tales of the Grim Sleeper*, which exposes the story, and some of the work we've been doing in the Black Coalition Fighting Black Serial Murders for many decades. From the beginning, in the mid-80s, our theme was that every life is of value. Black women's lives matter. Here we are today with the busting out of the Black Lives Matter movement. It's a shame that we must do these campaigns to draw attention to something that both law enforcement and city officials should be concerned about and let everybody know about.

DB: *How do you deal with the police?*

MP: With great difficulty. When we first found out about the murders, a group of us went to police headquarters to ask about it and to express our concern. They literally said to us, "Why are you concerned? He's only killing hookers." It's as though the lives of women who are sex workers have no value. It's the double standard that's all too frequent in our society that some lives are worth less than others — the lives of people of color, of women. Women are criminalized as a sex worker, or criminalized when caught up in the crack epidemic. Gary Webb and others have well documented that the Reagan administration and CIA turned a blind eye to the crack epidemic that came into south LA. Because these women, according to the LAPD, were "prostitutes, some of whom were addicts," it meant we should be less concerned, because they were less deserving. But they are some mother's daughters.

We want a Department of Justice investigation into the handling of the case. Why is it that one survivor of the case now known as the Grim Sleeper — the film shows there are other survivors — was only told by the LAPD 22 years later that she was a victim of the serial killer? It also took the LAPD 22 years before they released a 911 call of somebody talking about where the body of Barbara Ware was dumped in 1987. Barbara Ware's mother found out that her daughter was a victim of a serial killer decades later on television. Law enforcement didn't even have the decency to inform these families. It's been very difficult all along in dealing with law enforcement. We'll see how this plays out. There's someone in custody now charged with ten of the murders and one attempted murder. What about all these other murders? Are they going to be properly investigated or are they going to put all the murders on this one suspect? This is a story that is heartbreaking. Children were left behind because mothers were killed.

DB: *The film highlights the devaluation of Black women's lives and the lives of sex workers. Say how the film unfolded.*

MP: This shows that you should try to do your best every day, do good work and give it all you can. The filmmaker had won awards, but I was unfamiliar with his work. He tracked me down at the offices of KPFK radio. At the Coalition, we had become so mistrustful of the media because of their disrespect to the victims that initially I didn't want to talk to him. I sent him away. Fortunately, he was persistent and he had connections with south LA through the mother of his son, whose family had done social service work in south LA. So although he was based in the UK, he had some understanding of what had happened in south LA and the impoverishment there. Nick Broomfield, a world traveler, said that LA reminds him of Johannesburg. It's like apartheid. He was on the west side of town, with the people with more resources, and they knew nothing about what was going on in the inner city of south LA and other inner city areas like east LA. It's shocking how segregated we remain. A sheriff apparently said he saw a suspect in custody as a hero for cleaning up the street.

The US Prostitutes Collective is taking this up because we know that serial murderers tend to start with women who are vulnerable, women they think are illegal. They have been taking up the case of sex workers' increased vulnerability to violence because they are illegal. Other groups have joined in support, such as All of Us or None, The Erotic Service Providers Union, Global Women's Strike, In Defense of Prostitute Women Safety Project, and there are many endorsers including the San Francisco Bayview national Black newspaper, Critical Resistance, Free Marissa Caravan, Incite! Women of Color Against Violence, and others. We're hoping to build an outrage about this. Through the Black Lives Matter movement, the nation and world are beginning to learn about the devaluation of the lives of Black men and Brown men. What is less known is the devaluation of women.

DB: *The film deals with the vulnerability to violence of women who are considered illegal. There are many women in this country who under the law are considered illegal and that makes them even more vulnerable, because law enforcement is the enemy — as is the rapist on the street — so they don't know which way to turn. Many Brown women in this situation are extremely vulnerable, particularly in LA.*

MP: That's right. Recently there were pockets of serial murders of Latina sex workers in Orange County, California. There are pockets of Black women being killed in Cleveland, Ohio and Fresno, California. It's like there's certain kinds of woman who it's OK to hunt down, and a complacency — sometimes even among friends in the left — because they say it's a moral issue, maybe they were on drugs, maybe they were sex workers. We're saying their lives are of value. Remember the term the lumpen proletariat? The reality is that poverty, and deep poverty, has widened in our community. The nation doesn't want to talk about poverty anymore — they go on about income inequality. A lot of these women who were killed were impoverished women, homeless women. They are considered throwaway people. That gets to the heart of the lumpen proletariat. Those of us who want to "wear the mantle of respectability" and distance ourselves from women who are vulnerable — whether they are sex workers, on drugs, Black or Brown — must get past that. When they are vulnerable, all of us are vulnerable. What kind of message does that send to the nation, the world, or any maniac who is out there ready to do harm? Law enforcement must clean up their attitude and be held accountable for what happened.

Caitlyn Jenner and the Hijacking of Transliberation

Mattilda Bernstein Sycamore   June 2015

DB: *Described as startlingly bold and provocative by the late Howard Zinn, a cross between Tinkerbell and a honky Malcolm X, with a queer agenda — a gender plucking tower of pure pulsing purple fabulous — Mattilda Bernstein Sycamore is most recently the author of* A Memoir: The End of San Francisco, *which won her the 2014 Lambda Literary Award. Mattilda Bernstein Sycamore, what do you think about Caitlyn Jenner's changeover and the public response to it?*

MS: To start with, the amount of resources spent on the *Vanity Fair* cover story about Caitlyn Jenner and the related publicity alone, is more money than many trans women will see in their entire lives. Across the country, trans women are criminalized, brutalized, harassed, beaten and murdered on a daily basis with the full cooperation of the legal system. I think all the publicity about Caitlyn Jenner takes away from the issues that actually matter to most trans people, and from a more systemic analysis, which says that everyone deserves gender, sexual, social and political self-determination. Other crucial issues are access to basic needs like housing and health care, and an end to criminalization and mass incarceration. All over the country, including the Bay Area, trans women are routinely arrested on the streets for congregating in public. All the hoopla around Caitlyn Jenner's gender transition is a celebration of someone who is a wealthy celebrity and a conservative Republican. I'm worried that all this attention is adding a more conservative element to the trans movement rather than a broader focus on liberation.

DB: *Name some of the people you might choose to represent you in this community, state and country.*

MS: Many people point to Caitlyn Jenner as a trans elder. In the Bay Area there is a wonderful person, Miss Major Griffin-Gracy, who is the Executive Director of the Transgender, Gender Variant, Intersex Justice Project. She was active in the Stonewall rebellion, participated from inside prison in the Attica prison riot, and has continued her activism for over 40 or 50 years. We need to look to people like that who are still fighting for people on the margins. We could talk about CeCe McDonald, a young trans woman who was attacked by racist, homophobic, transphobic people in Minneapolis. She fought for her life and was imprisoned for that. We need to be talking about people who are on the margins, who are fighting for a more liberatory politics.

DB: *What about Laverne Cox and* Orange is the New Black? *Is that moving some walls?*

MS: Laverne Cox is great because she always manages to bring the focus away from herself. When there's an article about her, it's not only about her. She makes the connections and talks about the criminalization of Black trans women and trans women of color across the country. She talks about broader social struggles, and that isn't happening with Caitlyn Jenner. With her, it's the exact opposite. A few days ago, she tweeted that she spent a few days with the Human Rights Campaign [HRC], the largest LGBT lobbying organization. Every year the HRC gives an equality index, where they give 100% ratings to companies like British Petroleum, Exxon, Morgan Stanley. So they are giving awards to the worst companies in the world. I'm worried that all the attention on Caitlyn Jenner is going to end up as another screen for continuing some of the violence that the mainstream gay movement now enacts. That's my worry. Another example is Jennifer Pritzker, a member of a family that you've done a lot of reporting on, who is considered the first trans billionaire. She is single-handedly responsible for bankrolling the campaign for trans inclusion in the US military. She gave about $2 million to the Palm Center, and then suddenly this issue became a centerpiece of analysis in the media — out of nowhere.

DB: *You are talking about the cousin of the current US Secretary of Commerce. She's the heir to the Hyatt Regency.*

MS: Yes. She obviously has an extremely conservative agenda and has made this her particular issue. There are so many trans women in this country who are living in dire poverty, with no access to basic resources. Instead of talking about that, Jennifer Pritzker's agenda and the agenda of organizations like the HRC, is about allowing trans people to serve openly in the US military — go abroad, kill people and get away with it. I'm worried that when we have conservative celebrities like Caitlyn Jenner and they become so-called movement spokespersons, their priorities become the priorities of what is considered a movement. One of the reasons that gay marriage became so central to so-called LGBT organizing is because rich celebrities want tax and inheritance breaks, and that became the movement issue instead of gender, sexual, social, and political liberation for everyone.

DB: *You recently wrote that HBO's TV show* Looking *is an "advertisement for gentrified San Francisco masquerading as a portrait of contemporary gay life."*

MS: *Looking* was an HBO show that was celebrated across the country as providing an authentic look into San Francisco, the gay Mecca. But what's the biggest issue in San Francisco — gentrification.

DB: *Yes, I just had to move as a result.*

MS: Here's a series based in San Francisco, shot almost entirely in San Francisco, but it's essentially a tourist brochure that acts like displacement isn't happening at all — it's basically an advertising campaign with bodies as billboards. In this day and age, when the portrayal of gay lives is hardly more threatening than a trip to Pottery Barn, *Looking* makes sure that no hint of a radical queer alternative slips through the cracks in the glaze, even in the city where these alternatives are still most visible.

There's no mention of the violence of gay powerbrokers in San Francisco, who are more than happy to push aside queer and trans youth, elders, HIV-positive people without money, homeless queers, drug addicts, disabled queers, people of color, migrants from smaller towns and other countries, and anyone else unable or unwilling to conform to narrow notions of white middle-class respectability. The show prefers to focus on pop-up restaurants and shallow conversations about beaches and bodies and cock size, while reveling in standard beauty myth charades, rather than offering anything even hinting at a critical analysis. Luckily, the show was cancelled after two seasons, so we don't have to endure any more of that particular whitewashed version of what it is to be gay — advertising displacement as a consumer choice.

I tend to think of LGBT as an acronym that means lesbian and gay, throw out bisexual and throw in trans as a bit of window dressing. Trans people have always been excluded from institutions of power within LGBT communities. There's just as much transphobia within gay and lesbian cultures as there is in dominant straight cultures. It plays out differently, but I think there's as much of an exclusionary agenda.

For me, the policing of language never works. We need to talk about the actual structural violence, not the language. Personally, I'm a big fan of reclaimed speech. People have a right to reclaim the words that are used against them. When people start talking about who can say what, it ends up being that no one can say anything. We need to talk about transphobia, misogyny and racism in drag culture, which is very rampant. Just because people don't use certain words, it doesn't mean they aren't transphobic, misogynist or racist. We need to focus on challenging the structural issues, rather than word choices.

Whenever there is a "movement" that centers around the people with the most privilege, the same kinds of violence that are enacted on a daily basis outside of LGBT worlds are going to be played out. San Francisco is the perfect example, where gay people have become part of the power structure. That is the dream of the gay movement. We can look and see what gay people do when they access that power. What do gay political consultants do when they engineer the election of anti-poor, pro-development candidates over and over again? What does the so-called LGBT Center do when it hires police to serve at the front desk, keeps bathrooms segregated by outdated gender norms, and basically becomes nothing more than a meeting space for business people and recovery groups? What happens when gay people are arresting homeless queer youth for getting in the way of happy hour? Whenever the privilege is allowed to exist without being challenged structurally and on a daily basis, the same kind of violence is going to play out over and over again.

DB: *There have been some struggles with feminists about trans inclusion.*

MS: One of the beautiful things about the trans movement for me is challenging the notion that there is no one way to be a woman or a man, etc. — exploding these categories and trying to create something else from the ruins. Creating multiple categories with gender, sexual, social and political fluidity. It's the possibility of using gender as a starting point for challenging all the violence in the world — identity as a starting point rather than identity as an end point. Look at the mainstream gay movement, and increasingly, unfortunately, there's a trans movement that is mimicking the worst mistakes of the gay movement. Identity is offered as an end point rather than as a starting point. That's how you can see trans inclusion in the US military rather than the abolition of the US military as a centerpiece to the trans struggle.

Yes, there are some backward people who describe themselves as feminist, and to them this means subscribing to an outdated idea of what it means to be a woman, based on a biological purity test — to me, this is not feminist. Feminism should be about challenging power, not just accessing it, creating more space for complicated identities in all of their eccentricities and multi-faceted possibilities for transformation, not policing the borders. This is where the real possibility lies.

Raising Hell Against Patriarchy

Alex Petersburg   June 2015

DB: *Today the Supreme Court stayed the draconian Texas anti-abortion decision, but the right to abortion remains under attack. Alex Petersberg is a national abortion rights activist with Stop Patriarchy. Alex, tell us about this ruling.*

AP: In 2013, a package of anti-abortion legislation was passed. The four laws were all specifically designed to shut down clinics by imposing medically unnecessary requirements and then putting doctors in difficult positions. Probably the most nationally contested provision is the ambulatory surgical center law. Abortion is a simple and safe outpatient procedure but now only abortion clinics must outfit themselves like mini emergency rooms. These are $3 million renovations, which by design, require clinics across the country to close due to the exorbitant cost. Dozens have closed across the country, and it has the potential to close about half the clinics in Texas.

DB: *Why did you put your body on the line and get arrested?*

AP: Over the last couple of years there have been a historical number of restrictions against abortion — over 300 — more than in the entire decade before 2009. There is a rapidly escalating assault on this basic right. Last year, Texas Governor Rick Perry spoke on behalf of the anti-abortion groups, saying that his goal was to make Texas an abortion-free state. These people have a very specific goal for women in mind. The veil is about babies and life, but when you understand that 50,000 women die every year from illegal, unsafe abortions, you must take a step back and ask — How could a movement that opposes birth control and abortion be about anything other than establishing a particular role for women? Dennis, as you often bring to light, this movement is lead by terrorists, fascists, and fanatics who have a real beef with the fact that women have won any kind of independence in society at all, and they want to see that go backwards. They believe the only role in life for women is to be a mother, and that there's something wrong with her if she chooses not to be.

DB: *I wrote a book about Henry Hyde, who set the tone with his law that is still being used to brutalize these women. When you take them on, you get into their cross hairs as somebody they want to get rid of. They don't mess around.*

AP: It's true. There's a real need at this moment not to pander to that side or cede the moral high ground, even though they do it in the name of religion and babies. We need to step out in this emergency and demand that women are entitled to unrestricted abortion, anytime we need it, no questions asked, and without guilt or shame. There's nothing wrong with abortion, fetuses are not babies, and unless we want a future where women are treated as property, it's on us to stand up.

DB: *The Supreme Court stayed the worst of the law, which would have closed some clinics today, but this is a tight rope, isn't it?*

AP: While I plan on fighting this battle in perpetuity, we also aim to win it, and change the terms society-wide on how people think about abortion — when people consider women to be human beings and not objects, accessories, or baby makers. There's lots of evidence that we should not rely on politicians. With six states that have only one abortion clinic, this is a national issue. People across the country need to raise hell. Tomorrow, as part of a national day of protest, in San Francisco we'll be going to the home office of Archbishop Salvatore Cordileone who writes pro-life legislation. He has taken it upon himself to be the champion against women, a champion of old school, dark ages, and patriarchy. The people and institutions that are leading these attacks need to be confronted — challenged by people in no uncertain terms.

Selling Out the "Comfort Women," Again

Phyllis Kim & KJ Noh   December 2015

DB: *The corporate press announced that there was a major landmark deal between Japan and South Korea in which Japan apologized in a substantive way for the incredible tragedy of what's known as the "comfort women," the kidnapping of hundreds of thousands of women by the Japanese in a time of war. We are joined by Phyllis Kim, Director of the Korean American Forum of California, and KJ Noh, special correspondent. Phyllis Kim, you disagree that this is a landmark agreement ending the long running dispute. You don't think this is a real apology?*

PK: KAFC, the Korean-American Forum of California, the organization I work with, denounced the agreement that came from a meeting between the Korean and Japanese foreign ministers. The victims immediately rejected the agreement. If the two governments wanted to actually resolve the issue they should have listened to the victims. These victims didn't just sit and wait around for some kind of magic to happen. They have been active for the past 25 years, actively demanding an official government apology and legal reparations from the government of Japan, which *they did not get*. Including the victims' voices in any negotiations was extremely important, but that did not happen.

In addition, there were victims from eleven different countries. South Korea is just one of the eleven countries. Some estimate that as many as 400,000 women were victimized by the institutionalized system of sexual slavery from 1932 until the end of WWII. These victims are scattered among these eleven countries, including South and North Korea, China, Taiwan, Japan, Indonesia, Malaysia, the Philippines, Vietnam, East Timor, and some Dutch women. These victims deserve to be part of any negotiation or settlement with the Japanese government, but the women outside South Korea were completely excluded from these negotiations.

Another issue is that the heartfelt apology offered by Prime Minister Abe sounds sincere on paper, but the reasons the victims were not able to accept the previous apology was because the Japanese government has been relentlessly working to downplay, whitewash, and eradicate any responsibility the government of Japan bears for these war crimes.

There have been attempts to revise the Kono statement [the pro-forma apology issued by Chief Cabinet Secretary Yohei Kono in 1993] and to deny the Murayama statement [the statement of apology by the Japanese Prime minister in 1995]. Even in the US, there was an attempt to lobby against passage of House Resolution 121 [the House Resolution recognizing the facts of the military sexual slavery and urging Japan to make amends] in 2007. There were numerous attempts and lobbies against installation of "comfort women" memorials in the US. Japanese diplomats raised objections against McGraw Hill, the textbook publisher, for including a passage about comfort women in its history textbook.

Also, if the Japanese government is sincere about its will to resolve this issue once and for all, there needs to be an official government apology, which means the apology needs to be approved by the Japanese cabinet, which never happened. No previous apologies were ratified by the Japanese cabinet, which makes them unofficial, private statements. Those are the problems we see from the agreement.

DB: *KJ, what is your response to Ms. Kim?*

KJ: I absolutely agree with her. The main point is that the comfort women themselves and the organizations involved have denounced the agreement as a sham and a betrayal. It is a sham and betrayal because the women have been excluded. Their essential demands for an official state apology with legal force have not been listened to. It irrevocably commits the Korean government to silence going forward — it can no longer criticize the Japanese government. It's very clear the Abe government has not changed its ways, message, actions, or ideology. This is a continuation of the unequal, undemocratic, unpopular treaties pushed by US-influenced or US-manipulated Right-wing South Korean governments in the manner of what Park Chung Hee did in 1965. As dictator of South Korea, he signed a normalization treaty with Japan under pressure from Walt Rostow, the National Security Advisor of the Kennedy/Johnson administration. This agreement relinquished any future claims for reparation from Japan. It was widely opposed by the people. Park Chung Hee had to declare martial law in order to squelch opposition. All this ties back into this idea that South Korea, Japan and the US have to create a trilateral security collaboration, which forms the basis of an anti-communist or anti-Chinese bulwark in East Asia. This relates to the Pacific Pivot, and creating a military and political bloc against China.

DB: *This is the "why now?"*

KJ: Yes, this explains the "why now?" It's to create military and political coordination to contain China in the Pacific.

DB: *Now we are going to hear a survivor of this brutal program. KJ, can you tell us about who we are going to hear from?*

KJ: This is Halmoni, grandmother Yong Soo Lee, who was a comfort woman kidnapped — taken by the Japanese — and forced into sexual slavery. [Grandmother is a title of honor; the majority of these women were unable to have children, due to sexual trauma.] She's currently 88 years old and has spent most of the past 23 years trying to get the Japanese government to render a formal apology. At one point she attempted to kill herself in front of the Japanese embassy in order that they would listen to her. She believes that she has to do this work for all the women who did not survive — 75% of all the comfort women died during their enslavement, a higher rate of death than frontline combat troops — as well as for all the women over the world who suffer from sexual trafficking and abuse. We did this interview with her in Berkeley when she traveled 10,000 miles to the US, to ask the San Francisco Board of Supervisors to pass a resolution creating a "comfort women" memorial in San Francisco.

DB: *Which they did. Let's listen to her.*

YSL: When I tell my story to people it's like I am talking to my mom about what happened to me, things that happened to me. So it makes me cry...

For 23 years we have been demonstrating in front of the Japanese embassy, rain or snow. I sometimes wonder, why do we have to keep doing this? We are human beings. We are not animals roaming around the streets. When we started, I was still young. Now I am old, and it makes me wonder why I keep doing this.

The reason is that it was the difficult times our people went through, because of the war Japan started. Why were Korea's daughters taken away and abused?

When I go to Japan I tell them I am not a "comfort woman." I am Yong Soo Lee. That is the name my parents gave me. I tell them it was you, the Japanese, who took us away, took away our names, and made us into the "comfort women," so you have to take responsibility for it.

When they call us the "comfort women," it means we volunteered to go and give "comfort" to the soldiers. But Japanese authorities have already confessed that it was the Japanese government that created the system of comfort stations. Because it was you, Japan, that made us the "comfort women," you must be responsible and officially apologize and make legal reparations. Be responsible. That is what I am saying.

DB: *Why did you feel it was important to come to San Francisco now, at 88 years old?*

YSL: The victims have been shouting in front of the Japanese embassy in Seoul for 23 years. It was for them to listen. I did that as a *living witness* to this history.

We kept shouting, for 23 years, and all we were demanding was an official apology and legal reparations. If you heard the same thing for 23 years, you would have heard, even if you were deaf. You would have seen, even if you were blind. However the Japanese government hasn't done anything for 23 years. They are trying to deny history, saying nonsense, whitewashing, making history-distorting statements that don't make sense.

I started out as a victim. But now, as a woman human rights activist, I decided to go around the world and talk to the people in order to resolve this problem. I came to San Francisco because I heard that good people there are trying to build a memorial. I also heard that Japan is paying lobbyists in order to block the effort. That doesn't make sense, so I came here to express my love and respect for the people of San Francisco and to plead with the people of San Francisco to please erect the memorial, as an activist who works for women's rights around the world.

DB: *Is part of your message to communicate to young people what you've been through?*

YSL: I always emphasize my story to the students, and especially the younger people, because the younger people are our future and are going to protect the country and society. That's why I believe the younger people are so important. But the Japanese government is spending so much money to sabotage the plans to establish monuments in the US. That is very low, very bad behavior. They must be straightforward and accept responsibility. That is the only way they will regain their honor. I want to tell them to change their mind and stop harassing the good, respectful people in San Francisco and cooperate with their plan to erect the monument. More importantly, teach and tell the young people in their own country as well as the young people here, that what they did was wrong and they should work together to resolve this.

DB: *Phyllis Kim, can you respond and what comes next?*

PK: I have heard her testimony before, because I help the comfort women as an interpreter whenever they make trips to the US. It breaks my heart at the same time; it makes me feel embarrassed. Now she's 89, after her birthday on December 13. These women are trying so hard, and I can't even begin to imagine how difficult it must be for them to talk about the horrendous experiences they had to go through at their tender ages. She nonetheless stood up and made up her mind to demand what is right and what is justice — to recover their dignity. She told me she does this not only for herself but also for the grandmas who have passed away without seeing justice. She always talks about the young generation, and that the same tragedy should never be repeated in their generation. That is the lesson I take away from meeting with this incredible woman. It is heartbreaking that this so-called groundbreaking agreement failed to include the voices of these women who are incredible victims and incredible human rights activists. I hope that we keep an eye on what is going to happen next and how both governments will follow through on whatever has been agreed upon in the agreement. The major project now is education.

DB: *The activism continues. KJ, what is a real apology? What is real remorse for this extraordinary suffering?*

KJ: The grandmothers themselves have put it out clearly. They want full acknowledgement of the military sexual slavery that was coordinated and implemented by the imperial army and the government. They want a thorough and complete investigation. They want a formal apology in front of the National Assembly because if it's not done in front of the National Assembly, it doesn't have any legal or political force. It's just a nice statement. They want legal and full reparations to all victims. They want prosecution of the criminals responsible for the crime. They want full and ongoing education. They want the building of memorials in museums. This agreement stipulates that memorials should be dismantled.

DB: *The agreement says the memorials should be dismantled? They want forgetting?*

KJ: In this agreement, they asked that the "comfort woman" memorial in front of the Japanese embassy, on Korean soil, be removed. They said not one word about education. There is nothing to indicate this will be a legal apology. The reparations are being given indirectly, put into a pool, rather than coming directly from the Japanese government. These are all ways of avoiding official responsibility. And finally, what makes this the most astounding "apology," is that it comes with a *gag order.* I have never heard of an official acknowledgement of wrongdoing coming with a gag order. This one does. The Korean government will shut up once and for all when this agreement is enforced. War crimes and crimes against humanity do not come with a statute of limitations, nor do they come with a mandate of silence. But that is what the Korean government has agreed to. That is an unimaginable breach of ethics and sovereignty.

DB: *Phyllis Kim, what would you like to add?*

PK: We need to keep our eyes open and support those incredible victims. I appreciate the efforts made by the people in the San Francisco Bay Area to erect a "comfort women" monument. Let's keep working together. I can be reached at KAFCinfo@gmail.com.

Migration, Deportation, and US-Latino Culture

Educating and Organizing in Arizona

Dolores Huerta   January 2011

DB: *We are about to hear from legendary union organizer, co-founder of the United Farm Workers, Dolores Huerta. You've helped organize in Tucson. Talk about the shooting in Tucson last Saturday.*

[On January 8, 2011, US Representative Gabrielle Giffords was shot by Jared Lee Loughner in a mass shooting in Tucson where she was holding a constituent meeting. Eighteen others were shot. Six died, including a Federal Judge. *Ed.]*

DH: Tucson actually is a bright spot in Arizona. Congressman Grijalva is the co-chair of the Progressive Caucus. In Tucson we had Chicano Studies and Ethnic Studies in the grammar schools as well as the high schools. This is why Sarah Palin targeted the Tucson area congressional districts, which included Gabrielle Giffords.

[Sarah Palin's political action committee put out maps of Giffords' district with pictures of cross hairs on it. *Ed.]*

This person said he wanted to kill Gabrielle. The federal judge [Chief Judge John McCarthy Roll, District of Arizona] who was killed had received much hate mail because of his decision against parts of the enforcement of 1070 — the racial profiling law that passed in Arizona. The shootings in Tucson reflect the need for gun control but the focus on gun control has taken the focus away from the hate speech.

DB: *On January first a new law went into effect that bans teaching Mexican-American studies in the public school system. Tom Horne, former Superintendent of Schools and now State Attorney General, said he had complaints about this program being anti-American. He's also been furious about something you said several years back.*

249

DH: He objected to my making a speech at the high school in Tucson, where two high schools were brought together after the walkouts to oppose the Sensenbrenner Bill, which would have made people eligible for jail or prison if they helped somebody who was undocumented. The bill was defeated in the Senate after millions of people marched all over the country. The students in the Tucson school district walked out.

I also spoke about gay rights, although there was some objection to this. But why shouldn't I talk to high school students about human rights for people who are gay, lesbian and transgender? Then the state legislature passed a bill to try and remove the teacher, principal and other people in Tucson who brought me there to speak.

Ethnic Studies should be required at the grammar school level because it's how we're able to start fighting against discrimination. When a student learns about the history of discrimination against people of color in this country, and in the world, they can change their minds. They need to understand how it started with slavery, how many people have suffered and been killed because they just happened to be people of color. By banning Ethnic Studies or African American studies in Arizona they're perpetuating the racism that leads up to something like the shooting of Gabrielle Giffords and the others.

DB: *So Mr. Tom Horne, then Superintendent of Schools, took your reaching out to high school students, encouraging them to participate in the political process — like the young girl who got killed Saturday — and he turned that into you encouraging hate and violations of the constitution. You become a hater. He's now the Attorney General, the chief law enforcement official of Arizona.*

DH: Yes, everything in Arizona now is upside down and it's tragic. As we approach Dr. King's birthday, we see how hatred is spewed upon undocumented people, against Latinos. Several immigrants have been murdered, just like the lynchings in the South, and they still continue against African Americans.

It begins with hate talk and ignorance. The corporate media should refocus their attention about the shootings in Tucson and say, "Where did this young man form these ideas of hatred in the first place?" Gabrielle Giffords is also Jewish, and a lot of his rantings and ravings were against Jewish people, like they were first in line along with African Americans as targets of violence and discrimination.

DB: *There was a young man shot dead at the border a few days before the shooting of the congresswoman and the killing of the federal judge, but not much was said about that.*

DH: People rarely ask, "Why do people come here?" The Free Trade Agreements have displaced millions of people in Mexico. Immigrants try to cross borders to survive, whether it is from Mexico to the US, from Africa to Europe, or the Middle East to Europe.

We arrest the victims of our past and present economic policies. We have boats to travel oceans and send materials from here to Asia, where they are made into clothes and sent back to us to buy. Materials and capital can cross borders, jillions of dollars can cross borders, but don't let an immigrant cross a border to try to find work to feed their family because that person is a criminal in the eyes of the campaign against immigrants.

DB: *The federal judge who was killed, Judge Roll, approved the lawsuit brought by immigrants against John Barnett. This judge was in the middle of very controversial court cases about immigrant rights. Even though the congresswoman wasn't radical, she opposed SB 1070.*

DH: We have a horrible history of assassination: Gabrielle Giffords, President Kennedy, Bobby Kennedy, and leaders like Dr. King and Malcolm X. As Dr. King said, we must have a revolution of our values of peace and justice. To create any kind of peace and justice, people need to know about the histories of other peoples. Every child should know that the land that we are sitting on here in the US belonged to Native Americans. Now they have the highest infant mortality, due to their poverty.

Howard Zinn's *A People's History of the United States* needs to be taught in every school so that our Anglo children can understand history — so they can see where we're coming from. And our children of color need to know their history so that they can understand discrimination, and what their contributions have been to this country, so they can get the self-esteem to motivate them to participate in society and stay in school.

We need to expand ethnic studies to the grammar school level. We'll talk about Christopher Columbus, the genocide of the Indigenous Peoples of the Caribbean, the contributions of our Asian communities — the building of the railroads and tilling our fields. The Japanese Americans and the Mexicans — always contributing, and of course our African Americans who have always been doing the work. African slaves and their descendants built the White House and the Congress. People need to know this.

DB: *In founding the United Farm Workers with Cesar Chavez you faced a gauntlet of violence. In the Gandhian tradition, you all thought about how to deal with violence and fear.*

DH: Yes, and I, like many activists, am receiving lots of hate mail, both at my office and even on my cell phone. They managed to get hold of my e-mail and I'm getting very racist messages and...

DB: *You are getting racist and hate messages now?*

DH: Yes.

DB: *Where do we go from here?*

DH: We must commit ourselves to a campaign. During the sixties we had the Freedom Schools. In Arizona they've got to start Freedom Schools and violate the law — teach Ethnic Studies. I'll go to Arizona, do another lecture, get arrested, and we can appeal up to the Supreme Court based on First Amendment rights.

DB: *The education banned in Tucson was significant in keeping kids in school and encouraging them to go to college.*

DH: California banned bilingual education when a big wave of immigrants came into the country after the 1986 legalization bill passed, the IRCA. Because they got rid of bilingual education, many of our children are not proficient in the English language, so have a hard time learning, causing an enormous dropout rate.

We need to take over the school boards. Let's put in Ethnic Studies, Peace Studies, and Women's Studies. In Tucson, their Ethnic Studies started at the grammar school level.

DB: *Cesar Chavez, you, Martin Luther King, Mahatma Gandhi — it was about nonviolent civil disobedience. You are still a firm believer in non-violence?*

DH: Absolutely, and also in organizing. The Dolores Huerta Foundation raises money, trains organizers, and sends them into communities to get people organized to take on their issues and solve them. We form a volunteer army.

Banning Books in Tucson

Dr. Carlos Muñoz   January 2012

DB: *Outrage and disgust continue to build over the decision by the Tucson, Arizona Unified School District to ban books by Chicano and Native American authors. The punitive action follows on the heels of the decision by state politicians to shut down Tucson's highly effective Ethnic Studies Program that focused on Mexican-American life and culture. Over 60 percent of the students in Tucson are of Mexican descent, and the program was widely regarded as an educational success. However, the program drew the ire of some Arizona whites who were offended by lessons about white oppression of Chicanos and Native Americans.*

Among the banned books are: Pedagogy of the Oppressed by Paulo Freire, Occupied America: A History of Chicanos by Rodolfo Acuña, 500 Years of Chicano History in Pictures edited by Elizabeth "Betita" Martinez, Chicano! The History of the Mexican Civil Rights Movement by Arturo Rosales, Critical Race Theory by Richard Delgado, and books by Native American writers such as Leslie Marmon Silko, Buffy Sainte-Marie, and Winona LaDuke. According to various news reports and interviews with teachers directly affected by the book ban, the banned books were seized from classrooms right in front of students. The teachers were given a couple of days to figure out what to teach in place of the Mexican Ethnic Studies curriculum. Some students in these classes were in tears as the books were packed up and shipped off to a book depository.

Dr. Carlos Muñoz, one of the key pioneers in Ethnic Studies and Chicano Studies in the country was the founding chair of the first Chicano Studies Department in the nation at the California State University at Los Angeles in 1968, and the founding chair of the National Association of Chicana and Chicano Studies.

Dr. Munoz, it's good to have you with us, although it's a terrible situation, which, incredibly, started to unfold on Martin Luther King's birthday celebration. What was your initial response to what happened here?

254

CM: I don't have the words to express my anger at what's taken place in Tucson, Arizona. It's simply unbelievable. Never did I expect this — at this point in history, after over 40 years of scholarship generated, published and taught in universities across this country, specifically on the Chicano experience in the United States.

Scholars of Mexican-American background and other scholars of color have collectively made a profound, profound contribution to the body of knowledge of people of color in this country — and have rectified and documented a history that speaks the truth of what this country has been historically as an empire — a promoter of imperialism throughout the world, a racist white-supremacist nation, witnessed by the so-called Founding Fathers who were in many cases slave owners. This kind of truth doesn't speak well to what's going on in Arizona.

I think the people who are responsible for this particular tragedy in public education are either ignorant and never attended a university, were never educated, and/or are members of the Tea Party or some other extreme racist organization that is promoting anti-Mexican racist hysteria. What we see here is a situation where Right-wingers have collectively organized and made this an issue. A manifestation of the perceived threat, of what I call the "Brown invasion," has been encapsulated by a lot of the Right-wing politicians in this country. The increasing of what I call a demographic revolution that we are witnessing now has become a threat to many people in power, especially in Arizona. They are the ones who started this process of criminalizing Mexican undocumented workers and have set the tone for other states to follow under the tutelage of Right-wing political folks. I think it needs to be protested. People have to take to the streets, as they are doing in Tucson. It is an issue that has become very, very critical and deserves the support of all Americans, regardless of race or ethnic backgrounds. It is ridiculous.

DB: *Teachers and students say it was an incredibly effective program in which students who were dropping out before, were staying in school and going on to higher education. Talk about why it's so important for these students and the school system, which is 61 percent Mexican-American?*

CM: I think in any process of education, if you are a student and don't hear about people like yourself in the making of history in this nation, you are bound to feel somewhat inferior. I went through that when I was a kid — my God, it's all white history, and all the heroes were white. You never hear about the good things that were done by folks of color in our society, in the building of this nation. Prior to the emergence of Ethnic Studies and Chicano Studies in the universities, there were no books about the Chicano experience. The consequence of that, as I experienced, was an inferiority complex. All we hear about Mexicans, for example, is that they are criminals and drunkards, and the women are whores. There are racist, negative stereotypes promoted in the movies, television and newspapers. The consequence is what I call the colonization of the mind, where young people of Mexican descent were pushed into thinking they were inferior and their culture was inferior.

What's happened in Tucson has been a remarkable process of deep colonization, where public school issues were taken on by teachers, staff members, and the school district. They had the courage to develop a program of Mexican-American studies — the only one in the country at the public school level. This was a remarkable feat that ought to be celebrated and set up as an example of what other public school systems, including those in California, ought to pursue. The consequences have been remarkable. In Tucson, the Mexican-American studies program has resulted in a radical turnabout of young people taking pride, becoming proud of their heritage, proud that they learned they come from ancestors who made profound contributions to civilizations throughout the Americas. That fact alone is incredible — it's an intangible contribution to boosting the feeling of being worthy as human beings. That kind of feeling is very, very important to have in order for young people to succeed in life, beyond public school. I think what has been done in Arizona by these white politicians has been an effort to return to the days of the 1950s, previous to the Chicano movement and other civil rights movements in this country, to try to "Americanize" and re-colonize the minds of young people in the State of Arizona.

DB: *Banning this program in Tucson is almost like banning the speaking of Spanish in Mexico. It's Mexico, but called the United States. The decision was made for the teachers to box the books in front of the students. Kids were crying. When I was in Tucson broadcasting, one young student told me she was thinking about suicide and had once tried to take her own life until she got into a program like this and began to feel alive.*

CM: This is an example of what I was referring to. When young people are awakened by educators about who they are, where they come from, and why it's a source of pride — or should be a source of pride — it's incredible. You cannot put value on that kind of influential discovery and awakening of a young mind. It makes a world of difference to a young person to find meaning in their lives that carries them forth towards a positive direction in society. They become good citizens and critical-thinking people who are going to make contributions to the betterment of the society as a whole.

DB: *One gets the strong feeling they don't want these students to succeed because the program was so successful. The percentage of students who ended up going to college as a result of this kind of study was overwhelming. One has to think this is an attempt to cripple, undermine and keep these kids down, rather than to cheerlead that they are getting better and succeeding. It's racism at the core.*

CM: I wholeheartedly agree. With regards to the demographics, Arizona has become even more "Mexican" than ever. They envision that out of all these young people developing a critical thinking capacity and proud identity, some are going to become the future politicians of Arizona, and that's a scary thing for these guys. My God, we'll not only have undocumented workers who are poor and a cheap labor source, we're going to have people getting into powerful positions in the future who are going to take away what belongs to "us." I think that's the bottom line here. They want to put a stop to this process of producing young leaders who are going to speak truth to power, and are going to make a difference in the future in terms of turning the tide against racism and other things that are negative in Arizona for Mexican people as a whole.

DB: *Some of the people who have been banned are labeling this as a kind of inquisition. I thought that was maybe an overstatement, but now I'm thinking it's an understatement. Imagine, books that were banned include* The Pedagogy of the Oppressed *by Paulo Freire and* Occupied America, a History of Chicanos *by Rodolfo Acuña, a good friend of yours. We had both of you on the show not too long ago. Talk about what these white people might be afraid of that's inside these beautiful books.*

CM: They are afraid of the truth. The truth hurts, such as in the scholarship of Rodolfo Acuña's incredible path-breaking book. He was the first one to put out a true history of America, documenting beyond the shadow of a doubt, the nature of our society and how Mexican-Americans in particular have struggled for social justice throughout the history of this country. They have problems with it because Rody Acuña speaks the truth, as do all scholars.

Shakespeare speaks the truth. Even Shakespeare, an English white guy, had the audacity for his time to speak truth to power of the British Empire, and put out the issue of colonization and oppression. Even there they couldn't tolerate that particular scholarship.

An ideological struggle is going on, a cultural war is happening in Arizona between those who espouse the racist framework of analysis that white Eurocentrics thought should be predominant in public education, and those of us who have struggled against that and created a teaching of a more truthful history of our society, and who have gone out of our way collectively to push forward a more visionary process of education that is inclusive of not just Mexican-Americans, but all people.

We don't do what we are accused of doing — being divisive and un-American. To the contrary, we have been most American by continuing a process of creativity and intellectual thought that our ancestors started here in the Americas long before the white man arrived to conquer and engage in conquest. Our ancestors generated civilizations way back when, and our people as a whole have completed that process. We are remarkable because of what we represent as a people — not just being Indigenous Peoples, but also inclusive of other dimensions of reality that we represent, as a multi-racial, multi-ethnic, multi-cultural people in our society. These people don't want to acknowledge that — it's scary to them. Rightly so. It should be scary to them. That's the whole issue now.

DB: *Dr. Muñoz, I don't see your book,* Youth, Identity, Power, the Chicano Movement *on the list yet, but I guess it's going to become a kind of a diploma that you put on your wall along with the other ones that you have. "I was banned in Tucson and I'm proud of it."*

CM: I tell people that I think all these banned books represent quite an honorable group of people. It's incredible. I feel kind of ...

DB: *...left out?*

CM: I want the honor of being identified by this Right-wing. In the meantime, I'm very proud of all these folks in Arizona, how they have gone to bat and supported the defense of Mexican-American studies in Tucson.

DB: *It is troubling that this comes during the new civil rights movement for the rights of migrant workers, immigrant workers — the workers who do the hardest work in this country that we all depend on. It's a way to build the borders higher, even for those who are citizens in this country — it's building walls around their lives and condemning their kids to a life less than they deserve.*

CM: I agree. I think there's an effort to put down Mexican-Americans in Arizona, to criminalize them, put them as social outcasts, not worthy of being "American" unless, of course, they take the path of assimilation into the dominant culture, which, by the way, won't be so dominant down the road. The demographic revolution is a reality. Whether some white people like it or not, we're going to be the majority in this country.

DB: *Here in California whites are already the minority.*

CM: Exactly. So it's happening. We don't want to romanticize it because I always provide my critical analysis of the demographic revolution — it is not necessarily going to be a consequence of profound change. I cite President Obama as an example — big deal, we have a Black president, but where are we? We are worse off than we were during the Bush presidency. The point is not to romanticize that people of color are going to take "power." It's a question of looking at the reality that indeed, there is the potential to honor this diversity of American culture and there will come about a more humanistic society that is going to place its emphasis on social justice and peace, not war and violence, in our society and throughout the world.

DB: *Let's get back to the revenge aspect of this action taken in Tucson, and what may need to happen in terms of a fight-back. We understand that white politicians took this action starting while Dolores Huerta was in Tucson and talked about how white people hate Brown people, and white politicians there hate Brown people. Those politicians never forgot it. They are in positions of power now, and they are punishing the people. What should the fight-back look like?*

CM: I think there should be a revolution. This is the time for the revolution to emerge in the context of Dr. King's call for a revolution of values. I'm not talking about any Hollywood version, a Hollywood revolution of violence, but rather a non-violent revolution as Dr. King called for that's going to transform the value system we have now in our society away from a process of individualization — what's best for the individual, the banks, the 1% — to what is best for the 99% of our society. That's the majority of people of color and the white middle class. This is what I would like to see happen there. We also must make clear that it's not all white politicians — there are some good folks out there who are allies. The white politician we need to address is the Right-wing, Tea Party, white politician-type of person who is doing the evil deeds taking place in Tucson, Arizona.

Stepping into the Breach: Restoring Blood to Words
Martin Espada   September 2012

DB: The challenge of poetry is to reconnect words to reality. Martin Espada's poetry is transcendent and very precise at the same time. His poems are an act of love at every turn, and bear witness in a way that is poignant and unforgettable. Martin, your book of essays was banned in Tucson, along with the purging of Ethnic Studies, the Mexican American Studies Program. You've had a history of being censored.

ME: Yes. When this book *Zapata's Disciple* was banned in Tucson, my first reaction was, "Again?" This wasn't the first time I've been censored or the first time this particular book has been banned. *Zapata's Disciple,* a collection of essays and poems from South End Press, was banned once before, by the Texas state penal system. The publisher attempted to donate this book to the Texas penal system so that inmates in Texas might read it. A committee of some sort convened and decided this was a book that could not be allowed into the Texas prison system. They sent back a form with boxes checked stating the reasons why, which included that this book might lead to the incitement of rioting among the inmates.

Of course, it wasn't only *Zapata's Disciple* that was banned and literally taken out of the classroom in Tucson. It is a roll of honor if you look at some of the other authors who were banned there: James Baldwin, Howard Zinn, Cesar Chavez, Ana Castillo, Sandra Cisneros, Sherman Alexie, and the list goes on. I am in very good company and am glad and proud to be there. But once you get over that "not again" sensation, and that sense of pride in belonging to a select group of writers, you start to reflect that you live in a country where book banning is going on, openly. And here's the funny part: not too many people are upset about it.

DB: You read for Derechos Humanos *in Tucson and you had a little problem there!*

ME: There is an essay in *Zapata's Disciple* called "The New Bathroom Policy at English High School," which is about language politics in the US. The essays were published in 1998, but the issues are still very much the same. I wrote: The repression of Spanish is part of a larger attempt to silence Latinos, and like the crazy uncle at the family dinner table yelling about independence or socialism, we must refuse to be silenced.

On October 12th, 1996 — Columbus Day — I gave a reading at a bookstore in Tucson, Arizona co-sponsored by *Derechos Humanos*, a group which monitors human rights abuses on the Arizona-México border, and coordinated with the Latino March on Washington that same day. At 7 PM, when the reading was to begin, we received a bomb threat. The police arrived with bomb-sniffing dogs, and sealed off the building. I did the reading in the parking lot, under a streetlamp.

DB: *The liberals are in this.*

ME: The liberals are usually in there somewhere, absolutely. Here's an example. *All Things Considered* contacted me to commission a poem from me. I began making some connections with the case of Mumia Abu-Jamal, the African American journalist convicted of killing a Philadelphia police officer named Daniel Faulkner, many, many years ago. Many of us, myself included, feel that he did not receive anything resembling a fair trial, and that he is imprisoned unjustly.

So I wrote a poem about Mumia Abu-Jamal. I presented it to NPR for *Weekend All Things Considered*. They were suitably horrified, and refused to air the poem. A junior producer told me directly this was a poem they would not air for political reasons. This was splattered across the newspapers and magazines for about a year afterwards. The cover story in the *Progressive* was "All Things Censored: The Poem NPR Doesn't Want You to

Hear." It got a surprising amount of attention, considering how controversial Mumia was, and is to this day.

Why there was such an uproar when my poem about Mumia Abu-Jamal was censored by National Public Radio, but an entire academic program, the Mexican-American Studies Program in the Tucson Unified School District, has been censored and shut down in just the same way by the State of Arizona — and there's barely a peep? Why do we no longer, as a nation, even seem to make the attempt to live up to the rhetoric of free expression, the rhetoric of free speech, the rhetoric of academic freedom? Where is it?

DB: *What do you see as the work of a poet? Why is a poet important now?*

ME: We have reached such a gulf between language and the meaning of language. We live in an age of hyper-euphemism. That's why we can use language politically and bureaucratically the way we do. This is why the government, media, educational system, and big corporations use language the way they do. Language is increasingly divorced from meaning. Increasingly, there's a separation of words from what they actually mean. It's a tendency that's been going on for a very long time, but now it's been perfected. We call it "extraordinary rendition" when we refer to the kidnapping and incarceration of people around the world by this government. We use language like "weapons of mass destruction" in order to justify a war. They never found the weapons of mass destruction, but the words themselves did damage enough.

So how does a poet fit into this equation? If this hyper-euphemism drains the blood from words, poets can restore the blood to words. They can reconcile language with meaning. They can say what they mean and in so doing create a record, bear witness, give testimony, speak clearly about what is happening, both for the present generations and the generations to come, who will want to know what really happened at the beginning of the twenty-first century.

I see that as something poets can do. In some respects, this is not a new idea. You can go back to Percy Bysshe Shelley, who spoke of poets as the unacknowledged legislators of the world. Walt Whitman spoke of his role as a poet to advocate "for the rights of them the others are down upon." I am part of that tradition and that continuum. We live in an age where language is so depleted of its meaning, so divorced from itself, that we as poets have to step into that breach.

We are surrounded by poetry and don't even know it. What poets do, of course, is very much akin to what birds do when they are feathering a nest. You take something from here, something from there, and in the end it becomes a poem.

DB: *Can you read us "Isabel's Corrido?"*

ME: "Isabel's Corrido" is based on a true story. A "corrido" is a Mexican narrative song, a storytelling song, whether the subject is love or revolution. There's a phrase — "quiero ver las fotos" — which simply means, "I want to see the pictures."

I also refer to "the land of Zapata." Emiliano Zapata was one of the major leaders of the Mexican revolution of 1910. He came from the State of Morelos, which is the same place where Isabel was born. That's the connection between them. I reference the fact that this is based on my own life, some thirty years ago.

There was a time when I couldn't even talk about what happened to Isabel, much less write about it. But as I witnessed the increasing backlash in this country against immigrants and immigration, which has been building in intensity for so many years, I felt I had no choice but to finally write this poem down and speak out.

It's a very personal, very intimate poem at the same time it's a very political poem. Even though it's based on something that

265

happened three decades ago, it is very much a response to what's happening now with immigrants and immigration.

Isabel's Corrido
Para Isabel

Francisca said: *Marry my sister so she can stay in the country.*
I had nothing else to do. I was twenty-three and always cold, skidding
in cigarette-coupon boots from lamppost to lamppost through January
in Wisconsin. Francisca and Isabel washed bed sheets at the hotel,
sweating in the humidity of the laundry room, conspiring in Spanish.

I met her the next day. Isabel was nineteen, from a village where the elders
spoke the language of the Aztecs. She would smile whenever the ice pellets
of English clattered around her head. When the justice of the peace said
You may kiss the bride, our lips brushed for the first and only time.

The borrowed ring was too small, jammed into my knuckle.
There were snapshots of the wedding and champagne in plastic cups.
Francisca said: *The snapshots will be proof for Immigration.*
We heard rumors of the interview: they would ask me the color
of her underwear. They would ask her who rode on top.
We invented answers and rehearsed our lines. We flipped through
Immigration forms at the kitchen table the way other couples
shuffled cards for gin rummy. After every hand, I'd deal again.

Isabel would say: *Quiero ver las fotos.* She wanted to see the pictures
of a wedding that happened but did not happen, her face inexplicably
happy, me hoisting a green bottle, dizzy after half a cup of champagne.

Francisca said: *She can sing corridos,* songs of love and revolution
from the land of Zapata. All night Isabel sang corridos in a barroom
where no one understood a word. I was the bouncer and her husband,
so I hushed the squabbling drunks, who blinked like tortoises in the sun.

Her boyfriend and his beer cans never understood why she married me.
Once he kicked the front door down, and the blast shook the house
as if a hand grenade detonated in the hallway. When the cops arrived,
I was the translator, watching the sergeant watching her, the inscrutable
squaw from every Western he had ever seen, bare feet and long black hair.

We lived behind a broken door. We lived in a city hidden from the city.
When her headaches began, no one called a doctor. When she disappeared
for days, no one called the police. When we rehearsed the questions
for Immigration, Isabel would squint and smile. *Quiero ver las fotos,*
she would say. The interview was canceled, like a play on opening night
shut down when the actors are too drunk to take the stage. After she left,
I found her crayon drawing of a bluebird tacked to the bedroom wall.

I left too, and did not think of Isabel again until the night Francisca called to
say: *Your wife is dead. Something was growing in her brain.*

I imagined my wife
who was not my wife, who never slept beside me, sleeping in the ground,
wondered if my name was carved into the cross above her head, no epitaph
and no corrido, another ghost in a riot of ghosts evaporating from the skin
of dead Mexicans who staggered for days without water through the desert.

Thirty years ago, a girl from the land of Zapata kissed me once
on the lips and died with my name nailed to hers like a broken door.
I kept a snapshot of the wedding; yesterday it washed ashore on my desk.

There was a conspiracy to commit a crime. This is my confession: I'd to it
again.

DB: *Thank you. Now please read us your poem about the poet Ezra
Pound, who supported the Italian fascist Mussolini.*

ME: **How to Read Ezra Pound**

> At the poets' panel,
> after an hour of poets
> debating Ezra Pound,
> Abe the Lincoln veteran,
> remembering
> the Spanish Civil War,
> raised his hand and said:
> *If I knew*
> *that a fascist*
> *was a great poet,*
> *I'd shoot him*
> *anyway.*

DB: *Can you give us one last poem?*

ME: This is a poem about the discovery of poetry. I want to
conclude with this poem because there's some joy and exaltation
to it.

The Playboy Calendar and the Rubáiyát of Omar Khayyám

> The year I graduated from high school,
> my father gave me a Playboy calendar
> and the *Rubáiyát* of Omar Khayyám.
> On the calendar, he wrote:
> *Enjoy the scenery.*
> In the book of poems, he wrote:
> *I introduce you to an old friend.*
>
> The Beast was my only friend in high school,

a wrestler who crushed the coach's nose with his elbow,
fractured the fingers of all his teammates,
could drink half a dozen vanilla milkshakes,
and signed up with the Marines
because his father was a Marine.
I showed the Playboy calendar to The Beast
and he howled like a silverback gorilla
trying to impress an expedition of anthropologists.
I howled too, smitten with the blonde
called *Miss January*, held high in my simian hand.

Yet, alone at night, I memorized the poet-astronomer
of Persia, his saints and sages bickering about eternity,
his angel looming in the tavern door with a jug of wine,
his *battered caravanserai* of sultans fading into the dark.
At seventeen, the laws of privacy have been revoked
by the authorities, and the secret police are everywhere:
I learned to hide Khayyám and his beard
inside the folds of the Playboy calendar
in case anyone opened the door without knocking,
my brother with a baseball mitt or a beery Beast.

I last saw The Beast that summer at the Marine base
in Virginia called Quantico. He rubbed his shaven head,
and the sunburn made the stitches from the car crash years ago
stand out like tiny crosses in the field of his face.
I last saw the Playboy calendar in December of that year,
when it could no longer tell me the week or the month.

I last saw Omar Khayyám this morning:
Awake! He said. *For Morning in the Bowl of Night
Has flung the Stone that puts the Stars to Flight.*

Awake! He said. And I awoke.

Suffering in Every Bite: Migrant Workers' Bitter Fruit

Seth M. Holmes   July 2013

DB: The Obama administration presses forward with the most stringent deportation policies in modern history. Every week, thousands of migrant workers are arrested and deported. This harsh journey to the north, made by millions of migrant farmworkers, is invisible to most Americans, though they literally consume the fruit of this labor. But Dr. Seth M. Holmes hopes to change that invisibility with his new book, Fresh Fruit, Broken Bodies: Migrant Farmworkers in the United States.

Holmes, a cultural anthropologist, physician. and Martin Sisters Assistant Professor at UC Berkeley made the dangerous journey north from Oaxaca, Mexico, via a "coyote." His trek north ended in his arrest.

Seth, how did you come to go down and come back with a group of folk crossing over with a coyote?

SH: I'm a physician and anthropologist, and as an anthropologist I use the classic field research method of participant observation. We observe, but also participate and gain from our own bodies' data about what that way of life is like. For 18 months I lived and migrated with undocumented indigenous Mexicans from the State of Oaxaca starting in Washington State where we lived in a labor camp and picked strawberries.

In central California, I lived with this same group of people in a slum apartment. We pruned vineyards when there was work, went down to their home village in the mountains of Oaxaca to help plant and harvest corn, and then crossed the border back through northern Mexico into Arizona. I was put in the border patrol jail with them. I did this fieldwork to understand how ethnic hierarchies and hierarchies of citizenship and immigration work in the US today, and how that affects people's health and health care.

DB: *Was the work hard?*

SH: Yes. I never was able to keep up with the other folks. In fact, if I hadn't been a white person who was interesting to the farm owners, I would have been fired several times because I could not keep up. Farmworkers are not unskilled labor; they are very skilled. I worked as hard as I could to pick strawberries and I could never keep up. They had to pick 50 pounds of strawberries — the appropriate kind of ripeness, without any leaves — per hour, in order to make the minimum wage. If they pick less than that for a few days, they're fired.

DB: *These fruit and vegetables are full of the fingerprints of suffering. The senior producer of this show, Miguel Gavilan Molina, watched his mom die in the fields when he was a young farmworker. At what point did you decide to put your life on the line?*

SH: Many people I worked with were from the indigenous group known as the Triqui people from Oaxaca, and they spoke of *"sufrimiento"* — suffering as a major metaphor for what happens for them in the process of migration. They talked about the back and hip pain from picking, but also the *sufrimiento* of crossing the border.

A lot of people had stories of going across the border with a coyote whom they didn't know, who mistreated them and pushed them into a chemical tank and closed them in the train until they got to the US. Other people were told by someone, "I work for your coyote, come with me," and then were kidnapped. One man was told by a border patrol agent "I'll take you to border patrol jail unless you let me have sex with you, in which case, I'll let you go free."

I felt that to understand the health and suffering of these people — their work, their lives — I needed to understand both the farm and the border. The border crossing happened after a season picking berries in Washington State, winter in California pruning vineyards, then moving down to their home village in the mountains of Oaxaca to participate in the corn harvest there.

DB: *A coyote is the guide, the one responsible for bringing you across the border — not always the most trustworthy.*

SH: Let me clarify. A group of people in a relatively small village with extended families who know each other, tend to go with a coyote from their home village who is a friend of a friend, or a relative, or someone else with whom they are connected. For them, the coyotes are quite trustworthy and try to look out for the group. In my research, the people who are more unfortunate are people who come from other parts of Mexico, or even more so, from Central America. They arrive at the border without any contacts for a coyote and then try to figure out whom to trust. That's where people can really get into trouble.

DB: *Tell us about the struggles of that 49-hour ride from Oaxaca.*

SH: We started in the village in Oaxaca — up in the mountains. We rode a Volkswagen van down to a nearby town where every Saturday, from January until May, there is a bus full of people who want to cross the border. The bus takes them all the way up to the border in northern Mexico, in Sonora. Almost all of them are men. I was the only white person on the bus. Each time we arrived at a military checkpoint on the highway, the bus driver announced over the sound system — "Okay, everyone tell the military that you're going to Baja, California to pick tomatoes." If we tell them we're going to the border, they will ask more questions and it will take more time. Each time they told me "you tell them that you're going to" ... and then they'd pick a nearby tourist town — "Guadalajara," or something like that.

DB: *This is not an easy road.*

SH: The bus was packed full of people, without air conditioning, nonstop all night without being able to sleep, so when we arrived at the border town in northern Mexico, we were all — I was very exhausted.

DB: *What happened as you approached the border?*

271

SH: We arrived in Sonora, in a small town in northern Mexico. The driver let us out, out of town, in the middle of the blazing sun, and told us he wouldn't take us into town because there was too much border patrol activity. So we walked into town through the heat, and followed the cousin of our coyote down back streets to a little apartment where we stayed, with no furniture or running water. We slept on the floor, on swaths of old carpet, and waited. There was a shower out back made of sheets hanging above mud that was shared by all the apartments that opened up into this same backyard area. Other groups came and went from the apartment. People came in from time to time and told us, "You have to pay me for staying here." The first time, some of us did pay. Then we realized it was a scam and we didn't pay anymore. People came in and told us they were our driver, and they would pick us up tomorrow. But we didn't know whom to trust.

We went through the town, which was very clearly set up for border crossing. There were several money changers and places to wire money. There were places to buy dark-colored clothing and dark-colored backpacks — what you wear to cross the border. The grocery store had aisles and aisles of Gatorade, water bottles, and Pedialyte. We hid all our cash in zip lock bags in mayonnaise jars. The grocery store had aisles of different kinds of small mayonnaise jars, so apparently that wasn't only our group's plan.

We hid the money in the mayonnaise jars because in that town, or crossing the border, if you run into someone dressed in dark clothing, you don't know if they're someone else trying to cross the border for work, to support their family, to let their family survive, or if they're someone who is after your money. Everyone knows there are a lot of people with thousands of dollars cash in order to pay their coyote, and pay the drivers of the cars to get across the border. There was a lot of fear and anxiety.

DB: *What are the dangers of this so-called heightened security?*

SH: Several senators proposed a "border surge," which would take a $30 billion increase in funding.

DB: *Double the funding.*

SH: And roughly double the number of border patrol agents, with more drones, heat sensors and other kinds of militarization of the border. A study by the Binational Migration Institute at the University of Arizona showed the number of deaths in the borderlands has, in general, been increasing over the last decade or two. Several scholars, including myself, have written about the ways border patrol policies and actions contribute to those increased deaths.

The border patrol has used a policy called "prevention through deterrence," which puts more border patrol agents near the safer regions of the border, and less agents in the more dangerous areas. In essence, it redirects the flow of migrants into the most dangerous and risky areas. There have been statements by border patrol administrators and US government officials showing they know this policy will increase the danger for the people crossing. The study released by the University of Arizona argues that this policy is one of the reasons the numbers of deaths have been increasing. If this policy of redirecting migrants to the most dangerous areas of the border continues, then increasing the power and militarization of the border patrol may simply increase the number of deaths by putting people intentionally more and more into harm's way.

DB: *What do we know about the statistics?*

SH: Within the last 30 days, we know that 177 people were rescued by the border patrol from near death, according to the Border Patrol. We also know from organizations such as Humane Borders, which posts online maps with information from the Border Patrol, the Mexican Consulate and independent sources about exactly where and when different people died — but that's likely not everyone. It's been slowly increasing in general even though the number of people entering has decreased, so the risk of death for each individual who goes through this process is higher and higher.

I was continuously surprised by how dangerous it was. We ran into rattlesnakes, and people with guns — and weren't sure what their motivations were. We ran into other people through the desert and tried to avoid them. There were cactuses we'd run into in the middle of the night, because you can't use a flashlight if you're trying to hike in the darkness and not be seen. There are scorpions, etc., not to mention different kinds of vigilantes. We heard reports of what some vigilantes have done.

We saw hand-painted posters, each with a kind of danger in the border; a scorpion, cactus, rattlesnake, or a picture of someone dying of dehydration and heat stroke. At the bottom of each poster, in Spanish in red letters, the posters read, "Is it worth risking your life?" At first it seemed to me the answer had to be "Yes," because there are thousands of people who are trying to do this every year. But we must question the framing of the question itself. That question — "Is it worth risking your life?" — presumes that each immigrant is choosing based on pluses and minuses.

DB: *That they have an option...*

SH: The immigrants I know crossing from Mexico into the US do not experience this as a choice. One told me, "There's no other option for us." Another said, "It's either certain death, a kind of slow death in our villages where we can't survive, largely due to NAFTA..."

DB: *NAFTA, free trade — which has been a boon for drug traffickers, but not for everyday people.*

SH: They do not experience this as a voluntary choice and there are many ways that politics originating in the US, including NAFTA, relate directly to why they can't survive in their home towns anymore, and feel like they have to migrate so they and their children can live.

DB: *This is a terrible death. As an M.D., tell us what happens.*

SH: There are several ways people die in the border. Some people die violent deaths due to assailants — whether from Mexico or the US — looking for their money, or anti-immigrant assailants who are very angry at an immigrant for being there. There are also people who die related to rattlesnake bites or scorpion bites, but the most common way people die is from heat and dehydration. I drank through a gallon of water every few hours while I was hiking, and we took a relatively easy flat path through the desert. I had several gallons of water, and several bottles of Gatorade and Pedialyte with me. I had no idea where I was, and if I had gotten separated from the group I would likely have died. If someone gets separated and they only have enough water to make the trip under perfect circumstances, they can easily become dehydrated and perhaps experience heat stroke and die.

DB: *If you don't have a friendly coyote, you have less of a shot.*

SH: Right. There are some organizations — Humane Borders, Border Angels, No More Death, Samaritans — who leave water, walk through the desert, say, "We have water," and try to get people to the hospital if they need help. There is an arm of the border patrol that works on this as well. If they see people in distress, they try to take care of them. Ironically, last week, the *L.A. Times* wrote an article, which said, "Over the Past 30 Days Border Patrol Rescues 177 People." While that is important, and true, we also must remember the Border Patrol policies that increase the danger people are put in based on where they are intentionally encouraged and discouraged to cross in the first place.

DB: *A number of people were prosecuted as alien smugglers for going out and leaving water there — horrifying prosecutions.*

SH: People went to jail because they came across people who were dying in the desert and put them in their car to take them to the hospital, a clinic, refuge, shade — something. I saw water containers in the desert shot with bullets to drain them of water.

DB: *Water-leaving is a felony, but you're trying to prevent this horrible death. You had an encounter and got arrested.*

SH: I was a backpacking guide in California for several years, so I'm used to hiking long distances for many days, but I've never hiked as fast for as long a period of time — especially in the heat and dryness we experienced while crossing. Every once in awhile we would stop in a dried-up creek bed and share frijoles [beans] or different food with each other — dried grasshoppers — things like that. Then we'd hike again and stop sometimes to pull cactus spines out of each other's legs if we had crashed into cactuses in the dark.

When we got into Arizona, the driver told our coyote he wasn't driving anymore because there had been more and more border patrol activity in that area, so we were stranded in this dried-up creek bed. Eventually the coyote decided to go back to the driver he usually works with and asked whom else he could talk with. So he went back, found someone else who was going to give us a ride, and all of a sudden we see him run and jump down into the creek bed. Then two border patrol agents jump down after him, pull guns on us, and in Spanish say "Put your hands in the air." They looked at me and said, "This doesn't look good for you with a bunch of illegals." That's what they said. They held us in the desert then took us into the Border Patrol jail.

DB: *What happened?*

SH: They separated me from the group. They weren't sure what to do with a white US citizen. I had a passport and letters from my university,

DB: *That's what confused them — maybe we'd better be a little bit more careful with this white guy.*

SH: They put all of the Triqui men into the back of a Border Patrol truck that is like a pick-up with something like a small jail cell on the back. They put me alone in a different one. We went to the Indian Health Service Hospital, because one of the two Border Patrol agents was bit by a rattlesnake while following our coyote. We waited in the truck while he was treated there.

Eventually, we arrived at the Border Patrol jail. I was put alone in the women's cell because they were still confused about who I was — whether I was a coyote — and what they should do with me. All the Triqui people were put in a different cell. They told me I was not allowed to look at the Triqui people — that we couldn't look across the hallway at each other. The graffiti in my cell, mostly written by women, were hopeful messages, like "I'll see you in Chicago," and "Proud that I'm Mexican." I watched as the Triqui people, one by one, were taken, fingerprinted and photographed and taken back to their cell.

I motioned to them with my hand that I wanted to make my phone call. One of the agents shook his head at me, "No." Later, one of the agents came to my cell and asked if they could turn on my digital camera. I said, "I want to call my lawyer." I had contacted a few lawyers before doing this, asked about the implications, and had their cell phone numbers. I also had my mom and my dad's numbers and friends' numbers. I called my lawyer who told me that the Arizona legal system was backlogged and that it would be a couple of weeks before I would get another phone call and get to meet with her. She asked me if there was anyone I wanted her to call. I gave her my mom and dad's numbers and another lawyer's number. At that point I started to cry, just imagining being in this jail cell for two weeks, not being able to talk to anyone, not having a pen — as an anthropologist, not being able to write, and not sure what would happen to me. That's the moment my Triqui friends were taken out of their cell in a single file line — watching me cry as they were taken to a bus, and deported to Nogales.

DB: *I imagine they weren't crying.*

SH: They weren't crying.

DB: *Talk about the multiple misperceptions in the US press.*

SH: The first misperception is that these people coming to pick berries or work on farms in the US are coming here voluntarily. That framing is often done by US government officials and the media. The people who die in the desert are subtly blamed for their deaths.

DB: *For their own deaths ... they killed themselves...*

SH: They are understood to have chosen to take on that unnecessary risk. But the experience of the farmworkers I met was that they were forced to do this. There's no other option, so this idea that they deserve their death is a subtle, but very inhumane, way to think about people who are dying. This takes elected officials who make trade and border patrol policies that intentionally increase danger and risk — as well as the American public who support them — off the hook.

DB: *Multiple forms of racism.*

SH: Anti-immigrant prejudice, racism. Those deaths are mournable, should be grieved, and should count. A few weeks ago, several members of Congress stated they wouldn't vote for immigration reform unless newly legalized immigrants would not get health care in the US for roughly 15 years, despite paying taxes. The essence of the transaction between these farmworkers and the rest of us Americans who shop at grocery stores and farmer's markets, is that the farmworkers are going through dangerous border crossings, working bent over six or seven days a week, all day, getting back problems, hip problems, knee problems — essentially giving away their health — in order to pick fresh fruit, grapes, broccoli, asparagus, so the rest of us can be healthy. The title of the book, *Fresh Fruit, Broken Bodies*, was suggested by Philippe Bourgois, who wrote the book's foreword. There's an exchange that we are all implicated in farmworkers' bodies becoming sick and broken, in essence, to give us this healthy fruit, healthy food. If we are to respect this, we need at least to prioritize health care for these people who work for all of us be healthy.

DB: *Tens of millions of Americans depend on these workers to eat every day. Yet many of these people want these workers kicked out.*

SH: Yes. In the midst of debates on immigration and health reform, we must remember that immigrants are people. There's a lot of debate about immigrants in the abstract, without listening to the stories, voices, realities of immigrants themselves — they're fathers, sons, daughters, wives and mothers. I hope this will help Americans vote differently, think and listen differently when they hear about people dying on the border. When they taste their strawberries, they'll remember that the last person who touched these strawberries was probably the person who picked them. That's an intimate exchange that helps us have health — what do we owe in response?

Why the Honduran Children Flee
Adrienne Pine   July 2014

DB: *A flood of Central American children seeking safety in the United States has created a political and humanitarian crisis for border states, and left President Barack Obama lecturing parents not to send their children off on these long dangerous journeys as he requests $3.7 billion in emergency spending to step up border security and speed up deportations. But the crisis has a long back story, including the US militarization of Central America in the 1980s and Secretary of State Hillary Clinton's support for an anti-democratic coup in Honduras in 2009, which ousted a populist president and increased the exploitation of the population. Adrienne Pine, an American University anthropology professor, is the author of* Working Hard, Drinking Hard: on Violence and Survival in Honduras.

Adrienne, we are hearing that these kids, many from Honduras, are coming from a very violent situation. Could you give us a little background, since you were there so much in this last year?

AP: Honduras is generally recognized as the most violent country in the world, with a homicide rate over 90 per 100,000. Country number two's rate is in the 60s, so it's extremely high. The risk of being murdered is far higher than any other place in the world right now. But that only tells a partial story, of course.

To understand why not only the homicide rate, but also the rate of many other forms of violence is so high, is to understand the coup that happened in 2009, a coup that was carried out by military forces trained at the School of the Americas in Fort Benning, Georgia. It was, in effect, supported by the US, which refused to follow the unanimous decision of the OAS [Organization of American States] at the time to not recognize the usurping government. Instead, the US negotiated with it and has continued through all these years to send massive amounts of military and police aid to a government that has militarized the country and is murdering and terrorizing its citizens, both through militarization and direct violence. There is also the more indirect violence of neoliberal policy, which for many people isn't indirect at all. It includes the usurping of Indigenous Peoples' lands, of *campesinos'* or peasant farmers' lands. It includes the destruction of any notion of sovereignty and Honduran peoples' control of their land, water, sub-soil rights, and of their government itself. There are conditions of extreme violence in Honduras. Politicians say, "Well, this is all the fault of the gangs." But the reasons why there is so much violence are these bigger structural forces. Of course, the gangs are very dangerous. But if young kids had work opportunities and a chance to live a decent life, these gangs wouldn't be threatening people in the way they are.

DB: *Talk about the situation in terms of the social setting, the level of poverty, and how this violence unfolds.*

AP: It's hard to explain. I've just come back from a year of living in Honduras, teaching at the National University. You live a constant embodied state of terror in Honduras. It's hard to exaggerate it, because everybody is always afraid. I'm perhaps the only person I know who has lived a significant period of time in Honduras and has never been assaulted. I'm very lucky, in that sense. Every Honduran I know has been violently assaulted at one point or another — with a gun. It's happened in front of me on several occasions. It's something you become used to and expect. A month ago I walked by a man who had been killed in a targeted assassination ten minutes earlier, and was lying there on the ground. This sort of violence is day-to-day, and even more immediate for anybody who owns a small business. "War taxes" are basically bribery from local gangs who, in many cases, are affiliated with the police, as well as direct bribery on the part of the police. "You pay us this money" — like protection money — "and we won't kill you." They will kill people if they don't pay the money.

Recently, in one neighborhood, Flor del Campo, in the past few weeks, three taxi drivers were killed for not paying their war taxes. Bus drivers pay phenomenal amounts of money. What generally happens is that businesses close because they are not able to afford their war taxes and business costs. There are very few businesses open, except in malls. There is extreme privatization, closing off of public spaces because they have become so dangerous. The complicity between the police and military police was set up by the current president, who won in extremely fraudulent elections last year. He set up a new military police force and re-militarized the country. The gangs are involved in all of this business. Perhaps the most powerful actors in the country are the drug traffickers who are also very deeply involved in the financial sector and the government.

There is day-to-day embodied terror. All the US seems to want to do — or rather what the State Department seems to want to do — is pour more money into a military apparatus that is terrorizing people, and defending the neoliberal vultures who are stealing Honduran land and Honduran young people's possibilities for a future and survival.

DB: *President Barack Obama was lecturing the parents of Central America and of Honduras, telling them to keep their children home or they will be in danger and deported. It implies these parents don't love their children, and they just want to let them go. Talk about the life of the child and why a parent might try and get their kid out of there.*

AP: I think it's cynical that both the Honduran and the US governments are blaming the parents for this situation. Honduran parents love their children as much as parents do anywhere — a whole lot. If they are desperate enough to agree to let their kids go — and in many cases, kids decide to go on their own — it's not that the parents send them. But if the parents agree to let their kids go, it's because their life is at risk in Honduras. By their calculation, their life will be at less risk even with the massive dangers, in particular the "death train" through Mexico to the northern border of Mexico and the southern border of the US. It's a realistic calculation because the homicide rate in Honduras is 90 per 100,000, but for children it's much higher — so young people have a much higher rate of death by homicide than the general population.

DB: *Why? How do they die?*

AP: It didn't begin with the coup. A lot of these processes are ongoing, but they sped up with the coup. In 2002 and 2003, at the beginning of the Presidency of Ricardo Maduro — a big supporter of the coup in 2009 — he brought in Rudy Giuliani to consult for his campaign, to bring in a Zero Tolerance policy and change the laws to create an anti-gang law. In 2003, when Pepe Lobo was president of the Congress, [he later became President] he passed an anti-gang law which was modeled on the anti-loitering laws in the US that basically criminalize Black people, and people of color in general, when they are not working. This law did the same thing. It criminalized people without having to ever commit a crime. If they had a tattoo, were in a neighborhood where they were associating with gang members — in many neighborhoods, it's impossible not to associate with gang members because they control the whole neighborhood — they were considered criminal. Many people are criminalized by identity. In Honduras, there's a complete and total impunity for violent crime, especially against people who are labeled as criminals. It has been okay, since about 1998, to kill off young people. There's very little consequence for this. I've analyzed it as a sort of social cleansing program, which is how it is referred to in common language — the cleaning of the streets.

Young people, in particular young boys and men — since the labor sector has been feminized with the sweatshop industry that employs more women — are idle, because there are absolutely no jobs for them to obtain, and when they aren't working, they are seen as gang members. Regardless of whether they actually are, or whether they committed a crime, it is seen as justifiable to kill them. There are death squads, and there is plenty of evidence, over more than a decade, that these death squads are police who are either undercover, working off hours, or people who are working for some of the private security companies, many of which are run by the same leaders of the death squads from the 1980s — Battalion 3-16. It is, in effect, a genocidal policy. This isn't genocide in the way that many people are used to thinking about it. But it is a policy of social cleansing by an identity category that is, in effect, supported by the state, and which makes it impossible for people in this identity category — young, poor men — to survive.

Young, poor women are similarly threatened, although their homicide levels are not as high. This is curious. I've been carrying out fieldwork at the national teaching hospital, Hospital Escuela in Tegucigalpa, where it's been noted that among child migrants from Honduras — which has the highest number of migrants coming to the United States right now — there's a higher proportion of boys than girls, but more girls than from other countries. In inverse proportions, it seems that girls in Honduras are now killing themselves, or attempting to kill themselves. The doctors and nurses at the Hospital Escuela have shown me intake numbers to back this up. There's been a huge spike in suicide attempts among girls from age 9 to 14 in the past two or three years. Kids are trying to escape their reality, the dangers they live on a daily basis thanks to the US support for this coup and the militarization of the country, through whatever means they can. That means migration, or in some cases, tragically, death — killing themselves.

DB: *People have tried various legal ways to get out of the country, to save their children. There are many attempts at political asylum.*

AP: That's true. For over ten years I've been getting requests from lawyers to serve as an expert witness, and I've worked on dozens and dozens of these cases. In the past two years, since the coup, but in particular in the past two and a half years, there's been a huge spike in requests. I'm sometimes getting two or three requests a week from lawyers, which obviously is more than I can take on. It's a full-time job, and there aren't many other people doing this kind of work. The volume of requests is going up, not just for things that are obviously directly related to the coup, but also requests related to gang violence and domestic violence. It reflects the general precariousness of day-to-day life in Honduras. The increase in impunity following the coup — in a country where impunity already reigned — has meant that everybody is at greater risk. A survivor of domestic violence might have found shelter in Honduras prior to the coup, but it's impossible to be protected today because of the generalized violence and generalized impunity.

It's complicated to do asylum cases. Asylum functions to tell ourselves and the US a narrative that we are a country that respects human rights, whereas this other country, Honduras or other offending countries, don't respect human rights. We claim we are protecting these people from the human rights violations and the "cultural flaws" of these other countries. In reality, what I've seen over the past 17 years working in Honduras is a massive militarization and military occupation of Honduras by the US. According to my colleague David Vine, who is writing a book on military bases, there are over 14 US bases and installations in Honduras. If it weren't for our support for murderous military and police services in Honduras, most of these human rights abuses that are causing people to flee from the country would not be happening. People would not have to flee from Honduras.

Asylum is an important tool, but it is also complicated because these people aren't fleeing to the US because the US is a protector of human rights. The US is one of the primary actors in the violence that so many of these people are suffering.

DB: *What are the chances of an average Honduran, a ten year old, to make it through, graduate and study with you at the university?*

AP: I saw graffiti about this the other day. Less than 20 percent of students ever make it to the university — possibly around 13 percent. The Honduran national public university has historically been autonomous — it's even in the name. The National Autonomous University of Honduras, which has been the most important and prestigious university, is rapidly being privatized in various ways. There's also a growth of private universities that goes along with a neoliberalization of the whole educational sector, which was one of the major impulses of the coup. A year after the coup, it was one of the most important achievements of then-President Lobo's administration, which won in the 2009 fraudulent elections funded and supported by the National Endowment for Democracy and the US State Department. One of his major achievements was to destroy the teachers union, which was the most important defender of public education in Honduras. In doing so, they've managed to help destroy public education, and increase the possibility for profits for the owners of private schools, many of whom were strong supporters and central actors within the coup. So it has become more and more difficult for Hondurans to get an education. Honduras is an extremely poor country, but it's also extremely divided between rich and poor, so that over 70% live under the poverty level. The majority of Hondurans don't get through high school. I think most Hondurans get to third or fourth grade.

DB: *Third or fourth grade.*

AP: But there's almost no point in getting educated because there are no jobs — that's the crux of the matter. Even if kids want to better themselves by getting an education, and they fight, struggle, sacrifice and work full-time and their parents sacrifice and they get that university degree, there are no jobs available. For so many of them, their only chance is to flee. That's what is behind this.

DB: *Did Hillary Clinton play a role supporting the coup in Honduras?*

AP: Hillary Clinton was probably the most important actor in supporting the coup in Honduras. One of her best friends from law school, Lanny Davis, was hired immediately following the coup by the most powerful business group in the country, and supported the coup as the representative for the Micheletti coup government in Washington. In that capacity he was able to organize hearings in Congress through his friend, Eliot Engel, who at the time was the head of the House Committee on Foreign Affairs' Subcommittee on the Western Hemisphere, and he was able to have Hillary Clinton's ear. The initial signals from the White House, from Obama, were that indeed this was a coup and illegal, so the coup administration shouldn't be recognized, but Hillary Clinton vetoed that position, in effect. Alongside her friend Lanny Davis, the State Department took a couple of months to admit that a coup had happened, then made a previously unknown differentiation that this had not been a military coup, just a regular coup. It's a difference that didn't make much sense. The military, in effect, had carried out the coup.

DB: *If there ever was a distinction without a difference, it was that.*

AP: Hillary Clinton played a huge role in propping up the coup administration. The State Department went against the Organization of American States [OAS], which has had a positive impact hemisphere-wide because it provoked the creation of CELAC [Community of Latin American and Caribbean States]. CELAC is the new, parallel organization to the OAS that excludes the US and Canada because they have had such a negative impact within the OAS, pushing back against the progressive governments in the region that want to have a different kind of relationship with the North — not just be in a kind of ongoing imperialism. The State Department ensured that the coup administration would remain in place through the imposed negotiations, against the OAS' wish, and by continuing to provide aid and continuing to recognize the coup administration. So if it weren't for Hillary Clinton, basically, there wouldn't be this refugee crisis from Honduras at the level that it is today. Hondurans would be living a very different reality from the tragic one they are living right now.

DB: *Obama and the administration shouldn't lecture the parents of Central America that they shouldn't let their kids go.*

AP: It's incredibly offensive that that's the analysis they're taking. It's a culture of poverty discourse that is meant to take all the blame away from the people who deserve it, which are the governments who are carrying out this violence against families trying their best to stay together, and stay alive.

DB: *You mentioned that the drug trade is integrated with the economy. There are also lots of US military bases there. Don't the US and the military know about the trafficking operations interwoven with the financial community?*

AP: Sure, the US knows about them. From time to time the US Treasury Department will sanction one of the drug kingpins, as they call them, like they did with the *Los Cachiros* organization and another group last year. It tends to be the kingpins who have fallen out of their favor for some reason or another. I think the US has a good sense of who are the real players in drug trafficking in Honduras, as everybody does. Historically, the US military and the CIA were directly involved in drug trafficking in the region — there's plenty of evidence for that. Peter Dale Scott wrote about that in the early 90s and 80s. Of course the Iran-Contra affair was a big part of that. The Honduran military is deeply involved in the drug trade as well.

The drug war has never been an honest excuse for the massive military presence in Honduras. There is militarization of regions like the Mosquitia, as well as the north coast, which are incredibly resource rich regions being opened up for oil exploration, and used for hydroelectric projects. This is all carried out by international companies; British, Chinese and US companies. A recent article by Kendra McSweeney describes how the military is terrorizing the population, clearing these lands, helping with land grabs to remove the indigenous and other people who live on these lands, in order to pave the way for a complete exploitation of the water, land and subsoil resources of those regions. I agree with that analysis.

Obama: Deporter-in-Chief

Nativo Lopez   November 2015

DB: *Nativo Lopez, former president of the Mexican American Political Association, is a Mexican political leader and immigrant rights activist in Southern California. Nativo, we've seen four years of extraordinary deportation, suffering heaped upon the undocumented community through two terms of the current democratic president. How do you see this?*

NL: Why are we not riled up, mad as hell, not going to take it anymore at Obama, who by the end of his term will have deported close to three million immigrants, 96% of whom are Mexican and Central American? He's obligated more than 700,000 American citizen minors to accompany their deported Mexican parents to Mexico and they are now stranded in Mexico as undocumented American citizens in Mexico because they are with their deported Mexican parents. Obama is responsible for more deportations than any other US president.

DB: *Obama has also supervised a major expansion of the private prison program. Even as Obama goes to prisons to let people out early, he's supervised the expansion of a private prison structure that has been devastating to Brown people.*

NL: It's included in the budget that the federal government is obligated to keep those beds occupied to at least 35,000 nationally — individuals who have not committed a criminal offense. They committed a civil, administrative offense by entering the US without status. Obama released 6,000 federal prisoners because they committed non-violent drug offenses. Our call would be to release the 35,000 detainees who have not committed any criminal offense. They are being detained because they entered the US in an unauthorized manner. This private system, developed under the Bush administration, has been perpetuated by the Obama administration and Congress, so now it's an item in the budget that must be allocated in an ongoing basis.

DB: *There is cruelty in Obama's dreamer possibility, where at the last minute he has an amnesty, which disappears with the next presidency.*

NL: First, it's not amnesty, just a temporary stay and work visa. Yes, I believe it was a political maneuver. Nine months prior to his second term campaign, their internal poll showed that Latinos were staying home — wouldn't turn out to vote as they did in his first campaign. It was very politically calculated to create this program for the young Dreamers, who are quite vociferous in their critique of the president, disrupting numerous campaign stops and speeches. He was re-elected with the help of the Latino community, but his legacy will be that he was the president who deported more immigrants than any other president.

Dispossession at Home, Deportation Abroad

Pablo Alvarado   January 2016

DB: *Pablo Alvarado is the Executive Director of the National Day Laborer Organizing Network. In 2005, he was among* Time magazine's *25 Most Influential Hispanics in America. Pablo, the corporate press reports that President Obama, deporter-in-chief, and the federal government are planning massive ICE raids of people who came here in the last year. It's a dark turn for the folks who have faced some of the most difficult circumstances — to fill our tables full of vegetables. You work with migrant and undocumented workers across the country to defend them and their rights. What is this new plan for massive deportation?*

PA: It's no surprise, because it's very consistent with the deportation policy of this administration. That you need to deport some to provide relief to others, deport first and legalize later, that deporting some people is necessary for others to get relief. That's how the Obama administration has operated for the last seven years. The intention was that by being tough on immigrants, the xenophobes and nativists would support immigration reform. It's a failed policy.

This new wave of deportations comes at the worst time. Deportations are bad at any time, but at this time in particular, we're going into an electoral year. The sentiment created by Donald Trump has dominated American politics. Mr. Trump stigmatizes migrants with his derogatory and racist language, but the President is deporting them. There's no difference between what the Republicans and Democrats do when it comes to deportations. There is no political gain the President can make by spearheading this new wave of deportations of children and mothers. The only one who benefits from this type of initiative is the Right-wing — essentially the Republicans, xenophobes and nativists.

DB: *This is being pushed by the Department of Homeland Security. These people forced out of their countries due to draconian US policies and free trade are now seen as a danger in this heightened security state.*

PA: They see the refugee children and their mothers as a matter of national security. We see it as a matter of human rights, a humanitarian crisis. The administration claims they have the situation under control, that the surge — as they call it — has ended and the numbers of unaccompanied minors and mothers with children has decreased. However, the US government has invested a lot of money in a project called *Frontera Sud*. They are funding the Mexican government and its military and other repressive bodies to apprehend Central Americans in the southern border of Mexico. Many folks still make it to the US-Mexico border, but a significant number are apprehended in Mexico and deported from Mexico to Honduras, Guatemala and El Salvador. The Department of Homeland Security claims they are simply enforcing the law, that it has nothing to do with any political calculation. But that's hypocritical because they themselves claim the immigration system is broken. They know very well we have an obsolete set of immigration laws that criminalizes our community and needs to be modernized. They know they have not done that. Yet they continue to engage in human rights violations.

The standing of the US government in global politics has deteriorated because of this new wave of deportations. The US is supposed to be a beacon of how to treat refugees, but they have not lived up to those expectations. They are telling the world it's OK to grab and deport people even if you are deporting them to their death. If the US government believes that people are going to stop coming, they are wrong. As long as it is more dangerous to stay than leave, people will continue to leave their countries of origin looking for better horizons, particularly when the levels of violence are unbearable in those places.

DB: *The National Day Laborer Organizing Network represents thousands of undocumented workers in centers where workers gather, make arrangements with people who want to hire them, and get some protection from the attacks and threats they often face — always worried about not being deported. When workers are not paid and they demand it, the bosses call ICE. Pablo, you are from El Salvador. Can you tell us about your own experience in order to put a human face on this?*

PA: I migrated under different circumstances. I was 22 when I migrated with my 17 year-old brother. The violence in El Salvador then was more about political activity. Now it's more gang related activity and common criminal violence all over the country. The political circumstances in El Salvador were different at that time, but the process of migration was essentially the same. People are fleeing from El Salvador, Honduras and Guatemala due to extreme violence. I have relatives who live in El Salvador. Two of my brothers are teachers. They would love to have a business but it's impossible because the organized crime organizations come in and start taxing. That's happening in those three countries. The circumstances are unbearable, so people are leaving. They are either being recruited by gang members or they have already been subjected to extreme violence. It's happening every single day.

My cousin migrated a few months ago. She was caught at the US/Mexico border. She was a police officer in El Salvador and was investigating a case of extortion. Some of the other officers were involved in the crime. When she reported it, she began getting persecuted. She was deported a few months ago because she didn't qualify for political asylum. She was looking for ways not to go back to El Salvador, but to live in Guatemala — because of fear. If a police officer goes through these circumstances, imagine what happens to a little kid.

The reasons why people migrate are multi-causal. Violence is only one cause. There is also poverty and family reunification. There are hundreds of thousands of Salvadorans who live here and whose kids are back in El Salvador growing up with their grandparents. They want to be unified, to be together. We must find ways to ensure that we unify transnational families. That's the only way forward — when we put families first, people first, over politics — to try and alleviate the suffering of the most vulnerable members of society. We should not just care about the kids in the US, but also the kids in Mexico, El Salvador, Honduras and Guatemala.

DB: *You describe the economic desperation, the wars the US supported throughout Central America, the coup the US supported in Honduras. The other side of the failed US policies leads to forced migration. The US has been failing and undermining the people of Central America for some time and Obama continues his failed policy as deporter-in-chief. You must be outraged, and the people you represent must feel totally betrayed.*

PA: Not just by the US, but the governments in Central America as well, because they are not living up to their expectations. The US intervention in Honduras has had catastrophic consequences. Before President Zelaya was deposed, he was trying to bring a sense of equality and justice to impoverished communities. He was trying to increase the minimum wage for workers, to encourage people not to leave. Wages and working conditions are not the best in our countries of origin, so people tend to migrate. These are some changes President Zelaya was trying to make. The US government came in and supported a coup d'état against President Zelaya. Immediately after the coup, you could see the levels of violence skyrocketing, with San Pedro Sula and Tegucigalpa becoming some of the most violent cities on the planet. San Salvador is among them as well. These are places where the levels of violence are far worse than the levels of violence in Iraq. It's part of the US intervention, because they intervene to protect their national interest with protectionist policies. The free trade agreements were established to protect the interests of the US, not to create prosperity and equality for folks in Central America. If that were the case, then people would be choosing to stay, not leave and face a dangerous road.

DB: *It's like a hammer and anvil. On the one hand the US, through Obama, is supporting the policy that is driving people out of their country, then the hammer comes down to force them back. It's a cynical situation. When we talk about Honduras, don't we need to talk about Hillary Clinton?*

PA: Correct. I was in Honduras a few months ago, and met four young men who were deported from New Orleans. These men left Honduras to come to the US a few years ago because they were forced to grow African palm and give up their subsistence farming, but they couldn't compete in the market. They were growing African palm to produce oil because it's one of the crops promoted through the Central America Free Trade Agreement. This new policy displaced them by taking away their subsistence farming and they were forced to come north. They came north, helped reconstruct New Orleans, then they were sent back. These are the victims of these policies — workers of impoverished communities, poor people. The aristocrats in Honduras, the powerful families, continue to profit from those trade agreements. Of course the US corporations continue to benefit. But it's at the workers' expense. Hillary Clinton has promoted these trade policies since Bill Clinton was in power, and when she was Secretary of State she supported the coup d'état against President Zelaya.

DB: *The millions of undocumented workers face the reality of private prisons. People are living in fear and vulnerability, and private prison corporations make money hand over fist on this program of abuse.*

PA: I don't know if they've been involved in pressuring the administration to engage in this new wave of deportations but they will definitely benefit. That's their business mantra — incarcerate people so they can profit. They get as much money as they can for every person they incarcerate from the US government. The more initiatives there are, the better it is for them. They will make a lot of money.

DB: *How are you getting ready for this announced mass deportation?*

PA: We'll do what every vulnerable community under siege has done in the past. The most important thing is that migrants must resist the fear that these raids are instilling in their lives. The way to do that is to be sure migrants know their rights and how to exercise them — particularly when a deportation agent comes knocking on their doors. That's the first step — resist and overcome fear. We are teaching and bringing information to the people about exercising their rights. We will also push for more sanctuary policies to keep ICE out of jails across the country.

We will continue to protest the President. This has been his policy for the past seven years, and we will not stop until he changes course. He still has one year to change the legacy he leaves behind. Will he be the deporter-in-chief or will he take us in another direction? He still has time. Many migrant refugees don't have the time he has. We will continue to exercise pressure. We will work to ensure that Hillary Clinton takes a harsher stand against these raids, that she commits to not engage in this practice if she becomes president. We will continue to equate what the President is doing with what Trump is promoting. In our view, in our heart, we know that Mr. Trump stigmatizes migrants with his dehumanizing language, but the President deports them. We must de-link the fight for immigrant rights from partisan politics. Both parties must be held accountable. We must speak truth to power and denounce these inhumane, immoral raids the President is engaged in, as well as denouncing the vile, racist, fascist language that Mr. Trump is using to describe us.

DB: *Has Bernie Sanders shown sympathy?*

PA: Yes, Sanders has been very friendly and reached out to immigrant rights organizations to ask our opinions to shape their plans on what to do with the issue of migration. He has shown a lot of creativity and willingness to not continue what the traditional Democratic Party has done so far, which is use immigration as a wedge issue to get the Republicans going and attack migrants so the Democrats can secure the Latino vote. .

Global Militarization and Empire

The UN's Ugly Coup in Haiti

Kevin Pina   March 2012

DB: *Kevin Pina is an American journalist, filmmaker and educator. He serves as a Country Expert on Haiti for the Varieties of Democracy project sponsored by the University of Notre Dame. Kevin, what is happening in Haiti today?*

KP: Since the coup was on a leap year, although this is the eighth anniversary, it was only the second time Haitians were able to mark February 29, 2004 as the day Jean-Bertrand Aristide was taken out by US marines at gunpoint, forced onto a plane and flown to Binge, the capital of the Central African Republic, against his will. This ushered in two years of utter brutality and terror managed by the United Nations. Haitian police forces were murdering, falsely imprisoning, creating thousands of political prisoners, and forcing thousands more into exile — all backed up by UN guns between 2004-2006 for the two years following Aristide's ouster.

Today 15-20,000 Haitians marched in the capital, beginning at Aristide's former church. The first AP reports said only hundreds of Aristide supporters demonstrated in the streets. What they didn't say was that thousands of UN troops were blocking and cordoning off the poor neighborhood of Bel Air, where Lavalas support is strong. They also blocked the major thoroughfare coming out of Cité de Soleil. Both of these cities are bastions of support for Lavalas. There were thousands of UN forces going throughout the street, trying to intimidate the people not to demonstrate. But when the word got out that the UN troops had the strategy of blocking them, the press actually did their job and covered the UN blocking the thoroughfares and aiming their guns at the population. So the UN was forced to back down. The US is trying to give the veneer of normalcy and democracy coming to Haiti. The current president of Haiti, Michel Martelly, could not have come to power without a direct intervention of the US embassy and the international community. He was able to get elected with only 14% of the vote. Despite what the UN did, between 15-20,000 Lavalas supporters took to the streets today.

DB: *Remind us what happened on February 29, 2004.*

KP: I lived through that period in Haiti.

DB: *Yes, you reported to us contemporaneously what was happening on the ground. We have clear proof of a US, Canada, and French-backed operation.*

KP: This was preceded by at least a year of destabilization. The World Bank and the IMF cut off money. There were so-called opposition demonstrations demanding Aristide's resignation by an organization calling itself Group 184, a civil society organization of 184 people, which included sweatshop owners in opposition to Lavalas and which called for Aristide's resignation. Where are they today? If they had such roots in Haitian society, they would still be around. It vanished into the ether.

DB: *Those who did not vanish were the death squads that were welcomed back.*

KP: As well as the former brutal military, which actually performed this coup. Being on the ground, I remember that one day Colin Powell said we need to back the constitutional president of Haiti — we will not accept anything that is unconstitutional to remove the current leader. One week later, there was a well organized, USAID-funded demonstration of 15-20,000 people calling for Aristide's resignation, with US and French Embassy cars trailing the demonstration and lots of media transported on buses. This was a media coup. Those demonstrations dwindled to 600 in a week, and it was ugly. The very next day Colin Powell said Aristide had to go. Also the next day, the former brutal military and death squads led by Guy Philippe, former chief of police — a known human rights violator and cocaine trafficker — came over from bases they organized in the Dominican Republic and began seizing townships in Haiti. At that point Powell said Aristide must go. Once they lost the media war, when it was clear the opposition had no steam, the paramilitary forces come in from the Dominican Republic to give the real justification and rationale for forcing Aristide out.

DB: *They had a lot of weapons.*

KP: Brand-new M16s, which the Dominican Republic received just a year earlier. Flashpoints broke the story that the Dominican army received 20,000 brand new M16s from the Pentagon. These were many of the same weapons, including M50s, that showed up in the hands of Guy Philippe and the former brutal military that came from the Dominican Republic to overthrow Aristide.

DB: *Some members of the death squads convicted by a War Crimes Tribunal and investigated in Haiti were back in power. It was the beginning of the reconstituting of the brutal Haitian military.*

KP: At that point the entire police force was purged. The entire government was purged. It wasn't just Aristide who was overthrown. There were over 7,400 elected officials at the local and national level thrown out of office and driven into hiding. Some were murdered.

Currently, guys in red shirts are going into communities in Cité de Soleil and Bel Air to intimidate Lavalas supporters. Martelly has increased repression against Lavalas. He is the boy of the US.

Update: February 29, 2016

On leap year of 2016, the twelfth anniversary of the US led coup against the constitutional government of Jean Bertrand Aristide, more than 10,000 people demonstrated all around the country. There is a reemergence of former President Rene Preval, previously closely aligned with Lavalas and Aristide. However, he distanced himself from them in 2006 when he never fulfilled his campaign promises to help return Aristide from exile in South Africa after the coup, to release political prisoners, and to end the repression against Lavalas. Instead, Rene Preval began a campaign to co-opt Lavalas leadership and take the base of the party of the poor from the popular organizations and neighborhoods — not just from the capital, but also throughout the country. Of course that campaign failed. On the 12th anniversary, Lavalas, despite two coups, thousands of people killed, and losing nearly 25% of their supporters during the earthquake, can still turn out large crowds.

The Inverted Logic Behind the North Korean Crisis

Christine Hong   April 2013

DB: *US propagandists and the mainstream media present foreign crises, like the current one with North Korea, as black-and-white morality plays, with Official Washington behaving wisely and the adversaries as crazy. But the reality is always more complex. In early March, the US and South Korea launched an expanded set of war games on the Korean Peninsula, prompting concerns in some circles that the military exercises might touch off an escalation of tensions with North Korea. Christine Hong, professor at the University of California at Santa Cruz, is worried that the US "was lurching towards war" since "the military exercises that the US and South Korea just launched are not defensive exercises" but rather appear to promote a "regime change" strategy.*

There's a lot of disinformation and patriotic reporting coming out of the US. What is the situation and how dangerous is it?

CH: All we see is media reporting that singularly ascribes blame to North Korea, which is portrayed as a kind of unquestionable evil, so what the US is doing in response to the supposed provocation seems eminently justified. I think we are at a crisis point. It doesn't feel dissimilar to the kind of media rhetoric that surrounded the run-up to the US invasion in Iraq. During that time also, there was a steady drumbeat to war. What do the facts tell us? I will give one example of the inverted logic coming out of the media and US administration. In a recent Pentagon press conference, [Defense Secretary] Chuck Hagel was asked whether or not the US sending D2 stealth bombers from Missouri to fly and conduct a *sortie* over South Korea and drop what the Department of Defense calls inert munitions in a simulated run against North Korea, could be understood as provocative. He said no, they couldn't be understood as provocative. And it was dutifully reported as such. There is a distorted informational landscape in which the average person who listens to these reports can't make heads or tails of what is happening.

What has happened since Kim Jong Un came into his leadership position in North Korea is that the US has pursued a policy of regime change. We tend to think of regime change operations and initiatives as a signature or hallmark policy of the Bush administration. But we have seen under President Barack Obama a persistence of the US policy of getting rid of those powers it finds uncooperative around the world. After Kim Jong Il passed away in December 2011, the US and South Korea launched the biggest and longest set of war exercises they ever conducted. And for the first time it openly exercised OPLAN 5029, which is a US war plan that essentially simulates regime collapse in North Korea. It also envisions US forces occupying North Korea. What is routine during these war exercises, which are ongoing right now, as we speak, is that they simulate nuclear strikes against North Korea. These war games are a combination of simulated computer-assisted activities as well as live fire drills. Last year, the first year of Kim Jong Un's leadership, a South Korean official was asked about the OPLAN 5029 and why South Korea, in tandem with the US, was exercising this regime collapse scenario. He said the death of Kim Jong Il makes the situation ripe to exercise precisely this kind of war plan.

It's almost impossible for us in the US to imagine Mexico and the historic foe of the US, Russia, conducting joint exercises that simulate an invasion of the US and a foreign occupation of the US. That is precisely what North Korea has been enduring for several decades.

DB: *For some time now, the press have been stenographers for the State Department. We do not understand the level and intensity of the so-called war games offshore of North Korea. The press plays a key role in fanning the flames of a dangerous situation. How dangerous is it now?*

CH: I think it's hair-trigger dangerous. The commanding general of the US armed forces in Korea, James Thurman, said that even the smallest miscalculation could lead to catastrophic consequences. Even though many blame North Korea, I think everyone realizes this is a very volatile situation.

China has stepped up its military presence, amassing its forces along the North Korea-China border, sending military vehicles and conducting controlled flights over this area. It's also conducted its own live fire drills in the West Sea yet no one in the Western media is reporting on this. It is a situation eerily reminiscent of the Korean War, in which you can envision alliances like the US and South Korea, with China in some echo of the past aligning itself with North Korea. I think it's a very dangerous situation we are in right now. The abysmal nature of the reporting is reflected in the fact that all you hear is jingoism. US and North Korean relations must be premised on peace. For over six decades, the relations between the two countries have been premised on war. US policy toward North Korea throughout the existence of North Korea has been one of regime change.

War doesn't get conducted only on the level of battles or simulated battles. It gets conducted on a terrain of information. That's why misinformation and disinformation prevail with the reporting of US and North Korean relations in the western media.

DB: *Secretary of State John Kerry called North Korea's actions dangerous and reckless and he continues to be part of a policy to send the most advanced stealth fighting weaponry. Do you think there are countries cheering — maybe not in the foreground — that somebody finally said, "No, you can't make believe we are an aggressor. You can't turn us into an enemy when you are having exercises with 60,000 troops. You can't plan to invade us and expect us to just stand by."*

CH: Yes. That is the other inverted reality. There is the reality of those of us in the US — locked into the limitations of our positions here — and the rest of the world. This is classic US Cold War foreign policy. So much of what goes on in our name in US foreign policy is a blood-soaked history. If you pause to think about the lived reality of those unfortunate enough to be on the receiving end of US foreign policy, then you realize why George Bush had that plaintive cry, "Why do they hate us?" It was a soul-searching incapacity to understand the causes of anti-Americanism around the world. If we are going to have a sensible approach to procuring any common future with the rest of the world, we are going to have to reckon with our foreign policy.

DB: Is the US foreign policy predicated on keeping a divide between the North and the South?

CH: Since the inception of something called North Korea and South Korea, the US has been instrumental throughout. In 1945, scarcely three days after the bombing of Nagasaki, two junior US army officers, Dean Rusk and Charles Bonesteel, retired to a small room armed with nothing more than a National Geographic map of the Korean peninsula, with which, in a 30-minute session — with absolutely no consultation of any Korean — they divided the Korean peninsula. This division of the Korean peninsula at the 38th parallel into north and south, and the creation of a southern government, had no popular legitimacy.

North Korea, by contrast, emerged from a very long anti-colonial struggle against the Japanese. What was created by the US act of partition is a divided system in which one in three Korean families at that time were separated. A divided state was visited on the Koreans who were colonized by the Japanese and were not a war aggressor during WW II. What this eventually ensured is that there would be a civil war of national unification that would be fought by both sides, the North and South.

That tension has served US purposes. The US claims that it is doing these very provocative actions, deploying stealth bombers, etc, because it needs to give a show of support to its South Korean ally. But of course, this fundamentally misunderstands history and the fact that the US from the beginning has exploited the division for its own geopolitical advantage.

DB: *What is happening in the South? Is there a grassroots movement that includes unity and shows concern for this kind of US hegemony in the region?*

CH: Absolutely. The specter of a nuclear war and a US nuclear strike against North Korea would not just impact those people who live above the 38th parallel. It would inevitably impact the rest of the peninsula — environmentally, and in every possible way. These are two countries very much tied through families, communities, etc. Nuclear ruin is an unimaginable outcome for both sides. When the South Korean people have been polled as to which country they think is the greater threat, the US or North Korea, they point to the US.

In the South, as well as in the North, 60 years represents a full lifetime. South Korean progressive activists have said, "We had 60 years of a war system." This year is the 60th anniversary of the signing of the Korean War armistice that brought the Korean War to a temporary halt, but did not end the Korean War. After six decades of a war system, activists have declared 2013 as the first year of Korean peace. We've had 60 years of war, and we are inaugurating a new era of peace. Heaven forbid the US continues its strategy for denuclearizing North Korea. North Korea believes that nuclear power is the basis of its sovereignty. Heaven forbid that the US, rather than finding a way of co-existing with North Korea, actually deploys nuclear weapons to stop nuclearization. That would be the greatest irony of all.

DB: *If you had ten minutes to advise Barack Obama about what US foreign policy might be helpful, what would you say?*

CH: I would say that the US would secure many gains if it were to seriously consider peace. Donald Gregg, the head of the CIA in South Korea for many years and the former US ambassador to South Korea, and Franklin Graham, son of Billy Graham, who runs a humanitarian aid organization that provides food relief in North Korea, both said, after Dennis Rodman returned from

North Korea, that we had to heed the message he was conveying to Obama; "Call me. We don't want war." They both stated that however irregular the form of the message, it could not be ignored. Most US presidents get vision in their second term. In regard to North Korea, even G.W. Bush eventually came around to the position that engagement and diplomacy was the only way forward. I would only hope that Barack Obama would come to his senses about North Korea as well.

[Since this interview was conducted, the US and South Korea, in June 2015, agreed upon a new operational war plan, OPLAN 5015. Although kept largely under wraps, OPLAN 5015, like previous operational war plans, envisions a scenario of all-out war on the Korean peninsula, yet it also lays out an explicit blueprint for a preemptive strike against North Korea and the "decapitation" of the North Korean leadership. CH]

The Cuban Five

Danny Glover   September 2013

DB: *In the 1990s during a resurgent wave of terrorism inside Cuba, five Cuban intelligence agents infiltrated Cuban-exile groups in Miami seeking to uncover planned attacks that the US government was doing little to prevent, in line with its half century of hostility toward the Cuban revolution. The five agents were arrested on Sept. 12, 1998; they were tried in Miami, convicted of crimes related to espionage and given harsh sentences, including Gerardo Hernandez, who received double life plus 15 years. Despite questions about prejudice at their trials and international appeals for their release, four of the men remain in prison. [See Editor's Note below for update.]*

The case of the Cuban Five reflects the profound hypocrisy of the US "War on Terror," which has sent armies to faraway lands to battle al-Qaeda and its allies and has dispatched lethal drones to hunt down and kill suspected Islamic militants. But the same government has ignored the presence of well-known Cuban terrorists who live comfortably in Miami. Then, when the Cuban government sought to obtain information about planned terror attacks by sending intelligence agents to Miami, those agents are aggressively prosecuted and severely punished, even as Cuban-exile terrorists are treated as heroes by US politicians — including members of the Bush family.

Perhaps the best-known and outspoken supporter of the movement to free the Cuban intelligence agents is actor Danny Glover. Danny Glover, why are you engaged in this case?

DG: The case itself expresses the crux of what the dilemma is with Cuba, which is the US's inability or unwillingness to honor or respect Cuban sovereignty, the Cuban state, and the Cuban people's will. The case represents all of that. This is 50 years of failed policy. This War on Terror goes as far back as 1998 and the Cubans were certainly at work with the US, the FBI and other agencies to curb the terrorist activity that had gone on for years. Cuban exiles organized, conducted, or orchestrated attacks on Cuban people, including the explosion of the jetliner that killed children and the Olympic fencing team over 20 years ago. The Cubans have offered as much cooperation as possible to end the terror. Part of the cooperation was to provide the FBI and other agencies vital information as it was uncovered.

The Cubans infiltrated a group that was planning attacks and had carried out attacks against the Cuban people. One person who died from these attacks was an Italian citizen. The Cuban situation provides us with an opportunity to not only deal with the complexities of the legal situation, but also to address the historic relationship between the US and Cuba. Hopefully it is a relationship that will bring about another way of honoring Cuban sovereignty, self-reliance, and independence. Saul Landau made a wonderful documentary about who the real terrorists are. Gerardo Hernandez has the longest sentence — double life and 15 years.

DB: *You've been visiting him. Can we hear about those visits?*

DG: I can't recall a more remarkable man than Gerardo. His commitment to protecting his nation comes first. His incredible political sensibility came into this maximum-security prison in Victorville, which has transformed relationships so that even the hardened criminals have come to respect him. He shouldn't be in a maximum-security prison. It is a reflection of how mean-spirited this process has been. It is clear this is a man who would be at the forefront of work on behalf of transforming the relationship between the US and his own country. His infiltration of the terrorist group in Miami was part of that. Creating a situation where we have a just relationship with Cuba is vital. Every country in Latin America has some kind of working relationship with Cuba. All other countries honor Cuban sovereignty, which is the choice of the Cuban people to govern themselves as they see fit. The only country that doesn't respect Cuban sovereignty is the US.

DB: *Many Third World countries depend on Cuba for training doctors and creating a medical structure that wouldn't exist if it weren't for the Cubans.*

DG: The Cubans exemplify the morality of the code doctors take. They operate in countries around the world, often in situations where they are welcome by some groups and not welcome by others. They go to places that doctors from other nations generally don't go. Cuban doctors go where there is an absence of health care, like Zambia, rural areas of Venezuela and Brazil. So they have had an enormous impact on establishing an infrastructure and an idea of health care as a right and not a privilege. Wherever they go, they establish that as a foundation — health care is a right, not a privilege.

DB: *The Cubans represent one of the few counties in this world that has managed to resist the US hegemony. They took a stand against terrible things that happened in their region. The US seems to have it out for them.*

DG: My other love is a place called Haiti, and I often look at their struggle in the same way. The Haitian revolution, and the victory of the Haitian slave revolt, was unacceptable, and the Haitians are paying for that right now. The Cuban revolution of 1959 was unacceptable to the powers that be, and the Cuban people continue to pay for that. What we need is the release of a certain energy, so that in our deepest place, we ourselves would want to honor and respect the energy of these two countries.

[René González was released on October 7, 2011. Of the remaining four, Fernando González was released on February 27, 2014 and the rest were released on December 17, 2014, in a swap with Cuba for an American intelligence officer. Gerardo Hernandez stated after his release, "I'm ready to receive my next order. I can serve anywhere my country believes that I am useful." *Ed.*]

Pivoting Japan Back Toward Militarism

Tim Shorrock   July 2014

DB: *The Obama administration's much-touted "pivot" to Asia has a militaristic side that involves encouraging Japan to abandon its post-World War II pacifism and make its revamped military a US ally in containing China. US politicians are displaying a rare bipartisanship as they back policies to override Japan's longstanding opposition to militarism and thus make Japan a potent ally of the US strategy for containing China politically, economically, and militarily. Tim Shorrock, who grew up in Japan, is a journalist and author who strongly opposes the policy of remilitarizing Japan and is deeply concerned that it will have a devastating impact on Japan and its people.*

Tim, the wires report that, "Japan takes historic step from post-war pacifism." It talks about Japan's willingness to join this new strategic alliance. Can you talk about what's going on?

TS: This is a real tragedy. I grew up in Japan in the 50s and 60s, and always appreciated that they adopted a peace constitution under the US occupation, which kept them from taking up arms ever again. They were responsible for a terrible war in Asia, occupying China, Korea, the Philippines, and many other countries. No one in Japan after that war wanted a return to militarism.

Unfortunately, during the Cold War, the US moved away from helping them, pushing them to adopt democratic institutions. During the Cold War, US officials began a military alliance, which continues to this day, and began incorporating Japan into the US military framework in East Asia. Japan supplied the US materials and weapons during the Korean War and the Vietnam War as well.

The Japanese ruling party — the Liberal Democratic Party — ruled for most of the post-war period, although there were brief periods when they were out. But they've been the US's best friends in Japan. They're a very far-right party. Prime Minister Shinzo Abe comes from this very Right-wing faction of a very Right-wing party, which wanted to restore Japan's place in the world as it was during World War II, but in the alliance of the US. This is something the far right in Japan has been pushing for years. Both Democrats and Republicans have pushed it in the US as well. It's been a bipartisan policy to push the Japanese into remilitarization. Now the US can use their military overseas. This is a huge step, and it's very sad to see it happen.

DB: *The US foresees the China Century. US security interests are creating a security ring around China. Japan can play a key role.*

TS: Yes. We have a massive naval presence in Japan at Yokosuka and a few other bases. We practically control the entire island of Okinawa, which is a major Marine base, a forward basing platform for US Marines. All of this is integrated in US bases in South Korea and, of course, we have just reopened bases in the Philippines, and are building another Marine base in Australia. It's the biggest US military buildup in Asia since the Vietnam War, and Japan can play a critical role in this. During the last 15 years or so, under the LDP [Liberal Democratic Party] government, they were doing things like escorting US ships going to Afghanistan and Iraq. They're using China as the excuse for this, but it's been long in the planning, and our bases remain there. The Soviet Union collapsed, and nothing changed. The US bases remain there. There was never any kind of cut back in that base structure.

DB: *You grew up in Japan. What were the impacts of the base at Okinawa on the local life and politics of Japan?*

TS: The US military controls a huge percentage of the island of Okinawa. There's one Marine base there now. The city goes right up to the edge of the base. Planes fly over the neighborhoods constantly. There's a terrible footprint, as they like to call it. Okinawans live with constant noise, the possibility of plane crashes and, of course, the behavior of US troops — rape, drunkenness and that kind of thing. They have been putting up with it for almost 60 years now.

When I was growing up, some of the biggest demonstrations I ever saw in my life were against the US bases in Japan, which were used as a launching pad to bomb Vietnam. There was a huge Japanese citizens' movement at the time, which forced the US to stop using Okinawa as a base for B52s to bomb Vietnam. Those were removed to Guam.

The Japanese have put up with this militarism and the US bases for a long time. Now they are consolidated in Okinawa, with the exception of a few major bases on the mainland. In some ways, a lot of Japanese people think, "Well, that's down in Okinawa, so it doesn't affect us so much." But for Okinawans it's a terrible thing. Over the next few months, they're expanding one Marine base in Henoko Bay, where there's all kinds of marine life because it's very well protected environmentally. It's going to destroy that environment. We're going to see a lot of protests here because people in Okinawa are starting to demonstrate and block the construction of these bases. But, overall, it's a sad day, and I'm ashamed that my government has been pushing them into this, particularly a president like Obama, who comes out like he appreciates democracy and is liberal and progressive. He's siding with the most Right-wing elements in Japan.

DB: *You called this a tragedy.*

TS: I do. Here's a country that vowed never to make war again. It has a pacifist constitution, something that no other country had, which was widely supported by the Japanese population. It kept Japan from participating in wars, and the people wanted it that way. Looking back, World War II was horrific. Every city was bombed and people were starving towards the end of the war. People don't want that kind of war ever again.

The Japanese began to be concerned about the US bases during the Korean War. They saw the US bombing Korea the same way they bombed Japan. And that really began to turn people away from what at first they welcomed — the American occupation. The occupation did change things for the better in the first few years. But then that got sucked into the Cold War, opposing China and the Soviet Union. Japan got more and more integrated with that US military structure. For years the Japanese role was a kind of economic part of imperial power. The US supplied the bases, military hardware and so on. The Japanese would lend money to South Korea, support South Korea economically, and support Taiwan economically. They were the economic base of all of this.

That's going to continue, but now they're going to add the military component to it, so their military could easily expand. It's a very top heavy, officer-concentrated military. All they need to do is start bringing in the ground troops and they could have a very large military. They already do have a large military, so there are all kinds of repercussions for Japanese society through this.

DB: *Many Koreans are waiting for apologies from Japan about the brutalization of women.*

TS: Sexual slavery...

DB: *There is a seven-year demonstration in Jeju in South Korea because the US is in the middle of forcing the Koreans to build a massive base. No South Korean ships need a base that big. It's a new militarized unity forced by the US and its bipartisan Congress.*

TS: Yes. What's sickening about this issue of the apology about World War II is that in the 1990s, during a very brief period, when Japan had a Socialist Party prime minister who defeated the LDP, the ruling party issued an apology for Japan's role in World War II in Asia. Now they're talking about reversing that apology, or watering it down. The Japanese leaders have complete contempt for the people they invaded in World War II. Unlike the Germans, who have de-Nazified their country — now it is illegal to come out as a Nazi in Germany — in Japan there's a World War II revivalism. These people want to restore the

313

Japan that was so strong before it was defeated by the US. But they want to do it in conjunction, in alliance with the US because they know they can never be an independent power to the US. That's what they want. You hear people in the Japanese government say, "Colonialism was good for Korea, it was really good for China" and this kind of thing. That's the kind of people that our national security people work closest with and prefer in power over democratic elements in Japan.

DB: *This new, extreme Right-wing leader of the country is post-Fukushima and the tsunami. They are still struggling with Fukushima, but it seems like nuclear has come back to haunt the Japanese people.*

TS: There's a lot of sentiment in Japan against nuclear power because of Fukushima and the history of Hiroshima and Nagasaki. This summer is going to be the first nuclear-free summer in Japan for decades. Many of these power plants are shut down — some were built on fault lines. There's been a lot of controversy over many of the power plants, so they have had to shut many down to re-inspect them. The nuclear industry is part of the military industry. They don't have nuclear weapons but they could easily build nuclear weapons. They have everything they need except for actual bomb-making facilities. The Japanese defense industry is hungry for overseas markets, and that's what this is going to open up. There are giant Japanese conglomerates, like Mitsubishi, that already make weapons. American defense contractors, like Lockheed Martin and Northrop Grumman, are already getting lots of deals, and look forward to Japan being a big, expanded market in working Japanese companies, to export weapons. This is a big payoff for the defense/ military industry in Japan and the United States.

The Oil Wars: Iraq, Kurdistan, and the Islamic State

Antonia Juhasz   August 2014

DB: *President George W. Bush's invasion of Iraq gave US and other Western oil companies a major stake in the country's giant oil fields, a foothold now threatened by the offensive launched by the Islamic State and offering at least a partial explanation for President Barack Obama's decision to return the US military to the conflict. Another complicating factor is Kurdistan's control of some giant oil fields and its push for independence.*

Antonia Juhasz is an oil industry analyst and investigative journalist. Antonia, why are the Kurds and Kurdistan of great interest to the US?

AJ: We are clearly engaged in a military action for oil. But the Obama administration is not the Bush administration. If the only thing at stake in Kurdistan now was protecting oil interests, we would not be engaging militarily, but if the Bush administration were in power now, we would be. The 2003 invasion of Iraq was about many things, but one of the most dominant was oil and the desire to get western oil corporations on the ground in Iraq. That goal was achieved by the Bush administration. Today we have Exxon producing from some of the largest oil fields in the world. Other western companies like BP and Shell — all of the major western companies — are operating in Iraq and doing quite well.

From the very beginning of the invasion, however, there was a strong issue in the area of Iraq known as Kurdistan that wanted independence from the rest of Iraq, with the Kurds trying to garner western favor to achieve that goal. The Kurds have a tremendous amount of oil. While the Bush administration succeeded in getting very good access for western oil companies in the rest of Iraq, what it didn't get was the Iraq oil law which western oil companies helped draft and the Bush administration pushed.

The Kurdish government was basically opening up Iraq on the most favorable terms to the western oil companies. The central Iraqi government said no to that level of turning themselves over. The Kurds said yes. Very early on, the Kurds passed their own version of the Iraq oil law, and started signing contracts with western oil companies, letting them in under the most generous terms. I believe this is a way of saying, "We are helping you, and so you must help us gain independence." That never happened.

The US military never came in on behalf of the Kurds in any direct way, although western oil companies certainly tried to use this division between the Kurdistan region and the central Iraqi government in terms of how they dealt with oil countries. Companies like Genel, headed by Tony Hayward — the former CEO of BP who was ousted because of the Gulf oil spill — is very active in Kurdistan. We've seen US policy makers now coming out loudly in favor of aggressive military action who were former heads of the Bush administration, like Zalmay Khalilzad — who were heading, lobbying, and advising economic interests in Kurdistan — making a lot of talk about war.

Companies like Exxon, Chevron, and Marathon all have exploration contracts in Kurdistan but have not gone to work there because of the dispute about who owns the oil — the central Iraqi government or Kurdistan.

DB: *It was an important moment when the soldiers took over the oil fields there. This was a big sea change.*

AJ: A huge sea change. Now enters ISIS. I think ISIS has truly shocked the world in the power it has — the level it has in taking over Syria and Iraq. One of the things that aided their sheer force and success is oil. ISIS is fighting an oil war. They are taking over fields in Syria, selling the oil on the black market and using that money to fund their efforts. They are taking over refineries and using that gasoline to fuel their trucks and their jeeps. They are targeting oil fields and infrastructure.

When they went into northern Iraq, they tried to take the Kirkuk oil field, one of the largest oil fields in the world. The armed forces of the Kurds, the Peshmerga, did what the Kurds had never done before — they took back or took over the Kirkuk field. Once they had that field under their control, it was a decisive moment for the Kurds to say we have this oil and we are not going to give it back. We are going to take independence.

ISIS keeps going and threatening Kurdistan and their goal. Now all of those interests are in trouble because ISIS could succeed in taking over the capital of Kurdistan, Erbil, although they can't take over all of Kurdistan. The Kurds are saying we are not going anywhere. Even more than before, ISIS is more powerful than ever, and looking like it is truly threatening Kurdistan.

DB: *What is the US military trying to do, given this very fragile situation?*

AJ: Now the US military enters on the side of the Kurds. We start funneling weapons to the Peshmerga. We start bombing in and around Erbil. We say we are not going to let ISIS take over Kurdistan. We are not going to let ISIS have that oil. We are not going to lose that oil for the western companies and western interests. We are not going to lose the extreme support we have gotten from the Kurdish government.

But that is not the only thing happening. Simultaneously, the Obama administration is looking at the rest of Iraq and saying this is not working out the way it was supposed to. Things are disintegrating, we are getting blamed for it and we need to figure something out. Several months ago, or earlier, [Prime Minister Nouri al-] Maliki became the fall guy — earned by becoming a terrible leader — and was pinpointed as the problem to get rid of. The Obama administration is saying to the rest of Iraq and the Iraqi central government, "Get rid of Maliki and get someone in place who will abide by our interests broadly or we

317

are going to do something you don't want," which is aid the Kurds in their independence.

That would greatly upset the central Iraqi government for many reasons, including losing the very large fields of oil in the Kurdistan region. Bombing is a deadly tool of political influence, which says, "Do what we want or we will do something to you that you don't want — we will do it militarily."

DB: *ISIS is in Iraq. The border is disappearing with Syria. The US is supporting the supposed moderates in Syria. A version of ISIS appears to be calling the shots in Syria. There are 30 million Kurds in Turkey watching what is happening to the 5 million Kurds in Kurdistan. How do the politics intersect with the oil and the economies?*

AJ: Although I am not an expert on the surrounding areas, what is very clear is that oil is a part of the discussion with each country. But as you point out, it is not just oil. There are longstanding ethnic issues and identities — a group of people was broken up into three separate countries, although it is one group of people. But it also involves oil and oil power.

As I said earlier, the Obama administration is not the Bush administration. I don't believe the Obama administration, devoid of other more dominant interests in Iraq, would have entered into this dispute on Kurdistan solely to protect the interests of western oil companies, including Exxon and Chevron. But certainly those oil interests are part of the decision-making, what is unfolding, and what is bringing the military back into Iraq.

When we look at how to solve the problem, it's not just about exposing the oil agenda. It's about exposing the desire of the Obama administration to continue to control the broader political outcomes in Iraq through the military — that is part of the problem. There is renewed talk of the Obama administration breaking Iraq up and entering into this dispute to separate Iraq into pieces, including separating out Kurdistan. That was an interest within the Bush administration and with people like

[Vice President Joe] Biden and others who have said that might be a solution.

There is a difference between having a solution to separate Iraq and using the military to achieve that goal. I believe the Obama administration and the oil companies would prefer a unified and stable Iraq. This military action in Kurdistan is a tool to make that happen — to get the central Iraqi government in line with the threat of separating out Kurdistan. But if they can't succeed in creating a unified stable Iraq, a separate Kurdistan is a pill the Obama administration and western oil companies are willing to swallow.

DB: *Apparently, the Kurds have been able to sell oil to the Israelis. If there were an independent Kurdish country, what would their policy look like?*

AJ: The Kurds are just trying to make money. The central Iraqi government has said that all Kurdish contracts and attempts to sell oil are illegal, that only the central Iraqi government can sell oil — nobody else can sign contracts. They say that every contract and attempt the Kurds made to operate on their own are illegal.

The Kurds have tried to smuggle and sell their oil where and to whoever they can. The Kurdistan government is deeply, deeply in debt. I believe they smuggled and sold oil to Israel because they could. They could get money there. I don't know that it tells us anything about what they would look like as an independent country. It just tells us they are desperate for cash.

Thunder Wilder than Thunder: Mourning Many 9/11's

Martin Espada   September 2014

DB: *Time and history sometimes intertwine in ways more poetic than linear, such as the multiple crimes associated with the date September 11th. Most Americans associate 9/11 only with the tragic events in 2001 but the date has a very different meaning to Chileans and others who remember the US-backed coup in 1973 that overthrew Chile's elected President Salvador Allende and plunged that peaceful South American nation into the nightmare of military repression. Award-winning poet Martin Espada reflects on those mixed legacies.*

When people think about September 11th, almost overwhelmingly — especially if you are white — they think about the Twin Towers. But September 11th is an incredibly important date. On September 11th, 1973, the United States participated in a coup to overthrow the duly elected, socialist government of Salvador Allende. How do these come together for you — one date, two incidents?

ME: The poet and essayist Ariel Dorfman said, "11 September has been a date of mourning, for me and millions of others, ever since that Tuesday in 1973 when Chile lost its democracy in a military coup." The fact that people in this country only associate 9/11 with events of September 11, 2001, says something about our historical amnesia. It was only in 1973 — less than a generation before — when we as a nation hid our collective eyes at the sight of our government orchestrating a military coup in Chile.

This is what happens when you live in the belly of the beast, as they say in Latin America about the US. What happens when you develop historical amnesia? What are the consequences of forgetting? How is it that, in the end, countless numbers of innocent people are killed? Whether it's on this continent, or that continent, or lands thousands of miles away that have nothing to do with the Americas.

DB: *Please read "Alabanza: In Praise of Local 100." It covers that terrain.*

ME: Over the days and weeks following 9/11, a new story began to emerge very slowly through the BBC, about one particular restaurant called Windows on the World, and the members of a union there, Hotel Employees and Restaurant Employees, Local 100. Forty-three members of that union were killed that day, most of them immigrant and many of them undocumented. They were invisible in life and even more invisible in death — some families of these victims couldn't even come forward to claim benefits. They literally vanished without a trace. I consider it a mission of mine — in the tradition of Neruda and Whitman — to make the invisible visible.

Alabanza is the Spanish word for praise. I wrote "Alabanza: In Praise of Local 100," for the 43 members of Hotel Employees and Restaurant Employees Local 100, workers at the Windows on the World restaurant who lost their lives in the attack on the World Trade Center.

> *Alabanza.* Praise the cook with a shaven head
> and a tattoo on his shoulder that said *Oye,*
> a blue-eyed Puerto Rican with people from Fajardo,
> the harbor of pirates centuries ago.
> Praise the lighthouse in Fajardo, candle
> glimmering white to worship the dark saint of the sea.
> *Alabanza.* Praise the cook's yellow Pirates cap
> worn in the name of Roberto Clemente, his plane
> that flamed into the ocean loaded with cans for Nicaragua,
> for all the mouths chewing the ash of earthquakes.
> *Alabanza.* Praise the kitchen radio, dial clicked
> even before the dial on the oven, so that music and Spanish
> rose before bread. Praise the bread. *Alabanza.*
>
> Praise Manhattan from a hundred and seven flights up,
> like Atlantis glimpsed through the windows of an ancient aquarium.
> Praise the great windows where immigrants from the kitchen
> could squint and almost see their world, hear the chant of nations:
> *Ecuador, México, República Dominicana,*
> *Haiti, Yemen, Ghana, Bangladesh.*

Alabanza. Praise the kitchen in the morning,
where the gas burned blue on every stove
and exhaust fans fired their diminutive propellers,
hands cracked eggs with quick thumbs
or sliced open cartons to build an altar of cans.
Alabanza. Praise the busboy's music, the *chime-chime*
of his dishes and silverware in the tub.

Alabanza. Praise the dish-dog, the dishwasher
who worked that morning because another dishwasher
could not stop coughing, or because he needed overtime
to pile the sacks of rice and beans for a family
floating away on some Caribbean island plagued by frogs.
Alabanza. Praise the waitress who heard the radio in the kitchen
and sang to herself about a man gone. *Alabanza.*

After the thunder wilder than thunder,
after the shudder deep in the glass of the great windows,
after the radio stopped singing like a tree full of terrified frogs,
after night burst the dam of day and flooded the kitchen,
for a time the stoves glowed in darkness like the lighthouse in Fajardo,
like a cook's soul. Soul I say, even if the dead cannot tell us
about the bristles of God's beard because God has no face,
soul I say, to name the smoke-beings flung in constellations
across the night sky of this city and cities to come.
Alabanza I say, even if God has no face.

Alabanza. When the war began, from Manhattan and Kabul
two constellations of smoke rose and drifted to each other,
mingling in icy air, and one said with an Afghan tongue:
Teach me to dance. We have no music here.
And the other said with a Spanish tongue:
I will teach you. Music is all we have.

DB: *Beautiful.*

ME: We will see as we tie these disparate elements together —
9/11, the Villa Grimaldi poem — the urgent necessity to bear
witness, which is something poets ought to do.

DB: *As a tenant lawyer, you helped tenants deal with slumlords. You
were on the front line.*

ME: Yes. As a lawyer or as a poet, I believe in the principle of bearing witness. Likewise, when we talk about bearing witness, we must speak not only in terms of the present but in terms of the past, to see if we can connect the past with the present, and see to what extent we are making the same mistakes, ignoring the lessons of history.

DB: *Could you read the poem about Villa Grimaldi?*

ME: Yes. On September 11th, 1973, there was a military coup in Chile, which overthrew elected socialist president Salvador Allende, and brought to power the dictatorship of General Augusto Pinochet, who would not be dislodged for 17 years.

I visited Chile twice. The second time, some years after Pinochet was ousted, I went to a place called Villa Grimaldi. Chile is still very much coming to grips with the national trauma, the national devastation of the coup, with thousands killed, and tens of thousands tortured and incarcerated during the dictatorship. Chile is still coming to terms with that, still trying to tell the story, and still bearing witness to the crimes committed there. How do they do it? Well, one way is they create commemorations.

One such commemoration is at Villa Grimaldi. Villa Grimaldi was not a prison; it was a center of interrogation, torture and execution during the Pinochet dictatorship. It has now been reconstructed as a peace park. When the military pulled out of there, they tried to destroy the evidence of their crimes — cover their tracks. However, with the assistance of those who survived, and even a few guards, Villa Grimaldi was reconstructed.

There are also some parts of Villa Grimaldi that are original to the institution. One such original structure is, believe it or not, a swimming pool. That useful phrase "the banality of evil" comes to mind. Consider the whole concept of bearing witness as I read this poem. It is called "The Swimming Pool at Villa Grimaldi," Santiago, Chile.

Beyond the gate where the convoys spilled their cargo
of blindfolded prisoners, and the cells too narrow to lie down,
and the rooms where electricity convulsed the body
strapped across the grill until the bones would break,
and the parking lot where interrogators rolled pickup trucks
over the legs of subversives who would not talk,
and the tower where the condemned listened through the wall
for the song of another inmate on the morning of execution,
there is a swimming pool at Villa Grimaldi.

Here the guards and officers would gather families
for barbeques. The interrogator coached his son:
Kick your feet. Turn your head to breathe.
The torturer's hands braced the belly of his daughter,
learning to float, flailing at her lesson.

Here the splash of children, eyes red
from too much chlorine, would rise to reach
the inmates in the tower. The secret police
paraded women from the cells at poolside,
saying to them: *Dance for me.* Here the host
served chocolate cookies and Coke on ice
to the prisoner who let the names of comrades
bleed down his chin, and the prisoner
who refused to speak a word stopped breathing
in the water, facedown at the end of a rope.

When a dissident pulled by the hair from a vat
of urine and feces cried out for God, and the cry
pelted the leaves, the swimmers plunged below the surface,
touching the bottom of a soundless blue world.
From the ladder at the edge of the pool they could watch
the prisoners marching blindfolded across the landscape,
one hand on the shoulder of the next, on their way
to the afternoon meal and back again. The neighbors
hung bedsheets on the windows to keep the ghosts away.

There is a swimming pool at the heart of Villa Grimaldi,
white steps, white tiles, where human beings
would dive and paddle till what was human in them
had dissolved forever, vanished like the prisoners
thrown from helicopters into the ocean by the secret police,
their bellies slit so the bodies could not float.

DB: *The US played a crucial role in this slaughter, this undermining
of democracy on September 11, 1973.*

ME: Yes. Allende was seen as a threat for a variety of reasons. First of all, he was the first elected Marxist president of any country in the Western hemisphere. Castro, of course, came to power by revolution. Allende was elected. That was threatening. It was democracy in action, through the ballot box.

Secondly, Allende believed very much in the economic independence of his country. He went about doing something that caused grave offense to US economic interests: he nationalized the copper industry. This offended corporate giants such as Anaconda Copper, Kennecott Copper and I.T &T. Of course, they had a great deal of sway over what happened in Chile, and a great deal of sway over what happened in the White House.

So Richard Nixon and Henry Kissinger cooked up what was called the 40 Committee, overseeing the efforts to destabilize Chile economically and politically, setting the stage for the bloody military coup of September 11, 1973. That time, in some ways, is still upon us.

It is remarkable that, in the present day, we in the US, in the name of security, are debating the efficacy of torture — which torture works best, which torture is ethical, who to torture and who not to torture. As if you could have rules for this sort of thing. If anybody thinks that torture works as an instrument of social policy, all they have to do is look at Chile — that traumatized, and now transcendent, nation.

A New Cold War with Russia

Robert Parry   June 2015

[Robert Parry sadly passed away on January 27, 2018, but ConsortiumNews.com continues his incisive, scholarly legacy. Oliver Stone said of his passing, "Robert Parry's death Saturday night leaves a giant hole in American journalism. To my mind, he exists now alongside I.F. Stone, Drew Pearson, George Seldes, Gary Webb, and others as seekers of truth at the steep price you seem to have to pay to follow your common sense and your integrity when they are in direct opposition to the tyranny of mainstream media conformity." *Ed.*]

DB: *A new Cold War has taken shape between nuclear-armed Russia and the United States with very little public debate, just a return to hostile rhetoric and military moves and counter-moves over Ukraine. Journalist Robert Parry is a longtime Washington-based investigative reporter and editor of* Consortiumnews.com.

Robert, it looks like the US has entered what you call "the second Cold War." What do you mean by the second Cold War?

RP: There is a sharp increase in tension, obviously, between the United States and Russia. We've seen a very divergent way of looking at the problem. The US and mainstream media have taken a very propagandist view of what occurred in Ukraine. The Russians have taken a very different view, which, perhaps to our amazement, is more accurate than what the US is saying.

Because of these two divergent narratives, the countries have essentially plunged back into a cold war, where there's a lot of hostility, threats of military escalations, with the US sending military teams to essentially parade along the western border of Russia. Some of those countries are NATO allies, and others, like Ukraine, may want to become a NATO ally.

So these tensions are building up, that oddly don't have much direct connection to US national interests, but have become a kind of cause célèbre in official Washington, where everyone just wants to stand tough against the Russians and bash Putin. It's become almost a self-perpetuating dynamic.

The Russians have taken a very different perspective, which is that the United States is encroaching on its borders and threatening them in a strategic manner. They also look at what happened in Ukraine very differently. They see a US-backed coup d'état in February 2014 that ousted an elected president and put in a regime that is very supportive of free market, neo-liberal policies, but also includes very strong Right-wing elements, including neo-Nazis and far-right nationalists. A crisis was created and tensions continue to spiral out of control.

DB: *Barack Obama is leading the charge. He is a Cold War warrior.*

RP: He's certainly allowed some of his underlings to use very aggressive rhetoric against the Russians, particularly Assistant Secretary of State Victoria Nuland, who led the charge in supporting the coup in Ukraine in early 2014.

DB: *Most people don't know that occurred. Was there a coup?*

RP: Of course there was. There was an armed uprising that involved some very far right neo-Nazi militias that had been organizing and penetrating into what became the Maidan protests against the decision by the elected President Yanukovych not to go ahead quickly with an association with the European Union. That became increasingly violent; including some mysterious sniper attacks killing police and demonstrators, and getting the two sides to go at each other.

There was a political effort on Feb. 21, 2014, where Yanukovych agreed to reduce his powers and have early elections so he could be elected out of office. It was signed by three European countries to guarantee it. The next day there was a coup. These Right-wing groups surged forward, seizing buildings, and Yanukovych barely escaped with his life.

Very quickly, despite the unconstitutional change of power, the United States and European Union recognized this as legitimate. But it was obviously something the ethnic Russians, especially those in the eastern and southern Ukraine, found objectionable. They were the bases of support for Yanukovych — they rose up, and this coup d'état then merged into a civil war.

DB: You say the US played an active role in this coup.

RP: There's no question. The US was supporting, through the National Endowment for Democracy, scores of organizations working to overthrow the elected government. There were other US entities, like USAID, as well as members of the US government. Sen. John McCain went to Kiev and told a Right-wing group, "The US supports you and what you are doing."

Then there was the famous phone conversation that was intercepted between Assistant Secretary of State Nuland and Ambassador Geoffrey Pyatt where they discussed who was going to take over after the change of power. Nuland put forward that Yatsenyuk "is the guy," and after the coup he became the prime minister. There were all the markings of a coup d'état. Neutral observers who have looked at this, including the head of the Stratfor think tank, George Friedman, have called it the most obvious coup he's ever seen.

That was the reality, but the US news media and government presented it very differently. The Yanukovych government just left the scene, is how the *New York Times* presented it. It wasn't real, but it's how they sold it to the American people.

We have two very distinct ways of looking at this. One is the ethnic Russians of Ukraine who saw their president violently overthrown, and the other is the western Ukrainians, backed by the US, and in some degree the European Union, saying they got rid of a corrupt leader through a revolution. That became the core problem between the US and Russians. Instead of finding common factual points to agree on, there are these two distinctly different narratives about what went on there.

DB: *In Germany, Obama himself carried this forward.*

RP: Obama has been all over the map on this. In May, he sent Secretary of State Kerry to meet with President Putin and Foreign Minister Lavrov in Sochi, Russia. Those meetings, by all accounts, went very well in that Kerry was looking for Russian help on a variety of international problems, including Syria, Libya, the Iran nuclear talks, and so forth. These are areas where Putin has been very helpful in the past in terms of US policy. There was a general meeting of the minds, it seemed.

But after Kerry returned, Obama seemed to swing back, to go more with his hard-liners. That was followed by the recent G7 Summit in Bavaria, at which Obama pushed for a continuation of economic sanctions against Russia. He continued to blame Russia for all the problems of Ukraine. He pretended that the Russians were the problem for why the Minsk 2 Peace Accord had not been going forward, even though the accord was essentially Putin's idea that he sold to the Germans and the French. It's really the Kiev regime that has tried to derail the Minsk 2 agreement from the very time it was signed.

Now we are back into this idea that we must have a confrontation with Russia. We're seeing this play out not just at the government level, but now also at the media level. At the more popular level, the *New York Times* and other major news organizations essentially are acting as propaganda agents for the US government, by simply conveying whatever the government says as fact, not something to be checked out.

DB: *You are saying this as somebody based outside the Beltway?*

RP: No, I'm actually inside the Beltway.

DB: *Good, I feel better that you're in there. You've expressed concerns that we are dealing with two major nuclear powers. We have a man in Russia who will not be fooled with public relations, given that he was a master of it, as head of the KGB. Where is this going?*

RP: It's very dangerous. One hopes, of course, that cooler heads will prevail. But when people paint themselves into corners, they sometimes don't want to get into the embarrassment of getting themselves out. The more rhetoric and propaganda you throw into this, the harder it is for people to come to some common ground, reach an agreement and work things out.

There's this idea among the neoconservatives in Washington that the real goal here is to oust Putin. As Carl Gershman, president of the National Endowment for Democracy, said back in 2013, Ukraine is "the biggest prize." But he made clear that it was simply a stepping-stone to removing Putin as the President of Russia, doing some sort of regime change in Moscow.

What the neocons often fail to understand, as we've seen very painfully in places like Iraq, is they think things will be easy — they can simply put in somebody like Chalabi in Baghdad and everything will work out. But it's often not the way it goes. With Russia, the great danger is that if the US could destabilize Russia, somehow create a political crisis there, it's very possible that instead of an easily manipulated person like Yeltsin, there would be a super hard-line nationalist taking over, taking a harder line than Putin. Then you can get into a situation where a nuclear confrontation would become a very real possibility.

To deal with that kind of dangerous reality and be reasonable, the US needs to realize that the ethnic Russians in Ukraine have a legitimate beef, and they are not simply part of a Russian invasion or aggression. Both sides have some argument here. All the truth does not rest in Washington DC and I would argue that less of it rests in Washington DC. If you don't deal with people honestly and directly, and try to understand their concern, a manageable crisis can turn into one that spins out of control.

DB: *I have always thought that to some degree the* New York Times *and* Washington Post, *on foreign policy issues, have often acted as an arm, a public relations division of the State Department.*

RP: Yes, it's been a problem. In 2002 and 2003, the *Washington Post* and *New York Times* essentially led the drive for believing that Saddam Hussein had WMDs and the only answer was to invade Iraq. We've seen what that led to. The great irony here is that as much as the Washington press corps pretends it stands for truth and all these good things, there was virtually no accountability assessed upon people who misreported that story.

It's true there's safety in numbers. All the important journalists got the story wrong and almost none were punished. They were allowed to go on, many in the same positions that they held then. Michael Gordon is still the Pentagon correspondent for the *New York Times*. He was one of the co-authors of the famous aluminum tube story, that these tubes were being used for nuclear centrifuges, when they weren't fit for that at all. Fred Hiatt, the editorial page editor of the *Washington Post*, said as flat fact that Saddam Hussein had weapons of mass destruction back in 2002 and 2003. He's still in the same job.

There's a problem of no accountability, so many of these news organizations go from one catastrophic inability to report honestly about what is going on, to the next. Now they've upped the ante to a possible confrontation between nuclear-armed Russia and nuclear-armed United States. We are back into the Cold War mentality. The *New York Times* had a recent piece essentially suggesting that anybody who doesn't go along with the US version of events must be working for Moscow.

We are starting to see McCarthyism rear its ugly head. Once you get into propaganda wars, anyone who challenges or questions them has their patriotism questioned. In Iraq, people who questioned the WMD story early were called Saddam apologists. It's similar now. If you point out some of these inconvenient facts that don't make the Kiev regime look too good, you're accused of being a stooge of Moscow.

DB: *This kind of policy could continue. It's not Saddam Hussein now, but Vladimir Putin, who has extreme experience about how to play public relations games. And he has a nuclear arsenal.*

RP: The American propaganda barrage has not swayed the Russian people and government. The US says they are being propagandized by *Russia Today* and other Russian networks. One can argue with some ways some things have been reported by *RT* or other Russian sources, but they have been doing a more accurate, on-the-ground job than the US press corps has been.

You can point to a number of egregious major mistakes made by the major US news organizations. The *New York Times* went along with a bogus photograph from spring 2014 supposedly showing Russian troops in Ukraine. It turned out that some of the photographs were misrepresented and did not show what they were supposed to show. The *Times* writers were forced to retract that.

You can point to factual errors on both sides, but it's not that the facts as the *New York Times* tries to present them, are perfect and haven't been presented improperly, while the Russian media are all lies and propaganda. It's not true. But it's getting to the point where you cannot be a reasonable person, or look at things objectively, because you are pushed into taking sides.

That's where journalism is a very dangerous thing — especially here. There was a lot of dangerous reporting during the Cold War that in some cases pushed the two sides into dangerous confrontations. That can happen again. We were lucky to escape the 60s without a nuclear war. Now we are rushing ourselves back into something that William Polk, a writer and former diplomat of the Kennedy administration, has called a possible Cuban missile crisis in reverse. This time we're the ones pushing our military forces onto the Russian border, rather than the Russians putting missiles onto a place like Cuba. We know how Americans reacted to that. Now Russians are facing something very similar.

Systemic Solutions for the Global Refugee Crisis
Deborah S. Rogers   September 2015

DB: *Dr. Deborah S. Rogers is just back from Budapest, where she found herself in the middle of what unfolded into a huge crisis, with the entire world putting a spotlight on a train station. How did you end up in the middle of that situation?*

DR: I went to Hungary to speak at some meetings about corruption, which is a fitting place to talk about corruption. I had stopped in Prague, in the Czech Republic first, and then took the train from Prague to Budapest. When we rolled into the station, I learned of these human rights abuses, with literally thousands of people living in the tunnels and underground hallways that lead to the train station. When I got off the train, I looked down the staircase and saw this dramatic scene.

DB: *How did you join in?*

DR: First I went to my five days of meetings. When I got back from the meetings and back into Budapest, I was in touch with people. I have a number of friends in Budapest and other parts of Eastern Europe, so I talked with them, and I also went back to the train station several times to see what was going on for myself, and to get a sense of who was there and how they were being treated.

DB: *The world has seen many pictures. Where is the situation now?*

DR: There have been many ups and downs in the past week. It's been heart wrenching because people are flooding into Hungary, the entrance to the EU, from the southern border with Serbia — about 3,000 people a day. That's a huge number of people driven by the need to escape the conflicts they've been trying to live with. That train station in Budapest is still crammed with people. There were several times they let people leave — once, by train. Another time they let people walk, then took them to buses, which took them to the Austrian border. Another time they took them by train, then suddenly dumped them out about 30 miles outside Budapest in what I would have to call concentration camps. I will not dignify these camps with the words refugee camps, because refugee camps must meet international standards. They must meet the needs of food, water and shelter. These camps don't do that.

DB: *There is recent reporting of improvements. Where is the change?*

DR: There's some good news and some bad news. The human rights abuses in Hungary continue, and if anything, are getting worse. There's a place on Hungary's southern border with Serbia where, when people come across, they have to make their way through a razor-wire fence that Hungary has been putting up. If they are caught by the police, they are put into camps that are essentially like cages. People are treated like animals. There is no shade, no shelter. They lie on concrete with metal wires around them. I've seen videos that show the people who run the camp literally throwing the food at the people, throwing bread rolls at them.

People are coming in at a faster rate than they are leaving. Hungary is a bottleneck. People can't move through as fast as they are arriving into Europe. Hungary's response has not been helpful. They are building this razor wire fence now, but plan on building a wall later. The people call it NATO wire, and it causes many injuries. In a very, very troubling move, they have declared a state of emergency. Their military exercises are getting the military prepared to fend off what they are framing as an invasion by Muslim people. They are going to use the army to block the influx of refugees starting on September 15. I don't think it's a coincidence that this is a day after the EU will meet to set quotas of how many refugees each country in the EU must take. This is a threat they are making to the EU.

DB: *How many people in Hungary are facing these dangers?*

DR: I don't have any good estimates, but I believe it's about 10,000, based on how fast people are coming in and how fast they are being allowed to leave. In addition to the militarization, they have declared a police state, passing legislation to give the police all kinds of unconstitutional special powers. People I know living in Hungary are tremendously upset, because they are now living in a police state.

DB: *What kind of police powers do you mean?*

DR: The police have the right to do whatever they think is needed to stop refugees, regardless of what constitutional or human rights people might have.

DB: *They are doing this in the name of national security?*

DR: Yes it's being declared a national emergency. Many people in Hungary are beginning to call it Orbanistan, because Prime Minister Victor Orban is the architect of these policies. Of course, under international law, it's illegal not to accept refugees.

DB: *Who are the majority of refugees?*

DR: It's difficult to pin down. The numbers suggest that about 50% of them come from Syria, the rest from a scattering of countries, all of which are conflict zones that the US has been involved in. There are people from Afghanistan, Pakistan, Iraq, and other places having difficulties — in the Horn of Africa, such as Eritrea. This is the biggest refugee crisis since WWII. 400,000 refugees have entered Europe so far this year, and they predict a million by the end of the year.

DB: *Forced migration is a global problem. The responsibility lies in the West, in imperialism, which forces people off their land.*

DR: I have this image of the US standing on the sidelines, holding their breath, hoping nobody will look at them and ask, "What is your role, and what do you plan to do?" In Europe, there are a few flashpoints. Hungary of course is one, and another is Greece. The islands of Lesbos and Kos are packed with refugees. Again, the whole process to request asylum has broken down. About 30,000 people are crammed onto these two islands. No toilets, no place to sleep. They are lying on sidewalks and parking lots. It's a terrible crisis. These are the two places where very bad things are happening.

In the rest of Europe, the European Commission and other countries are working very quickly to find a way to break this logjam. The European Commission just announced they will relocate 140,000 people across Europe. They are setting up quotas for different countries, which are somewhat intelligent — based on the GDP and rate of unemployment in the country. They are funding refugees in the EU to the tune of 780 million Euros. There are current programs to try and prevent refugees coming from Africa, to see if problems can be solved there, rather than have another huge group of people coming into Europe. They've waived the Dublin Regulation, which caused problems because it required the initial countries to do the processing, which clearly wasn't realistic. They've also set up speedier procedures to help governments procure supplies, such as tents, food, etc. Europe is trying to do some things.

But this is not just a European problem. It's a global crisis. Currently, there are a record-breaking 60 million displaced people around the world. In June, the UN High Commissioner for Refugees reported that one out of every 122 people on earth is forcibly displaced. This is a massive, massive problem. The US can't just stand by and watch, saying let Europe handle it, and make a few token gestures like taking in a few Syrians. Here's why the US plays a central role in all this: the primary region generating the refugees — I'm getting this from the UN High Commissioner for Refugees — is Afghanistan, which the US invaded in 2001, but had been causing problems there long before that, giving funding to help set up the Taliban and Al Qaeda. The US war in Afghanistan has spilled over into Pakistan. Huge numbers of refugees from Afghanistan are in Pakistan, and people are continually being terrorized by US drone strikes in Pakistan. The US invaded Iraq in 2003, destroying the government and military, so they don't have a functional state any more. When you have a breakdown of the state and mechanisms of power, there is a training ground for extremism and things like ISIS to get going, so Iraq is a major contributor of these refugees.

Syria is also not just about Assad and Russia. The US is very involved there as well. They've been providing funds and equipment to some opposition factions since 2012, along with France, Britain and certain Sunni Arab states. We've been involved in that, and now we have a completely catastrophic, chaotic situation where any functioning state has broken down, and we have so many different warring factions, we can't even keep track of them. This is where ISIS steps in, because whenever there is chaos, there is a vacuum of power and of a functional state. Something's going to step into that, and in these parts of the world, unfortunately that's going to be ISIS. It's the same with Libya. Many of the refugees are from Libya, where there is an absolute catastrophe after the US-backed forces helped topple the Gaddafi government in 2011. It's now a failed state with multiple centers of power, each claiming to be the true authority in the country. Clearly, nothing is functional there. This the pattern: go in, cause trouble, invade or cause economic collapse, and you end up with a situation where there's so much chaos that extremism starts to multiply, and there are these ongoing conflicts that seem almost completely irresolvable.

DB: *The neocons' goal is to break up all the countries, to control the resources — oil. It was the imperialism in the region that led to purposely setting the Shiites against the Sunnis — a suicide game with entire populations. This forced migration is the aftermath of that failed policy. It's not only that the US isn't willing to play its part in the objective situation of how many refugees to take, but also the US is fueling the problem at the core. Turkey is now at major war with the Kurds, who work with the US, who were fighting with ISIS. Meanwhile, there's a purge of the Palestinians who are on their way to the border with Lebanon. How many times have they been refugees? Four?*

DR: Exactly. The role the US has been playing and continues to play is devastating. It is more than not helpful. It is actively destructive. Although Europe feels sorry for itself — suddenly experiencing this big influx — the primary host countries are not in Europe, but the developing countries. The primary host countries, in order, are: Turkey, currently with 1.6 million refugees; Pakistan with 1.5 million refugees; Lebanon, a tiny country, has 1.1 million refugees. Iran has 982,000. Ethiopia has 659,000 and Jordan has 654,000. Developing world nations host 86% of all the refugees. Europe doesn't have to feel so sorry for itself, and the US should not sit there holding its breath hoping nobody will look at it, because clearly it's very, very involved in all of this.

DB: *Europe and the US should be very aware that if they continue with this policy, the refugee problem of today will seem small.*

DR: Everyone is predicting that this refugee crisis is not just a flash in the pan. This may just keep going because there's almost an endless supply of these conflicts and reasons why people are driven out of their home countries. I haven't even mentioned Sub-Saharan Africa. I have a long list of statistics from there, but you can imagine how bad it is. In summary, all of that is very clearly resource-extractive economy driven. So in the Democratic Republic of Congo, people take minerals and timber, and all the various factions in the country are fighting for control of that money. That fuels terrible corruption and comes from multinational corporations.

DB: *In this hemisphere, 12 million people were forced to migrate due to failed trade policies. This is almost a Mafioso, World Bank policy. There's no real change in either the military or corporate side.*

DR: We had a token gesture by President Obama who offered to take 10,000 Syrians, which is a tiny drop in the bucket.

DB: *Human rights people say we should be taking at least 70,000.*

DR: Even 70,000 is too low. There are 60 million refugees now. 10,000 is just a drop.

DB: *What are potential solutions?*

DR: The terrible things that are happening in many countries are being perpetrated by governments and people who hold the reins of power. In many countries of Europe, the ordinary people are opening up their arms, hearts and even their homes, and taking refugees in. I've seen these beautiful scenes of refugees walking along the highway in Hungary, having a difficult time. It's hot, they're desperately tired, they're getting sick, and their feet are sore. People stop their cars on the highway and try to pick them up to help them. They have to fight with the police who represent the state and say no, do not help them.

These are beautiful human gestures that are very important, but there are some big policies and big money that must be used to solve this. There needs to be a real stepping up to the plate for an equitable sharing of the burdens, which includes financial and resettlement burdens. So the US and Australia, the EU and the Gulf States like Saudi Arabia — which has also been holding their breath in hopes nobody looks at them — must all step up. The very wealthy states need to step up. Also, we need to provide safe and legal routes for people to escape from conflict, to migrate, to become refugees. Right now they are trapped through EU policies that block people from coming in until they go through many steps. The airlines, at their ticketing desks, are enforcing these policies because they want to err on the side of caution and not get in trouble with the EU. Even people who bought tickets are prevented from flying. This must change.

We must process the requests for immigration and refugee status much, much quicker. The UN High Commissioner for Refugees is proposing mass-processing sites set up across Europe immediately to start processing people quickly and efficiently, but also humanely, where they're given food, water and shelter, and a place to sleep with their children — rather than treating people as criminals because they have the audacity to try to flee from warfare. We need massive resettlement programs, which look at each person's specific circumstances. A bad trend is they are developing a so-called safe list, where people from certain countries can be deported, no questions asked, because the country is deemed safe. It's ridiculous, because you must look at individual circumstances. Just because there's not an official, legally declared war in a country, it doesn't mean there is not a horrendous conflict with life threatening consequences. Nigeria, with the Boko Haram, is considered a safe country, but people are fleeing from there.

DB: *In the US we are more aware of this hemisphere, so thank you for painting a more global picture. Do you want to leave us with some closing thoughts?*

DR: The immediate things that must be done are all very doable. The money to do these resettlement programs and processing exists. This wealth is tied up somewhere else, and people aren't making it available. But the money exists and we need the political will to do this. The rich countries must step up. There are also longer-term, systemic changes that must happen so we don't keep generating more and more refugees. That's what you were mentioning earlier about what led to all these conflicts. We need to change they way we do business across the world. We need to change our systemic approach that prioritizes short-term profits over anyone's quality of life or wellbeing, or the environment, or sustainable economies and access to resources over time. We need to look seriously at systemic changes. A short-term or band-aid approach will not help.

Update: January 2016

Since September 2015, we've seen several significant developments: a worsening of the conflicts in Syria, Yemen, and now Burundi; the November 13th bombings in Paris — attributed to Islamists if not refugees; and the New Year's Eve large-scale sexual harassment of women in Cologne, Germany — linked to Islamic refugees among others. The European Right-wing has predictably responded by demanding an end to refugee resettlement. Meanwhile, in the US, we've experienced a Republican presidential candidate spewing vitriolic anti-immigrant rhetoric, while a sitting Democrat president activates a deportation crackdown against Central Americans fleeing the unendurable violence of the failed US war on drugs and abject poverty stemming from the failed US economic and political agenda in that region.

All these developments raise serious questions about the ability of the global North to deal with refugees and other consequences of its self-interested interference around the world. The mind-set underlying the anti-refugee backlash is the same as that underlying the exploitative actions that drive the conflicts generating refugees: a pervasive sense by people in the West that they are somehow separate from — and superior to — non-Western "others." If we don't want the refugee crisis to continue to go from bad to worse, we must quit demonizing, recognize our common humanity, address our cultures' shared failings (such as endemic violence and sexism), and move towards non-exploitative economic and political relationships. [DR]

Carnage in Paris
Vijay Prashad   November 2015

DB: *In Official Washington, the talk is all about expanded wars and how tough to be on Syrian refugees. But elsewhere there is some serious reflection on how the West went wrong in its approach toward the Middle East. After the Paris terror attacks and a bloody hostage standoff in Mali, the focus has been on the West's plans to "intensify" the war against Islamic terrorists, especially the Islamic State (or ISIS), but some more thoughtful thinkers are calling for a critical examination of the past mistakes made and the lessons that can be learned.*

Vijay Prashad, an Indian historian, journalist and commentator, writes, "A week of horrible carnage, bomb blasts in Beirut and Baghdad, then the cold-blooded shootings in Paris. Each of these acts of terror left dead bodies and wounded lives. There is nothing good that comes of them, only the pain of the victim, and then more pain, as powerful people take refuge in clichéd policies that once again turn the wheel of violence." *The BBC just announced* "France is committed to destroying the so-called Islamic State group after Friday's deadly attacks. President Francois Hollande has said France's military campaign against ISIS and Iraq will intensify." *Imagine, intensify. Vijay, what is your overview?*

VP: These attacks have been horrible. There's been an intensification of ISIS attacks — the one in Paris was part of a sequence. The reaction from the French president is to be expected. There's a kind of political grammar that he's forced to fall in line with. Two words apply here — you have to do something, and you have to appear strong. *Something* and *strong* are the keywords in order to understand the French reaction just as we are to understand the US reaction after 9-11. There's no worked out strategy after 15 months of US and Gulf bombing of Iraq and then Syria. The roll back, particularly in Syria, has been minimal. The French now want to intensify that. They were part of the coalition previously, so there's nothing new here. It's the same strategy, which is not bringing dividends. On the other hand, it's producing acts of terror. I'm afraid the prognosis is very poor for what Francois Hollande is recommending.

DB: *You have some suggestions for the French president. What are they?*

VP: First, grieve for those who have been killed. Grief is important for a family, neighborhood, city, country, and the planet. There are terrible stories, and each one should be told. A 41-year old woman at a cafe was shot in Paris. In Beirut, a four-month-old baby was sitting in his mother's lap. She cushioned the blow. Mother and father died, and the baby lived. These stories are educational. They tell us who the victims of these terror attacks are. There was the killing by drones of an entire family in Yemen. We need to know their names — their lives — so that people don't just see them as statistics. First we need an accounting of who they are, and then grieve for them.

Secondly, states need to not believe that a response to a terrorist action is military force. One needs to understand how this happened. How is it possible that the Turkish government handed over the names of one of these terrorists to the French — not once, but twice? Apparently, it was not acted upon. These are the kinds of questions that were not asked after 9-11. The 9-11 Commission ducked many serious questions about how people on a watch list were not discovered. It's the same thing with any terrorist action, whether it's 9-11 or the Oklahoma City bombing. These were known characters on a certain list. We're supposed to have this enormous surveillance, but instead of forensic surveillance, we have blanket surveillance. Everybody's emails are checked. There needs to be a proper police accounting of what occurred.

DB: *I like the next suggestion: Try to get to the root of the issue that provoked the inhumanity. This is one the US and the West aren't particularly interested in.*

VP: We used to joke that somebody needs to tell the CIA that highlighter pens are yellow and not black. The 9-11 Commission did some accounting of the reason it occurred, but most of the 9-11 report was entirely blacked out, particularly the section that involved Saudi Arabia and its involvement — not the country, but individual sheiks. There needs to be a very serious and honest appraisal, not only of the culpability of people in the Arabian Peninsula, but also in the French and American government. Just this year, the French government sent $10 billion of arms to Saudi Arabia. The US and Western Europe rely on Saudi oil money — not the oil itself, but the profits — to liquefy their banks. There's extreme complicity of the West with the Gulf Arab states. So any accounting of where this vicious ideology spawns from — who finances the network of mullahs, some of these extremist groups — none of that is taken in hand. Friends in Paris tell me that when a mosque is searching for a new cleric, often the government insists the cleric not be from the community, but they must be brought in from abroad. Often some Sauditrained cleric arrives, so people feel these clerics are foisted upon them. This is the nature of the accounting that's necessary. You can't just say ISIS is bad guys. It's much deeper than that, because our complicity is quite considerable in these cases.

DB: *Do you think US and Western terrorism in the Middle East are the driving force behind growing acts of terrorism against the West? They tried to put a cork in Allah's mouth, and the whole world blew up.*

VP: There's a lot of truth to what you are saying. There are different timelines by which you can sketch that story backwards, such as to the Iraq war of 2003. Now it's widely understood that the regime change in Iraq had a catastrophic impact on the region. It essentially produced the space for ISIS to grow, and brought us to where we are. But we can go earlier, to the way the West and the Gulf Arab states first collaborated to send the Mujahideen to Afghanistan. This was also a regime change in process, where we financed anybody, mostly the most

344

conservative and heinous forces on the ground. We legitimized them, gave them training, and then were surprised when out of the kernel of Afghanistan, Al Qaeda erupted.

Before that, in the 1950s, the US collaborated with the Saudis, largely to attack Arab nationalism, undermining and destroying the Left by promoting very virulent forms of Islam, pushed by the Saudis in particular. There's a lot to be said about the role of the West in producing the social conditions, which lead to ISIS. Many serious questions must be asked about the role Saudi Arabia has played in West Asia and across the Muslim world, with its collaborators in Morocco and elsewhere, pushing a very heartless politics against the social democratic politics that had emerged from the people of the Arab lands.

DB: *The more I see how the Saudis operate, the more they remind me of Israel.*

VP: The last UN report that came out from the Economic and Social Commission of West Asia addressed the sense of the Arab Spring, and stressed the importance of what happened in Tunisia. Then the report made a startling comparison. It had a section where it went after states that promote a kind of moral, ethnic, religious culture where there's no cultural diversity allowed or sanctified by the state. The countries it used as an example were Israel and Saudi Arabia. The report suggested that these two countries are creating an anachronistic form of nation for the world, and are not a good example for the region. Of course Israel is furious with the comparison, because it prefers to be compared to European states, and would hate to be compared to Saudi Arabia. But there's something to be said for the way in which Israel is increasingly showing a very narrow understanding of ethnic or religious nationalism. If you were very uncharitable, you might call it racist nationalism.

DB: *Do you see a light at the end of the tunnel?*

VP: There is the phrase, "May we always live in interesting times." In an essay I wrote after the Paris shootings, I called these pitiless times — not interesting, but times without pity. We are going to prosecute a ruthless, pitiless war. Our political leadership, across the planet, has the imagination of yesterday. They don't want to see new ways of doing things, or acknowledge we are dealing with people, not aliens who can be smashed out of existence. We need creative thinking. In Syria, as an example, all understand the West is trapped in a web of its relationships. Turkey is on one side, which understands terrorism to include the Kurds. The Kurdish fighters have been some of the most successful fighters against ISIS. Here's a major US ally, and NATO member, which wants to attack the Assad government in Damascus, and the Kurds. The Americans have been giving close air support to the Kurds against ISIS. Meanwhile, the US is so compromised with the Saudis that it's unable to pressure the Saudis to back down from their proxies. We live in an age where the politics is yesterday — they are not able to look forward. Yesterday, Obama and Putin had a private discussion for 35 minutes. My only hope is that they don't do more damage than they've already done. Our current political leadership is not capable of rolling back the damage, but we should have faith that they will not make it worse than it is already.

DB: *Following the Charlie Hebdo killing in Paris, we had the insanity of Netanyahu marching in the streets of Paris in solidarity with the people of France after he had slaughtered some 2,200 people, including many children. They say no peace in Palestine, no peace anyplace else in the world.*

VP: In 2003, it was very gratifying to see India, Brazil and South Africa take a very strong position against the American war in Iraq. Then in 2011, the five BRICS countries happened to comprise the Security Council. [BRICS is the acronym for an association of five major emerging national economies: Brazil, Russia, India, China and South Africa. The grouping was originally known as "BRIC" before the inclusion of South Africa in 2010.] Sadly, Russia, China, India and Brazil abstained when the West and the Gulf Arab states wanted to bomb Libya. Only

South Africa voted in favor, and President Jacob Zuma said that Obama personally called him to convince him to vote yes. So the five BRICS countries essentially allowed the West and Gulf Arabs to destroy Libya. Now we have an extraordinarily introspective BRICS bloc, particularly India, Brazil, South Africa and China. The four of them seriously regret their vote about Libya. Unfortunately they've gone silent, but my hope is that these four countries will assert themselves on the global stage, and argue that the approach the West has taken has been catastrophic, and another way must be put forward. Thus far they haven't had the confidence to articulate an alternative, but I very much hope that these countries, which are very chastised by the vote in 2011, might now come out and say the West doesn't have all the answers.

Ongoing Bloodshed in the Holy Land

UN Human Rights Adviser Blasts Israel
Richard Falk   June 2010

DB: *In a predawn raid on Monday, in international waters off the coast of the Gaza Strip, Israeli commandos seized the fleet of the Free Gaza Movement, which was carrying 10,000 tons of humanitarian aid, in an attempt to break the Israeli embargo against Gaza. Nine peace activists were killed and several dozen people were wounded.*

Professor Richard Falk, United Nations Special Rapporteur for the Occupied Palestinian Territories, stated that the Israeli commando raid against a humanitarian fleet of unarmed ships was "as clear a violation of international humanitarian law, international law of the seas, and international criminal law, as we're likely to see in the early part of the twenty-first century."

Israel admits they carried out this raid. What happened in terms of human rights violations and international law?

RF: It is fairly clear that these were ships carrying humanitarian supplies for blockaded Gaza, the passengers were unarmed, and at the time of the Israeli attacks they were situated on the high seas. These attacks, therefore, were unlawful and by most interpretations would be regarded as criminal. The statement of the Turkish Prime Minister that the attacks constituted state terrorism corresponds with the tragic reality we've been witnessing over the past twenty-four hours.

DB: *The Israelis say these commandos armed with handguns and paint guns were only defending themselves from armed and dangerous attacks by people on the boat. What is your response to that?*

RF: There are two lines of response, and this is an area where the facts are contested and difficult to disentangle at this stage. The witnesses on the boats, particularly the Turkish ship Mavi Marmara where most of the violence took place, claim that the commandos landed shooting, and that it was only after their

348

initiation of violence that there was some attempt at defense by very contrived and primitive weapons, as opposed to the kind of advanced weaponry the Israeli commandos were carrying. Beyond that, it's clear that if an unlawful attack of a vessel on the high seas is occurring, the passengers on that ship have some right to self-defense. That's one aspect. The second aspect is that even if there was some kind of defensive violence on the ship, that's no excuse for an unprovoked attack carried out in this manner. If Israel didn't want the ships to go to Gaza, they could have diverted them. It seems clear this was a deliberate attack designed to punish the effort to carry out this humanitarian mission, which would have disclosed the brutality of the blockade of the Gaza Strip, which has been going on now for almost three years. The Israeli arguments are not seriously plausible.

DB: *You are the UN Special Rapporteur for the Palestinian territories. What is your responsibility now? What is the United Nations' responsibility? What should happen?*

RF: My responsibility is to report to the Human Rights Council and the UN General Assembly on the Israeli violations of the human rights of the occupied Palestinian people. This incident is at the edge of my responsibility because it didn't occur within the occupied territories, but it so directly affects the people within, that I treat it as part of my responsibilities. In my judgment, the Security Council, if one takes the UN Charter seriously and avoids double standards, should do three things. One, it should condemn the attack as a violation of international law; secondly, it should demand an immediate lifting of the blockade of the people of the Gaza Strip, allowing food, medicine, reconstruction materials and fuel to enter freely; and thirdly it should refer the allegations of criminality associated with the attack to the International Criminal Court for investigation and action. Given the geopolitics within the Security Council, it is unlikely this course of action will be followed. The General Assembly could try and do these things if the Security Council fails to act, and it remains to be seen whether there's the political will to do this.

If the UN is stymied in this way, it shifts the responsibility and opportunity to civil society to augment the ongoing Boycott, Divestment and Sanctions campaign, which is gaining momentum. Presumably this latest incident will create a great deal more strength for that campaign, the form of action so effective in opposing the Apartheid regime in South Africa in the early 1990s and late 1980s.

DB: *Is there any kind of special protection for the people who risked their lives—and now we see that they really did risk their lives—going into a situation where the world knows there are terrible things happening? Is there a role for legal action within international law?*

RF: Yes. There is a great opportunity to provide protection to people who are courageous and morally motivated, and at the same time are vulnerable to this kind of violence and brutal treatment, but the political will is lacking at the governmental and international institutional level to provide that kind of protection. One has the norms, the responsibility to protect concept — endorsed by the Security Council and the support of international lawyers — but it can't be implemented without the requisite political will, and that's what's missing. Of course our government is the lynchpin of what makes effective or futile international initiatives of this sort. If the US government had indicated a firm desire to establish some kind of protective capability for missions of this sort, individuals like this would be protected.

I thought that however little Israel respects international law, they wouldn't do something as crudely violent and alienating as what they did with these commando attacks on the freedom flotilla. It was not in my political imagination that they would seek, by such means, to prevent the delivery of these humanitarian necessities that pose no security threat whatsoever to Israel — it only posed a public relations threat in that it would have revealed the inability of governments to break the blockade and placed pressure on them to do something in the future. At the same time it would have added to the willingness of activists around the world to push harder against the Israeli occupation policy so that what was at stake from Israel's point of view was the delegitimization of their policies. They apparently, and I think wrongly, calculated that they would lose less from the violent disruption of this humanitarian mission than it would have by allowing it to quietly deliver the humanitarian materials the ships were carrying.

DB: *They certainly could have gained a lot of supporters if they had shifted their policy and let the aid arrive. The US is supplying a good deal of the equipment that Israel uses and that these commandos may have been using. Does that make the US responsible?*

RF: The US is certainly morally and politically complicit and responsible in these kinds of Israeli tactics and undertakings. Whether we are legally responsible is a trickier question. There are American laws that forbid the equipment we provide from being used except in defensive roles. We've never taken this legislative restriction seriously in the context of Israel, but it is a definite legal concern, and could be pursued by those who are eager to test the degree of legal responsibility the US government possesses. I believe such a test would be beneficial for the American people because it would allow the public to express more of its changing view of the conflict, and send a message to Washington that it has yet to hear — that the American people would rather see our government pursue a genuinely balanced law-oriented approach to the conflict than this unconditional partisanship with the kind of criminal tactics that Israel just employed against the Freedom Flotilla.

Standing with the Palestinians

Alice Walker   September 2011

DB: *Pulitzer-winning author Alice Walker sees a reflection of the injustice done to African Americans in today's treatment of the Palestinians, leading her to object when the artwork of Palestinian children is barred from US museums and to join a flotilla that challenged Israel's blockade of Gaza. Alice, you wrote about the recent attempt by the Children's Museum of Oakland to prevent Palestinian kids from showing their art. Could you briefly outline what you wrote and your response to this censorship?*

AW: I said that the children need to have exposure of their art because it is a wonderful way to help them heal from the trauma of being bombed, and watching their friends, and sometimes parents, die. It's unconscionable that any adults, especially in this part of the world, and lo and behold in Oakland, would want to deprive these children of a venue in which they could expose some of their grief and pain through their art.

DB: *As a teacher, I saw the impact of very troubled, oppressed kids who got through it by self-expression. What bothered me the most was that the exhibit was advertised, invitations sent out, workshops set up, the kids were excited, and then they were told, "No, it isn't going to happen." Could you share the personal side of what you wrote?*

AW: As a child, I was injured. I was playing Cowboys and Indians with my brothers, and one of them accidentally shot me in the eye. That led to a lot of suffering, grief and pain. I started writing poetry at that time, when I was eight or nine years old. My relatives encouraged me to share it, to show it to people. That was part of my healing, so I could easily see that it could help these children. Having the venue denied them, keeps them locked in their own private suffering. Adults with money did this to these little kids. But they are doing this to children at great risk to their own souls; to force them to remain unexpressed or try to force them to remain unexpressed in their suffering.

What also came to mind was how in 1939 Marian Anderson, the great contralto, was denied a venue at Constitution Hall in Washington D.C. by the Daughters of the American Revolution, who were upset that the place was going to be integrated. So Anderson's friends, including President [Franklin] Roosevelt and Eleanor Roosevelt came to her defense and she was allowed to sing on the steps of the Lincoln Memorial. She attracted seventy-five thousand people of all colors and kinds. It was one of the biggest turnouts ever, up to that time, at the Lincoln Memorial. That is something to remember — these attempts to censor people often backfire.

It strengthens us as well, because we begin to see the forces that are against us. They are fleshed-out; they come out of the walls and woodwork, wherever they've been hiding and pretending to be upstanding, kind, and generous people. They suddenly stand revealed as the very narrow-hearted people they are, so we don't have to be fooled. It's a great thing not to be fooled by people, to have a little bit of consciousness about who is likely to try to trip you up as you start climbing towards your freedom.

DB: *If a very terrifying, tragic experience happens, you can express it to people who care and want to hear it, or it gets forced down inside and manifests as an illness in various ways.*

AW: It makes all the difference in the world. You learn from having dreadful things happen that you can survive and still be happy. I once came across a leper in Hawaii, on the island of Molokai. His face was almost dissolved by his illness, but his expression of absolute joy was shining through what was left of his face. He said, "One thing I learned from this hard life is that terrible things can happen to you and you can still be happy."

This is good news for anybody, but especially a child who feels completely squashed by an imperial power that bombs its communities and schools for twenty-two days, non-stop — a child who has lost parts of his body. It helps to know that somewhere is this teaching, and that someone is waiting for them on the other side of the trauma to share with them what they gained. You don't only lose; you sometimes gain a lot from suffering. People can stand with you. That's why I love the Middle East Children's Alliance [MECA]. They commit to these children and make it clear, not only to the children, but to the adults in the world, what we need to be doing together — bringing them along, helping them stand and see that there is still a possibility of being joyful little kids.

DB: *Why did you decide to join that Flotilla?*

AW: I believe it is our responsibility to do something when the world is out of whack, as it is almost everywhere you look. What do you do and where do you place yourself? How much do we believe what we say we believe about wanting to fight the good fight for the freedom and happiness of the people of the world?

I had been in Gaza and the West Bank and met my tribe of poets, singers, musicians, philosophers, historians and children — and we're just people. People everywhere deserve to be free of fear, free of people taking their land, bombing their schools, and taking their water. I'm sitting here looking at pictures of both my parents. Given my own background in the South with segregation, I have an obligation, given how deeply I understand this kind of pain, to try to be present, even if we don't get to where we were trying to get to.

We didn't get to Gaza. Armed commandos from the Greek coast guard turned us back, but we got ten miles off the coast of Greece. We never had a direct confrontation with the Israelis, but they were working against us the whole time. They had sabotaged the other ships, making it very hard for us to move.

Yet there again, I can't be discouraged, I feel strongly that if people would get off the couch, leave the house, head out to stand with their neighbor, even if they are ten thousand miles away, we are already there. Our intention, and the movement forward, is so important.

DB: *Alice, you got on a boat knowing that the last round of the Freedom Flotilla faced extreme violence by Israeli commandos — a number of people died and were wounded. Were you afraid?*

AW: Of course I was afraid. We're all afraid. I also realize that an earthquake could right this minute cover us up with rubble, we could be sucked out of our car by a hurricane, or drowned in the floods that are happening. I see that danger is everywhere, in every moment, so it is better to approach those areas that are dangerous and difficult in that spirit — I could lose my life here at home also. What I find remarkable, and I felt this way in Mississippi forty years ago, is reaching other people who are as determined and dedicated as you are, with the love that you have; it's a kind of heaven, and not to be missed if you can possibly manage to get to this kind of circle of people who have evolved. I felt it on the boat, in the presence of such goodness, such amazing spirit and heart. It made it worth whatever the sacrifice might have been. If I would go, I would go with these people — how blissful.

DB: *There are Israeli reports of a program of midnight kidnappings and torture of children as young as twelve years old by Israeli soldiers. Sometimes they are taken to the basements of the illegal settlements by hooded soldiers, then masked and questioned. What drives a people to go to these lengths to silence children and repress freedom?*

AW: I think one thing that probably should not have happened for so long is the constant reiteration of the Holocaust. I think if we had a slavery industry, so that every time you turn around you would hear horrible tales about the enslavement of black people, we would have some incredibly crazed black people who would be doing much more violent things because of their anger. Whatever happens, you are never permitted to evolve beyond your rage, so everything becomes an obstacle to your liberation from your own rage. Then you turn into quite dangerous entities in society.

Legal Intifada: Recognition and Sovereignty
Francis A. Boyle   December 2012

DB: *On November 29, the UN General Assembly overwhelmingly approved a resolution to upgrade the Palestinian Authority's observer status to a non-member state. According to various sources, the UN General Assembly voted to recognize Palestine as a sovereign state, despite threats by the United States and Israel that the Palestinian Authority would be punished by withholding much needed funds for the West Bank government. It was reported that Britain threatened to abstain from the vote for enhanced Palestinian status at the UN unless the Palestinians agreed not to take the Israelis to international courts.*

Dr. Francis A. Boyle, professor of International Law at the University of Illinois College of Law, and author of The Palestinian Right of Return Under International Law, *was advisor to the Palestinian Liberation Organization and its chairman, Yasser Arafat, on the Palestinian Declaration of Independence of November 15, 1988.*

Professor Boyle, why would the US threaten to cut off Palestine, and why are the Brits so upset?

FB: No member state of the United Nations organization has ever been destroyed or eliminated. Some of them have broken off into constituent units, but they have never been extinguished. Israel would like all of Palestine — the West Bank, and East Jerusalem — without the Palestinians. So it's important, as they see it, not to have recognition of Palestinian statehood by the United Nations organization. It's that simple.

I've been working with the Palestinians and their peace initiatives since 1987, and was legal advisor with the Palestinian delegation to the Middle East peace negotiations. The Israelis never demonstrated even one iota of good faith when negotiating a two-state solution with the Palestinians. The Zionists have always wanted all of Palestine, going back to the Basel Conference of 1897. That is still their agenda, and why they are vigorously fighting against recognition of Palestine by the UN. Last year they fought against our admission as a member state to the UN. This is an existential battle going on now for 115 years, and it's not about to end tomorrow.

DB: *Describe the six legal remedies the Palestinians would have available if the international community recognizes the Palestinians.*

FB: Obviously Palestinians could barely defend themselves because the US, the most powerful military power in the world, has given Israel every type of high-tech weapon system possibly imaginable. So their strong suit is international law. I already recommended to them, in Ramallah, that they consider implementing these steps, which I call a "legal intifada."

First, is becoming a party to the Rome Statute for the International Criminal Court. After Operation Cast Lead One, I advised President Abbas to accept the jurisdiction of the International Criminal Court [ICC] under Article 12, paragraph 3, which he did. Then we filed a long complaint with the ICC prosecutor over Operation Cast Lead One. The ICC prosecutor, Moreno Ocampo, announced that he was going to investigate two issues: Did Palestine have the capacity to accept the jurisdiction of the ICC under Article 12, paragraph 3? And did Israel create war crimes and crimes against humanity against the Palestinians during Cast Lead? The Goldstone Commission Report answered the second question in the affirmative; Israel had inflicted war crimes and crimes against humanity against the Palestinians.

As to the first point, just before he left office, Ocampo announced that he did not believe Palestine had the capacity to accept the jurisdiction of the ICC under Article 12, paragraph 3. In any event, he said it was not for him to determine whether Palestine was a state. This, despite the fact that Palestine was admitted as a full-fledged member state of UNESCO [United Nations Economic and Social Council], which is a UN specialized agency. Basically, Moreno Ocampo copped out. If he hadn't, there's a good chance Israel would not have repeated what I call Cast Lead Lite, which occurred for eight days in November. In his press conference, Ocampo said, "But of course, Palestine could ratify the Rome statute and then proceed as a member state, and that would solve the jurisdictional problem." All Palestine has to do once it becomes a UN member state is accede to the terms of the Rome statute and file that with the UN Secretary General, which is the depository for the Rome statute. The Secretary General will be obligated to accept that instrument of accession, and then Palestine can simply reactivate the complaint that's already there and add in Cast Lead Lite for November 2012. If they want to, they can also add the current settlements policy. The International Court of Justice ruled in its advisory opinion on the wall, that all the settlements in the West Bank and East Jerusalem violate the Fourth Geneva Convention of 1949. Of course, such violations are a war crime, and when they are widespread or systematic, which they certainly are in the West Bank and East Jerusalem, they become a crime against humanity.

DB: *The British foreign secretary says the Palestinians will not get their support unless they pledge not to sue Israel for war crimes.*

FB: Yes. And he doesn't understand that we already did that, so these are obviously highly technical matters that their international law staff will follow. We already filed that complaint, so we just need to reactivate the complaint we have filed. This would put us in the driver's seat with the settlement policy issue in the dock.

Britain created this problem in the first place with the Balfour Declaration. They've always been against us, so it doesn't surprise me that the Brits are still taking this position. They were behind the partition resolution 65 years ago.

It's not just Palestine. The Brits did the same to my country, Ireland — they partitioned us. The British partitioned the Indian subcontinent to India and Pakistan, creating a monumental human rights tragedy that's still going on. Britain also partitioned the Republic of Bosnia and Herzegovina, which remains a problem. It's a joke that the British say they are for peace. They've created so many of the problems that we confront today: India, Pakistan, Palestine, Ireland, Bosnia, The Falklands, Malvinas, for starters.

DB: *What could happen about the illegal siege of Gaza under the International Court of Justice?*

FB: Once it becomes a UN observer state, Palestine can then accede to the terms of the statute of the International Court of Justice [ICJ], which is the world court of the UN system. Palestine will — across the board on all these issues — be following the precedent of Switzerland, which did not join the UN until about five years ago. But during that period of time it had UN observer state status, and in that capacity Switzerland had most of the rights it needed to do whatever it wanted to do. Switzerland became a party to the ICJ statute. Palestine, I'm sure, will too. Palestine, by taking the Swiss instrument and filing it with the World Court, would be able to sue Israel at the ICJ. I've offered to President Abbas and the PLO executive committee to file this lawsuit, and try to break the genocidal siege of Gaza that is still going on today, as we speak. President Morsi of Egypt, despite all the rhetoric, still hasn't done anything about it. It's on a list of things the Palestinians can do once the dust settles.

Third, Palestine could then join the Law of the Sea Convention and get legal access and a legal right to these enormous gas supplies right off the coast of Gaza, which Israel has access to. Lebanon, Cyprus, and Turkey all have their claims in, but Palestine has a claim too. Indeed, a pretty substantial claim. If Palestine gets access to that gas, it can become economically self-sufficient, so this is a very important issue.

Palestine can become a party to the International Civil Aviation Organization and get legal, sovereign control over their own air space. By becoming a member of the International Telecommunications Union, they will get control of their airwaves, phone lines, band widths for internet and satellite access.

Those are some of the immediate consequences. Of course Palestine would also become a high contracting party to the four Geneva Conventions of 1949. Back in 1989 I recommended this step to President Arafat as a purely humanitarian measure. The US government applied massive pressure to the Swiss government not to accept our instrument of accession. So what the Swiss did — again, they copped out back in 1989 — was say, "Well, we're not in a position to determine whether or not Palestine is a state, but we will treat their declaration as binding." And they still carry us as a footnote.

Palestine will be upgraded to a high contracting party like all the 193 states in the world, with the right to demand that they all act to protect it as a fellow high-contracting party under common Article 1 to the four Geneva Conventions, where they have an obligation not only to respect the conventions themselves, but to ensure respect by Israel. These are the six steps, in terms of priority, that Palestine could get to work on tomorrow.

DB: *If the Law of the Sea Convention were applied, are the offshore gas fields so extensive they could help bring Palestinians out of poverty? Is this a battle around resources or a religious war?*

FB: This isn't a religious war. I've spent a lot of time in the Middle East and dealt with Palestinians, Christians, Muslims and Jews. This is a war over land, resources and water — that's what is going on here. Israel believes it's in its best interest to present this as a religious war, but it simply is not. Those gas supplies under the Mediterranean are enormous. The financial literature, including the *Wall Street Journal* and the *Financial Times*, have extensive discussions about how much natural gas is there. It certainly would be enough to make Palestine economically self-sufficient, along with the capacity of its people, who are highly educated and highly motivated. Israel would be entitled to its share as well. If you read the debates over the gas fields, of course no one mentions the Palestinians and their legitimate claim to the gas fields. Palestine, Israel, Lebanon, Cyprus and Turkey would have to sit down among themselves within the framework of the Law of the Sea Treaty and negotiate some type of equitable sharing of these gas supplies — fields — which in turn would be based upon the delimitation of their continental shelves.

That is where it stands. If this could not be resolved by negotiations, Palestine would have access to the UN's Law of the Sea tribunal in Jamaica. There are hundreds of billions of dollars worth of gas there. We really don't know precisely how much there is, but it's enormous, and it would help the Israeli people too. Right now, there is some gas being pumped out, but given the disputed status of the title, it's not much. So if there is massive exploitation of this gas, certainly Israel has a very long coastline there on the Mediterranean, but so does Gaza, and the Palestinians are entitled to their cut.

DB: *So when the Israelis fire at the Gaza strip from the water offshore, they are firing over these extensive oil resources? When these Israeli warships intercept boats coming from Turkey and other places trying to break the siege on Gaza, they attack the boats. The Israelis are killing international activists over the waters where these resources exist, which is an obvious attempt to defend the resources they want to steal.*

FB: That's correct. In theory it could be possible for the stakeholders, primarily Israel, Palestine, Lebanon and to a lesser extent Cyprus and Turkey, to sit down and establish an equitable but lawful sharing of these gas supplies. But Israel doesn't want to share it with anyone. Cyprus and Turkey seem to be enforcing what they believe are their claims, and Lebanon is doing the same, which means that all these conflicting claims to these resources make it difficult to agree on a viable exploitation of those resources.

This isn't only going on in Gaza. Israel is staking a de facto claim to these tremendous gas resources, which would probably make Israel energy interdependent as well. Israel currently has no domestic sources of energy supplies there at all. I've read estimates that there may be resources for the next hundred years, but that's cutting the Palestinians out of the picture. Now they get their oil and gas from Egypt but that's been disrupted — they have to scramble to get it somewhere else.

This is a very important factor in the equation, together with the water. Most of the water — the aquifers — is on the West Bank. This is Palestinian water and the settlers are stealing it. I once saw a Palestinian village literally thirsting to death because it had no water. I followed the pipeline upstream to Aerial, a settlement on the West Bank, where I could see the water being diverted from the village so the settlers could have an Olympic-sized swimming pool. Since then, I've read that they have two Olympic-sized swimming pools in Aerial. This is outrageous — unacceptable. Clearly it's plunder of Palestinian water resources.

In today's resolution submitted by the Palestinians at the UN they made it quite clear that any final settlement is going to have to involve water because it is their water that is being stolen by Israel. We see Israel stealing and plundering natural resources, certainly water on the West Bank, and now they're going after the gas fields in the Mediterranean. The Israelis have a valid claim, but it's not all theirs. They are going to have to sit down with Lebanon and Palestine and, to a lesser extent, Cyprus and Turkey, which has laid claims to some of these gas fields.

Justice for Palestine is Still the Fundamental Issue

John Pilger   May 2013

DB: *Noted documentary filmmaker and author John Pilger knows a great deal about the Gaza Strip, and the extreme conditions Palestinians there have been forced to endure under a brutal Israeli Occupation. Pilger has made two films about it with the same name, twenty-five years apart: "Palestine is Still the Issue."*

John, we're continuing to hear reports of massive bombing, with injury and death to civilian life — to children.

JP: We should be disgusted. That is a normal, human response to this latest Israeli atrocity. We ought not to be surprised, but we should also understand this has nothing to do with Hamas or rockets. It is an ongoing assault on the Palestinian people, especially the people of Gaza, which began a very long time ago. The plan is to effectively get rid of them as an entity. I'm not exaggerating. The historical record is clear. The infamous Plan D that was executed in the late 1940s, just before Israel came into being, was to expel the population of Palestine. There were 369 villages attacked, the people thrown out — the documented evidence is there. Israeli historians such as Benny Morris have documented this, and the Hebrew archives have thrown it up.

We see a form of genocide underway in Palestine. Although Israelis are doing the bombing, the US is pushing the buttons. Israelis are flying American planes, which are supplied for this very exercise — this very purpose. This is an American/Israeli assault on a people who effectively live in an open prison.

The United Nations Special Rapporteur, Richard Falk, has likened their situation to the Warsaw Ghetto. Fascism is not a word easily used, nor should it be. But we have close to a fascist state in Israel, and those historic parallels that Falk draws are correct.

DB: *Why did you do two films, and what does it mean that they have almost the same name twenty-five years apart?*

JP: The first film was in the late seventies and the second was made in 2002. I was reporting on the Middle East and Palestine since the mid 1960s. When I made the second documentary, what struck me, looking at the first, was that nothing had changed. The title still applied — Palestine is Still the Issue.

It is the single most pressing issue in the Middle East because it is about the most fundamental justice. It is about people fighting for their lives, literally, against an enemy that is a brutal, historical anachronism. As much of the world was decolonized following WWII, a new colony — very much in the 19th century tradition — was imposed on the Middle East. It can be said that what makes Israel unique is the control it would exercise over the policies of its current mentor and provider, the United States.

Against the historical tide, a new colony arose: Israel. It's an utter anachronism. It is not in any way, in any sense, at peace with its region. It's at war with its region. In fact, its raison d'être is war with its region. If it were to make peace with its region, then its reason for existing would disappear. This centers on the oppression and expulsion of Palestinians — the theft of their land, the theft of their resources. These are not opinions, but facts, which have been on the historical record for a long time. To almost everybody in the Middle East, ordinary people regard Palestine as 'still the issue'. This center of turmoil and war, this permanent flashpoint in the world, would lose its volatile and very dangerous status were the Palestinians to achieve the fundamental justice to which they have a right. It's basically Israel and the US that stand in the way. That's why to ordinary people in the streets of Tehran and Cairo, Damascus, and Beirut, Palestine is still the issue. And it should be the issue in Los Angeles, San Francisco, London, everywhere. Until the Palestinians have justice, the Middle East will be at war.

Hope for an Israeli-Palestinian State

Ali Abunimah   April 2014

DB: *Amid the impending collapse of Secretary of State John Kerry's Israel-Palestine negotiations for a two-state solution, Israel appears determined to expand settlements in the West Bank, while Palestinians are ratcheting up international pressure in pursuit of their human rights.*

In a new book, The Battle for Justice in Palestine, *Ali Abunimah sees surprising hope in the possibility of a democratic one-state solution achieved through growing global support for a boycott-divestment-sanctions movement targeting what he calls Israeli "apartheid" in Palestine.*

Co-founder and director of the Electronic Intifada, Abunimah is also the author of One Country: A Bold Proposal to End the Israeli-Palestinian Impasse.

Ali, are people better off now than 20 years ago in Occupied Palestine?

AA: I started *The Battle for Justice in Palestine* with a very short sentence: "The Palestinians are winning." That might sound out-of-touch given the fact that in so many ways Palestinians are actually worse off today than they were 20 years ago, after 20 years of the so-called Oslo Peace Process. I chronicle that in the book, from the siege of Gaza — which has absolutely devastated the economy there, devastated the foundations of civilized life — to the ongoing ethnic cleansing of Bedouins in the Negev, to the catastrophe facing Palestinian refugees in Syria.

But I think in terms of the public debate and public understanding of the roots of the violence and conflict in Palestine, things have never been better in many ways. There is an incredibly vibrant and growing movement for justice in Palestine that's like nothing I have seen in 20 years. In this book I wanted to lay out some of the realities that offer hope, that there is a path forward. And we are very much on it. That's what I hope *The Battle for Justice in Palestine* offers.

DB: *Israelis are continually supported by the US government, although the US government says, "No, you shouldn't expand those settlements" or "No, that's wrong. Don't knock down those houses. It's not going to help." What are the counter-balances to the extraordinary oppression that continues to exist in the isolated Gaza Strip? What gives you hope?*

AA: A few years ago when Barack Obama was elected I wrote a piece, looking forward, predicting what I thought would happen in the next few years, and I said two things: One is that there was going to be no two-state solution. And, the peace process would go absolutely nowhere. I was right about that — that's not too hard to be right about.

The other thing I said is that this was not going to remain static, and those who support justice in Palestine would have options. And a main option in North America and in many parts of the world for people who are fed up with this, is to support the Boycott, Divest, and Sanctions Movement. So a major change is that this movement is a real force now. It's a much more significant force than John Kerry's peace negotiations.

And you can see that in the fact that Benjamin Netanyahu devoted one-third of his recent speech at the AIPAC, Israel lobby conference, to attacking the BDS [Boycott, Divest, Sanctions] Movement. This is a factor on campuses all over the country. I was at the University of Michigan a few weeks ago, when there was the largest-ever attendance at any student government meeting. Thousands of people were there, either in person or watching on video feed, when divestment was being debated.

When that vote was lost because the students chickened out, in a sense, there was a spontaneous rally of hundreds of people. I have seen this kind of energy and mobilization before but it has always been around a military attack, Operation Cast Lead, or some other atrocity, like the war in Lebanon. But then it gradually died down and dissipated. What is different now is that this is a sustained movement.

People in power, institutions in power are being forced to react. They are being forced, they feel, to condemn the ethical movement that students are leading. And they are being forced to try and stamp this out through censorship, rather than to address it.

As powerful institutions, they don't take the ethical side. They have to be pushed and pressured and fought into doing the right thing eventually. The critical mass I'm seeing on campuses is like something I've never seen.

DB: *The boycott and divestment movement is taking hold in spite of quite a bit of repression on the campuses against the students and the teachers.*

AA: It's a lot of repression. I write in the book that since 2010, the Israel lobby and pro-Israel organizations have spent millions, if not tens of millions of dollars, trying to repress Palestine solidarity activism on campuses and particularly the BDS movement. They are not just targeting activists; they are also targeting educators, teachers and professors in the institutions themselves. One of the major groups in this campaign is something called The David Project, which is founded by a very extreme, pro-Israel Islamophobe.

They actually recommend accusing professors who teach about Palestine of academic malpractice. They try to bring in all of the disciplinary proceedings against students and teachers. We've seen that in a big way. We saw it in the Irvine 11 trial where the University of California, Irvine, colluded with Orange County prosecutors to bring their own students to trial. For what? For protesting against the Israeli ambassador. We've seen the abusive use of US civil rights law to try and stifle activism on campus.

367

In the past few weeks we've seen absolutely astonishing acts of censorship and repression. Northeastern University in Boston became the first US University to have the distinction of banning outright a Students for Justice in Palestine group. Last week, the spoken word poet and activist, Rami Nashashibi had his event at Washington University in St. Louis canceled and they tried to tell him what he could and could not speak about.

This is happening nationwide, and it's unprecedented. There's a free speech emergency. On the positive side, the taboo is being broken with the American Studies Association's vote on boycotting Israel. Judith Butler, the philosopher who's at Berkeley and is now at Columbia wrote — and I quote her in the preface to the book — that just in the past two years she's seen a change. People are coming out of the silence. They are starting to speak.

Israel does not have an answer to this except repression. They cannot win the argument — all they can do is try and stop it. But it's too late — it's happened.

DB: *Do you see any change in the way the press has dealt with the issue? It's one of the most censored stories of our time, and I think it's worse on the liberal channels — the Rachel Maddows who have taken up the role of being the protector of the President.*

AA: It's worse than ever, and sometimes even worse on the Left, sadly enough. But here's a story we've been covering on the Electronic Intifada in the past few days. We exclusively published the secret court transcripts that everyone else refused to publish — the *New York Times*, the Associated Press. This was a secret court transcript of a hearing where a judge allowed the incommunicado detention — effectively the fourth disappearance — of Majd Kayyal, a Palestinian journalist who's a citizen of Israel.

Because we published it, and a few other independent media outlets published it, the judge was forced to lift the gag order. Today, only after the gag order was lifted, the *New York Times* published the story and they even linked to the Electronic Intifada's coverage. That's another example that time and again, media like ours are setting the agenda. We are reaching people directly. Over the past week when Israelis could not get this news in their own censored media, they were coming by the thousands to the Electronic Intifada to read about what was happening in their own country — where the secret police had disappeared a journalist.

So, on the one hand corporate media is worse than ever — more cowardly and censored than ever — but our ability to reach past it and talk to people directly is greater than ever before. I think we are able to set the terms of discussion. It's worse, but there are so many things on the other side that are allowing us to fight it.

DB: *Is there support around the globe for this divestment movement? Has it been growing in other countries?*

AA: It's never looked better. One of the frustrations I've had over the years is that there's always been very strong latent support for justice in Palestine in many countries around the world, but it wasn't mobilized. People would go out and do opinion polls and find that people object to Israel's occupation as apartheid, as violence. But other than occasional street demonstrations — which can be important — it wasn't translating into effective pressure.

The change now is that the BDS campaigns all over the world take so many forms. In Europe, it's incredible what's been achieved in the past couple of years. They are giving people a way to have an impact on the situation, to get involved. BDS was initiated by Palestinians almost a decade ago. It's still led by Palestinians but as more and more Palestinians see the response around the world, there's kind of a virtuous circle where Palestinians who were skeptical about BDS, or skeptical about its potential, are saying, "Well, actually this is something that we can get behind and we can encourage."

That momentum has been very positive and Israel doesn't know what to do about it. In *The Battle for Justice in Palestine,* I write about the Reut Institute, a think tank, which set the strategy that Israel adopted in 2010 of how to sabotage the Palestine Solidarity Movement. They were going to focus on what they called hubs of delegitimization, which included the Bay Area and UC Berkeley, which were perceived to be places particularly hostile to Israel. They say in their strategy that the most valuable support for Israel, or the most valuable criticism of BDS, is going to come from the Left.

Israel's strategy has been to target the Left through a kind of carrot-and-stick approach. On the one hand, the carrot is presenting Israel as this haven of green technologies, of LGBT rights, which is all bogus. In the book, I show how Israel's claims on these things are absolutely false. Its environmental record is horrific — disastrous. On the other hand, is the stick — repressive measures, lawsuits — which the Israeli consulate in San Francisco has been very involved in. They were involved in the lawsuit against the Olympian Food Co-op — repression.

It's amazing that with all these resources they are putting in, it's not working. This [BDS] movement is growing and growing. That's the story that needs to be told. People should understand that we're powerful. We don't have to sit and wait for John Kerry or Barack Obama or anyone else to pull something out of their hats. We can set the agenda and that's what's happening on this issue.

The Path Ahead for Palestine
Mustafa Barghouti   July 2015

DB: *The ongoing occupation and ethnic cleansing of Palestinians from their homeland by Israel continues unabated. Israeli forces continue to demolish Palestinian neighborhoods in East Jerusalem, while they step up the pace of illegal settlement building on the West Bank. In Gaza, the situation is beyond bleak. It is a major feat even to get fresh water. Thousands of children have been sickened because of this, and are suffering major health defects and learning disabilities as a result. Meanwhile, they are traumatized on a daily basis by the continuing military assaults and constant drone presence on the strip.*

Mustafa Barghouti is a physician, activist, politician, and General Secretary of the Palestine National Initiative. He's been a member of the Palestine Legislative Council and is a member of the Palestine Liberation Organization, PLO Central Council. He was nominated for a Nobel Peace Prize in 2012.

Welcome Dr. Barghouti. What brings you to the United Nations in New York?

MB: We had a conference at the UN of 151 parties from all over the world, within the framework of the so-called socialist international. It was a very important platform to present the Palestinian issue. We reached the best resolution ever issued by all these parties supporting the right of the Palestinian people to end the occupation, to have freedom and justice. It calls for the right of the Palestinian refugees to return to their homes, and to support the immediate end of occupation and all illegal Israeli settlements in the occupied territories, as well as the release of Palestinian prisoners held by Israel, especially the young people — the children and the Palestinian elected members of Parliament who are held in Israeli jails.

It was a very good conference inside the United Nations. I hope these resolutions will help advance the Palestinian cause and explain to the world that we are struggling not only for the freedom of the Palestinian people, but also to liberate the Israeli public from its own Israeli government, which is consolidating a system of occupation, oppression, and segregation in the form of an apartheid much worse than what was in South Africa.

DB: *In September 2014, following Israel's brutal 51-day massive assault and slaughter [on Gaza], you said, "This inhumanity can't continue. There is only one way out — to establish a boycott, divestment, sanctions movement (BDS) against Israel in order to dismantle the occupation and this apartheid."*

MB: Palestine agreed to the two-state solution and the PLO recognized Israel while Israel still does not recognize the Palestinian state. Many Palestinians thought that by accepting the two-state solution — which is really unfair, but is a painful compromise that Palestinians can accept — this would end the occupation and that Israel would finally let Palestinians be free and dignified. Unfortunately it turned out that after 22 years of useless negotiations, these negotiations became a cover for Israeli illegal expansion of settlements, and the negotiations became a cover for the destruction of the very last opportunity for a two-state solution and peace.

After 22 years, Palestine discovered that the so-called peace process has itself become a substitute for peace. That's why we first need to change the balance of power before we speak about negotiations. The last atrocity in Gaza was the attack of 51 days that took the lives of 2,270 Palestinians, who were 85 percent civilians, including 580 children. This was one last episode of a series of massacres that have been waged against the Palestinian people.

When we speak about the balance of power, it cannot only happen with the resistance on the ground, which is a nonviolent resistance — it requires an international factor. That is what happened in South Africa. Without the boycott, divestment, and sanctions against the system of segregation and apartheid, the South African injustice would not have ended. That's what we are saying today. BDS is one international instrument to make the Israelis understand that their government is dragging them into a terrible situation. BDS is not against the Israeli people as people, or against Jewish people at all. Many Jewish people are supporting this, including many famous people, such as Daniel Barenboim, the famous musician, Ilan Pappe, the great historian, and other very well known Israelis. BDS is not against the Israeli people, but against the Israeli government policy.

As we tell Israeli soldiers when they try to arrest us during non-violent actions, we are not struggling only for the Palestinian people but also to liberate the Israeli people from the system of apartheid. Israelis will not be free from fear and the terrible system of apartheid until the Palestinians are free from occupation. This is the message. It is very peaceful message, about a very nonviolent form of struggle, but also about the determination of the Palestinian people to be free and dignified.

I hope that many Jewish people in the US will understand that the Israeli government policy is destroying not only the future of the people in the region, but it is also harming the image of Jewish and Israeli people everywhere. It's time for people to understand that Palestinians deserve freedom and justice like everybody else. It's time for people to understand that Palestinians need to be free and will be free. Nothing will break us after 67 years of dispossession and displacement, 48 years of occupation — the longest in modern history — and now a system of apartheid and segregation.

All of that will not break our will because we are determined to be free like African Americans are determined to get their rights in the US, the people of Algeria struggled for their freedom, and the American people struggled for their independence. It's the same. People aspire to freedom and nothing can stop that.

DB: *We often hear the Israelis say they are looking for peace, but they don't have a partner.*

MB: I think that is incorrect, because they have had partners from the Palestinian side and they had the chance to conclude peace with the Camp David meeting, but instead of accepting Palestinians' right to have a state, they proposed that Palestine would remain under Israeli slavery.

DB: *What do you mean by Israeli slavery? That's not hyperbole, is it?*

MB: For 48 years, the Israeli government has been exploiting the Palestinians in several respects; by taking away our land, confiscating more than 90 percent of our water, then selling us the water back at twice what the Israelis pay — and a system of segregation where many major roads inside the Palestinian territory are exclusively for the use of Israelis. If a Palestinian is caught driving or walking on them, he could be sentenced to six months in jail. People like me, born in Jerusalem, are prevented from reaching Jerusalem, although I worked there for 15 years as a medical doctor. Yet the Israeli army doesn't want me to be in Jerusalem. People in Gaza cannot reach out to their relatives in the West Bank and vice versa. Our movement and lives are restricted by Israeli military orders and a legal system created to establish apartheid.

Apartheid means two systems of rules for two people living in the same area. That's exactly what we have today. Many people in the US avoid using the word apartheid, but it means segregation, injustice, and discrimination. That's exactly what we have. We don't have the right to be free, to move freely from one part of the country to another, the right to determine our future without Israeli control.

When I spoke of the system of oppression imposed on us, I meant a situation where the Israeli government is practicing racism. When you listen to Israeli officials, they frequently say very serious racist remarks, depriving and denying Palestinians the same rights that are supposed to be allowed to everybody. We are talking about inequality. That is the reality on the ground.

DB: *What are your hopes and the hopes of a free Palestine in the face of this extraordinary violent war in Syria, which is again making refugees of thousands of Palestinians who were living in Syria. How do you see this terrible and bloody war playing into the future of your people?*

MB: What's happening around us is very sad and horrible. We feel very sorrowful about what is happening to the Syrian people, as well as the people of Iraq and Yemen today. These explosions are the result of lack of democracy and opportunity for people, especially young people. These are the core causes of the terrible violence we see, including the terrible forms of terrorism committed by the so-called ISIS, ISIL, etc. All of these are horrible things.

We, the people who have suffered so long, understand the suffering of others more than anybody else. But this suffering of the people in Syria, and the violence that is practiced there, as well as in other places, present no justification for Israel to practice violence against the Palestinian people, as some Israeli government people would think or try to claim. Because thousands of people are killed in Syria, that does not justify killing thousands of people in Gaza. We want the situation to improve in all these countries. We want the people in these countries to be able to practice democracy and have their rights. But at the same time we also want our rights as Palestinians to be free from occupation and oppression and free from any form of discrimination — through the longest occupation in modern history.

The problem with the two-state solution is that while negotiations keep failing, Israel claims there are no partners for the Palestinian state. The truth is that there are partners all the time. The problem is that Israel does not want a partner, but wants an operator, a leader who would sacrifice and give up the rights of his own people and cooperate with Israel to give up those rights. This is the kind of leader Israel wants to see, and they keep failing because there is no Palestinian leader who respects himself who will sell out his country and his people to the occupiers. That's why Israel keeps claiming there are no Palestinian partners.

DB: *Many in the movement for a free Palestine feel the days of a two-state solution are long gone. The Palestinians have lost so much land. I try to imagine what the map would look like, for a free Palestine with contiguous borders and airports. Do you have a map in your mind?*

MB: If there was a will on the side of the international community, especially the US — being the greatest supporter of Israel — if there was a will for a real two-state solution, they could easily force Israel to stop the occupation and they could easily force Israel to remove the settlements from the occupied territories, in which case there would be a chance for a Palestinian state in the West Bank and Gaza, including East Jerusalem, according to the 1967 borders. There would be a corridor linking the West Bank to Gaza.

But none of that is happening, because the US government, and many other governments, are either afraid or do not want to pressure Israel. Because of that, we see the evaporation, disappearance, withering of the possibility of a two-state solution. That's what some Israeli leaders also say.

Israel must confront three choices: either they accept to take out the settlements, remove their army from the West Bank and Gaza and allow the Palestinians to have a Palestinian state on 1967 borders, or they must sustain the existing situation — but the existing situation is not sustainable because it's a system of segregation, apartheid, and occupation. This is not sustainable because no people in the world can accept being slaves of occupation forever. Then, the only possible third solution if Israel completely strikes the possibility of two-state solution, is the one-state solution with equal rights. I would prefer to have one-state solution immediately, where Israelis and Palestinians have equal rights and equal duties.

We *can* live together. We lived together with the Jewish people before Israel was established. Palestine was not a place where

Jewish people were persecuted or discriminated against. On the contrary, as was the case in most European countries. I understand the suffering of the Jewish people. I understand how they went through the Holocaust, which was the most horrible thing, and the suffering in the pogroms in Russia, and the suffering during the Inquisition time.

One thing that many Israelis forget is that all of these atrocities had nothing to do with Palestinians. Palestinians were never part of any oppression of any Jewish population. That suffering of the Jewish population doesn't justify in any way Israel's oppression of the Palestinian people. Because of that suffering, I think the Israelis should be more sensitive about injustice and oppression of another people than anybody else.

Unfortunately, that is not the case in Israel today. That's why you see many Jewish people in the US and in many other countries, joining and supporting the Palestinian struggle in solidarity with Palestinians because they care about the moral values.

That's why I say that if Israel prevents the two-state option — and it would be Israel's responsibility — there would be no other alternative than one-state solution with equal rights and equal duties. Such a state would not be a Jewish state. It would be a mixed state. That's what people need to understand. If the two-state solution vanishes, the Israeli government is responsible.

DB: *Isn't it just as unrealistic to expect a two-state solution in Israel as it was to expect a two-state solution at a certain point in South Africa?*

MB: Exactly. A friend of mine was a Jewish white minister in the first South African government that brought down the apartheid system. I told him that I thought the situation for the Palestinians was similar to the apartheid in South Africa. He stopped me and said what you have in Palestine is much worse than the apartheid system we had in South Africa. In South Africa people were not forced out of their country and did not suffer from this horrible system of oppression that Israel delivers.

In South Africa, the only solution was one-state with democratic rights for everybody. And this would not have happened if it weren't for the BDS, which eventually made the South African apartheid system understand that they would lose everything unless they stopped the system of apartheid. I believe there is a lot of similarity between our situation and South Africa's situation, and that's why I hope that some of the strategies that they used then can also work for Palestine today.

There is No Plan(et) B

BP's Gulf Coast Ecocide

Dahr Jamail   April 2011

DB: *On April 20th, 2010, the BP [British Petroleum] owned Deepwater Horizon oilrig exploded and sank, triggering the largest marine oil spill in history. The total discharge, lasting 87 days, was estimated at 210 million gallons (4.9 million barrels). "Gross negligence and willful misconduct" within systemic industry practices of cost-cutting and inadequate safety were determined to be the cause. Dar Jamail, who focuses on anthropogenic climate disruption and the environment, joins us.*

It is one year after the massive BP oil spill, the largest oil spill in history. Dahr Jamail, who is Ryan Lambert and why is he enraged?

DJ: Ryan Lambert owns one of the largest charter fishing businesses in the Gulf region of Louisiana. He did very well with that charter fishing business until April 20th of last year. During that time, before the disaster started, he always supported the oil industry in his home state, had plenty of friends in that industry, and trusted that if something went wrong, they would do the right thing — clean it up and compensate people adequately. Not anymore. Recently he said, "I am absolutely outraged. My business is down 94% in the last year. I've lost over a million dollars. I've filled out one information request packet after another from the Gulf Coast Claim Facility [GCCF], which is run by Kenneth Feinberg. Ryan keeps sending them forms, and they keep asking for more, so he recently snapped. He said, "Don't send me any more of your damn packets. I'm not going to send out anymore. I see you starving people out. There are thousands of people I know in the fishing industry who are literally being starved out. I do not know one person who is being made whole yet, as BP promised." So he has come out as a fierce critic of BP and the entire oil industry in the Gulf of Mexico. He traded in his accountant helping him get compensation, for a lawyer to go after BP.

DB: *This is a businessman. You have been talking to the Center for Biological Diversity. What is the scientific perspective?*

DJ: The Center for Biological Diversity released a report this month. In Louisiana, Alabama, and Florida there are daily dead endangered sea turtles and dead neonatal dolphins washed ashore. The CBD report estimated that about 6,000 sea turtles, 26,000 dolphins and whales, and 82,000 birds, as well as countless fish and other invertebrates, were harmed or killed by BP's oil disaster. These are staggeringly high numbers. The outlook is very grim. I've been speaking with Dr. Ed Cake, an oceanographer and marine biologist who is an expert on oysters. He fully expects it to take up to 20 years to get back to the day before the BP disaster.

There are countless other oil spills, like the 1979 spill in the Bay of Campeche in Mexico, which hasn't yet recovered. Many of the fisheries in the area of the 1989 Exxon-Valdez disaster in Alaska still haven't recovered. It's alarming to see these large numbers of sea turtles and dolphins washing ashore. To see this number of neonatal dolphins dead, and their numbers increasing daily — during their birthing season — is very worrisome.

Divers doing environmental assessments in the Gulf are coming up sick. They are wearing full, thick wetsuits, for a 45-minute dive, maybe twice a day, and coming up sick. Picture a dolphin whose skin is directly exposed to the waters in the Gulf of Mexico, eating the seafood. This is how fast they are dying. We're just a step up from the dolphins on the food chain; so this is a very telling, as well as alarming, sign.

DB: *The 1989 Exxon-Valdez spill is a reference point to the magnitude of the BP disaster. Are patterns repeating? Are people undermined, not being dealt with medically, or their economic losses ignored?*

DJ: Yes, to all of the above. We see the media working the same way. This one-year anniversary, they are saying, "It's not over yet, there are some issues, but clearly the Gulf hasn't had the apocalyptical environmental disaster people warned about. It's getting back to normal, people are eating the seafood, so it's not quite as bad as everyone had feared." That was the brunt of the media. Downplay the disaster. Don't alarm people.

There are people sick to this day from the dispersants used in the Exxon-Valdez spill. There were a huge number of lawsuits filed after that disaster, and many plaintiffs have already died. There are lawsuits that have still not been resolved from that 1989 spill. These are giant companies with ungodly amounts of money that can afford to litigate people to death, literally. That's what Exxon did, which is why ultimately they paid one-tenth of what people were hoping for restitution.

BP had a so-called $20 billion compensation fund. Kenneth Feinberg recently announced that he fully expected to pay less than half that to settle all the claims. They've paid out between 3.6 and 3.7 billion dollars as they continue to drag out the process and starve people out. It's the same pattern where the companies continue on with business as usual. The petrochemical industry lobby groups have been burning the candle at both ends, so we've had not one piece of legislation passed in the year after the biggest oil disaster in US history.

No law to change regulations of the oil industry for deep water drilling or improvements to a response plan. Not one piece of legislation passed. Ken Salazar, the Secretary of the Interior who Obama appointed, has issued permits, saying there's no foreseeable environmental risk with continued deepwater drilling. These permits further deepwater exploration. As we go into the future and oil continues to run out, we see these rigs going into deeper and deeper water because that's where the last oil is located. It's not if this happens again, but when.

DB: *Obama brought Kenneth Feinberg into this for the illusion that he was a representative of the US government, not BP. What happened?*

DJ: He was appointed as the so-called independent administrator of the fund. But this has been a stacked deck from the beginning. Feinberg is the guy who dealt with the aftermath of 9-11 and gave the shaft to the rescue workers and their families. Those are the workers who died or were made sick from the contaminants there — of course after the EPA gave it the "all clear." These are direct parallels with Feinberg. The remaining 9-11 rescue personnel — those still alive — called down to people in the Gulf. I heard the rescue responders from 9-11 trying to tell them how to prepare themselves for basically a slime bag like Feinberg. Obama appointed Feinberg as administer because he's great at working with corporations, and minimizing, mitigating their loss in situations like this. He did it well in the wake of 9-11, and he's doing it extremely well for BP.

Feinberg's firm is being paid one and a quarter million dollars a month directly by BP to basically act as a defense attorney for BP and save as much of that $20 billion compensation fund as possible. He's doing a very good job of that, while he's starving people out along the Gulf. People are taking $5,000 compensation claims because people are literally that desperate. If they don't take the claim, they don't eat. If you were a deckhand on a shrimp boat, the shrimping industry has already been decimated. Other species, such as red snappers, have also seen immediate huge impacts. This is much more dramatic than what we saw with the Exxon-Valdez. The people dependent on this for their livelihood are literally being starved out by BP, and settling for claims that are a drop in the bucket in the bigger picture, but they can pay the rent and feed their families for a few months, so they feel like they must do it. That comprises the vast majority of the claims that BP is so happy to tell the press they settled.

DB: *People are getting sick in a variety of ways and the press isn't picking that up. Can you say more about that?*

DJ: This is a huge component of the story — the physical human impact — which is second only to the massive destruction of the ecosystem of the Gulf. The psychological impact is as deep as the physical effects. Already I've come upon at least five deaths directly attributable to people suffering acute exposures to BP's oil and dispersants. Sick people are coming into the clinics daily. Doctors I spoke with say that most of the MDs along the Gulf coast don't know how to treat people coming in with headaches, rashes, chronic respiratory, sinus and kidney problems. They don't understand that they must treat it like workplace medicine, like somebody working in a chemical lab, who just suffered an acute serious exposure to toxic chemicals and their body is reacting to that. People in some areas, where much of the chemicals are blowing ashore on a regular basis, are being chronically exposed. A three-year-old boy, Gavin Tillman, had 29 doctor visits, and was on 10 different rounds of serious antibiotics. They finally took a blood test and he has massive exposure to these chemicals. He hasn't eaten any of the seafood. Since he's sick, he drinks only filtered water, doesn't go down to the beach. Shirley Tillman, his grandmother, says, "I've ruled out everything but the air. My three-year old wasn't on the clean-up crew. He is sick just from being near the coast and breathing the air." The chemicals are out there, and it will keep coming up over the years.

Unending Danger from Fukushima

Helen Caldicott   August 2012

DB: *At the 67th anniversary of the US bombing of Hiroshima, Dr. Helen Caldicott, a co-founder of Physicians for Social Responsibility, pediatrician and anti-nuclear campaigner, reflected on the 2011 nuclear accident at Fukushima and the continuing threat from its radiation.*

Dr. Caldicott, I read an interview with Yasuteru Yamada, the president of the skilled veterans corps for Fukushima. This is the group of old people who volunteered to sacrifice themselves because they had fewer years to live.

HC: The report was commissioned by the Diet, or the Japanese parliament, and said that the results of Fukushima were caused by human error, a result of the Japanese culture. It could have just as easily been applied to the American culture — however you are not as autocratic. The whole nuclear enterprise is totally controlled by the weapons makers, designers and nuclear power people.

The corruption is vast and they are all interlocked, as they were in Japan. There is no independent body — none — that is not paid for by the nuclear industry, which is overseeing the whole process — both weapons and nuclear power production. They cut corners continuously; they lie and don't inspect the reactors adequately or in time. Sometimes they do, but sometimes they don't. There have been some very close calls in America. When I read that report for the Diet on the Japanese situation, it made my blood curdle because I realized it was just as applicable — or even more so — to the American situation.

The situation in Fukushima is dire. They've examined 38,000 children under the age of 18 in the Fukushima prefecture, and 36% of them — over one-third — have thyroid cysts and nodules, almost certainly related to their exposure to both external gamma radiation and inhaling and ingesting radioactive iodine and cesium which also concentrates in the thyroid in their food. Children are extremely sensitive to radiation — 10 to 20 times more so than adults. Little girls are twice as sensitive as little boys, and we don't know why. You would normally expect solid tumors not to occur for another 10 to 15 years, and this data is coming within the first year after the accident. So it clearly indicates these children got a whopping dose of I-131 [radioactive Iodine-131] and cesium. The nodules were diagnosed by looking at the thyroids by ultrasound examination. They have not been biopsied, but should be. Thyroid nodules in children are, as we'd say in Australia, "as rare as hen's teeth." They occur occasionally as congenital abnormalities, but they're virtually never seen. In my years of pediatric practice, I never saw any thyroid lesions like this. When they occur, they should be biopsied either by sticking a fine needle in, sucking out some cells and looking at them under the microscope, or taking out the lesion and examining it to see if it is malignant. This is not being done.

These children are being "followed up" with another ultra-sound in a couple of years. Some of the bigger lesions are followed more closely, but they're not being biopsied, so no diagnosis can be made. If some are malignant — and almost certainly some are — these children will not be diagnosed. Malignancy would require the removal of the thyroid and very close follow-up. Some will die — these children who are not being biopsied are condemned to a certain death if they are malignant.

I've never read anything in the medical literature so absolutely irresponsible. The parents are told about the thyroid lesions but don't see the ultrasound. The ultrasound examinations are being done by, in some cases, very unqualified and unskilled people, but that is just the tip of the iceberg. Those reactors released 200 or so radioactive materials and isotopes, some with half-lives ranging from seconds to millions of years.

All cancers and leukemias can be induced by radiation. These isotopes go to many different organs. Cesium goes to the brain, thyroid muscle, testicles and ovaries, where it can induce malignancies. Strontium 90 goes to the bone, where it can cause bone cancer or leukemia. Plutonium goes to the lung where it can cause lung cancer. If lymph glands are also affected, it can cause lymphomas, or Hodgkin's disease. If the bone marrow and hemoglobin are affected, it can cause leukemia or bone cancer; if it affects the liver, it can cause liver cancer. Like thalidomide, it crosses the placenta and can kill a cell in a fetus that's going to form the left half of the brain or the right arm. It also deposits in the testicles where it can damage genes in the sperm and damage the very building blocks of life.

These aberrant genes are passed on generation after generation, like cystic fibrosis, diabetes and hemochromatosis — known as iron overload. There are over two thousand such inherited genetic diseases. Once you get these elements into an organ, the radiation is persistent. Many of these isotopes last for a long time within the body, consistently irradiating small volumes of cells, which get a very high dose. So they are very mutagenic, very carcinogenic.

The cedar pollen in Fukushima was so full of cesium it was almost unbelievable. It was blown all over the place. Someone tested dust in a tenth floor apartment in Tokyo recently, and there was a lot of cesium 137 and 134 in it, and uranium 238 and 235 from the Fukushima accident — the tenth floor of a Tokyo apartment! Much of the food is radioactive. Much of the rice grown in Japan is grown in the Fukushima prefectures. It's being harvested with cesium in it so they're mixing it with non-radioactive rice, but it doesn't matter because it re-concentrates back in the body. Sixty-three percent of the fish caught 100 kilometers from Fukushima have cesium in them. Tuna being caught off the coast of California is carrying cesium from Fukushima. Spinach and mushrooms are full of cesium and other isotopes, but they're only measuring cesium. Cesium lasts for 600 years and it's in the soil. Every time it rains it gets washed down from the hills, into the rivers and the ocean, concentrating in the food chain consistently. So the food will be radioactive for hundreds of years. It's not just that people have radioactive elements already in their bodies, which will continue to be there for some years, until they're excreted, finally. They will be eating radioactive foods for hundreds of years and the food is not being consistently tested. You can't taste, smell or see radioactive elements in the food.

Someone asked me to write an article about what I would suggest medically. There are children now living in areas so radioactive that they were evacuated around Chernobyl — evacuated, exclusion zones. Two days after the accident occurred, it hit me in the guts — my God, there's absolutely nothing anyone can do to reverse the accident, which is still ongoing and very, very critical. And there's nothing we can do as physicians about the people who will be contaminated. That's what the situation is now.

If Building Four collapses, which is very delicate and damaged from the previous earthquake, on top of Building Four is a cooling pool of spent fuel rods over a hundred tons, a hundred feet above the air. It's very damaged. If there's an earthquake greater than 7.0 on the Richter scale, they predict Building Four will collapse and down will come the cooling pool. The zirconium clouding of the fuel rods will burst into flames, reacting with air at very high temperatures. Ten times more cesium and radioactivity will be released from that cooling pool than from Chernobyl. Senior politicians in Japan are talking about evacuating Tokyo, should that happen. Then it will contaminate the northern hemisphere enormously. What really worries me is the vast cover-up in the American media and throughout the world. People are not learning what's going on.

DB: *I live in northern California and my partner's parents live in Hawaii. Should people in Hawaii and at the US coastline be worried the way Europe was worried after Chernobyl?*

HC: Some areas of America initially got quite a high fallout from Fukushima. The ambient levels of radiation in Seattle went up 40,000 times above normal. There was radioactive iodine in the kelp off Anaheim, where Disneyland is. It was brought through the currents in the air, and then fell down with the rain. As I said, tuna caught off the coast of California contained cesium. It's quite dilute but the dilution doesn't matter. If you eat tuna with some cesium in it, the cesium goes to one of your muscles or your brain. Cesium is the potassium analogue; it's like potassium and our bodily cells are reaching for potassium. You only need a single mutation in a single cell induced by a very small amount of cesium to induce cancer. The incubation time for cancer is anytime from five to 17 years. When the cancer arrives — say you get a headache or lose your vision and you are diagnosed with a cerebral tumor — the cause will not be noted. It doesn't say, "I was made by some cesium in some tuna, 20 years ago."

Chernobyl: Radioactive Tinderbox

Linda Pentz Gunter   April 2014

DB: *It's Earth Day, and we're looking at the health of the earth. On April 26th it will be the 28th anniversary of the nuclear reactor explosion at Chernobyl. Joining us to talk about this is Linda Pentz Gunter, founder and international specialist of Beyond Nuclear. A newly published study uncovered alarming indications of biological loss and ecological collapse in the area around the Chernobyl nuclear reactor, which exploded in Ukraine. The results of this report are not happy.*

LG: No. This is coming on the heels of other alarming indications that all is not well in the so-called Garden of Eden in Chernobyl. We already know about the shortened life span of birds there, the compromised immune system and mutations of plants and insects. But this study, which was done by a team of a friend and colleague of ours at the University of South Carolina, throws up a big question about what happens to the ecological environment as a whole when it's contaminated long-term with radioactivity. They found a lack of organic decay. Trees that fell at the time of the explosion are still lying on the forest floor and haven't disintegrated into sawdust, which changes the whole natural cycle of life. We hope we're not seeing what is called a potential advance of a silent spring there, but it appears that microbes are not present to decay the material. One of the most alarming things in the short-term is that the buildup of leaf matter invites tinderbox conditions for forest fires. That could spread radioactivity beyond the already contaminated areas.

DB. *How would that unfold?*

LG: In 2010, Russia was plagued with terrible wildfires, which threatened Moscow with smoke and smog. It was the result of record high temperatures and drought, which are clearly results of climate change. So the awful confluence of the impact of the Chernobyl nuclear explosion in 1986 and our national government's terrible, criminal inability to act quickly enough on climate change, means we could see Chernobyl contributing directly to the spread of contamination because the warming world make fires more prevalent. When you've got dry leaves sitting on the forest floor, it's a tinderbox waiting to be lit up.

DB: *What else in this report concerns you?*

LG: One of the facile arguments we encounter amongst the "nuclear deniers" is they say, "Look human beings aren't in the Chernobyl zone anymore, so now it's teaming with wildlife." This is naive. We recognize that we've contributed to a very negative environment for wildlife, through pollution and habitat destruction. Some also naively believe that if we vanished, the wildlife would be better off. But we've set up a dependency for wildlife. *The World Without Us* describes what would happen if we weren't around to run things, including nuclear power plants, which would melt down if we weren't around. The idea that the animals in the Chernobyl zone are frolicking, procreating, and glad we're gone is a complete myth — an illusion only in visual terms. If you look at their biology through long-term exposure of radiation, the DNA affects the offspring. The study compounds the eerie feeling that we're looking at a dystopian environment, very popular in current pop culture films, but we'd rather not see it in our lifetime. Possibly we will.

DB: *We also have Fukushima now. On Earth Day, are we in a safer nuclear world than we were 28 years ago, when Chernobyl exploded?*

LG: There are things to be hopeful about, such as the lowering of price for wind and solar, which are coming on fast, and with nuclear on the decline. But the decline sounds another warning, which is that the regulatory and safety oversight is not great, and the people with experience operating the nuclear power plants are retiring in huge numbers and are not being replaced at the same speed. Aging reactors are much more dangerous than midlife reactors. The economics of nuclear are so poor that we see companies walk away from nuclear. We've got aging reactors with huge inventories of nuclear waste in their pools, which could dwarf, if something happened to them, what occurred in Chernobyl and even Fukushima.

DB: *So 25 years later where are we?*

LG: We're not learning some of the lessons that we needed to learn, and could have learned many, many decades ago. The Paley Commission of 1952, under the Truman administration, did a study on the US energy future, and concluded that the US would be best served through "aggressive research in the whole field of solar energy, an effort in which the US could make a huge contribution to the rest of the world." That advice was not heeded. The Eisenhower administration turned that around into so called "Atoms for Peace" and we went down the nuclear road instead of the solar world in 1952. Imagine, you wouldn't need Earth Day if the US had led the world in the solar revolution in 1952. I don't think we're in a safer place from a nuclear power or weapons position than we've been. But the good news is that we've got lots of alternatives ready to go into production now, ready to be deployed. As the latest UN report shows, solar and wind can make the difference on their own, to supply what we need for developing as well as developed countries. There are lots of positive developments, although the nuclear picture is still dire. But nuclear power is on the decline worldwide, so that's a good sign. The economics and safety culture of nuclear is not attractive anymore — certainly not to Wall Street, Main Street, or even the boardrooms of utility executives.

DB: *What is your assessment of the situation at Fukushima, now that the new Japanese leadership is pro-nuclear on steroids?*

LG: Terrible. It's a disastrous turn of events. The prime minister who oversaw the beginning of the disaster has become a champion of ending the nuclear age, but unfortunately he's no longer in office. It's very difficult to know exactly what the situation is now at Fukushima because there's been an incredible suppression of information coming out of Japan from the beginning, not only from the government, but also from Tepco, the utility. We hope there will be no major earthquake in the near, or even indefinite, future, because all the reactors are still vulnerable. Just because they are shut down doesn't mean they are safe. No reactors are operating in Japan now, but they all have their fuel inventories on board.

The incredible human toll — people's lives, families, homes, work, health and culture have been wrecked by this, and it's not discussed. We get very caught up in the technological analysis and forget about the human tragedy, which at the end of the day is what it amounts to. Three Mile Island, Chernobyl, Fukushima and the unfortunate next one will undoubtedly happen, unless we see the light and say OK, we've got to shut these down ASAP. We can do wind and solar. The biggest US-missed opportunity is offshore wind. We looked at the Atlantic seaboard, and Rhode Island to Virginia could power 1/3 of the US in offshore wind alone. Thank goodness it's starting to happen, but it's a disgrace that the US still has no offshore wind power. The tide is turning on that front as well, and we will see a good deployment of wind, both on and offshore, and maybe start to see more nuclear plants shut down as we did last year.

DB: *Tell us about the recent UN report. There's some good news.*

LG: The UN's Intergovernmental Panel on Climate Change — the most prestigious, powerful scientific and political organization that deals with our climate — just released their fifth report, in which they gave a powerful endorsement of renewable energy. It's a definitive confirmation that renewable energy can take the lead and a major role in providing energy to our civilization. The full report says that only renewable energy can solve the climate crisis, and we can afford it. The transition to a green powered earth can be paid for and will help the economy. The deniers of the ability of renewables to supply energy are very powerful — funded by the fossil fuel and nuclear industries. But this panel said it's time to move ahead with renewables.

The Arctic Endgame

Zach D. Roberts and Steve Horn   September 2015

DB: *We turn our attention to President Obama "going environmental" off the coast of Alaska. What does the trip mean? We will speak with Zach Roberts, who writes for Alaska-based themudflats.net. And we have Steve Horn, who writes the DeSmogBlog, which deals with the public relations pollution that clouds climate science. Zach, what comes to mind when you see Obama "going environmental" in Alaska?*

ZR: Right before he got to Alaska, Obama approved Shell's offshore drilling in the Arctic Circle, which will dramatically affect environmental policy in the whole area. Hypocrisy? A greenwash? He wants to use the state as a nice backdrop, but not speak about what is one of the top three environmental issues of the state — the potential disaster of Shell drilling offshore. It's not even a conversation for him.

DB: *People in Alaska are very mindful of the dangers they're facing.*

ZR: We know it. We've seen it first hand — like the people in the Gulf of Mexico and New Orleans. We saw it in 1989 with the Exxon spill. We know what can happen. That's why many people in Alaska are very concerned about Shell, which has an incredibly long history of complete and total disaster. One official safety report said that during a test, one of the containment drums flew to the surface and was crushed like a beer can. No safety report with that information can be good. Now we're going to trust this company to drill offshore in Arctic waters with the oil industry's current technology for clean ups? We're still getting BP's oil coming into the Gulf, and you can't get better conditions for clean up oil than the Gulf of Mexico. Try doing it in -35* air temperature and 30-60 mph winds. Good luck.

DB: *Steve Horn, what are your thoughts on Obama's visit to Alaska?*

SH: I think it's a greenwashing trip. Obama is doing a big push for his "climate legacy" because groups are trying to shame him for his legacy to date. But the big picture is a president who after almost two terms, has approved rampant fracking on both public and private lands, offshore drilling in the Arctic and the Gulf — re-opening it to drilling after the BP disaster — and now in the Atlantic, and using the State Department as a mechanism to promote fracking technology around the world under the name of the Unconventional Gas Technical Engagement Program. Obama talks of climate change a lot, but he's done nothing about changing relevant policy whatsoever. Even in the Alaska trip where he's expressed concern for climate change, he approved a technology that will expedite drilling, including more ice pickers going up to the Arctic, allegedly to prevent Russia from getting the oil first. On the same trip, he talked about climate change, and expedited the drilling he had agreed to earlier.

DB: *Zach, what are the corporate interests involved? There's a lot of money for those icebreakers and other equipment in the Arctic Circle.*

ZR: This is the legacy of the governor after Palin. There is a long-term vision of what I call a mad, mad future, where trade will be able to go through the Arctic Circle, and Alaska will become a futuristic hub of industry. It's great that Alaska might have something other than oil, fish and minerals. But the Native populations survive off the scarce resources around there, and have for thousands of years. Let's face it. Oil runs Alaska. The reason many Alaskans don't support the offshore drilling is because Alaskans aren't going to get a penny of it. In Louisiana, they drill like crazy, destroy the environment, and people from Louisiana don't get any benefit from it. We saw what Katrina did to the wetlands. The same thing will happen in Alaska — it's inevitable. Shell has made no promises about clean up, and there's no new technology since the BP spill. There are hundreds of leases for inland oil that are not being explored because the oil companies — Shell, Exxon, Conoco Phillips, BP — would pay higher taxes for it. So they claim there's not a lot of oil, that

393

drilling is good for the economy, while the Arctic oil is much harder and more expensive to drill. This is a policy move from the oil industry, clearly not an economic one.

DB: *This has gone to steroids since the trillion dollar mineral find in Bristol Bay, Pebble Mine.*

ZR: If that goes through it will wipe out at least 25% of the wild Alaska salmon, which is a massive part of the Alaskan economy. Salmon is a renewable resource, unlike oil, where once it's sucked up out of the ground, it's gone. Pebble Mine is going to be the legacy of the Northern Dynasty, a Canadian mining company, which has both no record and a disastrous record of mining safety in large mining projects. That will end in nothing but tears if it goes through because the long picture is that if they go through with it, the waste water they use to mine gold and related minerals will be sitting there for 1000s of years in an earthen tailing dam, in an earthquake zone half the size of Manhattan, in one of the world's largest fresh water supplies. Water is another resource Alaska has just sitting there. A former senatorial candidate has already suggested selling Alaskan water from a melting glacier to India.

DB: *Steve, this trillion-dollar mineral find in Bristol Bay sounds like if the oil companies find gold, there's no way to stop them.*

SH: That's the premise of this Arctic drilling. The National Petroleum Council is an advisory body of the Department of Energy in existence since 1946, which consists of oil and gas executives and CEOs who advise the US on energy policy and its portfolio. Their 2015 report says that Arctic drilling is needed because at the end of the decade there will not be as much oil and gas from fracking as they had previously predicted. They had advertised 100 years of oil and gas, but it's beginning to run dry already, so it will be more expensive to drill for it. Arctic drilling is seen as the new frontier.

DB: *Zach, what about the resistance? The ice breaking boat was blocked for a while.*

394

ZR: Alaskans need to do the protesting. The Native populations have been speaking out against this. The conflict is that some Alaskans will get jobs from this industry — though many short-term. Many people spoke out against Pebble Mine, saying they will do more than just lie down to block machines — they will do a lot more. Alaskans are used to drilling, so they need to be convinced that this is potentially the endgame of everything in their environment in order to see a large resistance.

DB: *Steve, where do you see strong resistance?*

SH: That Greenpeace USA joined the kayactivists and other resisters who temporarily blocked the icebreaker in Portland shows that resistance has reached a new level. Unfortunately, many big green groups are hesitant to criticize the president or do much to stop his actions in a meaningful way.

DB: *And we can expect tons of money to be spent by the corporate elite during the election period to ensure these corporate drilling policies aren't undermined.*

SH: Absolutely.

Mother Earth and her Indigenous Peoples

Andrea Carmen   December 2015

DB: *The Climate Summit is in progress in Paris. Andrea Carmen is the Executive Director of the International Indian Treaty Council [IITC], and is there with a delegation of the IITC in Paris working with representatives of Native peoples from across the hemisphere. Andrea, what is the agenda for the Native peoples you are representing?*

AC: We're keeping our future generations first and foremost in our minds as we do this work. I'm one of two representatives on the global steering committee of what's called the International Indigenous Peoples Forum on Climate Change, which represents Indigenous Peoples from all seven indigenous regions in the world. Chief Bill Erasmus, from the Canadian Northwest Territories, and I represent the Indigenous Peoples of North America. We have about 20 Indigenous Peoples with us from the US, Canada and Mexico. There are also large delegations from Latin America, the Caribbean, the Pacific Islands, the Arctic, Africa, Asia, and Russia. We're very excited to be working with a very large team here. We have collective consensus points that we're working on with the UN States, which is what countries of the UN are called. I was selected by the whole indigenous caucus that met to finalize our positions and strategy for getting the rights of Indigenous Peoples recognized in the final legally binding agreement. This Paris agreement will hopefully come out by the end of the two weeks.

I was at the opening plenary and heard President Barack Obama, Vladimir Putin, Angela Merkel, Prince Charles, the King of Jordan, and Canadian Prime Minister Trudeau, the only one who mentioned Indigenous Peoples. It was very appreciated by the Canadian representatives here who worked on him hard to be sure he mentioned the issue. President Obama didn't mention either Indigenous Peoples rights or human rights. We hoped he would at least talk about human rights.

We're concerned that an agreement on climate change will make a difference on the ground. Some of the countries, like the US, are settling for working towards an agreement of no more than a 2° Centigrade temperature increase globally, but many scientists, including the UN scientists, say that degree of temperature rise will have a devastating impact on the traditional life ways and ecosystems of Indigenous Peoples — in many places, not just the Arctic and island communities, but everywhere. We're joining with over 100 countries, including small island states, to try and keep an agreement of a temperature rise no greater than 1.5° Centigrade. It makes a huge difference. Where I'm from, the Sonora Desert in Arizona and Northern Mexico is experiencing drought. Corn isn't growing like it used to. There is an increase in tornadoes in places like Oklahoma, and increased forest fires in California, the Pacific Northwest and British Columbia. Salmon are dying at unprecedented rates. The coho salmon run are not expected to even survive beyond this century in central California because of the warming temperatures. This is all over the planet.

DB: *You were disappointed in President Obama, and his lack of recognizing the importance of considering indigenous communities within climate concerns. What are some of the key issues impacting indigenous communities now?*

AC: We're experiencing an impact here. The UN General Assembly adopted the UN Declaration on the Rights of Indigenous Peoples in 2007, and of course the US was the last country to come on board in 2010. The Declaration says that Indigenous Peoples have the right to participate in decision-making that would affect our rights. But during the negotiating sessions here on different parts of the text, we're not even allowed to come into the room, even to observe and listen. Some of the Indigenous Peoples from the Pacific and Canada managed to get credentialed, so they are able to get in there and report out to us. Since we are not at the table to participate in the negotiations of text and decisions that will dramatically affect our rights, our rights are being violated right here, at COP21

[Council of Parties]. We are taking note of that. But we are talking to many countries. Today I talked to at least 20 countries, such as New Zealand, Ecuador, Iraq, and of course the US and Canada, about our position to include phrasing that says "respect, promote, protect and fulfill human rights, including the rights of Indigenous Peoples." That must be a fundamental principle of how this agreement will be carried out.

We know, as Indigenous Peoples, that a lot of our land is still protected, pristine, with healthy ecosystems, because we protected it. Yet when they talk about adaptation and mitigation, our land, water and resources will be a target for use by the states as they look for ways to try to resolve the problems they created around climate change. We want to make sure that our rights to our land, our traditional economy, and subsistence, are respected, as well as traditional knowledge and ways we can contribute to solve some of these problems using our traditional understanding of our relationship to the earth. Our original seeds, our practices, have not contributed to climate change. We have something to offer these discussions. Our traditional knowledge must be protected and respected.

There are some elements in the text that we are working on that we want to make sure are included. It's an uphill battle. The US and Canada today — a result of much pressure from Indigenous Peoples and other organizations here — are beginning to look at supporting our language. We are fighting to have the language in the operative, but they are only suggesting it for the preamble at this point. There is much common ground with human rights in general — such as gender equity, intergenerational equity of youth and elders — so there was much agreement on our concerns and proposed language. We work on mutually agreed on language that can take everyone's concerns into consideration. But there are countries here that don't want human rights at all.

DB: *These are struggles crucial to Indigenous Peoples. Can you put a human face on the suffering of people from environmental racism?*

AC: We are emphasizing what Indigenous Peoples call food sovereignty, or a right to food. Many communities, not just Indigenous Peoples, can't grow traditional corn anymore because of the climate changes and lack of rainfall. Traditional people from the salmon areas along the Pacific coast are saying there is an 80% salmon die off of the coho salmon run on the Columbia River this year because of the warming water temperatures. These are real issues that affect Indigenous Peoples' lives, their culture, their ceremonial ways of life.

DB: *The Columbia River wraps around the Hanford nuclear facility — a disaster waiting to happen and affecting indigenous communities.*

AC: The dams there have already affected the salmon run, so this is one more thing to add to a very struggling species. Salmon is called an indicator species. We heard from Indigenous Peoples of the Great Lakes area how the wild rice they live from is diminishing and is a fundamental part of their culture. We heard from Indigenous Peoples in Alaska that they are not able to hunt seals or walruses — what they have always lived off of. These are isolated communities. They don't have another resource to turn to, and this is part of their culture as well. Indigenous Peoples' relationship to our traditional food is not just economic and nutritional. It's our identity. Spiritual and clan relationships are all included. We're giving people the opportunity to talk about that here. The tar sands directly affect Indigenous Peoples from Canada. An elder spoke about the victory we all had with defeat of the Keystone XL pipeline. We give Obama credit for doing the right thing by standing up to the political opposition and denying the permit that would bring filthy oil down from tar sands — devastating for the communities of Alberta, Canada — down into the middle of the US, just waiting for a spill. As a sign of important solidarity between indigenous nations in the US and Canada, yesterday we presented some videos. We have an Indigenous Pavilion and the opening with North America Day was packed — standing room only — as people from the communities as well as delegates from countries listened to Indigenous Peoples tell their stories.

399

We started with a panel of elders talking about traditional knowledge of climate change, and how it's been prophesized — predicted to occur — if we continue to misuse the natural resources of the earth. We have a lot to contribute here.

DB: *In Canada, there are indigenous communities that have already lost their land. This isn't something happening in the future.*

AC: It's absolutely happening now. There is a relationship between what Indigenous Peoples are going through on the ground, to mega-projects like tar sands in the far north of Alberta, which used to be forest and clean rivers but is now devastated, contaminated. That tar sands project alone produces more greenhouse gases that cause climate change than all of the other sources in Canada — cars, buses, planes, factories. What Indigenous Peoples are defending with their homeland struggle on the ground is also a major part of fighting global climate change. We heard from representatives from the Navajo Dine Nation about the fight against coal mining there, which is also a fight against global warming, because burning fossil fuels is the biggest cause. We heard about some of the impacts of fracking in Oklahoma — the earthquakes, devastation of water supplies.

DB: *A record number of earthquakes. Talk about the fight against the coal miners and its impact on indigenous communities.*

AC: The biggest single emitter of greenhouse gases, mainly from burning coal, is China. Much is from indigenous land in the Americas as well as other places. The big debate is about the responsibility of the different countries, which they call differentiated responsibilities. Africa produces 7% of the total greenhouse gases. Obama recognized that the US has been a major contributor to climate change. It still has the largest output per capita. That gets back to demanding a change in energy policy as well as our own individual carbon footprint. China is still considered a developing country, so should they cut back as well? The US is pushing hard for that. Countries are talking about economics. We're talking about survival, as Indigenous

Peoples — not in the future, but now. It's coming down to a political and economic debate among countries about who is to blame, and who should do more. We're saying we are being killed off, literally, by this climate crisis. And the cause of the climate crisis is fossil fuel extraction.

DB: *Groups like the United Farm Workers stand against environmental racism because of the pesticides and other deadly chemicals used on the land. This is a workers' struggle as well.*

AC: Absolutely. And a human rights struggle. We are fighting this battle in our Yaqui communities of northern Mexico. We just brought a case against Mexico for importing pesticides that are exported by the US. We've also taken the US to the United Nations on this because they are the biggest exporter of pesticides they ban for use in the US. They ship it to Mexico and Guatemala, and spray it from airplanes over schools and communities. We documented 39 cases of children who died from direct exposure to these pesticides in small Yaqui communities. We got the United Nations Committee on the Rights of the Child to declare that environmental health was a human right that all children have, which relates to maternal health, which relates to pesticides. There is a strong connection between that kind of chemical contamination of indigenous and farming communities and what's happening with climate change, both in cause and effect. Many insects are now moving further and further north. Over 38,000 acres of forest have been killed by an invasion of bark beetles — forests from Alaska, British Columbia, California and Montana. That's a direct impact of climate change. But of course the industrial solution is to spray pesticides on them. This is strongly connected to climate change and we are beginning to talk about that.

DB: *If you could sit down with the people calling the shots there, what would your speech be?*

AC: We all have children, grandchildren, nieces, nephews, and children in our communities. Think about their lives, and what it will be for them in 25 years if this situation isn't radically changed. Not just a little, but a radical withdrawal from the fossil fuel-based economy to a sustainable way of life. What is their life going to be? They will look back at us and say, "What did you do for us in Paris? You knew what was happening. What are you going to do to put whatever comes out of here into action on the ground — to make a difference for the future?" We need to appeal to hearts and souls of the countries, heads of states, and state negotiators, so we all realize we all live on the same planet. Our future generations will look back and judge us to see what we did so they could have a life that was just and livable — where they and the natural world can thrive.

We have a lot of opportunity to interact with the countries, the States, and present our positions to them. We might not be in a certain room, but we catch them when they go in and come out, and we talk to them in their offices. We talk as a human family about how Indigenous Peoples have a lot to offer in this dialogue for solutions based on our traditional knowledge and practices. We want to offer as solutions how we maintained our relationship with the Mother Earth and natural world. All of our lives are at stake, particularly our children and grandchildren. I think we're making an impact. We ask for thoughts and prayers from everybody. We're all in this fight together.

Flint's Water Poisoned for Profit

Marsha Coleman-Adebayo   February 2016

DB: *The case of Flint, Michigan and its lead-poisoned water supply has exposed a US political disgrace, treating poor and minority communities with shocking disregard — and showing little interest in punishing the officials responsible.*

When I was a teacher in the mid-1970s, my middle-school students in Far Rockaway, Queens — one of the poorest communities of New York City — were celebrating May Day, the international workers holiday. Marilyn, the proud queen of the May Day show, was dressed in a redesigned wedding gown, surrounded by the girls in the class who were admiring her classy attire.

When it came time to kick off the May Day festivities, Marilyn rose to take her place at the Maypole, but she never made it to a full standing position. She grew extremely dizzy, fell back into her chair and was taken to the emergency room. I then learned that places where my students lived, played and studied were laced with lead-based products and their minds were being dulled and poisoned, even as I tried to expand them.

Now, four decades later, there is the case of Flint, Michigan, where an entire city has had its water systems poisoned by lead. Many in the community and environmental activists around the country are outraged at what was allowed to happen to Flint and the slow reaction of state and federal officials. And the more the people of Flint find out about what their politicians and officials knew and didn't do, the angrier the citizens are getting.

According to the Centers for Disease Control, "Lead is a neurotoxic substance that has been shown in numerous research studies to affect brain function and development. Children who have been exposed to elevated levels of lead are at increased risk for cognitive and behavioral problems during development. Exposure to lead can result in a variety of effects upon neuropsychological functioning including deficits in general intellectual functioning, ability to sustain attention on tasks, organization of thinking and behavior, speech articulation, language comprehension and production, learning and memory efficiency, fine motor skills, high activity level, reduced problem solving flexibility, and poor behavioral self-control."

Dr. Marsha Coleman-Adebayo, an Environmental Protection Agency whistleblower, worked at the EPA for some 18 years and is the author of No Fear: A Whistleblower's Triumph over Corruption and Retaliation at the EPA. *Her lawsuit led to the "No Fear Act," passed to protect government whistleblowers from intimidation and retaliation.*

Dr. Coleman-Adebayo, does the EPA have the resources to investigate and the criminal mandate to do so? Do they have the will to do it? What's possible? What could and should the EPA be doing?

MC: The EPA has the legal authority to prosecute. There are criminal violations and there are provisions of the Clean Air Act that provide for criminal prosecutions. Many people don't understand the breadth of the EPA, and the legal provisions the EPA has to go against environmental criminals. The EPA has 200 fully authorized federal law enforcement agents who are authorized to carry firearms in order to carry out their responsibility.

At the EPA we have about 70 forensic scientists and technicians and 45 attorneys who do nothing but litigate environmental criminals. It's not the most extensive array of personnel, but we definitely have the resources. It certainly does not take the 200 environmental law enforcement officers to arrest a governor, or other people involved in this criminal act in Michigan. We have the authority.

But the second question you asked, "Do we have the will?" That's where the fault line lies. The agency has shown that it may have the authority, but it certainly does not have the will to protect the people of this country from environmental criminals.

DB: *The EPA made an institutional decision not to prosecute in certain communities. Describe the so-called sacrifice zones.*

MC: Sacrifice zones are essentially primarily African American, Hispanic communities, and low-income white communities that no longer have the economic ability to flex their muscles in the overall environment and economics of our country.

Flint, Michigan, used to be an area where many African Americans moved to who were escaping from state-sponsored violence in the South, from the Ku Klux Klan, the White Knights, and all the organizations that were dedicated to killing black people in the early 1920s, 30s, 40s.

So many of these people who live in Flint now migrated from the rural South into cities like Detroit, and into Flint, trying to escape state-sponsored violence. They went to Flint seeking economic value, jobs in the auto industry.

Then, of course, it's another economic betrayal, where these industries pick up and leave these cities through NAFTA and other kinds of economic incentives. They go to Mexico or some other place where they can pay workers very low wages, with almost no benefits, leaving these communities without a way of recovering from that kind of economic devastation.

Those kinds of communities, where the economy is almost non-existent in terms of supporting human activities — good schools, and now, of course, even water, it seems — we call sacrifice zones. These communities no longer have the ability to demand from the political system that they are treated as equal citizens in this country.

DB: *There are various ways to blame the victims for poisoning themselves. "Well, these people are too poor and stupid to know what's happening to them."*

MC: It's a pathetic argument. This community started complaining almost two years ago that the water had turned various colors — gray, brown — and that there was an odor emanating from their faucets. The governor, all the other city officials and the EPA ignored them, made fun of them, told them that there was nothing wrong with water that has this brown color.

There's an interview of some government officials in Michigan shown drinking, supposedly, the water from Flint. The reality is that there are a number of people who knew there was something terribly wrong. Ford Motor Company realized that something was wrong when they refused to use the water because it was corroding the various car parts they were creating. They received special compensation, so they could bring water in for the parts they were creating.

So they had enough sense to make sure the water they used to build cars was not polluted. But they were allowing the children and the men and women of Flint to bathe in the water, to drink the water. It is a crime of such unbelievable proportion. The fact that no one has been charged with a crime at this point is, in fact, absolutely astounding.

DB: *I spent about 14 years teaching in various very poor communities in New York City and saw the impact when kids were exposed to lead. There is not even a clear and wide-ranging education program of how to deal with it. Many people still don't know all the dangers.*

MC: Lead poisoning is irreversible. It's an inter-generational poisoning. So the children of the fetuses who have been poisoned through their mother's womb — their grandchildren will most likely be lead poisoned.

These children will never, to a large extent, see their God-given potential because of this lead poisoning. President Obama hasn't even gone to Flint to kiss these babies or hold their hands, or just make a head bow to the incredible disaster that Flint has become. What would have happened if ISIS, for example, had lead poisoned an American city? How would the response have been different if "a terrorist" had poisoned hundreds of

American children and thousands of adults? How would we have dealt with that situation?

It's sad that a lot of the people who are responsible for this poisoning will get away with it. They will get away with it. We've already seen one sacrificial lamb pushed under the bus and that was Susan Hedman, who was Region 5 Administrator in the EPA.

DB: *I believe she tried to blow the whistle in April of 2015.*

MC: No, she didn't. There was an EPA whistleblower named Miguel Del Toral and he tried to blow the whistle in April. The EPA's culture is that if you try to blow the whistle, the first thing they do is demean you. They start spreading rumors that you've got mental illness or that you're not quite up to par in the EPA.

They demeaned his work and discredited what he tried to do. What's fabulous about this particular man is that he refused to allow the people of Flint to be poisoned, on his watch, without sounding the alarm. So he joined with a Virginia Tech scientist named Mark Edwards, who was the person who exposed the lead poisoning in Washington, D.C. The EPA and the CDC did the same thing to this professor. They demeaned him and tried to discredit him but he refused to be intimidated by the EPA and the CDC.

Also, a medical doctor noticed that a lot of her patients were bringing their children in to see her. When she evaluated them and performed tests she realized they had three to four times the amount of lead in their system that's allowed. So there are some real heroes in this story. There's one EPA employee who has been battered, but he's still standing. Of all the officials from Region 5 — Chicago all the way to Washington, D.C. — none of them lifted a finger to help the people of Flint, Michigan.

DB: *The statement from the EPA administrator talked about letting Susan Hedman take the brunt of it, calling her the scapegoat and saying, "Susan's strong interest is insuring that the EPA Region 5's focus remains solely on the restoration of Flint's drinking water." She's resigning.*

MC: You have to laugh at this. It's so silly. We are asking Congress, when Gina McCarthy — head of the EPA — knew about this crisis, and what did she do about it when she found out? We need to see the emails stream — the email traffic from Susan Hedman to Gina McCarthy. We need to find out when the head of the EPA found out that an American city had been poisoned. And then, what did she do about it?

And if she didn't know that Susan Hedman was inadequate and should have been removed, was there any conversation between the head of the EPA and the White House? Like, "I have an employee in Region 5 who's not up to snuff, who shouldn't be there." Either way, it seems to me that we need to focus on the head of the EPA instead of all the people that she's basically pushing under the bus.

DB: *You say there should be a criminal investigation.*

MC: At the very least.

DB: *Not only of the people at the EPA, but the role of the governor, the various officials and appointed administrators — the decisions made at all levels. How might you carry out the investigation?*

MC: The responsibility to carry out this investigation lies with Congress. We need to get to the bottom of what happened. How were these people poisoned? Flint is not the only city being poisoned. There are cities and municipalities around this country who are also being impacted by lead in the water. So if people think, "Well this is just a problem for Flint," I think they're in a fool's paradise at this point.

DB: *Examples of other cities?*

MC: I found out about three cities in Pennsylvania today that also have very high levels of lead. Perhaps we'll do another piece for the *Guardian* on those cities. There are some municipalities that people are complaining about in California now.

Citizens have a right to know whether the water coming from their faucet is clean and safe to drink. It sounds like such a simple statement but it's very powerful. What could the EPA have done in Flint? I'm pointing my baton at the EPA, because it has the power of the federal government behind it. Even if state officials and the governor in Michigan had decided to hide the information from their citizens, the EPA had the overall responsibility, as the federal government, to inform the citizens of Flint that their water was not safe.

They could have given the governor ten days to inform the citizens of Flint that there was a possibility their water was not safe. They could have said, "Until we've confirmed the results, we advise you to drink bottled water." That didn't happen. If the governor decided he was not going to inform, it was the responsibility of the EPA to inform the citizens of Flint that there was a possibility their water was not safe.

The EPA could have ordered a cease-and-desist order. They could have told the state, "You do not have the right to poison your people. And we are now going to step in as the federal government and we're going to take over this responsibility." The EPA did not do that.

They could have referred the governor to the Department of Justice for criminal prosecution — for poisoning his residents. They didn't do that. There were so many tools the EPA had at its disposal to step in and make a profound statement about the sanctity of life. Not only the planet, but also the sanctity of human life. That's why I'm pointing my baton at the EPA, because that's the responsibility of the agency — when states fail to protect their population, the federal government must step in and protect the people.

DB: *Michigan Governor Rick Snyder is turning down a request from the House to testify about his role in Flint. Would you suggest that Congress subpoena him rather than offering him the possibility of not showing up?*

MC: Absolutely. At the hearing, many times, Democratic members of Congress strongly urged the chairman of the committee, Chaffetz, to subpoena the Michigan governor — to force him to stand before Congress and explain what happened in Michigan. We're still waiting to see that kind of Congressional action.

Congress has now subpoenaed a Michigan official, and the chairman has actually ordered US Marshal service to hunt him down. Direct quote, "hunt him down," and bring him to Congress. Congress can do the same thing with the Michigan governor. They could order the US Marshal service to serve a subpoena against this governor and order him to stand before Congress. That's the kind of action we're looking for because this criminality deserves that kind of commitment to justice. So we must put a lot of pressure on Congress to carry out its oversight responsibilities.

DB: *So you would advocate subpoenaing the governor, and if he doesn't show up, just tracking him down and taking him into Congress?*

MC: Absolutely. That is what the law provides. We can't have two systems of justice where now a Michigan official has been subpoenaed and ordered to appear before Congress, but the governor is of out of bounds for that kind of action. We can't have citizens treated so differently in this country.

A two-tier system of justice in this country is that we have young men in prison for possessing a couple of grams of marijuana, sentenced to 10, 20 years, and we have federal and state government employees who poisoned an entire city and no one has been charged. We can't allow the government to operate with this two-tier system of justice. This isn't a democracy at this point. We need to focus in on this. And the people of Flint need to understand how the federal government is going to assist these families, going forward, with major medical and educational challenges before them.

These families are going to suffer a lot. They're already suffering because they're living in an economically depressed community, but now they're going to have children who are going to find it very difficult to learn. They're going to have other medical problems as a result of the lead poisoning. We need to understand how the government is going to assist these families, helping the children with these enormous, enormous challenges that lie before them.

DB: *What do you think would have happened if you were in the EPA and you tried to go to the President, or send an epistle through somebody who might be a little bit closer?*

MC: Many of us at the EPA have gone to Congress, tried to go through the bureaucratic channels, about communities being poisoned. I also reported that a community had been poisoned.

DB: *Where did that get you? It got you a lot of hell.*

MC: Exactly. It was hell because you become the target. I became the target of death threats and rape threats. Eventually I was fired. It is a process. We don't know what the President knew and we don't know when he found out. Did the President find out about the lead poisoning when all of us found out about it? Did he find out about the lead poisoning six months ago, or three months ago? If he did, what did he do about it? We don't have any of those answers, yet.

We must rely on Congress to help us figure out this puzzle. It's the same puzzle they grappled with at Watergate. What did you know, and when did you know it? We need to find that out. Once we have those answers, the officials who for six months, or four months, or three months, or a month or whatever it was, allowed the residents of Flint, Michigan to continue to drink poisoned water, bathe in poisoned water, feed their children, allow their children to drink poisoned water must be held accountable.

DB: *The President might have learned more if he had gone there for a few days to hand out water and talk with the people who were poisoned.*

MC: Those residents are getting only a few bottles of water a day. They have to bathe in that one bottle of water, bathe their children using that one bottle of water. It's almost too sad to talk about. Yet we haven't seen the National Guard sent out to put up tents, and places where people can take a bath once a day. We do that when we have disasters. The Red Cross and other emergency operations go out and put up large tents, allow people to take a bath, or have a place to have clean water. But we haven't seen that happen in Flint. This story remains a very heartbreaking, very sad story.

List of Contributors

Dennis J. Bernstein lives in San Francisco and is a long-time front-line reporter, specializing in human rights and international affairs. Prior to his work for Flashpoints, Dennis was an associate editor with the Pacific News Service. His awards for investigative reporting include the Jessie Meriton White Service Award in International Journalism, The Art of Peace award, the National Federation of Community Broadcasters Gold Reel award, the American Arab Anti-Discrimination reporting award, and the Media Alliance/Media Bash Investigative Reporting award. His investigative reports have been recognized numerous times by Project Censored. He was chosen by Pulse Media as one of the "20 Top Global Media Figures of 2009." Most recently he was the recipient of a 2015 Pillar Award for his work as a journalist whistleblower. He is the author of *Special Ed: Voices from a Hidden Classroom*.

Riva Enteen was raised as a socialist and has been an activist since the 1960s. While she attended Hastings College of the Law in San Francisco, she became active in the National Lawyers Guild, and then worked as its Program Director for 12 years. Riva was the first chair of KPFAs Local Station Board and led the successful efforts to bring Sovietologist Bill Mandel back to the KPFA airwaves. She raised two children in San Francisco, where they used to think every crowd was a demonstration. Riva now lives in S. Lake Tahoe.

Mumia Abu-Jamal is an award-winning journalist who authored nine books from prison, including bestseller *Live From Death Row*. In 1981 he was elected president of the Association of Black Journalists (Philadelphia chapter). That same year he was arrested for allegedly killing a white police officer in Philadelphia. He was convicted and sentenced to death in 1982, in a process called an epic miscarriage of justice. In 2001, after he had spent more than 29 years on death row – mostly in solitary – and 37 years in prison, his death sentence was vacated when the Supreme Court allowed stand the federal court finding that his death sentence was unconstitutional. He is now serving a life sentence without the possibility of parole. In addition to his books, which have sold more than 100,000 copies and have been translated into seven languages, he's also done thousands of radio commentaries (www.prisonradio.org). He holds a B.A. from Goddard College, an M.A. from California State University, Dominguez Hills, and is working on his Ph.D.

The New and Not So New Police State

Mara Verheyden-Hilliard co-founded The Partnership for Civil Justice Fund in 1994. The Partnership focuses on free speech, domestic spying, surveillance, police misconduct, government transparency and educating the public about their rights.

Jeff Cohen founded the media watch group FAIR in 1986. He is a media critic, lecturer, and founding director of the Park Center for Independent Media at Ithaca College.

Darryl Cherney of Earth First! produced the award-winning documentary, *Who Bombed Judi Bari?* In 2016, he ran in the Green Party primaries as a candidate for President of the US.

Shahid Buttar is a civil rights lawyer, singer, songwriter, poet, rapper, DJ, electronic music producer, dancer, grassroots organizer, and independent columnist based in Washington, DC.

Christopher Simpson, author of *Blowback*, is a professor of Journalism known for his expertise in propaganda, democracy, and media theory and practice.

Marjorie Cohn is a professor at Thomas Jefferson School of Law, former president of the National Lawyers Guild, and deputy secretary general of the International Association of Democratic Lawyers.

Birgitta Jonsdottir is a poetician, member of the Icelandic Parliament for the Pirate Party, and Chairperson of the International Modern Media Institution.

Katharine Gun is a former Linguist/Analyst for the British Government Communications Headquarters, equivalent to the US National Security Agency [NSA].

The Class War

Ai-jen Poo is director of the National Domestic Workers Alliance (NDWA) and co-director of the Caring Across Generations campaign.

Arturo S. Rodriguez, as president of the United Farm Workers of America, is continuing to build the union Cesar Chavez founded.

Gray Brechin is an historical geographer, a visiting scholar in the UC Berkeley Department of Geography, and founder and project scholar of the Living New Deal Project.

Manuel Pérez-Rocha is an Associate Fellow of the Institute for Policy Studies in Washington and an Associate of the Transnational Institute (TNI) in Amsterdam.

Richard D. Wolff was Professor of Economics Emeritus, University of Massachusetts, Amherst, and is now a Visiting Professor in the Graduate Program of International Affairs of the New School University, New York.

Domestic Dissent

S. Brian Willson, a peace and justice activist for over 40 years, is also a lawyer, published author, and regularly rides his adaptive bicycle with his prosthetic legs in order to reduce his carbon footprint.

Phillip John "Phil" Donahue is an American media personality, writer, and film producer. The Phil Donahue Show focuses on issues that divide liberals and conservatives.

Laura Flanders is an English broadcast journalist living in the US who hosts The Laura Flanders Show, a TV and radio program. She is the niece of Alexander Cockburn.

Marjorie Cohn (see above)

William Ramsey Clark is a lawyer, activist and former federal government official. He occupied senior positions in the US Department of Justice under Presidents Kennedy and Johnson, serving as the US Attorney General from 1967-1969.

Bill Means is a co-founder of the American Indian Movement, the International Indian Treaty Council and the UN Working Group on Indigenous Populations.

Diane Wilson is an American environmental activist, anti-war activist, author and co-founder of CODEPINK. She is the subject of an award winning 2005 documentary, *Texas Gold*.

Brandon Toy is politically active in the Detroit area, serving on the Board of Directors of The Michigan Coalition of Human Rights. An army veteran, he was deployed to Baghdad in 2005.

Oliver Stone, five-time Oscar award winner, wrote and/or directed over 20 full-length feature films, including some of the most influential and iconic films of the last two decades.

Miguel Gavilan Molina founded the first bilingual radio station in the US, KBBF. A Flashpoints and *La Onda Bajita* producer, he is long active in the Chicano and farmworker movements.

Black Bodies

Kevin Cooper, a death row prisoner at San Quentin, claims to be wrongfully convicted of murder, due to police and prosecutorial misconduct, evidence tampering, and constitutional violations.

Benjamin Todd Jealous is a venture capitalist, civic leader and former president and chief executive officer of the National Association for the Advancement of Colored People (NAACP).

Kevin Alexander Gray was among the first Blacks to attend an all-white elementary school in 1968. A community organizer, he serves on the national board of the ACLU and as president of the S. Carolina affiliate of the ACLU. He is also an author.

Michael Kroll is a writer and activist specializing in the American criminal justice system. He was the first executive director of the Death Penalty Information Center.

Walter Riley grew up in segregated Durham, NC, the ninth of 11 children. In high school, he joined the NAACP campaigns for jobs, voting rights, and desegregation. He is an attorney in Oakland and works with Haiti Action Committee.

Vernellia Randall, a professor at the University of Dayton School of Law since 1990, writes extensively on and speaks internationally about race, women, and health care.

Mohamed Shehk is the communications director at Critical Resistance, an organization that works to abolish the prison industrial complex. **Marie Levin** is an organizer working with the Prisoner Advocacy Network, which advocates for those experiencing human rights violations in solitary confinement.

Greg Palast is a *New York Times*-bestselling author and a freelance journalist for the BBC as well as the British newspaper *The Guardian*.

Church, State, Women, and the Criminalization of Sexuality

Terry O'Neill, a feminist attorney, professor, and activist, is president of NOW. She is also president of the NOW Foundation and chair of the NOW Political Action Committees.

Helen Benedict, professor at Columbia Journalism School. She broke the story about the epidemic of sexual assault of US military women serving in Iraq and Afghanistan.

Blase Bonpane moved back and forth from Central America through his work as a Maryknoll missionary. He is the Director of the Office of the Americas, which is now World Focus.

Margaret Prescod emigrated as a teen with her family from Barbados and became involved in the civil rights movement. She is the radio host and producer of "Sojourner Truth."

Mattilda Bernstein Sycamore's activism has included ACT UP in the early '90s, Fed Up Queers in the late '90s, Gay Shame, and numerous other groups. Mattilda is the author of two novels.

Alex Petersburg is an activist with Stop Patriarchy.

Phyllis Kim is the executive director of the Korean American Forum of California. **K. J. Noh** is an activist, writer, educator, and member of Veterans for Peace.

Migration, Deportation and US-Latino Culture

Dolores Huerta is an activist and labor leader who co-founded with Cesar Chavez what became the United Farm Workers. Huerta is the originator of the phrase, "Si se puede."

Dr. Carlos Muñoz, the son of Mexican immigrants, was the founding chair of the first US Chicano Studies Department at California State University, Los Angeles and founding chair of the National Association of Chicana and Chicano Studies.

Martin Espada, called "the Pablo Neruda of North American poets" by Sandra Cisneros, was born in Brooklyn, NY. He has published almost twenty books as a poet, editor, essayist and translator. He is a professor of poetry at U Mass, Amherst.

Dr. Seth M. Holmes is Associate Professor of Medical Anthropology and Public Health at UC Berkeley. As a cultural and medical anthropologist and physician, he works to understand alternatives to ethnicity and citizenship hierarchies.

Adrienne Pine is a medical anthropologist who has worked in Honduras, Mexico, Korea, the US, Egypt, and Cuba. Her most recent book is *Working Hard, Drinking Hard: On Violence and Survival in Honduras*.

Nativo Lopez is a Mexican political leader and immigrant rights activist inspired by Cesar Chavez. Lopez is the former president of the Mexican American Political Association (MAPA).

Pablo Alvarado is the Executive Director of the National Day Laborer Organizing Network, which focuses on migrant rights, labor rights, day laborers, and their health and safety. He has been called the Cesar Chavez of day labor organizing.

Global Militarism and Empire

Kevin Pina is Country Expert on Haiti for the Varieties of Democracy Project of the University of Notre Dame and teaches Media Studies Cal State East Bay.

Christine Hong is assistant professor of Literature and Critical Race and Ethnic Studies at UC Santa Cruz. She is on the board of the Korea Policy Institute, the coordinating committee of the National Campaign to End the Korean War, and the Working Group on Peace and Demilitarization in Asia and the Pacific.

Danny Glover is a prominent actor, producer, and political activist. He is an active board member of the TransAfrica Forum and a board member of The Black AIDS Institute.

Tim Shorrock is an expert on US-Korean relations, US intelligence and foreign policy, the World Bank, IMF, trade and labor, debt relief, Japan and trade agreements.

Antonia Juhasz is an award-winning policy-analyst, author, and journalist, covering oil and energy policy. She exposes the role of oil in conflict, particularly the US wars in Iraq and Afghanistan.

Martin Espada (see above)

Robert Parry was a George Polk award winning Washington-based investigative reporter who broke many of the Iran-Contra scandal stories before founding Consortiumnews.com as the first investigative news magazine based on the internet in 1995.

Deborah S. Rogers, PhD, is president of Initiative for Equality, a global network of 300 organizations working towards greater social, economic, and political equality in over 90 countries.

Vijay Prashad is an Indian historian and Marxist intellectual. The George and Martha Kellner Chair in South Asian History and Professor of International Studies at Trinity College, he served as the Edward Said Chair at the American University of Beirut.

Ongoing Bloodshed in the Holy Land

Richard Falk is a professor emeritus of International Law at Princeton. In 2008, the UN Human Rights Council appointed him as UN Special Rapporteur on "the situation of human rights in the Palestinian territories occupied since 1967. "

Alice Walker, a novelist, poet, and feminist is the youngest daughter of sharecroppers whose mother worked as a maid to help support the family's eight children. Her novel, *The Color Purple,* won the Pulitzer Prize for Fiction.

Francis A. Boyle is a leading American expert in international law, serving as legal adviser to the Palestinian Delegation to the Middle East peace negotiations from 1991-1993. He teaches international law at the University of Illinois, Champaign.

John Pilger, journalist, filmmaker and author, has an Emmy and a British Academy Award for his documentary films. His 1979 film *Cambodia Year Zero* is ranked by the British Film Institute as one of the ten most important documentaries of the 20th century.

Ali Abunimah is a journalist and the co-founder and executive director of The Electronic Intifada, a nonprofit, independent online publication focusing on Palestine.

Dr. Mustafa Barghouthi is a physician and political activist, advocate for Palestinian grassroots democracy, international spokesman for the Palestinian NGO sector, and organizer of international solidarity in the Occupied Palestinian Territories.

There is No Plan(et) B

Dahr Jamail was one of the few unembedded US journalists to report extensively from Iraq during the 2003 Iraq invasion, between 2003 and 2005. He now also focuses on anthropogenic climate disruption and the environment.

Dr Helen Caldicott, a Nobel Laureate, has devoted over forty years to an international campaign to educate the public about the medical hazards of the nuclear age and the necessary changes in human behavior to stop environmental destruction.

Linda Pentz Gunter is a founder of Beyond Nuclear and serves as the organization's international specialist and director of media and development.

Steve Horn is an Indianapolis, IN-based Research Fellow for DeSmogBlog. He was a reporter and researcher at the Center for Media and Democracy. **Zach D Roberts** is a photojournalist who splits his time between Alaska and the lower 48. For the last decade he's been a researcher and producer for Greg Palast.

Andrea Carmen, Yaqui Nation, has worked for the International Indian Treaty Council since 1983 and is its Executive Director. She was a human rights observer and mediator in crises in the US, Mexico, Canada, Alaska, New Zealand and Ecuador.

Dr. Marsha Coleman-Adebayo had no idea that standing up for human rights as an employee of the Environmental Protection Agency would lead to a 15-year fight which inspired and shaped the first major piece of civil rights legislation of the twenty-first century. She is an editor and columnist of Black Agenda Report.

Praise

Ralph Poynter is the son of a union organizer in steel. He was a founding member of The Teacher's Freedom Party Caucus in the UFT. Jailed during the human rights struggle for community control of schools in the sixties, he organized the first successful prison protest during incarceration. He supported recently deceased spouse Lynne Stewart in her lifelong struggle against the judicial double standard and successfully led the worldwide movement to free her from Carswell Federal Prison.

Larry Pinkney is a veteran of the Black Panther Party, the former Minister of Interior of the Republic of New Africa, a former political prisoner and the only American to have successfully self-authored his civil/political rights case to the United Nations under the International Covenant on Civil and Political Rights. William Mandel, in his book *Saying No to Power: Autobiography of a 20ᵗʰ Century Activist and Thinker*, recounts how Larry, when a prisoner, used KPFAs airwaves to expose and remedy prison malfeasance. He was on the editorial board of the *Black Commentator* and co-founded the Black Activist Writers Guild.

Frances Goldin has worked in publishing for over six decades and founded the Frances Goldin Literary Agency in 1977. Reflecting her radical politics, the Agency has long concentrated on serious, controversial, progressive non-fiction and literary fiction that addresses issues of social justice and the impact of culture and politics on human relationships. The agency has represented such luminaries as Mumia Abu-Jamal, Barbara Kingsolver, Adrienne Rich, Martin Espada and Staughton Lynd. Her lifelong commitment to social justice extends to her work with the Cooper Square Committee, an organization she co-founded in 1959 that advocates for tenant-rights, community-based planning, and affordable housing. She is featured in a soon-to-be-released film, *It Took 50 Years: Frances Goldin and the Struggle for Cooper Square.*

To be of use
By Marge Piercy

The people I love the best
jump into work head first
without dallying in the shallows
and swim off with sure strokes almost out of sight.
They seem to become natives of that element,
the black sleek heads of seals
bouncing like half-submerged balls.

I love people who harness themselves, an ox to a heavy cart,
who pull like water buffalo, with massive patience,
who strain in the mud and the muck to move things forward,
who do what has to be done, again and again.

I want to be with people who submerge
in the task, who go into the fields to harvest
and work in a row and pass the bags along,
who are not parlor generals and field deserters
but move in a common rhythm
when the food must come in or the fire be put out.

The work of the world is common as mud.
Botched, it smears the hands, crumbles to dust.
But the thing worth doing well done
has a shape that satisfies, clean and evident.
Greek amphoras for wine or oil,
Hopi vases that held corn, are put in museums
but you know they were made to be used.
The pitcher cries for water to carry
and a person for work that is real.